PRENTICE HALL LITERATURE

PENGUIN EDITION

Teaching Resources

Unit 6
A Time of Rapid Change

The British Tradition

PEARSON

Prentice Hall

Upper Saddle River, New Jersey
Boston, Massachusetts

ISBN 0-13-165323-7

2 3 4 5 6 7 8 9 10   10 09 08 07 06

Contents

UNIT 6

"In Memory of W. B. Yeats" and **"Musée des Beaux Arts"** by W. H. Auden

"Carrick Revisited" by Louis MacNeice

"Not Palaces" by Stephen Spender

"Shooting an Elephant" by George Orwell

"The Demon Lover" by Elizabeth Bowen

"The Soldier" by Rupert Brooke

"Wirers" by Siegfried Sassoon

"Anthem for Doomed Youth" by Wilfred Owen

"Birds on the Western Front" by Saki (H. H. Munro)

"Wartime Speech" by Winston Churchill

"Defending Nonviolent Resistance" by Mohandas K. Gandhi

"Follower" and **"Two Lorries"** by Seamus Heaney

"Outside History" by Eavan Boland

"No Witchcraft for Sale" by Doris Lessing

"The Lagoon" by Joseph Conrad

"Araby" by James Joyce

"The Lady in the Looking Glass: A Reflection" by Virginia Woolf

"The First Year of My Life" by Muriel Spark

Unit 6: A Time of Rapid Change

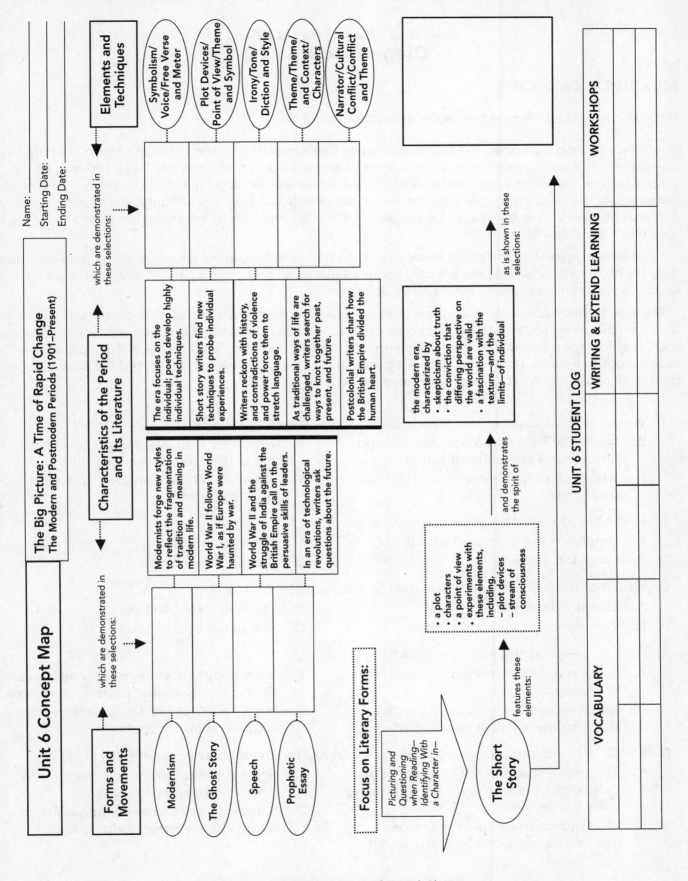

Name: _____

Unit 6 Concept Map

The Big Picture: A Time of Rapid Change
The Modern and Postmodern Periods (1901–Present)

Starting Date: _____
Ending Date: _____

Forms and Movements

which are demonstrated in these selections:

- Modernism
- The Ghost Story
- Speech
- Prophetic Essay

Characteristics of the Period and Its Literature

- Modernists forge new styles to reflect the fragmentation of tradition and meaning in modern life.
- World War II follows World War I, as if Europe were haunted by war.
- World War II and the struggle of India against the British Empire call on the persuasive skills of leaders.
- In an era of technological revolutions, writers ask questions about the future.

- The era focuses on the individual; poets develop highly individual techniques.
- Short story writers find new techniques to probe individual experiences.
- Writers reckon with history, and contradictions of violence and power force them to stretch language.
- As traditional ways of life are challenged, writers search for ways to knot together past, present, and future.
- Postcolonial writers chart how the British Empire divided the human heart.

Elements and Techniques

which are demonstrated in these selections:

- Symbolism/ Voice/Free Verse and Meter
- Plot Devices/ Point of View/Theme and Symbol
- Irony/Tone/ Diction and Style
- Theme/Theme/ and Context/ Characters
- Narrator/Cultural Conflict/Conflict and Theme

the modern era, characterized by
- skepticism about truth
- the conviction that differing perspective on the world are valid
- a fascination with the texture—and the limits—of individual

and demonstrates the spirit of

as is shown in these selections:

Focus on Literary Forms:

Picturing and Questioning when Reading— Identifying With a Character in—

The Short Story

features these elements:

- a plot
- characters
- a point of view experiments with these elements, including,
  - plot devices
  - stream of consciousness

UNIT 6 STUDENT LOG

VOCABULARY	WRITING & EXTEND LEARNING	WORKSHOPS

1

Unit 6: A Time of Rapid Change
Diagnostic Test 10

MULTIPLE CHOICE

Read the selection. Then, answer the questions that follow.

A solar eclipse occurs when the Moon is between Earth and the Sun and Earth, the Moon, and the Sun are aligned. This configuration causes the Moon to cast a shadow that hides the Sun from view. As the eclipse begins, the Moon's shadow begins to move across the Sun and the light from the Sun begins to decrease. At the height of the eclipse, the Sun is completely blocked, and although it is daytime, the sky darkens. Eclipses vary in degree: some are partial, blocking only part of the sun, while others are total—they block the entire Sun.

Total solar eclipses happen about every year and a half. However, many people mistakenly believe that they are quite rare, since eclipses are only visible from a small section of Earth. At any given spot on Earth, a total solar eclipse only occurs every 360 years.

Because daylight suddenly disappears during a solar eclipse, many cultures have developed legends based on these strange events. Some people came to view an eclipse as a sign of an impending calamity, such as a flood or a tornado. Others, including many native Alaskans, held the belief that eclipses presaged a positive event. According to one legend, an eclipse occurs when the Sun and the Moon leave their positions in the sky to check that everything on Earth is okay.

1. Which of the following best describes a solar eclipse?
   A. when the Sun and Moon are at opposite ends of the poles of Earth
   B. when Earth's shadow hides the Sun from view
   C. when the Sun casts a shadow that hides the Moon from view
   D. when the Moon's shadow hides the Sun from view

2. How often do solar eclipses usually occur?
   A. roughly every year-and-a-half
   B. every ten years
   C. once per century
   D. during the evening

3. Which of the following happens during a solar eclipse?
   A. The sky darkens.
   B. The sky becomes totally black.
   C. The stars are blocked.
   D. The moon disappears.

4. Why do people think solar eclipses are rare?
   A. Solar eclipses happen only once every 360 years.
   B. Astronomers are unable to predict when eclipses will occur.
   C. Most people never see an eclipse since they are only visible from a small area.
   D. Most people never see an eclipse since eclipses occur at night.

5. Which best explains why some cultures told myths about solar eclipses?
   A. An eclipse was a strange, rare event that they were unable to explain using their five senses.
   B. All cultures in the past developed myths and legends about the world.
   C. Solar eclipses are interesting events that inspire storytelling.
   D. Solar eclipses were so common that many stories arose about them.

6. Which of the following best describes what some cultures have believed about solar eclipses?
   A. They were a blessing from the gods.
   B. They were a sign of a calamity to come.
   C. They were a punishment from the gods.
   D. They were an astronomical event.

7. What did many native people of Alaska believe about solar eclipses?
   A. They were caused by the sky gods.
   B. They signaled a tornado or flood to come.
   C. They foretold a positive event to come.
   D. They predicted the end of the world.

Read the selection. Then, answer the questions that follow.

No one is certain how the term "Yankee" originated. Some researchers claim that it evolved from the Dutch name *Jan*, and its nickname *Janke*. Others suggest that it comes from the Dutch phrase *Jan Kaas*, which means "John Cheese," a perjorative term used to describe Dutch pirates in the Caribbean Sea.

The colonial settlers of North America came to be known as Yankees. The British initially wielded the term as an insult against the settlers, but the name soon took on a more positive connotation. Mark Twain considered a Yankee to be a resident of New England.

The phrase "Yankee ingenuity" can be applied to someone who can find solutions to tough problems, who is thrifty, or who knows how to use resources wisely. "Yankee ingenuity" also describes the ability to contrive an effective solution with whatever resources are available. For example, when faced with a task that seems impossible to finish, a Yankee might invent a new tool that gets the job done in half the time.

On the other hand, Yankees never boast about their accomplishments, despite having a strong sense of pride. While Yankees may appear grave and serious, most have a dry sense of humor.

8. From what group of people is the term "Yankee" thought to originate?
   A. Americans
   B. the Dutch
   C. New Englanders
   D. the British

9. To what does the term *Jan Kaas* refer?
   A. Dutch pirates
   B. British soldiers
   C. American colonists
   D. New Englanders

10. How did the British use the term "Yankee"?
    A. to refer to New Englanders
    B. as an insult to American colonists
    C. to insult Dutch pirates
    D. to praise the thriftiness of Americans

11. How did the meaning of the term "Yankee" change over time?
    A. It came to refer to Dutch pirates.
    B. It became an insult.
    C. It came to have a positive meaning.
    D. It came to refer to the British.

12. How did Mark Twain use the term "Yankee"?
    A. to insult the British
    B. to insult American colonists
    C. to refer to the Dutch
    D. to refer to New Englanders

13. Which of the following best describes the character of a Yankee?

    A. someone who is rich

    B. someone who is talented

    C. someone who is clever

    D. someone who is a pirate

14. Which of the following best describes "Yankee ingenuity"?

    A. the ability to invent new tools and new ways of doing things

    B. the quality of cleverness possessed by people from New England

    C. the willingness to work hard no matter what to get the job done

    D. the ability to solve problems with whatever resources are at hand

15. Which of the following is a true statement about Yankees?

    A. They are modest but have a strong pride.

    B. They do not take things seriously.

    C. They have no sense of humor.

    D. They are proud and boastful.

Name _____ Date _____

Unit 6 Introduction
Names and Terms to Know

A. DIRECTIONS: *Match each name or term on the left with its fact on the right. Write the letter of the fact on the line before the name or term it defines.*

<table>
<tr><td colspan="2">Names and Terms</td><td colspan="2">Facts</td></tr>
<tr><td>___ 1.</td><td>Edwardian Age</td><td>A.</td><td>global conflict triggered by the expansionist policies of the German leader Adolf Hitler</td></tr>
<tr><td>___ 2.</td><td>World War I</td><td>B.</td><td>dominant literary style from 1946 to the present, marked by "continuance and completion"</td></tr>
<tr><td>___ 3.</td><td>Lost Generation</td><td>C.</td><td>a trading bloc comprising Britain and other European countries with a combined population of several hundred million people</td></tr>
<tr><td>___ 4.</td><td>World War II</td><td>D.</td><td>era in which the rigid class distinctions and moral certainties of the Victorian Age lingered on</td></tr>
<tr><td>___ 5.</td><td>European Community</td><td>E.</td><td>twentieth-century style in the arts that stressed a commitment to new forms and often presented experiences in fragments</td></tr>
<tr><td>___ 6.</td><td>Modernism</td><td>F.</td><td>disillusioned British youth of the period between the world wars</td></tr>
<tr><td>___ 7.</td><td>Postmodernism</td><td>G.</td><td>conflict sparked by long-standing tensions among the nations of Europe, which exploded in 1914</td></tr>
</table>

B. DIRECTIONS: *Write an additional fact about each of the following names and terms.*

1. World War I: _____

_____

2. World War II: _____

_____

3. Modernism: _____

_____

4. Postmodernism: _____

_____

Name _____ Date _____

Unit 6 Introduction
Focus Questions

DIRECTIONS: *Use the hints below to help you answer the focus questions. You will find all of the information in the Unit Introduction in your textbook.*

1. What was the impact of two world wars on Britain?
   Hint: What realities in World War I came as a shock to the British? _____
   _____
   _____

   Hint: What were the darkest days for Britain in World War II? _____
   _____
   _____

2. Describe the influence of Modernism and Postmodernism on the writing of this period.
   Hint: How did the Modernists often present human experience? _____
   _____
   _____

   Hint: What is the link between such poems as T. S. Eliot's *The Waste Land* and the technique of collage in the visual arts? _____
   _____
   _____

   Hint: What features characterize the dramas of such postmodernist playwrights as Harold Pinter and Tom Stoppard? _____
   _____
   _____

Vocabulary Warm-up Word Lists

Study these words from the selections. Then, complete the activities that follow.

Word List A

amid [uh MID] *prep.* in the midst of; among
   The one red rose stood out <u>amid</u> all the white ones in the bouquet.

consume [kuhn SOOM] *v.* to use up or waste, as money or time
   Jennifer's part-time jobs <u>consume</u> all her free time.

core [KAWR] *n.* the central or innermost part of anything
   A burning desire to help others is at the <u>core</u> of Anna's heart.

glade [GLAYD] *n.* an open place in a forest
   Walter and Maria had a picnic in the <u>glade</u>.

innocence [IN uh suhns] *n.* freedom from guilt, blame, or sin
   The accused person declared his <u>innocence</u> in a loud voice.

murmur [MER muhr] *v.* to make a low, unclear, steady sound
   The two friends <u>murmur</u> between themselves in the shade of the oak.

sensual [SEN shoo uhl] *adj.* having to do with the body or the senses
   The aroma of the flowers was quite a <u>sensual</u> treat for all of us.

twilight [TWY lyt] *n.* the light of the sky just before sunrise or after sunset
   Having missed the sunset, Janet and Carl met at <u>twilight</u>.

Word List B

commend [kuh MEND] *v.* to speak highly of; praise
   Hal and Ivy <u>commend</u> Harry on his violin performance.

intellect [IN tuh lekt] *n.* the power of the mind to think and know
   Although she is young, Myra exhibits great powers of <u>intellect</u>.

magnificence [mag NIF uh suhns] *n.* impressive grandeur or beauty
   Stan was highly impressed by the <u>magnificence</u> of the statue.

monuments [MAHN yuh muhnts] *n.* things built in memory of an event or person
   Paul visited several important <u>monuments</u> while in Washington, D.C.

mysterious [mis TEER ee uhs] *adj.* difficult to explain or understand
   The message from Pedro's mother was quite <u>mysterious</u>.

neglect [ni GLEKT] *v.* to fail to attend to or care for
   If you <u>neglect</u> your homework, you will fall behind in your classes.

revelation [REV uh lay shuhn] *n.* something made known, especially something surprising
   The students held their breath as the important <u>revelation</u> was made.

vexed [VEXT] *v.* irritated or annoyed; troubled or afflicted
   The waiter's poor service <u>vexed</u> us.

Poetry of William Butler Yeats
Vocabulary Warm-up Exercises

Exercise A *Fill in each blank below with the appropriate word from Word List A.*

Every Friday, at [1] _____, Matt and a group of his friends met in the forest. There, in a [2] _____ not far from the forest's edge, they enjoyed a [3] _____ celebration of the season. Included in the celebration were all kinds of gourmet foods to [4] _____. The [5] _____ of the evening's entertainment was the learning of a new song, which everyone enjoyed singing together. The lyrics of tonight's song were about two young people and the [6] _____ of their love. As Matt learned the song [7] _____ all his friends, he was grateful for their friendship. As the evening came to an end, Matt heard the owls [8] _____ in the trees. No doubt the owls were glad to see the people leave.

Exercise B *Determine whether each statement is true or false. Circle T or F, and explain your answer.*

1. <u>Monuments</u> are usually small trinkets you can put on a bracelet.
   T / F _____

2. Something that is very beautiful might impress you with its <u>magnificence</u>.
   T / F _____

3. If someone makes a <u>revelation</u>, it would come as no surprise to anyone.
   T / F _____

4. You would probably be quite amused at something that <u>vexed</u> you.
   T / F _____

5. A person who has a fine <u>intellect</u> is not very smart.
   T / F _____

6. If you <u>neglect</u> your dog, he or she would probably be very unhappy.
   T / F _____

7. You would <u>commend</u> your friend for making a serious mistake.
   T / F _____

8. Something <u>mysterious</u> is difficult to understand.
   T / F _____

Name _____ Date _____

Reading Warm-up A

Read the following passage. Pay special attention to the underlined words. Then, read it again, and complete the activities. Use a separate sheet of paper for your written answers.

Trumpeter swans are the largest swans in the world, growing to a length of 58 to 72 inches with a wingspan of eight feet. Trumpeter swans, like all swans, are graceful birds whose lovely appearance has a <u>sensual</u> appeal to all bird-lovers. Their long, bendable necks, interestingly, have more bones than a giraffe's neck.

Trumpeter swans live on lakes and rivers in the grasslands and forests of the northwestern United States and western Canada. If you happen to be walking through the center, the <u>core</u>, of a forest some lovely day, strolling <u>amid</u> the tall trees, and come to a <u>glade</u> near a body of water, you might have the good fortune to see one or more of them. Listen closely! You might even hear the low sounds they make as they <u>murmur</u> to each other.

Because mature swans are covered in white feathers, they can be seen as symbols of <u>innocence</u>. They have dark brown eyes and long black legs and feet. Cygnets (juvenile swans) are mostly gray. They slowly turn whiter in their first year of life. It's hard to imagine a lovelier sight than a family of swans at sunset, just before <u>twilight</u>, with the colorful sky reflected in their watery surroundings.

When swans are three years old, they mate for life. Unlike other birds, swans do not build nests in trees. They are too heavy for that. The female lays three to nine eggs, which are guarded diligently by the male until they can safely hatch. The cygnets stay close to their parents as they learn to find food and to fly. Swans <u>consume</u> a diet of aquatic insects and mollusks. The cygnets can fly at about 14 weeks of age. However, they stay with their parents for about a year. At age three, they start families of their own.

1. Underline the words in this sentence and a nearby sentence that hint at the <u>sensual</u> appeal swans have. What does **sensual** mean?

2. Circle the word that means about the same as <u>core</u>. What do you find in the **core** of an apple?

3. Underline the words that tell what you might stroll <u>amid</u> in a forest. Use **amid** in a sentence.

4. Circle the word that tells where you would find a <u>glade</u>. Describe what you might see in a **glade**.

5. Underline the words that describe what you might hear as swans <u>murmur</u> to each other. If you were to **murmur** something to your best friend, what might it be?

6. Circle the words that tell why swans might be seen as symbols of <u>innocence</u>. What do you consider a symbol of **innocence**?

7. Underline the word that describes a time just before <u>twilight</u>. What activity are you usually doing when it is **twilight**?

8. Circle the words that tell what swans <u>consume</u>. What do you normally **consume** at lunchtime?

Poetry of William Butler Yeats
Reading Warm-up B

Read the following passage. Pay special attention to the underlined words. Then, read it again, and complete the activities. Use a separate sheet of paper for your written answers.

The Great Pyramid of Khufu in Egypt, is one of the most famous <u>monuments</u> in the world, and we should <u>commend</u> its builders for a job well done; however, it has a rival for <u>magnificence</u>, grandeur, and size nearby—the Pyramid of Khafre, the next Egyptian pharaoh to rule after Khufu. Close to these two pyramids stands the Great Sphinx, a <u>mysterious</u> creature with the head of a human and the body of a lion; unlike the pyramids, the Great Sphinx has no rivals there or anywhere else.

The stone that forms the head of the Sphinx is of much better quality than the stone in the rest of the body. One would think that the head, being better material, would be in better condition, but the entire nose is missing, and the eyes and upper lip are seriously disintegrated. The Egyptian government did not <u>neglect</u>, or fail to care for, the Sphinx; rather, natural erosion is responsible for some of this damage. However, most of the disfigurement was caused by Napoleon's army, who used the Sphinx's face for target practice; one has to assume that the men who did this were lacking in <u>intellect</u>, for even a person with average brainpower would realize that such unrivaled and ancient art should be protected.

The Great Sphinx is thought to be about 4,500 years old. An interesting story is told about a <u>revelation</u> made to King Thutmose IV, who reigned about 3,400 years ago: when still a prince, he had fallen asleep in the shade of the Sphinx, and in his dream the Sphinx talked to him, saying he was <u>vexed</u> because of the sand that was choking him. He asked Thutmose to clear the sand away, and his reward would be a kingship—Thutmose did what was asked, and he soon became king.

1. Underline the words that name one of the most famous <u>monuments</u> in the world. Name two famous *monuments* that you have visited or would like to visit.

2. Circle the words that explain why we should <u>commend</u> the builders of the Great Pyramid. For what accomplishment do you wish someone would *commend* you?

3. Underline the word that means about the same as <u>magnificence</u>. Use *magnificence* in a sentence.

4. Circle the words that describe a <u>mysterious</u> creature. What does *mysterious* mean?

5. Underline the words that tell what <u>neglect</u> means. Tell about a time you had to *neglect* something that was important to you.

6. Underline the word that relates to <u>intellect</u>. Describe a person whose *intellect* you admire.

7. Underline the words in nearby sentences that tell about the <u>revelation</u> made to King Thutmose IV. Use *revelation* in a sentence.

8. Circle the words that tell why the Sphinx was <u>vexed</u>. Tell about a time that you were *vexed* about something.

Poetry of William Butler Yeats
Literary Analysis: Symbolism

A **symbol** is a word, character, object, or action that stands for something beyond itself. To determine whether a word has symbolic meaning, consider it within the context of the poem. For example, the city of Byzantium, which symbolically represents the poetic imagination, is central to the meaning of "Sailing to Byzantium." It is in Byzantium that the speaker finds "the singing masters of (his) soul." That Byzantium is part of the title is another clue to its significance.

The following is an anonymous poem. Read the poem and answer the questions that follow.

In the Garden

In the garden there strayed

A beautiful maid

As fair as the flowers of the morn;

The first hour of her life

She was made a man's wife,

And buried before she was born.

1. The "maid" of this poem is an allusion to Eve in the Biblical story of creation. What evidence in the poem indicates that "maid" is symbolic?

   _____

   _____

   _____

   _____

   _____

   _____

2. According the Bible, God created Adam's mate, Eve, by fashioning her from one of Adam's ribs. This means that Eve was never actually "born" in the normal sense of the word. Given this information, how can Eve be interpreted as a symbol for women in general?

   _____

   _____

   _____

   _____

   _____

   _____

   _____

Poetry of William Butler Yeats
Reading Strategy: Apply Literary Background

Many readers focus closely on the words of a poem for understanding. After understanding the writer's work as it exists on the page, though, readers may find it helpful and interesting to consider a work in the larger context of the artist's life. What might have led a writer to a specific subject? What was he or she doing when this work was composed? What was the social or historical climate of the period?

It is not necessarily safe or correct, however, to assume that what is in a writer's work gives the exact story of his or her life. Events in writers' lives may not adequately explain their work. For example, one need not know or understand the full details of Yeats's involvement with Irish politics to appreciate his poetry. In some of his poems, however, having knowledge of the issues helps explain references and attitudes.

DIRECTIONS: *For each poem, use the third column to write the impact the information in the second column might have had on the poem's composition. Cite specific lines or sections when you can.*

Poem	Background Information	Impact on the Poem
1. "When You Are Old"	Actress Maud Gonne, a founder of Sinn Fein, met Yeats three years before the poem was written. She starred in his first play. He proposed, but she married another Irish revolutionary.	
2. "The Wild Swans at Coole"	Yeats summered for years at Coole Park, elegant home of Lady Gregory, founder of the Irish National Theater.	
3. "The Second Coming"	The poem was written in 1920. After the Russian revolution in 1917, counterrevolution, chaos, and famine persisted in the new state into the 1920's.	
4. "Sailing to Byzantium"	In a prose work, *The Vision*, Yeats wrote "I think that if I were given a month of antiquity . . . I would spend it in Byzantium [circa 535 AD] . . ."	

Poetry of William Butler Yeats
Vocabulary Builder

Using the Root -ques-

The root -ques- derives from the Latin verb *quaerere*, which means "to ask."

A. DIRECTIONS: *The words in the list use the -ques- root. Choose the word that best completes each sentence and write in on the line.*

request   quest

1. The explorer's _____ for adventure caused him to undertake a voyage around the world.

2. The employee had to _____ another copy of the company's pension plan.

Using the Word List

clamorous	conquest	anarchy
conviction	paltry	artifice

B. DIRECTIONS: *Each item consists of a word from the Word List followed by four lettered words or phrases. Choose the word or phrase most nearly* opposite *in meaning to the Word List word. Circle the letter of your choice.*

1. clamorous
   A. miserable
   B. joyful
   C. quiet
   D. timid

2. conquest
   A. defeat
   B. plunder
   C. strategy
   D. battle

3. anarchy
   A. faith
   B. order
   C. power
   D. hope

4. conviction
   A. freedom
   B. certainty
   C. weakness
   D. doubt

5. paltry
   A. simple
   B. valuable
   C. clear
   D. kind

6. artifice
   A. destruction
   B. ingenuity
   C. dumbness
   D. incivility

Poetry of William Butler Yeats

Grammar and Style: Noun Clauses

Subordinate clauses of every type can function as single parts of speech. One type of clause, a **noun clause**, can serve any function that a noun can serve in a sentence. Here are examples of noun clauses:

Subject:	*What Yeats believed about history* shows in his poems.
Direct Object:	Yeats thought *that history runs in cycles.*
Indirect Object:	Yeats gives *what he believes* free rein in some poems, but not all.
Object of Preposition:	His general theory of *what determines history* produces sometimes complicated imagery.
Predicate Noun or Subject Complement:	The important thing to remember is *that one need not understand all Yeats's theories to enjoy the poetry.*
Appositive:	The essential thing, *what one should go by,* is whether a poem speaks to you.

A. PRACTICE: *Underline the noun clauses in the following sentences. Above each, indicate how the noun clause functions.*

1. In "When You Are Old," the speaker expresses an idea of what the thoughts of a woman he once loved might one day be.

2. Who you are may determine whether you believe "The Lake Isle of Innisfree" refers to a type of place or a kind of work.

3. Knowledge that the world will go on without you, that stark recognition, glides also across the water in "The Wild Swans at Coole."

B. Writing Application: *Write a sentence that uses the noun clause in the way indicated in parentheses.*

1. That Yeats is the best Irish poet (subject)

_____

_____

2. How Yeats creates memorable images (complement)

_____

_____

3. What Yeats says about aging (direct object)

_____

_____

Poetry of William Butler Yeats
Support for Writing

Review Yeats's poetry to find examples of "dreamlike symbols" and "symbols expressing conflict." Write examples in the chart. Think about whether your examples support Brower's statement that Yeats succeeded by letting these symbols express conflict he could not deal with outside of his poetry. Write your opinion below.

"dreamlike symbols"	"symbols expressing conflict"

My opinion:

_____

_____

_____

_____

_____

On a separate page, use the statement of your opinion to write a thesis statement for your response to criticism. Then, use details from the chart to support your thesis statement as you write.

Poetry of William Butler Yeats
Support for Extend Your Learning

Listening and Speaking

Use the following checklist as you practice your **oral interpretation** of Irish poems. Continue practicing until you are satisfied with your use of each technique.

Checklist for Speaking

✓	Techniques	Where I Can Use These Techniques
	Slow down or speed up your rate of reading.	
	Raise or lower your voice to stress certain phrases.	
	Change your tone of voice.	
	Emphasize certain words and phrases.	
	Use hand gestures and facial expressions.	

Research and Technology

Use these prompts to write questions for researching your visual display of Byzantium's treasures.

What characteristic of Byzantium art . . . _____

_____

_____

When did Byzantium art . . . _____

_____

_____

Why did Byzantine artists . . . _____

_____

_____

Name _____ Date _____

Poetry of William Butler Yeats
Enrichment: Philosophy

Spiritual Eclecticism

The work of W. B. Yeats contains a clear spiritual sense, but his plays were denounced as irreligious. Yeats was a spiritual eclectic. The word *eclectic* means "composed of various sources," and comes from a Greek word meaning "to pick out." Yeats chose elements of diverse beliefs that appealed to him. Eclecticism borrows and combines ideas from various contexts, but may ignore their fundamental differences.

The idea that no one belief has a monopoly on truth was strong as early as the second century B.C., when Greek thinkers tried to unify many philosophies. Early Christian philosophers adapted Greek metaphysics and borrowed from other religions.

Modern eclectic philosophy was advanced by French philosopher Victor Cousin in the nineteenth century. Yeats, a student of French thought, joined a Theophilosophical Society when he was twenty-two, seeking to promote brotherhood through mysticism. He never felt completely at home in either Protestant or Catholic Ireland, nor in England. Amid political strife, Yeats sought unity in a mysticism deeper, he felt, than the troubles he knew, hoping to heal with art what had not been healed with politics and religion.

DIRECTIONS: *Use critical thinking skills and your understanding of Yeats's work to answer the following questions.*

1. What might be the advantages and disadvantages of eclectic spiritualism?

_____

_____

_____

2. In what way might Yeats's attitude toward death, as expressed in these selections, depart from a traditional Christian attitude? _____

_____

_____

3. What ideas or images in "The Second Coming" seem to combine differing philosophies?

_____

_____

_____

4. Identify three suggestions of spiritual eclecticism in "Sailing to Byzantium."

_____

_____

_____

Poetry of William Butler Yeats
Selection Test A

Critical Reading *Identify the letter of the choice that best answers the question.*

_____ 1. What can you conclude about the speaker in "When You Are Old"?
A. He is sad because a woman never returned his love.
B. He is happy with the life he has lived.
C. He is angry about they way he has been treated.
D. He is thankful for the love a woman has shown him.

_____ 2. The man in "When You Are Old" says he "hid his face amid a crowd of stars." Why?
A. The woman he loves is famous.
B. The woman he loves has other admirers.
C. The woman he loves has died.
D. The woman he loves has many dreams.

_____ 3. In "When You Are Old," what is the book that the poet wants the woman to read when she is older?
A. a photo album with pictures of friends
B. a diary that belongs to a friend
C. a book that describes his love for her
D. a book of stories about women

_____ 4. Where is the speaker when he remembers the sound of water in "The Lake Isle of Innisfree"?
A. in a boat on a lake
B. lying awake on the Isle of Innisfree
C. standing on roadways and pavement
D. alone on the shore of the lake

_____ 5. What is the mood created by "The Lake Isle of Innisfree"?
A. danger and suspense
B. anxiety and dread
C. sadness and disappointment
D. peace and longing

_____ 6. What do the swans symbolize in "The Wild Swans at Coole"?
A. freedom and timelessness
B. sorrow and despair
C. youth and childhood
D. stars and the moon

_____ 7. What is the speaker's concern in "The Wild Swans at Coole"?
A. Other humans will disturb the swans.
B. He will not see the swans anymore if they fly away.
C. The swans will become old and eventually die.
D. The lake will become too crowded with swans.

____ 8. What does the speaker mean in "The Second Coming" when he asks about a "rough beast" that "slouches towards Bethlehem to be born"?
   A. He asks about how nature might be affected by changes in technology.
   B. He asks about the changes Christianity will need to make in the modern world.
   C. He asks about the animal that will symbolize British power.
   D. He asks about the civilization that will replace the Christian civilization.

____ 9. Yeats believed in cycles of world history. How does this belief reveal itself in "The Second Coming"?
   A. He uses images of circles.
   B. He refers to religious symbols.
   C. He describes the Sphinx.
   D. He talks about nightmares.

____ 10. In what stage of life is the speaker in "Sailing to Byzantium"?
   A. youth
   B. early adulthood
   C. middle age
   D. old age

____ 11. What does the city of Byzantium symbolize in "Sailing to Byzantium"?
   A. war
   B. art
   C. love
   D. kings

____ 12. In "Sailing to Byzantium," why does the speaker want to go to Byzantium?
   A. to find love
   B. to pray
   C. to find hope in art
   D. to become young again

Vocabulary and Grammar

____ 13. *Clamorous* children cause adults to tell them to be quiet. Why?
   A. They are young.
   B. They are noisy.
   C. They are ill.
   D. They are late.

____ 14. Which sentence includes a noun clause that contains a form of *what, how,* or *who* as a subject?
   A. "The falcon cannot hear the falconer."
   B. "The ceremony of innocence is drowned."
   C. "Upon the brimming water among the stones . . ."
   D. "Whatever is begotten, born, and dies."

Essay

15. William Butler Yeats was deeply in love with Maude Gonne, who did not return his love. However, he still wrote poems about her. In an essay, explain the role that Maude Gonne plays in "When You Are Old." Whom is the speaker addressing? How does the speaker describe the subject of the poem? Use information from the poem to support your explanation.

16. In "The Wild Swans at Coole," the speaker says that "All's changed" since he first heard the sound of the swans' wings. In an essay, compare the swans and the speaker. How has the speaker's life changed? How have the swans' lives remained the same? Give examples from the poem to support your ideas.

Name _____   Date _____

Poetry of William Butler Yeats
Selection Test B

Critical Reading *Identify the letter of the choice that best completes the statement or answers the question.*

____ 1. "When You Are Old" is addressed to
   A. the speaker considering his advancing years.
   B. a woman once loved by the speaker.
   C. the speaker's mother.
   D. all readers as they consider the future.

____ 2. Which is possible to infer about the speaker of "When You Are Old"?
   A. He is saddened by rejection.
   B. He conceals his love out of pride.
   C. He remembers with great pleasure.
   D. He enjoys the peace and solitude of old age.

____ 3. In "When You Are Old," the speaker's love of "the pilgrim soul" and "the sorrows of your changing face" means that he loved the
   A. woman for who she really was.
   B. way the world changed her.
   C. causes she believed in, whether they succeeded or failed.
   D. way the time took its toll on her.

____ 4. Knowing Yeats's relationship with actress Maud Gonne helps explain why "When You Are Old" is about
   A. the shallowness of public affection.
   B. the sacrifices of political life.
   C. the fleeting nature of beauty.
   D. deep love not returned.

____ 5. What is the main idea expressed in Yeats's "The Lake Isle of Innisfree"?
   A. a love of cities
   B. a feeling of longing
   C. contempt for urban life
   D. nostalgia for youth

____ 6. The island in "The Lake Isle of Innisfree" is a symbol for
   A. isolation.
   B. mystery.
   C. contentment.
   D. effort.

____ 7. Which statement best summarizes the central idea of "The Wild Swans at Coole"?
   A. Nature cares nothing for human feelings.
   B. People need to feel powerful emotions.
   C. The beauty of nature is temporary.
   D. Human passions cannot remain the same.

____ 8. Which best reflects the central message of "The Second Coming"?
  A. In world history, a cycle of order follows a cycle of chaos.
  B. Society is doomed to revert to its barbaric origins.
  C. Humanity is powerless to do anything against the forces of time and nature.
  D. A dark future is foreshadowed by the violence of the present.

____ 9. Yeats's belief in a cyclic theory of world history reveals itself in "The Second Coming" through
  A. images of circling and completion.
  B. symbols of birds and the Sphinx.
  C. references to stone and violence.
  D. allusions to religious prophecies.

____ 10. The "lion body and the head of a man" and "the rocking cradle" in "The Second Coming" symbolize
  A. Yeats's ideas of communism and capitalism.
  B. systems of philosophy alternating in power.
  C. adult knowledge and childhood innocence.
  D. England and Ireland's political relationship.

____ 11. In "Sailing to Byzantium," Yeats implies that the natural world is
  A. cold in its destruction of life.
  B. adverse to the life of the mind.
  C. chaotic in its proliferation of species.
  D. blind to the horrors of death and disease.

____ 12. For Yeats, Byzantium symbolizes
  A. the mind's eternal life.
  B. the perfect social order.
  C. the distant quality of hope.
  D. divine revelation.

____ 13. When he wrote "Sailing to Byzantium," Yeats believed that the world of art and thought is superior to the life of body and feeling. This idea exhibits itself in the poem in
  A. a sea voyage as a means to escape old age.
  B. the admiration of Eastern "singing-masters."
  C. a movement from natural "birds in the trees" to mechanical ones "upon a golden bough."
  D. the image of a "drowsy Emperor."

Vocabulary and Grammar

____ 14. A *clamorous* gathering of people is one that is
  A. joyful.
  B. angry.
  C. noisy.
  D. religious.

___ **15.** A person without *conviction* has no
   A. strategies.
   B. offenses.
   C. procedures.
   D. beliefs.

___ **16.** A noun clause acts in a sentence
   A. anywhere in the subject.
   B. as a direct or indirect object, but not a subject.
   C. in any way that a noun can.
   D. as an independent clause.

Essay

17. All five poems in this selection reveal a sense of longing, of wanting something not available. What Yeats yearns for may vary from poem to poem, and he may express his wishes with images, symbols, or direct statement. What is Yeats seeking in each of these poems, and how does he disclose that longing? Write an essay in which you identify what Yeats longs for in any three of the poems in this selection, and discuss the way he conveys that sense of longing in each poem. Use specific examples from the poetry to support your ideas.

18. A symbol is a word, character, object, or action that stands for something beyond itself. Yeats employed and invented symbols throughout his poetry. What symbols appear in this selection of Yeats's work? Write an essay in which you discuss the symbols and what they may symbolize in any three of the poems in this selection. Explain how they fit with both the poem and the world beyond it, using specific examples from the poetry.

Vocabulary Warm-up Word Lists

Study these words from the selections. Then, complete the activities that follow.

Word List A

consciousness [KAHN shuhs nuhs] *n.* awareness; a conscious condition
   After being in a coma for a week, Marvin regained <u>consciousness</u>.

constituted [KAHN stuh toot id] *v.* made up; composed
   Four quarts have always <u>constituted</u> a gallon.

deliberate [duh LIB uhr it] *adj.* done on purpose; thought about; intended
   Linda's <u>deliberate</u> attempt to annoy me just made me laugh.

gesture [JES chuhr] *n.* a motion of the head, hands, or other part of the body expressing some idea or feeling
   Orlando's <u>gesture</u> indicated that we should come in and sit down.

grimy [GRY mee] *adj.* full of or covered with dirt
   The mother sent her <u>grimy</u> child directly to the bathtub.

regretted [ri GRET id] *v.* felt sorrow or grief about something
   Alma forever <u>regretted</u> ending her friendship with Tameka.

satisfactory [sat is FAK tuhr ee] *adj.* good enough to meet expectations
   Steve's job performance was <u>satisfactory</u> but not outstanding.

temperate [TEM puhr it] *adj.* moderate in temperature; mild
   San Diego has a pleasant, <u>temperate</u> climate all year long.

Word List B

conception [kuhn SEP shuhn] *n.* the act of forming an idea
   The <u>conception</u> of the project differed from the final result.

essence [ES uhns] *n.* basic quality; that which makes something what it is
   Playfulness is the <u>essence</u> of childhood.

folly [FAHL ee] *n.* foolishness; lack of sense
   I wish my dog could understand the <u>folly</u> of chasing cars.

grumbling [GRUM bling] *v.* complaining in a grumpy way; muttering unhappily
   The workers started <u>grumbling</u> about having to work late.

hostile [HAHS tuhl] *adj.* showing dislike or hate; unfriendly
   The <u>hostile</u> mother bird clearly did not want me to approach her nest.

insistent [in SIS tuhnt] *adj.* demanding or persistent
   Brian's sister was <u>insistent</u> that he play a game with her.

potency [POH tuhn see] *n.* force; power; strength
   The <u>potency</u> of that medicine is more than I need for this little cough.

sordid [SAWR did] *adj.* foul or unclean; morally impure
   The movie was about the main character's <u>sordid</u> desire for cruel revenge.

Name _____ Date _____

Poetry of T. S. Eliot
Vocabulary Warm-up Exercises

Exercise A *Fill in each blank below with the appropriate word from Word List A.*

Patricia thought that Calvin had made a [1] _____ effort to get extra dirty that afternoon. She thought she might lose [2] _____ because he smelled so bad. As she looked at his [3] _____ clothes, she wondered with annoyance why he did it. Didn't he understand what [4] _____ careful behavior as opposed to careless behavior? With a [5] _____ of anger, she sent him to his room. Immediately, she [6] _____ being so hard on the little boy. After all, they lived in a lovely, [7] _____ climate. It was normal for a young boy to play outside and get dirty on such a beautiful day. Patricia apologized to Calvin, and he smiled to show that her apology was [8] _____ and acceptable.

Exercise B *Find a synonym for each word in the following vocabulary list. Then, use each vocabulary word in a sentence that makes the meaning of the word clear.*

Example: Vocabulary word: *hostile* Synonym: *opposing*
   Sample sentence: When <u>opposing</u> forces arrived, the soldiers retreated.

1. Vocabulary word: folly Synonym: _____
   _____

2. Vocabulary word: insistent Synonym: _____
   _____

3. Vocabulary word: sordid Synonym: _____
   _____

4. Vocabulary word: potency Synonym: _____
   _____

5. Vocabulary word: conception Synonym: _____
   _____

6. Vocabulary word: grumbling Synonym: _____
   _____

7. Vocabulary word: essence Synonym: _____
   _____

Poetry of T. S. Eliot
Reading Warm-up A

Read the following passage. Pay special attention to the underlined words. Then, read it again, and complete the activities. Use a separate sheet of paper for your written answers.

The journey of the Magi, also called the Three Wise Men or the Three Kings, to see the newborn baby Jesus is a popular story from the Christian tradition. It is interesting to imagine the journey these three men might have taken. According to the story, they set out from Persia, or present-day Iran. The distance from there to Jerusalem is between 1,000 and 1,200 miles and would have taken three to twelve months by camel. This perhaps <u>constituted</u> the longest trip they had ever taken.

As they traveled across the land, through weather that must have ranged from <u>temperate</u> to cold, we can imagine that they <u>regretted</u> their decision to make the trip. They must have been tired, hungry, and dirty to the point of looking <u>grimy</u> as they traveled between rest points. Still, they must have made a <u>deliberate</u> decision to keep going. Uppermost in their <u>consciousness</u> would have been an awareness of how important it was to find the newborn king and pay their respects.

When they finally arrived, so the story goes, they took turns kneeling in a <u>gesture</u> of respect and adoration. The youngest magi, Caspar of Tarsus, was a European. He knelt first and presented his gift of gold, which symbolized Christ's immortality and purity. In exchange, Caspar received the gifts of charity and spiritual wealth. Melchior, a middle-aged Persian, knelt next, offering myrrh, a fragrant resin, which was believed to make children stronger. In exchange, he received the gifts of humility and truth. Finally, Balthasar, an elderly Ethiopian, offered a gift of frankincense, a resin that symbolizes prayer and sacrifice. In exchange, he received the gift of faith. The gifts of the magi must have been <u>satisfactory</u> and acceptable to the tiny king, for they received priceless gifts in return.

1. What <u>constituted</u> the longest trip the three magi had ever taken? Define **constituted**.

2. Underline the word that means about the opposite of <u>temperate</u>. Name a city that enjoys **temperate** weather.

3. Circle the words that tell what the wise men might have <u>regretted</u>. Tell about something a movie character did that he or she **regretted**.

4. Circle the word that means about the same as <u>grimy</u>. If you were **grimy**, what is the first thing you would do?

5. Underline the words that tell what <u>deliberate</u> decision the men might have made. What does **deliberate** mean?

6. Underline the word that means about the same as <u>consciousness</u>. Use **consciousness** in a sentence.

7. Circle the words that describe the <u>gesture</u> made by the magi when they found the baby king. Describe a **gesture** that can indicate confusion.

8. Underline the word that means about the same as <u>satisfactory</u>. How do you know if an assignment you turn in is **satisfactory**?

Name _____   Date _____

Read the following passage. Pay special attention to the underlined words. Then, read it again, and complete the activities. Use a separate sheet of paper for your written answers.

The story of Guy Fawkes and the Gunpowder Plot begins in May 1604. The new king of England, James I, had promised to relax the anti-Catholic laws, but it now appeared that he would be even more <u>hostile</u> to the Catholics than the former king had been.

A Catholic gentleman named Robert Catesby decided to do something; he asked his cousin, Thomas Wintour, to meet him at the London home of his friend John Wright. After <u>grumbling</u> about the situation for a while, the three discussed a foul, <u>sordid</u> plot to blow up the King and the House of Lords and kidnap the young prince and princess. Their <u>conception</u> of the plot was to begin a revolution that would restore Catholicism as the official religion of England. They soon had enlisted a large group to help in the conspiracy; included was Guy Fawkes, a mercenary soldier.

The group managed to rent a cellar right under the House of Lords. Fawkes's job was to fill the cellar with thirty-six barrels of gunpowder. There was great <u>potency</u> in that gunpowder—enough to blow the House of Lords off its foundations.

One of the conspirators, though, had second thoughts—perhaps he had friends who would be in Parliament that day, or perhaps the <u>folly</u> of the plot scared him. A letter was sent to Lord Monteagle, a member of Parliament, warning him in an <u>insistent</u> tone of the danger. The identity of the letter writer has never been identified with certainty, but one of the conspirators, Francis Tresham, was Lord Monteagle's brother-in-law.

All the conspirators were caught and, except for Tresham, executed; Tresham died while a prisoner in the Tower of London. To this day, England observes Guy Fawkes Day, in <u>essence</u> a celebration of the uncovering of the plot.

1. Underline the words that would show the opposite of <u>hostile</u> treatment of the Catholics. How might a cat show **hostile** feelings?

2. Underline the sentence in the first paragraph that tells what Catesby, Wintour, and Wright were <u>grumbling</u> about. Describe a time you were **grumbling** about something.

3. Circle the word that means about the same as <u>sordid</u>. Use **sordid** in a sentence.

4. Circle the words that explain the <u>conception</u> Catesby and his friends had of their plot. What does **conception** mean in this case?

5. Underline the words that indicate the <u>potency</u> of the gunpowder. How can you increase the **potency** of chili?

6. What is another word for <u>folly</u> as it is used in the passage? Describe something that you consider to be pure **folly**.

7. Underline the word that tells what the letter-writer was <u>insistent</u> about. What is one situation in which a person should be **insistent**?

8. Circle the words that describe the <u>essence</u> of Guy Fawkes Day. What does **essence** mean?

"Preludes," "Journey of the Magi," and **"The Hollow Men"** by T. S. Eliot

Literary Analysis: Modernism

Modernism was a literary movement of the early-to-mid twentieth century in which writers attempted to break away from traditional forms and styles of the past. Modernist literature was highly influenced by industrialization and by World War I, which many writers felt left the world chaotic, fragmented, and sad. In poetry, the Modernist movement brought forth a technique known as imagism. Imagist poets, including T. S. Eliot, stood back from their subjects, not commenting outright on feeling or meaning. They used suggestive, musical language and clear images to evoke emotions in readers. Their images are like snapshots, which capture important moments of perception.

DIRECTIONS: *Connect the elements of Modernism with the following excerpts from the Modernist poems you have read.*

1. The morning comes to consciousness . . . From the sawdust-trampled street / With all its muddy feet that press / To early coffee-stands. / With the other masquerades / That time resumes, / One thinks of all the hands / That are raising dingy shades / In a thousand furnished rooms.

   In what way is the style and theme of this excerpt from "Preludes" uniquely Modernist?

   _____

   _____

   _____

2. And the night-fires going out, and the lack of shelters, / And the cities hostile and the towns unfriendly / And the villages dirty and charging high prices: / A hard time we had of it. / At the end we preferred to travel all night. / Sleeping in snatches, / With the voices singing in our ears, saying / That this was all folly.

   In what way is the style of this excerpt reflective of the Modernist movement? In what way does the subject matter of "The Journey of the Magi," and the faithful dedication of the Magi revealed in this excerpt, set it apart from the strictly Modernist viewpoints expressed in the other two poems?

   _____

   _____

   _____

3. The eyes are not here / There are no eyes here / In this valley of dying stars / In this hollow valley / This broken jaw of our lost kingdoms / In this last of meeting places / We grope together / And avoid speech / Gathered on this beach of the tumid river

   What attitude toward people and the modern world is expressed in this excerpt from "The Hollow Men"? In what way is its style and theme similar to that of "Preludes"?

   _____

   _____

   _____

Name _____ Date _____

Reading Strategy: Interpret

In order to understand the themes in T. S. Eliot's poetry, you must **interpret**, or find meaning, in repeated images, words, and phrases. By linking these elements, you can find the meanings they suggest. For example, notice the images Eliot presents of urban life in "Preludes." If you put these images together, what do you learn about Eliot's view of the modern world?

DIRECTIONS: *As you read the poems, use the following questions as a guide to search for meaning in the images and patterns of Eliot's poems.*

1. What images does Eliot use to describe the city in "Preludes"? What feeling is created by these images? What do these images say about his perception of modern, urban life?

   _____

   _____

   _____

2. What images in "Preludes" relate directly to the actions of humans in the urban setting? What does the pattern of these images suggest about the lives of the people?

   _____

   _____

   _____

3. In "Journey of the Magi," what images does Eliot give of the journey? What do these images suggest about the journey?

   _____

   _____

   _____

4. What images and repeated words in "Journey of the Magi" describe the feelings of the Magi after their journey? What do these elements suggest about the importance of the journey?

   _____

   _____

   _____

5. What images in "The Hollow Men" describe specific limitations of the hollow men? What do these details reveal about the men's situation in life?

   _____

   _____

   _____

"Preludes," "Journey of the Magi," and "The Hollow Men" by T. S. Eliot
Vocabulary Builder

Using the Root -fract-

In "Journey of the Magi," T. S. Eliot describes camels as "sore-footed and *refractory*." The word *refractory* means "stubborn" or "hard to manage." It contains the root *-fract-*, meaning "to break." A *refractory* camel is one that breaks away from the path which you want to take.

A. DIRECTIONS: *Complete each sentence with a word from the following list.*

          refract   fractional   fractious

1. He ate only a _____ portion of his meal.
2. Guards were trying to control the loud and _____ crowd.
3. A prism hanging in a window will _____ sunlight into different colors.

Using the Word List

galled	refractory	dispensation
supplication	tumid	

B. DIRECTIONS: *Choose a lettered pair that best expresses a relationship* similar *to that expressed in the numbered pair. Circle the letter of your choice.*

1. GALLED : FRICTION ::
   A. worked : accomplishment
   B. consume : food
   C. rested : sleep
   D. injury : sore

2. REFRACTORY : STUBBORN ::
   A. generous : unselfish
   B. organize : arrange
   C. ancient : contemporary
   D. quietly : whisper

3. DISPENSATION : BELIEF ::
   A. creation : invent
   B. theory : philosophy
   C. operation : machine
   D. thought : concentrate

4. SUPPLICATION : PRAYER ::
   A. organization : society
   B. belief : knowledge
   C. education : lesson
   D. instruction : learn

5. TUMID : SHRIVELED ::
   A. pester : annoy
   B. heat : scorching
   C. massive : miniature
   D. simple : plain

"Preludes," "Journey of the Magi," and **"The Hollow Men"** by T. S. Eliot

Grammar and Style: Adjectival Modifiers

An **adjectival modifier** is any word or word group that functions as an adjective. The poems of T. S. Eliot contain many examples of prepositional phrases, participial phrases, and adjective clauses used as adjectival modifiers. For example:

Prepositional phrase: "In this valley of dying stars"

The prepositional phrase of *dying stars* modifies *valley*.

Participial phrase: ". . . And the silken girls bringing sherbet."

The participial phrase *bringing sherbet* modifies *girls*.

Adjective clause: "I am moved by fancies/that are curled around these images . . ."

The adjective clause *that are curled around these images* modifies *fancies*.

A. PRACTICE: *For each of the following excerpts from "Preludes," "Journey of the Magi," and "The Hollow Men," underline the adjectival modifier and circle the word it modifies. Then, on the line following the excerpt, identify the modifier as a prepositional phrase, a participial phrase, or an adjective clause.*

1. And now a gusty shower wraps / The grimy scraps / Of withered leaves . . . _____

2. The worlds revolve like ancient women / Gathering fuel . . . _____

3. Those who have crossed / With direct eyes . . . _____

4. And newspapers from vacant lots . . . _____

5. With all its muddy feet that press . . . _____

6. Then the camel men cursing and grumbling . . . _____

B. Writing Application: *Write a description of the scene in "Preludes," using a variety of adjectival modifiers. Experiment with prepositional phrases, participial phrases, and adjective clauses. Underline each modifier in your paragraph.*

_____

_____

_____

_____

_____

_____

_____

_____

Name _____ Date _____

"Preludes," "Journey of the Magi," and **"The Hollow Men"** by T. S. Eliot
Support for Writing

Review "Preludes" and "Journey of the Magi" and think about the quotation that suggests that "humanity is trapped in a dreary, meaningless cycle of time." As you read, gather details about time and the human sense of not belonging. Record your details in the organizers.

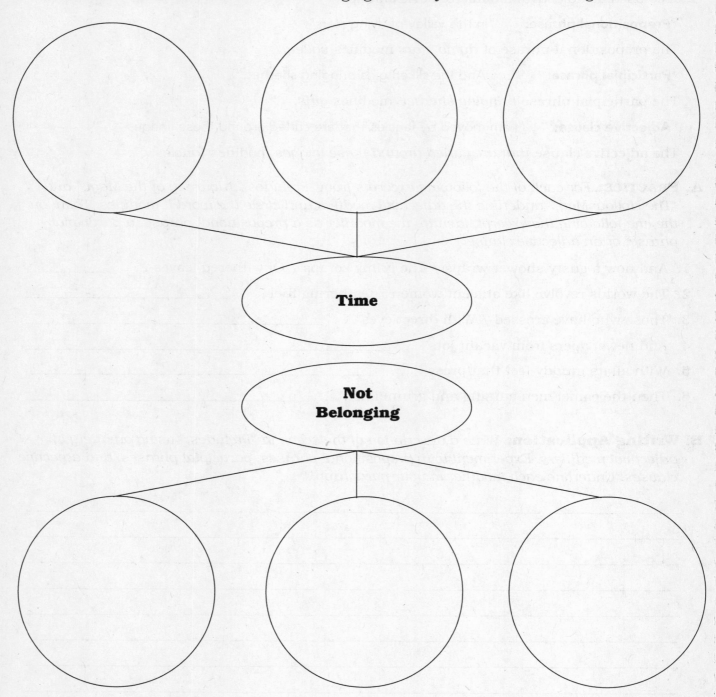

Look at the details you have collected and draw conclusions about Eliot's attitude toward these themes. Then, on a separate page, write your response to criticism.

"Preludes," "Journey of the Magi," and **"The Hollow Men"** by T. S. Eliot
Support for Extend Your Learning

Listening and Speaking

Use these questions to think about and collect ideas for your **debate on Modernism.** Remember to use an analogy (a comparison) and induction (a general conclusion based on specific examples) to help you prepare your arguments.

What is my strongest argument? _____

_____

_____

What objections might my opponents raise to this argument? _____

_____

_____

What is my opponents' strongest argument? _____

_____

_____

What objections can I raise to this argument? _____

_____

_____

Research and Technology

Use the following chart to compare and contrast Eliot's subject matter and techniques to Modernist visual art such as collage and Cubism. Use the details to write your **cultural report.**

T. S. Eliot's Subject Matter and Techniques	Modernist Developments in Visual Art

"Preludes," "Journey of the Magi," and **"The Hollow Men"** by T. S. Eliot
Enrichment: Music

Modernist Compositions

Modernism introduced great change not only to literature, but also to art and music. Modernist poets, including T. S. Eliot, experimented with forms and styles that were distinctly different from those used by poets in previous eras. At the same time, several composers introduced striking changes into the world of music, opera, and ballet. These changes signaled a break from the traditional sounds of classical compositions, to draw themes and styles from primitive folk tunes and jazz. Musicians Arnold Schoenberg of Austria and Igor Stravinsky of Russia created controversy when they wrote musical compositions in no particular key with irregular rhythms and conflicting sounds. Béla Bartók of Hungary created music that was simplified and emotionally restrained. American composer George Gershwin blended the techniques of popular music and jazz into his musical compositions. These composers influenced the contemporary music of today and represented a break from classical compositions such as those written by Franz Joseph Haydn, Wolfgang Amadeus Mozart, Ludwig van Beethoven, Franz Schubert, and Johannes Brahms.

DIRECTIONS: *The chart below lists the names and works of some of the most renowned Modernist musicians and composers. At a library, try to locate a classical musical selection by Haydn, Mozart, Beethoven, Schubert, or Brahms. Then try to locate the pieces by Modernist musicians. If you find other musical selections by the same composers, you may use those instead of the titles suggested. Listen to the pieces you find. Record your observations about the compositions in the space below. Think about how the Modernist pieces are different from the classical selections, and about how their style compares with the poetic innovations of T. S. Eliot.*

Composer	Observations of Style
George Gershwin *Rhapsody in Blue* **(1924)**	
Igor Stravinsky *The Rite of Spring* **(1913)**	
Arnold Schoenberg *Fourth Quartet* **(1936)**	
Béla Bartók *Cantata Profana* **(1930)**	

"Preludes," "Journey of the Magi," and **"The Hollow Men"** by T. S. Eliot
Selection Test A

Critical Reading *Identify the letter of the choice that best answers the question.*

____ 1. What setting does Eliot use in the first stanza of "Preludes"?
   A. winter evening in a city
   B. summer morning in the country
   C. summer evening in the country
   D. winter morning in his home

____ 2. How is the phrase "Six o'clock" a useful image in "Preludes"?
   A. It makes readers think of poetry.
   B. It makes readers think of love.
   C. It makes readers think of eating lunch.
   D. It makes readers think of the end of a day.

____ 3. In "Preludes," Eliot uses the Modernist technique of imagery. Which of the following uses an image of something that is not living to create a feeling of sadness?
   A. time resumes
   B. withered leaves about your feet
   C. You dozed
   D. across the skies

____ 4. In "Preludes," Eliot compares the planets to ancient women who are "Gathering fuel in vacant [empty] lots." What conclusion can you draw about the mood he creates with this line?
   A. The mood is fearful.
   B. The mood is innocent.
   C. The mood is hopeless.
   D. The mood is happy.

____ 5. Why did the speaker in "Journey of the Magi" make a long journey?
   A. to escape a war at home
   B. to see the newborn Christ
   C. to trade for goods
   D. to find his friends

____ 6. The speaker in "Journey of the Magi" says that the magi (wise men) traveled all night, even though there were "voices singing in our ears, saying / That this was all folly." What does the speaker mean?
   A. They sang to take their minds off the folly of their journey.
   B. Their journey was filled with singing and hopeful companionship.
   C. They were so tired that they sang to keep themselves awake.
   D. Even when they were tired and had doubts, they remained faithful.

____ 7. Based on the end of "Journey of the Magi," why were the magi no longer at ease in their kingdoms?
A. They were no longer welcome in the land they had left.
B. They no longer trusted people where they had lived.
C. The birth of Christ changed their lives and religion.
D. Their health had been destroyed by the journey.

____ 8. Why does Eliot use the word *we* in the line "We are the hollow men" from "The Hollow Men"?
A. to show that he is part of an important community
B. to show that people should all believe as he does
C. to show that he is a member of a large family
D. to show that he is referring to all modern people

____ 9. Who are the hollow men in Eliot's poem?
A. the nation's leaders
B. people who are starving
C. those who live meaningless lives
D. people who want to change the world

____ 10. What is one of the main ideas of "The Hollow Men"?
A. Religion is out of place in modern life.
B. People need to be saved to gain hope.
C. Most of us cannot control how we act.
D. Everyone today has strong faith.

____ 11. In "The Hollow Men" why does the poet say "There are no eyes here / In this valley of dying stars"?
A. No one speaks to anyone else.
B. Modern life is full of hopelessness.
C. The stars in the sky are dying.
D. Few people pay attention to nature.

Vocabulary and Grammar

____ 12. Which word could replace *tumid* in this sentence: "We could not cross the *tumid* river after the rains"?
A. shallow
B. dry
C. swift
D. swollen

____ 13. Which phrase from Eliot's poems includes an adjectival modifier, or a phrase that describes a noun?
A. "Lips that would kiss"
B. "The eyes are not here"
C. "We grope together"
D. "And the response"

Essay

14. Tone is the speaker's attitude or feelings toward his subject. The tone is different in the different parts of "Preludes" as well as within different lines of each part. In an essay, describe the overall tone of the poem. Give examples to support your description.

15. "Journey of the Magi" is a story told by a speaker who participated in a journey. In an essay, summarize the story. Who were the magi? Where were they going? What happened to them? Use examples from the poem to support your answers.

"Preludes," "Journey of the Magi," and "The Hollow Men" by T. S. Eliot
Selection Test B

Critical Reading *Identify the letter of the choice that best completes the statement or answers the question.*

____ 1. In the first stanza of "Preludes," what setting is described?
  A. a rural area in the stifling heat of summer
  B. a rural setting on a rainy winter evening
  C. a city on a rainy, winter evening
  D. a city on a foggy morning

____ 2. According to the speaker in "Preludes," what happens in the morning?
  A. People carry on with their various masquerades.
  B. People greet each other warmly at early morning coffee stands.
  C. People watch a thousand sordid images.
  D. People gather fuel.

____ 3. What does Eliot suggest about modern urban life with the images in the passage from "Preludes"?

  And now a gusty shower wraps / The grimy scraps / of withered leaves about your feet . . . The showers beat / On broken blinds and chimney-pots, and at the corner of the street / A lonely cab-horse steams and stamps.

  A. It is filled with hidden, natural beauty.
  B. It is lonely and sad until rain cleanses it.
  C. It is lonely, ugly, and filled with despair.
  D. It is filled with energy and life.

____ 4. What feeling or idea does Eliot express in the final lines of "Preludes"?
  A. that human beings are hopeless and doomed to suffer
  B. hope that the human spirit might move beyond its dreary circumstances
  C. that there is much laughter in the world
  D. that people are unable to recognize what is gentle and humorous

____ 5. What do repeated details in the poem "Journey of the Magi" reveal about the journey?
  A. The journey helps the Magi to appreciate humanity and nature.
  B. The journey brings the Magi into contact with interesting and friendly people.
  C. The journey is filled with excitement and adventure.
  D. The journey is long and difficult.

____ 6. What do the lines reveal about the Magi?

  At the end we preferred to travel all night, / Sleeping in snatches, / With the voices singing in our ears, saying / That this was all folly.

  A. They remained faithful, even when they had doubts and their journey became difficult.
  B. They were tired and resentful throughout their journey.
  C. They were continually in search of fun and folly.
  D. They did not want people to discover them, so they were forced to hide at night.

____ 7. Why are the Magi no longer at ease when they return to their kingdoms?
   A. They wanted more journeys and adventure.
   B. After the unfriendly journey, they no longer had respect for people.
   C. The birth of the baby changed their lives and their faith.
   D. They no longer believed in any form of religion.

____ 8. The allusion to Mistah Kurtz in "The Hollow Men" implies that
   A. the hollow men were corrupted by outside influences.
   B. one may become hollow by living among hollow men.
   C. the hollow men will cause the end of the world.
   D. self-delusion is the hollow men's greatest folly.

____ 9. Which image from "The Hollow Men" suggests the corruption of modern life?
   A. ". . . wind in dry grass"
   B. ". . . crossed staves / In a field"
   C. ". . . the eyes are / Sunlight on a broken column"
   D. "This broken jaw of our lost kingdoms"

____ 10. In "The Hollow Men," how might you interpret Eliot's use of the words *hollow, dried,* and *broken* to describe the hollow men?
   A. The hollow men spend their lives making repairs and gathering supplies.
   B. The lives of the hollow men are empty—void of spirituality or meaning.
   C. The hollow men suffer from the damaging effects of heat and wind.
   D. The hollow men are without money that would allow them to repair their homes.

____ 11. The passage that begins "Here we go round the prickly pear" from "The Hollow Men" conveys the idea of
   A. people's adaptability to progress and new developments.
   B. the perpetuation of childhood innocence in adulthood.
   C. people's ability to amuse themselves.
   D. the meaningless and repetitive behavior of modern life.

____ 12. One of the main ideas of "The Hollow Men" is that
   A. religious writings are irrelevant to modern life.
   B. salvation requires an act of will.
   C. life is too brief to be wasted.
   D. adults must avoid childish behavior.

Vocabulary and Grammar

____ 13. The camels used by the Magi are called *refractory* because they are
   A. tall and lean.
   B. exhausted.
   C. difficult to manage.
   D. calm and gentle.

____ 14. In "The Hollow Men," people are gathered on the beach of a *tumid* river, which is a river that is
  A. swollen with excess water.
  B. icy and cold.
  C. shallow and muddy.
  D. cluttered with leaves and trash.

____ 15. Identify the adjectival modifier in "You clasped the yellow soles of feet."
  A. You clasped the yellow soles
  B. You clasped
  C. the yellow soles
  D. of feet

____ 16. Which sentence contains a prepositional phrase used as an adjectival modifier?
  A. The worlds revolve like ancient women.
  B. The smell of steaks fills the winter evening.
  C. You tossed a blanket.
  D. I am moved by fancies.

____ 17. Which sentence contains an adjective clause used as an adjectival modifier?
  A. We preferred to travel at night.
  B. Then at dawn we came to a temperate valley.
  C. This was birth, certainly.
  D. We are people who are no longer at ease.

Essay

18. In an essay, describe the journey that is the focus of "Journey of the Magi." How do the Magi feel while on this journey? How do you know the journey is important to them? In what way does it change their lives? What specific images add to the meaning of the poem?

19. In an essay, describe why the poems "Preludes" and "The Hollow Men" are expressions of Modernism. In your essay, answer the following questions: What attitude toward humanity in the modern world is expressed in both poems? What style does the poet use to express this attitude? What specific images in both pieces convey the poet's meaning?

Vocabulary Warm-up Word Lists

Study these words from the selections. Then, complete the activities that follow.

Word List A

concealment [kuhn SEEL muhnt] *n.* the act of hiding
   The <u>concealment</u> of the moon behind clouds made the night quite dark.

emphasis [EM fuh sis] *n.* a stressing by the voice of a particular syllable, word, or phrase
   His mother's <u>emphasis</u> on the word *no* meant Raj would not get his way.

interlude [IN ter lood] *n.* a short interval of time that interrupts something
   Kevin enjoyed his <u>interlude</u> at the park between work sessions.

intolerant [in TAHL uhr uhnt] *adj.* unsympathetic
   Mr. Larson is <u>intolerant</u> of students who do not do their homework.

isolation [eye suh LAY shuhn] *n.* the state of being alone
   Mimi endured weeks of <u>isolation</u> in the cabin during the harsh winter.

leisurely [LEE zher lee] *adv.* in a slow, relaxed manner
   Carlos and Maria <u>leisurely</u> enjoyed their iced teas on the porch.

miraculous [muh RAK yuh luhs] *adj.* seeming to be impossible
   The friendship between the lion and the lamb was <u>miraculous</u>.

rapture [RAP chuhr] *n.* very great or complete pleasure or delight
   In a <u>rapture</u>, Marla danced gracefully in Pedro's arms.

Word List B

accumulation [uh kyoom yuh LAY shuhn] *n.* material gathered together
   Pete's <u>accumulation</u> of rare art was quite valuable.

acquired [uh KWYRD] *adj.* attained through one's own efforts
   The enjoyment of coffee is an <u>acquired</u> taste.

architectural [ahr kuh TEK chuhr uhl] *adj.* having to do with the science of designing and putting up buildings
   The old hotel was an excellent example of Victorian <u>architectural</u> style.

dreadful [DRED fuhl] *adj.* causing fear or uneasiness; terrible
   The <u>dreadful</u> threat to our safety was met by a show of force.

fashionable [FASH uhn uh buhl] *adj.* stylish; acceptable to wealthy or powerful people
   Darla lives in a <u>fashionable</u> part of the city.

modified [MAHD uh fyd] *v.* made less extreme
   After hearing the debate, Skip <u>modified</u> his political views.

reverently [REV uhr uhnt lee] *adv.* showing great respect
   Sylvia <u>reverently</u> curtsied when she met the queen.

tamper [TAM puhr] *v.* to interfere, as by mishandling or misusing
   Please do not <u>tamper</u> with my new camera.

Poetry of W. H. Auden, Louis MacNeice, and Stephen Spender
Vocabulary Warm-up Exercises

Exercise A *Fill in each blank below with the appropriate word from Word List A.*

Joyce was getting tired of the [1] _____ attitude of her friends and family, who just would not understand or respect her desire to be alone. She thought she would enjoy the [2] _____ of her family's mountain cabin. In no hurry, she [3] _____ packed up and left. When she got there, she went into a [4] _____ over the beauty of the surroundings. Sunset over the lake was so beautiful that first night that it seemed like a [5] _____ event. She was determined to put the [6] _____ on relaxing, for she felt that she needed a good rest. She enjoyed watching the squirrels as they worked hard on the [7] _____ of their winter food supply. Joyce enjoyed every moment of her one-week [8] _____ among the pines.

Exercise B *Decide whether each statement is true or false. Circle T or F, and explain your answer.*

1. The roof of a house is an <u>architectural</u> element.
   T / F _____

2. A room with an <u>accumulation</u> of dust probably has to be cleaned.
   T / F _____

3. An <u>acquired</u> talent is something that you were born with.
   T / F _____

4. If you heard a bear roar near your campsite, you might get a <u>dreadful</u> feeling.
   T / F _____

5. A crowd shouts <u>reverently</u> when its team is losing a game.
   T / F _____

6. When you <u>tamper</u> with something, you leave it completely unchanged.
   T / F _____

7. A <u>fashionable</u> place is one that wealthy and stylish people would avoid.
   T / F _____

8. If you refuse to change your mind about something, people might say you have <u>modified</u> your attitude.
   T / F _____

Name _____ Date _____

Poetry of W. H. Auden, Louis MacNeice, and Stephen Spender
Reading Warm-up A

Read the following passage. Pay special attention to the underlined words. Then, read it again, and complete the activities. Use a separate sheet of paper for your written answers.

According to Greek mythology, Daedalus was a talented architect, inventor, and master craftsman from Athens. He moved to Crete and started to work for King Minos and his wife, Queen Pasiphae.

Daedelus soon angered King Minos, who was <u>intolerant</u> of even the slightest disrespect—he simply would not allow it. Minos sent Daedalus and his son Icarus away to the Labyrinth, a giant maze, where their <u>isolation</u> from society would be their punishment. Minos knew that being alone all the time would be a terrible fate for the father and son.

Daedalus had built the Labyrinth many years before for the imprisonment and <u>concealment</u> of the Minotaur, a half-man, half-bull that had been born on the island. Because Daedalus had been the architect of the Labyrinth, he knew his way out of it, but escape by land or sea was not a possibility. Since Minos controlled the sea around the island, Daedalus knew that the only way out was by air.

Daedalus constructed wings for himself and his son. He made them with feathers held together by wax. Daedalus put the <u>emphasis</u> on safety, stressing that his son not fly too close to the sun, for it would melt the wax. Soon, father and son were ready to attempt the seemingly impossible. It was truly a <u>miraculous</u> accomplishment when they took off and flew like birds.

As the two began to fly <u>leisurely</u> and slowly away from Crete, Icarus forgot his father's warning. In a <u>rapture</u> of delight with his new-found freedom, he flew higher and higher, until the wax holding his wings together melted. His happy <u>interlude</u> in the air over, Icarus plunged quickly to the sea. His father, unable to save him, could only watch helplessly as his son disappeared beneath the surface.

1. Circle the words that tell what <u>intolerant</u> means. Then, explain how King Minos showed that he was *intolerant*.

2. Circle the words that mean about the same as <u>isolation</u>. Tell about a time you found yourself in *isolation*.

3. Underline the word that tells what was meant for the <u>concealment</u> of the Minotaur. What might be a good place for the *concealment* of a small treasure?

4. Circle the word that means about the same as <u>emphasis</u>. What is one safety rule that you think deserves great *emphasis*?

5. Circle the words in a nearby sentence that mean about the same as <u>miraculous</u>. Use *miraculous* in a sentence.

6. Underline the word that means about the same as <u>leisurely</u>. What is one activity of yours that you do in a *leisurely* fashion?

7. Underline the word that means about the same as <u>rapture</u>. Use *rapture* in a sentence.

8. Circle the words that tell what Icarus did during his <u>interlude</u> in the air. What is an *interlude* you might enjoy?

Poetry of W. H. Auden, Louis MacNeice, and Stephen Spender
Reading Warm-up B

Read the following passage. Pay special attention to the underlined words. Then, read it again, and complete the activities. Use a separate sheet of paper for your written answers.

Bauhaus was a school of applied arts, founded in Germany in 1919. The founders of the school wanted to bring together building designers who worked in the architectural field as well as those who worked in modern technology and the decorative arts. Their aim was to change not only building design, but also to influence industrial art and art in general. The idea was that creative minds could work together and learn from one another.

The Bauhaus school developed a style that can be characterized as spare, functional, and geometric. Bauhaus designs were not immediately popular or fashionable when they were first developed, but apparently they are an acquired taste because they are highly prized today. Anyone who has an accumulation of Bauhaus-inspired art has a valuable collection indeed.

Walter Gropius, an architect who was one of the founders of the school, wrote a manifesto stating his aims. He said, "The ultimate aim of all creative activity is a building! The decoration of buildings was once the noblest function of fine arts, and fine arts were indispensable to great architecture. Today they exist in complacent isolation, and can only be rescued by the conscious cooperation and collaboration of all craftsmen."

In 1933, the Nazi government, convinced that the Bauhaus architects were trying to tamper with German culture, closed the Bauhaus school. They claimed that the Bauhaus artists were producing dreadful art. In fact, they called it "cosmopolitan rubbish." Many of the Bauhaus staff and students moved to Chicago, where the New Bauhaus was founded in 1937. There, the original philosophy of Gropius and the other founders was modified slightly to meet American requirements. The New Bauhaus merged, in the 1950s, with the Illinois Institute of Technology; the school is still rated, almost reverently, as a highly respected school of design.

1. Underline the words that explain what people in the architectural field do. Then, give an example of something *architectural*.

2. Circle the word that means about the same as fashionable. Name a *fashionable* clothing style.

3. According to the passage, why is it apparent that the Bauhaus style is an acquired taste? Define *acquired*.

4. Circle the word that means about the same as accumulation. What might you do with an *accumulation* of old CDs?

5. Underline the words that tell with what the architects were accused of trying to tamper. What might happen if you *tamper* with a camera?

6. Circle the words that tell exactly how dreadful the Nazi government thought Bauhaus art was. Then, use *dreadful* in a sentence.

7. What word could replace modified in the passage without changing the meaning? What might you expect if a friend told you she *modified* her hairstyle?

8. Circle the words that are a clue to the meaning of the word reverently.

"In Memory of W. B. Yeats" and **"Musée des Beaux Arts"** by W. H. Auden
"Carrick Revisited" by Louis MacNeice
"Not Palaces" by Stephen Spender
Literary Analysis: Theme

A poem's **theme,** which is its central idea, concern, or purpose, may be directly stated. In some cases, theme may be implied by the poet's choice of words, images, tone, or mood.

DIRECTIONS: *State what each set of lines indicates about the poem's theme. Determine whether the lines express theme directly or indirectly.*

"In Memory of W. B. Yeats"

1. Now he is scattered among a hundred cities
   And wholly given over to unfamiliar affections;
   To find his happiness in another kind of wood
   And be punished by another code of conscience.
   The words of a dead man
   Are modified in the guts of the living.

   _____

   _____

"Musée des Beaux Arts"

2. . . . the expensive delicate ship that must have seen
   Something amazing, a boy falling out of the sky,
   Had somewhere to get to and sailed calmly on.

   _____

   _____

"Carrick Revisited"

3. Torn before birth from where my fathers dwelt,
   Schooled from the age of ten to a foreign voice,
   Yet neither western Ireland nor southern England
   Cancels this interlude; what chance misspelt
   May never now be righted by my choice.

   _____

   _____

"In Memory of W. B. Yeats" and **"Musée des Beaux Arts"** by W. H. Auden
"Carrick Revisited" by Louis MacNeice
"Not Palaces" by Stephen Spender

Reading Strategy: Paraphrase

When you **paraphrase** a poet's words, or restate them in your own words, you can check your understanding of the poem's basic idea. Then you can interpret the poet's original work and appreciate how its language, imagery, and tone add depth to its meaning.

A. DIRECTIONS: *Write a paraphrase for each set of lines.*

"Musée des Beaux Arts"

1. . . . even the dreadful martyrdom must run its course
   Anyhow in a corner, some untidy spot
   Where the dogs go on with their doggy life . . .

   _____

   _____

"Carrick Revisited"

2. Time and place—our bridgeheads into reality
   But also its concealment! Out of the sea
   We land on the Particular and lose
   All other possible bird's-eye views, the Truth
   That is of Itself for Itself—but not for me.

   _____

   _____

"Not Palaces"

3. It is too late for rare accumulation,
   For family pride, for beauty's filtered dusts;
   I say, stamping the words with emphasis,
   Drink from here energy and only energy
   To will this time's change.

   _____

   _____

B. DIRECTIONS: *Write an explanation of how each paraphrase in Part A helps you understand the poet's original words.*

1. _____

2. _____

3. _____

"In Memory of W. B. Yeats" and **"Musée des Beaux Arts"** by W. H. Auden
"Carrick Revisited" by Louis MacNeice
"Not Palaces" by Stephen Spender

Vocabulary Builder

Using the Root -top-

A. DIRECTIONS: *Knowing that the word root -top- means "place" and drawing upon your knowledge of other word roots, circle the letter of the best answer for each question.*

1. What does a *topographer* do?
   A. designs buildings
   B. plans cities
   C. records geographical features
   D. studies the use of electricity

2. Where would you find a *utopia*?
   A. in someone's imagination
   B. in the ocean
   C. on a plain
   D. in a distant galaxy

Using the Word List

sequestered	topographical	affinities
prenatal	intrigues	

B. DIRECTIONS: *Choose the phrase that is the most appropriate description for each numbered word. Circle the letter of your choice.*

1. sequestered
   A. a small fish in a big pond
   B. a knight on a mission
   C. a dancer on a stage
   D. a patient in quarantine

2. topographical
   A. a political map of Britain
   B. a spinning carnival ride
   C. a relief chart of a park
   D. a featureless, grassy plain

3. affinities
   A. a group of total strangers
   B. a network of interpersonal relationships
   C. an endless universe
   D. a structure made of building blocks

4. prenatal
   A. a ship being repaired
   B. a poet's first book
   C. a check-up for a mother-to-be
   D. a cat lapping up a large saucer of cream

5. intrigues
   A. conspirators' plots
   B. pilots' instruments
   C. students' textbooks
   D. priests' vestments

"In Memory of W. B. Yeats" and **"Musée des Beaux Arts"** by W. H. Auden
"Carrick Revisited" by Louis MacNeice
"Not Palaces" by Stephen Spender

Grammar and Style: Parallel Structure

Parallel structure is the repeated use of the same grammatical form or pattern. Poets may use parallel structure to create a natural rhythm or flow in their writing or to emphasize an idea. In the following lines from "Not Palaces," the parallel prepositional phrases are underlined:

It is too late for rare accumulation,
For family pride, for beauty's filtered dusts.

A. PRACTICE: *Rewrite the italicized words to make the sentence structures parallel.*

1. W. H. Auden wrote poetry and *was a teacher* in numerous universities.

   _____

2. Auden speaks of Yeats as a poet and *he was* a man.

   _____

3. Returning to his childhood home makes MacNeice recall his youth and *he considers* his identity.

   _____

4. For Spender, poetry has a way of changing attitudes and *it can promote* social equality.

   _____

B. Writing Application: *Rewrite each of the following sentences, incorporating parallel sentence structure.*

1. Yeats died on a day that was dark, and it was cold.

   _____

   _____

2. The "Old Masters" refers to artists from Belgium and Holland and others from Italy.

   _____

   _____

3. Bruegel enjoyed painting scenes of laborers, including harvesters and hunting scenes.

   _____

   _____

4. The speaker in "Carrick Revisited" admires the landscape and is remembering his childhood.

   _____

   _____

Name _____ Date _____

"In Memory of W. B. Yeats" and **"Musée des Beaux Arts"** by W. H. Auden
"Carrick Revisited" by Louis MacNeice
"Not Palaces" by Stephen Spender
Support for Writing

Write the details and images about the artwork you chose in the chart below. Then, list words and phrases to describe these details. Try to think of vivid and precise words and phrases that will help the reader "see" the details in the painting.

Images and Details	Vivid Words and Phrases

On a separate page, use the ideas you have gathered to draft your poem about the artwork. Try to get across one main impression in your work.

"In Memory of W. B. Yeats" and **"Musée des Beaux Arts"** by W. H. Auden
"Carrick Revisited" by Louis MacNeice
"Not Palaces" by Stephen Spender

Support for Extend Your Learning

Listening and Speaking

Prepare for your **group reading** by analyzing the mood and tone in Yeats's poem. Write words and phrases that describe the mood and tone of each section. If the mood or tone changes within a section, tell how. Discuss your analysis with your group.

Analysis of the Mood and Tone in "In Memory of W. B. Yeats"

Section	Mood	Tone
1		
2		
3		

Research and Technology

List Spender's ideals for art, based on "Not Palaces," in the left column. Then, list an artist and one of his or her works that illustrates the ideal. Use your ideas as you work with your group to assemble an **art exhibition.**

Spender's Ideals	Artist/Work of Art

"In Memory of W. B. Yeats" and **"Musée des Beaux Arts"** by W. H. Auden
"Carrick Revisited" by Louis MacNeice
"Not Palaces" by Stephen Spender
Enrichment: Social Studies

The Great Depression

For many people, the 1920s was a time of economic prosperity. Growing economic problems, however, culminated in the Great Depression. Throughout the decade, prices for farm products dropped dramatically. Many farmers, unable to sell their crops, lost their incomes and their farms. Despite a fifty-percent increase in industrial production, wages for industrial workers rose very slowly. Unable to afford products, workers curtailed their spending, and as a result, business sales suffered. Finally, when stock prices dropped in October of 1929, a record number of stocks were sold. The pressure on investors to sell their stocks caused the stock market to crash. Over the next three years, stock prices fell, thousands of banks failed, and millions of people lost their jobs.

This economic disaster soon affected the world economy. Countries like Great Britain, with war debts from World War I, were seriously hurt financially. The British economy experienced a cycle of decreased production due to decreased demand, and by the spring of 1931, unemployment in Great Britain had risen to twenty-five percent. In Germany and Italy, depressed economic conditions contributed to the rise of fascism. The depression continued with little improvement until the outbreak of war in 1939, when war demands increased production.

DIRECTIONS: *Read the following lines from "In Memory of W. B. Yeats," which Auden wrote in February of 1939. Explain how the social conditions of the time might have influenced Auden's writing.*

1. In the nightmare of the dark
   All the dogs of Europe bark,
   And the living nations wait,
   Each sequestered in its hate;

   _____

   _____

   _____

2. With the farming of a verse
   Make a vineyard of the curse,
   Sing of human unsuccess
   In a rapture of distress;

   _____

   _____

   _____

"In Memory of W. B. Yeats" and **"Musée des Beaux Arts"** by W. H. Auden
"Carrick Revisited" by Louis MacNeice
"Not Palaces" by Stephen Spender

Selection Test A

Critical Reading *Identify the letter of the choice that best answers the question.*

___ 1. What does Time respect more than beauty or bravery in "In Memory of W. B. Yeats"?
    A. Time respects people who love with all their hearts.
    B. Time respects people who not care about death.
    C. Time respects people who give life to language.
    D. Time respects people who devote their lives to others.

___ 2. Which is the best paraphrase for these lines from "In Memory of W. B. Yeats"?
    William Yeats is laid to rest: / Let the Irish vessel lie / Emptied of its poetry.

    A. William Yeats's body has been put on a ship to go to Ireland for burial.
    B. William Yeats is dead; the Irish nation has lost its poetry.
    C. William Yeats is dead and will not be able to travel on the Irish ship.
    D. William Yeats is resting on an Irish ship that will soon sail.

___ 3. What is the theme of "In Memory of W. B. Yeats"?
    A. Yeats will be long remembered as a great leader.
    B. Now that Yeats is dead, his poetry will be forgotten.
    C. Yeats lived an unhappy life and welcomed death.
    D. Yeats is dead, but his poetry still inspires readers.

___ 4. What painting that Auden describes in "Musée des Beaux Arts" is ignored by most people?
    A. a painting of children playing and skating
    B. a painting of a person eating at a window
    C. a painting of the fall of Icarus
    D. a painting of an older person who is suffering

___ 5. What can you infer about Auden's attitude toward art in "Musée des Beaux Arts"?
    A. Art can help us understand everyday life.
    B. People should study art in schools.
    C. Art of the past is not appreciated today.
    D. Not all art is important to all people.

___ 6. Which sentence paraphrases: "Our past we know / But not its meaning" from "Carrick Revisited"?
    A. Sometimes events happen, without any meaning or purpose.
    B. We cannot know how past experiences shaped our lives.
    C. We can learn about our past by revisiting our childhood homes.
    D. People should forget about their pasts and live for the present.

___ 7. What is the theme of "Carrick Revisited"?
  A. Western Ireland had a lasting influence on the speaker's poetry.
  B. Childhood experiences are quickly forgotten as people grow older.
  C. People want to know how their past influences their lives.
  D. Most people value their childhood experiences above all others.

___ 8. What are the "palaces" that Spender refers to in "Not Palaces"?
  A. large buildings
  B. homes of the wealthy
  C. traditional art
  D. modern art

___ 9. What does the speaker in "Not Palaces" want people to do?
  A. write poetry
  B. feed the hungry
  C. live in palaces
  D. accept new ideas of art

___ 10. What is the theme of "Not Palaces"?
  A. In the past, art was for the few; now it should be for all.
  B. Average people do not have the taste to appreciate great art.
  C. Art that is created for common people is not very good.
  D. Not all people can know and appreciate art.

Vocabulary and Grammar

___ 11. Which phrase best defines *prenatal* in the following sentence?
  During her *prenatal* examination, Sarah was told that she was in good health.

  A. in history
  B. before college
  C. before birth
  D. without expectations

___ 12. Which line from "Musée des Beaux Arts" contains an example of parallel structure?
  A. "While someone else is eating or opening a window or just walking dully along"
  B. "They never forgot / That even the dreadful martyrdom must run its course"
  C. "the sun shone / As it had to on the white legs disappearing into the green / Water"
  D. "the expensive delicate ship . . . Had somewhere to get to and sailed calmly on."

Essay

13. The theme of a poem is its main purpose or concern. Choose one of the poems from this group: "In Memory of W. B. Yeats," "Musée des Beaux Arts," "Carrick Revisited," or "Not Palaces." In an essay, identify the main theme. Then, identify images, symbols, examples, or other evidence from the poem that helps support the theme.

14. "In Memory of W. B. Yeats" is an elegy, a poem written to honor someone who has died. In an essay, explain what Auden thought of Yeats. What does he say about his personal life and personality? What does he think of his poetry? Describe details from the poem that support these ideas.

"In Memory of W. B. Yeats" and **"Musée des Beaux Arts"** by W. H. Auden
"Carrick Revisited" by Louis MacNeice
"Not Palaces" by Stephen Spender
Selection Test B

Critical Reading *Identify the letter of the choice that best completes the statement or answers the question.*

_____ 1. "In Memory of W. B. Yeats" is an unusual elegy because the speaker claims that
   A. Yeats was foolish in some ways.
   B. Yeats's death was mourned by nature.
   C. Yeats will eventually be forgotten.
   D. Yeats's poetry is vitally important.

_____ 2. According to the speaker in the poem "In Memory of W. B. Yeats," Yeats's poetic legacy is his
   A. readers' individual reactions to his verse.
   B. rejuvenation of Irish poetry in the modern world.
   C. radicalization of Irish politics.
   D. influence on Modernist poets.

_____ 3. Which is the best paraphrase of the following lines from "In Memory of W. B. Yeats"?
   The words of a dead man
   Are modified in the guts of the living.
   A. The living don't understand Yeats's poetry.
   B. After his death, Yeats became a more important poet.
   C. The speaker does not agree with some interpretations of Yeats's poetry.
   D. Yeats's poetry inspires his readers in different ways.

_____ 4. What is the theme of "In Memory of W. B. Yeats"?
   A. Yeats's personal life was painful and tragic.
   B. Yeats changed the course of Irish politics through poetry.
   C. Yeats's poetry continues to inspire his readers.
   D. Many people failed to appreciate Yeats's gifts.

_____ 5. What does Auden imply about art in "Musée des Beaux Arts"?
   A. People should venerate the work of great artists.
   B. Art can be relevant to everyday life.
   C. Art speaks only to its own generation.
   D. Only the well educated fully appreciate art.

_____ 6. What is the theme of "Musée des Beaux Arts"?
   A. Society should do more to help the unfortunate.
   B. There are as many interpretations of a painting as there are viewers.
   C. Tragedy means nothing to those who are unaffected by it.
   D. The Old Masters were obsessed with human suffering.

____ 7. What does the speaker of "Carrick Revisited" mean when he says he was "schooled from the age of ten to a foreign voice"?
A. The speaker did not attend school until age ten.
B. Born in Ireland, the speaker was educated in England.
C. The speaker forgot the language of his birth.
D. The speaker now refuses to speak English.

____ 8. Which is the best paraphrase of the following lines from "Carrick Revisited"?
. . . Our past we know
But not its meaning—whether it meant well.

A. Memories of childhood are painful.
B. The speaker understands his past by returning to his childhood home.
C. We can never truly understand how past experiences have shaped us.
D. One should live in the present, not the past.

____ 9. Which statement best summarizes the theme of "Carrick Revisited"?
A. Artists are more sensitive to their surroundings than other people.
B. A conflict of national identity can result in a personal identity crisis.
C. Artists draw their inspiration from childhood memories.
D. An artist yearns to understand the influences that have shaped his identity.

____ 10. What does the speaker of "Not Palaces" urge the audience to do?
A. build palaces
B. change ideas about art
C. become poets
D. feed the hungry

____ 11. Which is the best paraphrase of the lines from "Not Palaces"?
Touch, love, all senses;
Leave your gardens, your singing feasts,
Your dreams of suns circling before our sun,
Of heaven after our world.

A. Abandon simple pastimes.
B. Open yourselves up to new interpretations of art.
C. Consider new scientific theories.
D. Focus on sensory details.

Vocabulary and Grammar

____ 12. This atlas indicates _____ details, such as mountains and rivers.
A. sequestered
B. topographical
C. affinities
D. prenatal

___ 13. _____, such as a love of poetry, drew Auden to Yeats and his poetry.
   A. Intrigues
   B. Sequestered
   C. Prenatal
   D. Affinities

___ 14. Which set of lines best demonstrates parallel structure?
   A. "It is too late for rare accumulation, / For family pride, for beauty's filtered dusts;"
   B. "Earth, receive an honored guest; / William Yeats is laid to rest:"
   C. "They never forgot / That even the dreadful martyrdom must run its course"
   D. "Back to Carrick, the castle as plumb assured / As thirty years ago—Which war was which?"

___ 15. Which italicized part indicates parallel structure?
   A. *Yeats,* who was Irish, and MacNeice, who was British, both wrote about Ireland.
   B. Yeats, who was Irish, *and* MacNeice, who was British, both wrote about Ireland.
   C. Yeats, who was Irish, and *MacNeice, who was British,* both wrote about Ireland.
   D. Yeats, who was Irish, and MacNeice, who was British, *both wrote about Ireland.*

Essay

16. As in all literary works, theme in poetry can be either stated directly or implied. In an essay, identify the theme of two of the poems, and explain whether the poets state the theme directly or imply it. Support your conclusions about theme with evidence from the poems.

17. Of these three poets, whose interpretation of poetry and art resonates most with your own? Why? In an essay, explain the poet's views and why you agree with them. Contrast this poet and his views with the poet whose views are most in conflict with your own.

Vocabulary Warm-up Word Lists

Study these words from the selections. Then, complete the activities that follow.

Word List A

alternative [awl TER nuh tiv] *n.* either of two or more choices
  We had no <u>alternative</u> but to turn right onto the one-way street.

certainty [SER tuhn tee] *n.* the fact or condition of being sure
  Darlene competed with the almost complete <u>certainty</u> that she would win.

committed [kuh MIT id] *v.* obligated, bound, or pledged to do something
  Amy had <u>committed</u> herself to a life of service to others.

futility [fyoo TIL uh tee] *n.* complete lack of effectiveness; uselessness
  The <u>futility</u> of trying to move the huge boulder by myself was obvious.

intention [in TEN shuhn] *n.* plan, purpose, or aim
  My <u>intention</u> was to hit the bull's-eye, but I missed the entire dartboard.

invariably [in VEHR ee uh blee] *adv.* without change
  Mark tries to dress well, but <u>invariably</u> his shirt clashes with his pants.

motives [MOH tivz] *n.* reasons or causes that make a person act
  Carl's <u>motives</u> for wanting to help homeless children were honorable.

wretched [RECH id] *adj.* utterly miserable
  The <u>wretched</u> conditions in the primitive hospital made the patients sicker.

Word List B

Buddhist [BOO dist] *adj.* pertaining to the Asian religion of Buddhism
  While in Tibet, George visited a <u>Buddhist</u> temple.

comparable [KAHM puh ruh buhl] *adj.* similar enough to be compared
  Don and Alan are <u>comparable</u> in their excellent soccer skills.

inflicted [in FLIK tid] *v.* gave by striking
  The blows that were <u>inflicted</u> on the boxer caused permanent damage.

innumerable [in NOO muhr uh buhl] *adj.* too many to be counted
  Erin has <u>innumerable</u> freckles on her face.

oppressed [uh PREST] *v.* burdened or kept down by unjust use of force
  The greedy king <u>oppressed</u> the peasants for years before they rebelled.

petty [PET ee] *adj.* of little importance; minor
  Molly and Dee had a <u>petty</u> argument, but they made up quickly.

squeamish [SKWEE mish] *adj.* easily made a little sick at the stomach
  Because she was so <u>squeamish</u>, Betsy closed her eyes at the gory part.

tyranny [TEER uh nee] *n.* absolute power used unfairly
  We cannot allow the <u>tyranny</u> of the strong over the weak.

Name _____ Date _____

"Shooting an Elephant" by George Orwell
Vocabulary Warm-up Exercises

Exercise A *Fill in each blank below with the appropriate word from Word List A.*

After a totally [1] _____ week with the flu, I decided that I needed a
reward. My [2] _____ was to cheer myself up and have some fun. Carol
suggested biking, and Chad suggested fishing, but neither [3] _____
appealed to me. I knew what their [4] _____ were—those were their favorite activities, and they wanted to tag along. But I knew with [5] _____
what to do. When I take a walk on the beach, I am [6] _____ cheered up.
I knew the [7] _____ of any other plan. Without much coaxing, I was
[8] _____ to taking that walk.

Exercise B *Use complete sentences to answer the questions below.*

1. Name two things in nature that are <u>innumerable</u>.

   _____

2. If a group of people were <u>oppressed</u>, what might one of their complaints be?

   _____

3. What do you think is the difference between <u>petty</u> theft and grand theft?

   _____

4. If you could have talents <u>comparable</u> to those of someone you admire, what would
   those talents be?

   _____

5. What do you think is the best way to stop the <u>tyranny</u> of a bully?

   _____

6. What is one type of food that makes you feel a bit <u>squeamish</u>?

   _____

7. If a government <u>inflicted</u> unfair taxes, what might the people do?

   _____

8. If you met a <u>Buddhist</u> priest, what question would you like to ask him?

   _____

"Shooting an Elephant" by George Orwell
Reading Warm-up A

Read the following passage. Pay special attention to the underlined words. Then, read it again, and complete the activities. Use a separate sheet of paper for your written answers.

Except for minor physical differences, African elephants and Asian elephants are quite similar. In the Asian elephant, only the male has tusks. Both male and female African elephants have tusks. Tusks grow throughout the lifetime of the animal. That is why they are almost <u>invariably</u> larger in older animals.

Elephants live in small migratory herds of eight to thirty animals. A dominant female leads the herd. When the males mature, they leave the herd. Their <u>intention</u> is to live alone or in small bachelor herds. Elephants eat grasses, leaves, twigs, and bark. A food source <u>alternative</u> is agricultural crops, such as bananas and sugar, if they are available.

The greatest threat to elephants is loss of habitat when humans move into their territories. As elephants raid farms in search of food, they are killed by farmers who consider them pests. Another great threat to elephants is poaching by humans whose <u>motives</u> include harvesting their tusks. The ivory in the tusks is quite valuable. Even though an ivory ban was enacted in 1989, ivory is still traded legally in Japan. Many countries claim that the ivory trade helps them control their elephant populations and reduce losses in agriculture. These countries can now legally sell limited amounts of ivory to Japan. Because illegally obtained ivory can easily be included in these sales, the <u>futility</u> of the ban is obvious.

Those in favor of a continued ivory trade say it is a <u>certainty</u> that the sale of ivory helps local and national economies. They say the animals would suffer <u>wretched</u> lives of starvation and misery if allowed to grow in numbers. Those who are <u>committed</u> to banning ivory sales say that any ivory trade will lead to increased poaching. They fear a dangerous decline in the elephant population.

1. Underline the words that tell why tusks are almost <u>invariably</u> larger in older animals. Then, tell what *invariably* means.

2. Underline what the <u>intention</u> of the male elephant is when he leaves the herd. Then, use *intention* in a sentence.

3. Circle two things elephants might use as a food source <u>alternative</u>. Then, tell what an *alternative* might be to cereal for breakfast.

4. Circle the words that describe one of the <u>motives</u> of humans who kill elephants. Then, tell what *motives* means.

5. Underline the words that best explain the <u>futility</u> of the ivory ban. Use *futility* in a sentence.

6. Circle the words that tell what is a <u>certainty</u>, according to those in favor of ivory trading. What is one thing that you think is a *certainty*?

7. Underline the words that tell why the animals' lives would be <u>wretched</u>. Then, tell what *wretched* means.

8. Circle the words that explain the position of those who are <u>committed</u> to banning ivory sales. What is one idea, belief, or goal to which you are *committed*?

Name _____ Date _____

"Shooting an Elephant" by George Orwell
Reading Warm-up B

Read the following passage. Pay special attention to the underlined words. Then, read it again, and complete the activities. Use a separate sheet of paper for your written answers.

The use of working elephants in Southeast Asia has been going on for thousands of years. Once trained, these large creatures are used in <u>innumerable</u> ways in the logging and tourism industries. Logging teams are made up of five or six elephants and about fifteen men.

You might wonder why the huge elephant would allow a <u>petty</u> human to dominate it, for it is obvious that in size and strength, the two creatures are not even <u>comparable</u>— the elephant is at least ten times larger. Nevertheless, the elephant eventually submits to the <u>tyranny</u> and oppression of its human masters. A <u>squeamish</u> person, easily shocked, might think that elephants should be allowed to live in the wild, with no interference from humans. However, the argument can be made that the animals are not really being <u>oppressed</u> by being forced to work. In fact, some might say that they are being protected from the wild, where all sorts of hardship and danger might be <u>inflicted</u> on them.

Elephant trainers are called *mahouts*. Elephants get used to their own mahouts and will not take orders from anyone else. Elephants train every day for six hours in the morning, learning how to handle logs and do other tasks. A mature elephant can lift logs that weigh over a thousand pounds and can drag loads of up to one and a half tons. Once trained, an elephant will work its entire life; average life expectancy for elephants is less than fifty years, but if an elephant lasts until age sixty, it is usually allowed to retire. The only other time they can rest is on <u>Buddhist</u> holy days and for three months during the dry season when, like their mahouts, they do not work.

1. Underline the words that tell where elephants are used in <u>innumerable</u> ways. What is a word that means about the same as *innumerable*?

2. Circle the words that tell why a human might seem <u>petty</u> in comparison to an elephant. Then, describe a *petty* fault that a friend of yours has.

3. Underline the words that tell why the elephant is not <u>comparable</u> to a human. Then, describe two items in a classroom that are *comparable* in size or shape.

4. Circle the word that means about the same as <u>tyranny</u>. Tell what *tyranny* means.

5. Underline the words that mean about the same as <u>squeamish</u>. Use *squeamish* in a sentence.

6. Underline the words that tell how some people feel that elephants are <u>oppressed</u>. What might make you feel *oppressed*?

7. Circle the words that tell what might be <u>inflicted</u> on elephants in the wild. Tell what *inflicted* means.

8. Circle the phrase that indicates that the word <u>Buddhist</u> has something to do with a religion. Use *Buddhist* in a sentence.

Name _____ Date _____

"Shooting an Elephant" by George Orwell
Literary Analysis: Irony

Irony is a literary device that brings out contradictions between appearance and reality, or between expectation and reality, or between words and reality. In **verbal irony,** the intended meaning of words clashes with their usual meaning, as when Orwell describes the dangerous elephant as "grandmotherly." In **irony of situation,** events contradict what you expect to happen, as when the young Buddhist priests are revealed to be the most insulting toward the British.

DIRECTIONS: *Explain what is ironic about the following facts, events, or descriptions.*

1. Orwell's attitude toward Buddhist priests

_____

_____

2. Burmese population's lack of weapons

_____

_____

3. "Grinning" mouth of man trampled by elephant

_____

_____

4. Crowd gathering to watch shooting of elephant

_____

_____

5. Value of a living elephant compared to a dead one

_____

_____

6. Orwell's assessment that it was "perfectly clear" what he should do about **killing the elephant**

_____

_____

7. Comparison of rifle to something "beautiful"

_____

_____

8. Orwell's gladness that the coolie had been killed by the elephant

_____

_____

Name _____ Date _____

Reading Strategy: Recognize the Writer's Attitudes

Orwell reveals in his essay that his attitudes toward British rule in Burma are not always clear cut. At times, he expresses conflicting attitudes. When you recognize the writer's attitudes, you uncover clues to the meaning in a literary work.

DIRECTIONS: *Complete each cluster diagram by writing words and phrases, including quotations from the essay, that reflect Orwell's conflicting attitudes. Add branches to the diagram as needed. On the lines following each diagram, write your conclusion about Orwell's attitudes.*

1.

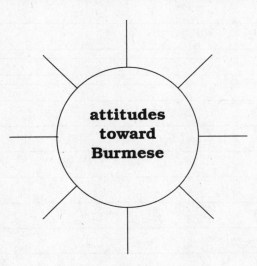

attitudes toward Burmese

_____

_____

2.

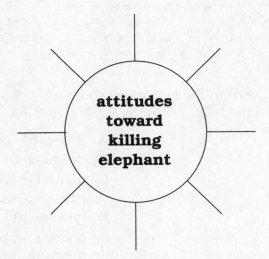

attitudes toward killing elephant

_____

_____

Name _____ Date _____

"**Shooting an Elephant**" by George Orwell
Vocabulary Builder

Using Words About Politics

A. DIRECTIONS: *In a few sentences, describe Orwell's experiences as a British police officer in Burma. Use the following words:* imperialism, despotic, dominion.

_____
_____
_____
_____
_____
_____
_____
_____
_____
_____
_____
_____

Using the Word List

| prostrate | imperialism | despotic |
| squalid | dominion | senility |

B. DIRECTIONS: *Match each word in the left column with its definition in the right column. Write the letter of the definition on the line next to the word it defines.*

___ 1. prostrate

___ 2. imperialism

___ 3. despotic

___ 4. squalid

___ 5. dominion

___ 6. senility

A. miserably poor; wretched

B. defenseless; in a prone or lying position

C. mental or physical decay due to old age

D. rule or power to rule; a governed territory

E. tyrannical

F. policy and practice of forming and maintaining an empire in order to control raw materials and world markets by the conquest of other countries and the establishment of colonies

"Shooting an Elephant" by George Orwell

Grammar and Style: Restrictive and Nonrestrictive Participial Phrases

Participial phrases, or groups of words with a participle, modify nouns and pronouns. A **restrictive participial phrase** is essential to the meaning of the word it modifies and is not separated by commas. A **nonrestrictive participial phrase** is not essential to the meaning and can be separated by commas. Note the differences in the following examples:

Restrictive: I . . . saw a man's dead body *sprawling in the mud.*

Nonrestrictive: Some more women followed, *clicking their tongues and exclaiming . . .*

A. PRACTICE: *For each sentence, underline the participial phrase. On the line, indicate whether it is restrictive or nonrestrictive, and write the word it modifies.*

1. " . . . the insults hooted after me when I was at a safe distance got badly on my nerves."

   _____

2. "It was a very poor quarter, a labyrinth of squalid bamboo huts, . . . winding all over a steep hillside."

   _____

3. "An old woman with a switch in her hand came round the corner of a hut, violently shooing away a crowd of naked children."

   _____

4. "He was lying on his belly with arms crucified and head sharply twisted to one side."

   _____

5. "Here was I, the white man with his gun, standing in front of the unarmed native crowd . . ."

   _____

B. Writing Application: *In a few sentences, describe a situation in which you felt uncomfortable in front of an audience or crowd. Use at least one restrictive participial phrase and one nonrestrictive participial phrase in your description.*

_____

_____

_____

_____

_____

_____

_____

_____

"Shooting an Elephant" by George Orwell
Support for Writing

Make an outline of the experience you will describe in your essay written in Orwell's style. First, write a sentence identifying your experience. Then, list events that were part of the experience in the order they happened. Finally, go back and fill in details about each event.

Experience: _____

_____

Event: _____

   Details: **1.** _____

          2. _____

          3. _____

Event: _____

   Details: **1.** _____

          2. _____

          3. _____

Event: _____

   Details: **1.** _____

          2. _____

          3. _____

Event: _____

   Details: **1.** _____

          2. _____

          3. _____

On a separate page, as you begin to draft your essay in Orwell's style, first write about your response to the experience. Then, draw on information in your outline to illustrate and explain what happened. Present details in a clear order.

"Shooting an Elephant" by George Orwell
Support for Extend Your Learning

Listening and Speaking

Record facts and events relating to Burma's path to independence in the left column of the following chart. List ideas for audiovisual aids in the right column. Use your ideas as you discuss your **audiovisual presentation** with your group.

Facts and Events About Burmese Independence	Ideas for Audiovisual Aids (Timeline, Photographs, and Recordings of Music)

Research and Technology

Use the following chart to compare and contrast Aung San Suu Kyi's (San's) political positions and practices with Orwell's. Draw on the information as you write your **biography** on a separate page.

San's Political Positions and Practices	Orwell's Political Positions and Practices

"Shooting an Elephant" by George Orwell
Enrichment: Social Studies

From Imperialism to Self-Rule in Burma

Various powers have ruled the nation of Burma, now Myanmar, in its long, embattled history. From 1885, Britain ruled Burma as a province of India, another of its territories. By the 1920s, when Orwell served in Burma as a police officer, Burmese protests against British rule were growing stronger. In 1937, Britain granted Burma some rights to self-government. However, in 1942, Japan occupied the country, which it ruled until 1945. At the end of World War II, Britain resumed control of Burma. Finally, in 1948, Burma gained independence.

Self-rule in Burma, however, did not bring peace. From 1948 to 1962, various political factions struggled to gain power. The established government was threatened by Communist and ethnic groups. With a military coup in 1962, the Revolutionary Council was set up. General Ne Win assumed leadership and eventually established a one-party system in Burma, outlawing the existence of any political party except the Burma Socialist Programme Party (BSPP). Ne Win remained in power until July of 1988, when protests and rioting against the BSPP forced him to resign. Military control was seized by a new faction later that year.

In 1990, free multiparty elections were held, resulting in an overwhelming victory for the main opposition party. The military government, however, refused to honor the election, imprisoned many protesters, and maintained control. Many nations have imposed economic sanctions against Burma in protest of the country's human rights violations. In 1991, the Nobel Peace Prize was awarded to the leader of the opposition, Daw Ang San Suu Kyi, for her human rights work. Under house arrest in the Burmese capital of Rangoon, Suu Kyi was unable to travel to Stockholm to accept the award.

DIRECTIONS: *To compare and contrast imperialism and self-rule in Burma, write your answers to the following questions.*

1. How does British imperialism contrast with Burmese self-rule?

   _____

   _____

   _____

2. Did the end of imperialism in Burma eradicate the oppression that Orwell describes? Explain.

   _____

   _____

   _____

   _____

   _____

   _____

Name _____   Date _____

"Shooting an Elephant" by George Orwell
Selection Test A

Critical Reading *Identify the letter of the choice that best answers the question.*

_____ 1. What was Orwell's attitude toward the English occupation of Burma in "Shooting an Elephant"?
   A. He knew England had the right to occupy Burma.
   B. He believed it was an evil situation.
   C. He thought it was England's responsibility.
   D. He knew it was the only way for Burma to progress.

_____ 2. What damage has the elephant done in "Shooting an Elephant"?
   A. destroyed a rice field
   B. it has not done any damage
   C. killed a man
   D. stampeded a herd of elephants

_____ 3. In "Shooting an Elephant," which word best describes Orwell's attitude about the elephant that "looked suddenly stricken, shrunken, [and] immensely old"?
   A. pitying
   B. satisfied
   C. pleased
   D. angry

_____ 4. What is Orwell's attitude toward the Burmese in "Shooting an Elephant"?
   A. respect
   B. anger
   C. fear
   D. love

_____ 5. In "Shooting an Elephant," Orwell describes the Burman who tripped him during a football game and about the Buddhist priests who jeered at Europeans. Why does Orwell tell these stories?
   A. to justify his action in killing the elephant
   B. to explain why he wanted to leave Burma
   C. to explain why he feared the Burmans
   D. to show why he was a police officer

_____ 6. As a British police officer in "Shooting an Elephant," Orwell is placed in an irony of situation. Why?
   A. He is a writer.
   B. He is not a police officer.
   C. He likes the Burmese.
   D. He dislikes imperialism.

____ 7. Why does Orwell finally kill the elephant in "Shooting an Elephant"?
   A. so the Burmese will not laugh at him
   B. because the elephant charges him
   C. because the elephant has killed a man
   D. to prevent further destruction

____ 8. What mistake does Orwell make in shooting the elephant in "Shooting an Elephant"?
   A. He tries to shoot it in the heart.
   B. He is too far away.
   C. His aim is poor.
   D. He does not shoot it in the brain.

____ 9. What is Orwell's purpose in giving details about the elephant's slow death in "Shooting an Elephant"?
   A. to make the event as dramatic as possible
   B. to make the scene more realistic
   C. to emphasize how unnecessary it was
   D. to demonstrate how unprepared he was

____ 10. Which line from "Shooting an Elephant" expresses verbal irony?
   A. ". . . the whole population of the quarter flocked out of the houses and followed me."
   B. ". . . there was something the children ought not to have seen."
   C. ". . . when the white man turns tyrant it is his own freedom that he destroys."
   D. ". . . an immense crowd, two thousand at the least and growing every minute."

____ 11. Orwell walks away from the dying elephant in "Shooting an Elephant." Why?
   A. He finds it painful to watch it suffer.
   B. He has other duties he must take care of.
   C. He must talk with the elephant's owner.
   D. He is afraid the people will riot.

Vocabulary and Grammar

____ 12. Which word best replaces *despotic* in this sentence: "The *despotic* government had complete control over its people"?
   A. poor
   B. tyrannical
   C. shrunken
   D. stubborn

____ 13. Which sentence contains a nonrestrictive participial phrase (does not tell which people it refers to)?
   A. Various Burmans stopped me, telling me about the elephant.
   B. I marched down the hill like the fool I felt I was.
   C. I knew I had to shoot the elephant.
   D. The impact of the bullet killed the elephant.

Essay

14. Orwell says in "Shooting an Elephant" that the white imperialist "wears a mask, and his face grows to fit it." In an essay, explain what he means. Consider these questions: What is the mask? How does the face "grow" to fit it? Why does Orwell kill the elephant? Use examples from the story to help you answer these questions.

15. Near the end of "Shooting an Elephant," Orwell says that he was "very glad that the coolie had been killed." In an essay, discuss whether you think he really meant this. Think about these questions: What was his attitude toward the Burmans? What was his attitude toward imperialism and his ideas about how it affected Europeans like himself? Give examples and details from the account to support your response.

"Shooting an Elephant" by George Orwell
Selection Test B

Critical Reading *Identify the letter of the choice that best completes the statement or answers the question.*

____ 1. What is Orwell's purpose in writing "Shooting an Elephant"?
A. to describe life in Burma
B. to expose the evils of imperialism
C. to argue for wildlife conservation
D. to promote Burmese independence

____ 2. What attitude does Orwell's description express?
> wretched prisoners huddling in the stinking cages of the lockups, the gray, cowed faces of the long-term convicts . . .

A. curiosity
B. embarrassment
C. indifference
D. rage

____ 3. Why does Orwell object to the Burmese's prejudice against him?
A. He isn't important enough to worry about.
B. The Burmese injure him whenever they can.
C. He opposes British imperialism.
D. He thinks the British behave impeccably.

____ 4. Orwell's resentful feelings toward the Burmese are ironic because
A. the Burmese do nothing to hurt him.
B. the British are naturally superior.
C. he professes to be a pacifist.
D. he believes the Burmese are oppressed by the British.

____ 5. Why is Orwell asked to do something about the elephant?
A. The Burmese refuse to control the elephant.
B. He has experience handling elephants.
C. Only the British police force has weapons.
D. The mahout has requested his assistance.

____ 6. What irony is expressed in the statement?
> A sahib has got to act like a sahib; he has got to appear resolute, to know his own mind and do definite things . . .

A. Orwell objects to the term *sahib*.
B. Although he knows his own mind, Orwell cannot do what he thinks he should.
C. Orwell does not appear resolute in front of the crowd.
D. Orwell cannot make a decision about the elephant, even though he knows he should.

_____ 7. When he states that it "would never do" to have the Burmese laugh at him, Orwell reveals his
   A. anger.
   B. embarrassment.
   C. pride.
   D. frustration.

_____ 8. What is ironic about the description?
   thick blood welled out of him like red velvet . . .

   A. The elephant's thick, rough skin contrasts with the smoothness of velvet.
   B. The luxurious image contrasts with the brutal reality of the elephant's dying.
   C. The mahout would be too poor to afford an expensive material like velvet.
   D. Orwell did not want to kill the elephant.

_____ 9. In his description of the dying elephant, what tone does Orwell create by repeating the word *tortured*?
   A. detached
   B. anguished
   C. hostile
   D. respectful

_____ 10. In the years since he worked in Burma, Orwell believes he has become
   A. sophisticated.
   B. ineffective.
   C. prejudiced.
   D. contented.

_____ 11. What is the theme of "Shooting an Elephant"?
   A. The British civil service is a model of efficiency.
   B. An individual's livelihood is as important as public safety.
   C. Rarely can anyone fully understand another culture.
   D. Anyone working for an imperialist power is morally compromised.

Vocabulary and Grammar

_____ 12. The British had _____ over the Burmese for more than fifty years.
   A. despotic
   B. squalid
   C. dominion
   D. senility

_____ 13. The _____ conditions of the holding cells were a testament to the _____ regime.
   A. prostrate, imperialism
   B. despotic, dominion
   C. senility, squalid
   D. squalid, despotic

_____ **14.** Which sentence contains a restrictive participial phrase?
   A. The crowd gathered to watch Orwell as if he were performing.
   B. The mahout, heading in the opposite direction, lost the elephant.
   C. Orwell, pressured by the crowd, changes his mind about shooting the elephant.
   D. The man trampled by the elephant was a poor laborer.

_____ **15.** Which sentence contains a nonrestrictive participial phrase?
   A. The Burmese, crowding around Orwell, want some fun.
   B. The rifle that Orwell brings is too small for the job.
   C. After the killing, people run to get knives and baskets.
   D. The elephant gasped and slowly collapsed to the ground.

Essay

16. Orwell states that the incident with the elephant "gave me a better glimpse than I had had before of the real nature of imperialism—the real motives for which despotic governments act." In an essay, explain Orwell's statement. Use examples from his essay to support your main points.

17. Orwell writes that "when the white man turns tyrant it is his own freedom that he destroys." Using this statement as a starting point, analyze Orwell's use of irony in "Shooting an Elephant." Include specific examples of irony in your essay.

Vocabulary Warm-up Word Lists

Study these words from the selection. Then, complete the activities that follow.

Word List A

alight [uh LYT] *adj.* lit up
    The room was <u>alight</u> with the glow of ten candles.

apprehension [ap ree HEN shuhn] *n.* a worried expectation
    With great <u>apprehension</u>, Nora crept into the cobweb-covered crawl space.

assent [uh SENT] *n.* consent or agreement
    We cannot go ahead with the plan without the manager's <u>assent</u>.

caretaker [KAIR tay kuhr] *n.* a person hired to look after a place
    The morning after the big party, the <u>caretaker</u> tidied up the yard and the pool area.

dependability [di pen duh BIL uh tee] *n.* the quality of being reliable
    Maureen's <u>dependability</u> is her greatest qualification for this job.

heightening [HYT uhn ing] *adj.* increasing or intensifying
    The ticking clock added to the <u>heightening</u> terror Charles felt.

knowledgeably [NAHL uh jib lee] *adv.* in an informed way
    Paul spoke <u>knowledgeably</u> about baseball history at the sports dinner.

perplexed [puhr PLEXT] *adj.* doubtful; confused; bewildered
    Angela was <u>perplexed</u> about how to use the new software for her computer.

Word List B

accelerating [ak SEL uh ray ting] *adj.* increasing in speed
    The car, <u>accelerating</u> as it went down the hill, was difficult to control.

acuteness [uh KYOOT nis] *n.* severity; sharpness
    The <u>acuteness</u> of the patient's pain can be described only by the patient.

consolation [kahn suh LAY shuhn] *n.* the act of comforting
    It was of some <u>consolation</u> to Jane that Larry sent a card.

console [kuhn SOHL] *v.* to comfort in sorrow
    After Allen lost the race, June tried to <u>console</u> him with a hug.

resumed [ri ZOOMD] *v.* started again after stopping
    Work <u>resumed</u> after a fifteen-minute break.

resuming [ri ZOOM ing] *v.* starting again after stopping
    "Now where was I?" asked Janet, before <u>resuming</u> her story.

sinister [SIN is tuhr] *adj.* threatening
    The three men discussed their <u>sinister</u> plot to take over the company.

ventilation [vent uh LAY shuhn] *n.* the act of filling with fresh air
    For better <u>ventilation</u> in the baby's room, Shirley opened all the windows.

"The Demon Lover" by Elizabeth Bowen
Vocabulary Warm-up Exercises

Exercise A *Fill in each blank in the paragraph below using each word from Word List A only once.*

Noticing that all the rooms in the corner apartment were [1] _____, Carol wondered who could be inside. She had had the job of [2] _____ for a few months, but she had never seen anyone occupying that unit. Very sensible and known for her [3] _____, Carol was also very concerned about conserving energy. She was [4] _____ about who might be wasting so much electricity. She was sure she had met all the tenants before and she [5] _____ matched their names and apartments in her mind, continuing to wonder about the corner apartment. She began to feel some [6] _____ as the day went on, for the lights remained on, even during daylight hours. With rapidly [7] _____ concern, she walked to the apartment and knocked on the door. A tiny old woman answered. When Carol asked her about the lights, the woman said, "I thought I could turn on my own lights without your [8] _____!"

Exercise B *Answer the questions with complete explanations.*

1. How would you rate the <u>acuteness</u> of pain from a paper cut, on a scale from one to ten?
   _____

2. If a <u>sinister</u> man spoke to you, would you feel frightened or safe?
   _____

3. If a storyteller was <u>resuming</u> her story after a short break, would you wait?
   _____

4. If you wanted to <u>console</u> your friend for losing a game, what might you say?
   _____

5. If your friend had <u>accelerating</u> spending habits, what advice would you give?
   _____

6. If the <u>ventilation</u> in a room were poor, what would you do?
   _____

7. What <u>consolation</u> might a mother offer if her child hurt her knee?
   _____

8. If two people <u>resumed</u> their friendship, would they exchange fewer phone calls?
   _____

Name _____ Date _____

"The Demon Lover" by Elizabeth Bowen
Reading Warm-up A

Read the following passage. Pay special attention to the underlined words. Then, read it again, and complete the activities. Use a separate sheet of paper for your written answers.

If you are confused, underlined perplexed, or simply wondering about how you might be able to support yourself in the future, one job you might want to consider is that of a caretaker of an estate or hotel grounds.

The job of a caretaker is to make sure the property is kept clean, tidy, and in good repair. If you have any apprehension—any worry at all—that you might not be up to the task, here is a list of questions; if you can answer *yes* to all of them, then you could probably do the job well.

- Do you know how to use basic tools, such as hammers, screwdrivers, and drills?
- If someone asked you a question about basic landscaping and maintenance, do you know enough to answer knowledgeably?
- Do you have excellent communication skills?
- Can your employer count on your dependability as a worker? Can someone else vouch for your reliability?
- Do you have a current driver's license?
- Are you physically fit, able to bend and lift, and willing to work hard?
- Can you work odd hours, including some evenings and weekends?
- Would you be able to deal with rapidly heightening demands from increasing numbers of people during possible emergencies?
- Would you be able to check that, at night, common areas are properly alight and therefore more secure? If need be, can you replace any burned-out bulbs in lamps?

If you are interested in being a caretaker, fill out an application for the job; as a qualified candidate, you can look forward to a job offer. All that would be needed is your assent, and once you communicate your agreement to work in this position, you can start immediately.

1. Underline two words that mean about the same as perplexed. Tell about something that once caused you to feel *perplexed*.

2. Circle the words that describe the job of a caretaker. What is something you would want a *caretaker* to do at your home?

3. Underline the word that means about the same as apprehension. Name one thing that gives you some *apprehension*.

4. Circle the words that indicate that a person is answering a question knowledgeably. Use *knowledgeably* in a sentence.

5. Underline the word that is close in meaning to dependability. Name one area in which you demonstrate *dependability*.

6. Circle the word that is close in meaning to heightening. How do you usually react to *heightening* demands on your time and patience?

7. Circle the word that is described as alight. What does *alight* mean?

8. Underline the word that means about the same as assent. To what job offer would you eagerly give your *assent*?

Name _____ Date _____

"The Demon Lover" by Elizabeth Bowen
Reading Warm-up B

Read the following passage. Pay special attention to the underlined words. Then, read it again, and complete the activities. Use a separate sheet of paper for your written answers.

The Henderson family was getting ready to move from their apartment in London to a lovely home in the countryside, but young John Henderson was not happy about the move. To <u>console</u> him and make him feel better, his mother proceeded to tell him how much their lives would improve in their new home.

She told him about her own fears in the city, reminding him of the afternoon she had been followed for several blocks by a rather <u>sinister</u> character dressed in black, who stopped following her only when he saw an police officer nearby. John was still not convinced that it was a good idea to move; he told his mother, for the tenth time, that the danger posed by that character was probably all in her imagination. <u>Resuming</u> her story, Mrs. Henderson reminded John about how nervous she had been. This was no <u>consolation</u> to John, who found no comfort in her story; he <u>resumed</u> telling her his own theory that it was probably a coincidence that the guy stopped when he did.

Fear was not the only compelling reason for the move. Mr. and Mrs. Henderson wanted to reduce the rapidly <u>accelerating</u> pace of life that they were experiencing in the city; the country, they felt, would slow them down a bit and allow them to enjoy themselves more. In addition, they were sure that their new house would allow much better <u>ventilation</u>. More windows would assure better circulation and air quality, which would surely improve their health. John realized he could not change her mind and began to feel homesick with some <u>acuteness</u>. Even though he had not yet moved, thinking about leaving his friends only added to the sharpness of his sense of loss.

1. Underline the phrase that means about the same as <u>console</u>. When you are unhappy, what can *console* you?

2. Circle the words that tell what the <u>sinister</u> character did. What does *sinister* mean?

3. Circle the words that tell what Mrs. Henderson said when she was <u>resuming</u> her story. Use *resuming* in a sentence.

4. Underline the word that means about the same as <u>consolation</u>. What *consolation* have you offered to a friend who was feeling unhappy?

5. Circle what John said when he <u>resumed</u> telling his mother his theory. Tell about an activity that you once dropped and then *resumed*.

6. Underline the words that describe what is <u>accelerating</u>. What does *accelerating* mean?

7. Underline the words in a nearby sentence that mean about the same as <u>ventilation</u>. Name two ways to improve the *ventilation* in a room.

8. Circle the word in a nearby sentence that means about the same as <u>acuteness</u>. Describe a feeling that once hit you with great *acuteness*.

Name _____ Date _____

"The Demon Lover" by Elizabeth Bowen
Literary Analysis: The Ghost Story

During the nineteenth-century Romantic movement, the focus of literature turned to the personal lives of everyday people. Some of these stories were of people with dark or mysterious events in their lives. One of the offshoots of this movement was the development of gothic novels, so named for settings that often included castles or other buildings of gothic architecture. Inevitably such stories began to include tales of folklore and other metaphysical events. Others were written with an emphasis on the supernatural. The **ghost story,** long an oral tradition, became a popular literary form as well.

Part of the appeal of a good ghost story is that it is about normal people who do everyday things. Somehow, though, their normality is disrupted by something that cannot be easily explained or dismissed. Readers relate to the ordinariness of the characters, and are, therefore, intrigued when something unusual happens. Most writers of ghost stories build tension throughout the story by dropping hints or including small details that could be interpreted in more than one way.

DIRECTIONS: *Use the following chart to record the "normal" elements in "The Demon Lover" as well as the unusual aspects that creep in almost from the very beginning.*

Scene or Detail	What is normal?	What is unusual?
outside Mrs. Drover's house		
inside Mrs. Drover's house		
the letter		
the farewell, 25 years ago		
Mrs. Drover's marriage and family		
catching the taxi		

Name _____ Date _____

"**The Demon Lover**" by Elizabeth Bowen
Reading Strategy: Respond to the Story

When you are reading and interpreting fiction, try to find the relationship between the details the author presents and the meaning of the piece. One way to find that meaning is to think about your own **response.** Did the piece grab your attention? Were you frightened? Did it remind you of something in your own life? Identify your own reaction and judge whether your response was intended by the author, and how he or she evoked it.

DIRECTIONS: *Use the following questions to record your own response to "The Demon Lover."*

1. What was your response to the mood set at the beginning of the story?

_____

_____

_____

2. What was your response to the letter sent to Mrs. Dover?

_____

_____

_____

3. What was your response to the story's ending?

_____

_____

_____

_____

4. Were there parts of the story that reminded you of your own experiences? If so, what were they?

_____

_____

_____

_____

5. What parts of the story grabbed your attention or emotions? Why?

_____

_____

_____

_____

6. Do you think the author intended to get these responses from you? Why would the author want this kind of response?

_____

_____

_____

_____

"The Demon Lover" by Elizabeth Bowen
Vocabulary Builder

Using the Root -loc-

A. DIRECTIONS: Each word in the following list contains the root -loc-, meaning "place." Choose the word from the list that correctly completes each sentence, and write it on the line.

allocation   localism   locality

1. Based on her accent, it was apparent that the _____ of her upbringing was the deep South.

2. The residents' customs gave the town its sense of _____.

3. Each employee received a memo about the _____ of bonuses at the end of the year.

Using the Word List

spectral	dislocation	arboreal
circumscribed	aperture	

B. DIRECTIONS: *Match each word in the left column with its definition in the right column. Write the letter of the definition on the line next to the word it defines.*

___ 1. spectral   A. a condition of being out of place

___ 2. arboreal   B. ghostly

___ 3. circumscribed   C. limited

___ 4. dislocation   D. opening

___ 5. aperture   E. of, near, or among trees

"The Demon Lover" by Elizabeth Bowen
Grammar and Style: Sentence Beginnings—Participial Phrases

A participle is a verb form that functions as an adjective. Most participles end in *-ing* or *-ed*. A **participial phrase** is made up of a participle and its modifiers and complements.

The Londoners, *dreading nightfall,* listened for the drone of the German planes.

In this sentence, the participial phrase "dreading nightfall" modifies *Londoners.*

To create variety in your writing, you can begin sentences with participial phrases. Make sure, though, that the word your participial phrase modifies follows soon after the phrase.

Confusing:　　Looking about her, the unfamiliarity of her own home perplexed her.

Clear:　　Looking about her, she was perplexed by the unfamiliarity of her own home.

A. PRACTICE: *Circle the number of each sentence that begins with a participial phrase. For each sentence that begins with a participial phrase, underline the phrase and circle the word it modifies.*

1. Everything smelled vaguely of ashes from the unused fireplace.

2. Proceeding upstairs, Mrs. Drover had not yet shaken her discomfort.

3. On the table lay a letter addressed to her.

4. Annoyed at the caretaker, she picked up the letter, which bore no stamp.

B. Writing Application: *Revise the following paragraph so that three of the sentences begin with participial phrases. You may either combine or rearrange the existing sentences, or add your own details to create the participial phrases. Rewrite the paragraph in the space provided.*

Elizabeth Bowen, described as a writer of "finely wrought prose," is praised highly for her stories. Her characters are mostly from the upper middle class in England and Ireland. Bowen "knew" her characters well, for she was born into that class. Her novel *The Hotel,* published in 1927, contains a typical Bowen heroine. The girl, trying to cope with a life for which she is not prepared, might remind some of a young Elizabeth Bowen.

_____

_____

_____

_____

_____

_____

_____

_____

_____

82

Name _____ Date _____

"The Demon Lover" by Elizabeth Bowen
Support for Writing

Plan your sequel using the graphic organizer that follows. First, write a question that "The Demon Lover" leaves unanswered. Then, answer the question with an action or event.

Question that needs to be answered:
Action or event that answers the question:

↓

Question that needs to be answered:
Action or event that answers the question:

↓

Question that needs to be answered:
Action or event that answers the question:

↓

Question that needs to be answered:
Action or event that answers the question:

On a separate page, use information from your diagram to organize your ideas as you draft your sequel. Make sure that the events are in a logical order that helps you tell a story.

"The Demon Lover" by Elizabeth Bowen
Support for Extend Your Learning

Listening and Speaking

Prepare for the **reading** of your ghost story. Decide where you can use each of the strategies below.

Techniques	Where I Can Use These Speaking Strategies
Use a hushed tone to give a chill.	
Use a higher voice to express fear or anxiety.	
Read more rapidly to suggest suspense.	
Use Visual effects.	
Use sound effects.	

Research and Technology

Do research for your **history report** on London during the Blitz. Write your topic in the center circle of the organizer. Write details in the surrounding boxes.

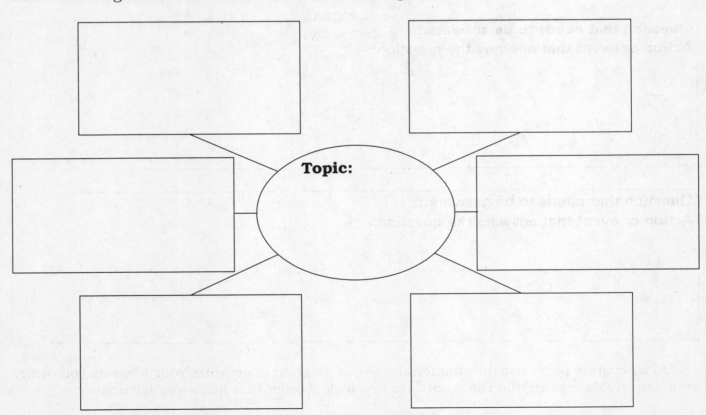

"The Demon Lover" by Elizabeth Bowen
Enrichment: Social Studies

The London Blitz

The eeriness of "The Demon Lover" may stem from Elizabeth Bowen's experience living in London during the Second World War. During the London Blitz, which lasted from September 1940 to May 1941, German planes dropped bombs on London every night. As an air raid warden, Bowen witnessed first-hand the horrors of the bombs' destruction.

DIRECTIONS: *Find out more about the London Blitz. How much of London was destroyed? How many children were evacuated to the safety of the country? When were they evacuated and where did they go? How did people cope in the air raid shelters? Use library resources and the Internet to explore one aspect of life during the London Blitz. Use the lines provided to take notes. Then present the information to the class in an oral report.*

_____

_____

_____

_____

_____

_____

_____

_____

_____

_____

_____

_____

_____

_____

_____

_____

_____

_____

_____

_____

_____

_____

_____

_____

"The Demon Lover" by Elizabeth Bowen
Selection Test A

Critical Reading *Identify the letter of the choice that best answers the question.*

_____ 1. Which of the following lines creates suspense in the beginning of "The Demon Lover"?
A. "Shifting some parcels under her arm, she slowly forced round her latchkey."
B. "Mrs. Drover went round to her shut-up house to look for several things."
C. "The part-time caretaker she shared with some neighbors was away this week."
D. "She stopped dead and stared at the hall table—on this lay a letter addressed to her."

_____ 2. In "The Demon Lover," why has Mrs. Drover come to London?
A. to fulfill a promise made twenty-five years before
B. to pick up things at her house and to check on it
C. to meet her husband and children
D. to visit a friend

_____ 3. Why are the house and neighborhood empty in "The Demon Lover"?
A. All the homes were destroyed by bombs.
B. Everyone left to join the army.
C. People have been frightened away by demons.
D. People have left the city because of the war.

_____ 4. Who has sent the letter that frightens Mrs. Drover in "The Demon Lover"?
A. a friend who died long ago
B. her son
C. a man she was engaged to
D. her husband

_____ 5. In "The Demon Lover," why does the letter frighten Mrs. Drover?
A. She has not kept in touch with the sender.
B. She thought the author of the letter was dead.
C. She had forgotten the sender lives in London.
D. She thinks the letter is from her husband.

_____ 6. How does the war setting make the setting of "The Demon Lover" more believable?
A. It provides a good reason for the house's emptiness.
B. It creates a situation in which bombing could occur.
C. The war makes it likely for ghosts to roam the streets.
D. During the violence of war, innocent people are often victims.

_____ 7. Which word best describes Kathleen as she said goodbye to her fiancé in "The Demon Lover"?
A. frightened
B. deeply in love
C. angry
D. peaceful

____ 8. Which line from "The Demon Lover" helps establish a suspenseful atmosphere?
   A. "The things she wanted were in a bedroom chest."
   B. "She picked up the letter."
   C. "Down there a door or window was being opened."
   D. "The rain had stopped."

____ 9. In "The Demon Lover," Mrs. Drover is unable to keep her back exposed to the empty room and changes her position. Which choice is an example of a reader responding to this event?
   A. When I'm nervous, I can't help turning around to see what might be behind me.
   B. My mother has a chest where she keeps tablecloths that she doesn't often use.
   C. I don't think upright chairs are very comfortable. I like to lean back more.
   D. My knees hurt if I kneel very long. I have to get up and stretch once in a while.

____ 10. Why is Mrs. Drover comforted by the idea of getting a taxi in "The Demon Lover"?
   A. She knows the taxi driver.
   B. She will not have to walk to the train.
   C. She will not be alone as she collects her things.
   D. She will not have to carry all her items.

____ 11. Why does Mrs. Drover scream when she sees the taxi driver in "The Demon Lover"?
   A. She remembers she forgot the letter.
   B. She recognizes the driver as her old fiancé.
   C. She is feeling the fear that gripped her at her house.
   D. She is frightened by the dangerous way he drives.

Vocabulary and Grammar

____ 12. Which word best replaces *aperture* in this sentence: "The woman looked outside through a small *aperture* in the door"?
   A. lock
   B. key
   C. opening
   D. doorbell

____ 13. Which sentence based on "The Demon Lover" contains a participial phrase that modifies a noun?
   A. She planned to move many of her belongings to the country.
   B. She married Mr. Drover, and they settled in Kensington.
   C. The room looked over the garden as the sun went away.
   D. Her child, fighting a serious illness, caused her to worry.

Essay

14. One of the characteristics of many ghost stories is the uncertain nature of a threat. In "The Demon Lover," Mrs. Drover is threatened by her old fiancé, who was "reported missing" and assumed to have been killed in the first world war. In an essay, tell whether you think he was a real person or a demon. Give reasons and examples from the selection to support your answer.

15. "The Demon Lover" is set in wartime London in about 1941. Much of the action takes place in a deserted neighborhood and in an ordinary but unoccupied house. In an essay, explain how the setting contributes to the mood, or atmosphere, of the story. Give examples from the story to illustrate your ideas.

"The Demon Lover" by Elizabeth Bowen
Selection Test B

Critical Reading *Identify the letter of the choice that best completes the statement or answers the question.*

_____ 1. Why is Mrs. Drover in London?
A. to check on the house and make sure the caretaker is doing his job
B. to meet her husband and sister
C. to fulfill a promise she had made twenty-five years ago
D. to do some shopping and get some things from the house

_____ 2. What significance do the stained mantelpiece and bruised wallpaper have?
A. They are familiar details that seem somehow strange.
B. They tell of further damage from bombings.
C. They put further burden on Mrs. Drover's need for repairs.
D. They indicate the destructiveness of the Drover children.

_____ 3. Which detail from the story helps emphasize the abnormality of the city?
A. Mrs. Drover's use—and mistrust—of a caretaker
B. the shortness of the taxi line
C. the fact that "no human eye" watched Mrs. Drover
D. the lack of telephone service

_____ 4. Why does a war setting make a ghost story believable?
A. Amid violent fighting, innocent people often get hurt.
B. So many people die that having ghosts as characters seems reasonable.
C. Once the expectation of normality is gone, anything can happen.
D. Deserted houses are appropriate settings for ghosts.

_____ 5. Why might the author of "The Demon Lover" want you to think about times when you have been lonely or vulnerable?
A. By remembering your own experiences, you identify with the situations in the story and understand the author's purpose.
B. The author wants you to pay attention to your own memory rather than the story.
C. The author wants you to see how bizarre Mrs. Drover is.
D. You are more likely to read more of the author's books if you remember your own experiences.

_____ 6. In what way does Mrs. Drover's response to her reflection in the mirror provide a typical ghost story element?
A. The whiteness of her lips hints at a ghostly element.
B. Her response is very normal, and ghost stories contain "normal" elements.
C. The fact that she has to clear a patch in the mirror suggests mystery.
D. Mrs. Drover reveals uncertainty about herself, which can hint at supernatural occurrences.

_____ 7. How does Mrs. Drover control her fear?
   A. She refuses to acknowledge it.
   B. She turns it into anger.
   C. She focuses on practical activities.
   D. She gives herself a pep talk.

_____ 8. In the flashback, the image of "spectral glitters in the place of his eyes" indicates that Kathleen was
   A. fearless.
   B. imaginative.
   C. literary.
   D. romantic.

_____ 9. If you responded to the beginning of the story with apprehension or dread, what excerpt best shows how the author has evoked that response?
   A. "Toward the end of her day in London Mrs. Drover went round to her shut-up house to look for several things she wanted to take away."
   B. "Mrs. Drover put down her parcels on the escritoire and left the room to proceed upstairs . . ."
   C. "She stopped dead and stared at the hall table—on this lay a letter addressed to her."
   D. "She thought first—then the caretaker *must* be back."

_____ 10. Why does Mrs. Drover become comforted at the thought of the taxi?
   A. The idea of not being all alone appealed to her.
   B. She knew the taxi driver.
   C. The presence of taxis meant that normal activities were once again operating in London.
   D. It gave her something else to think about.

_____ 11. Which is an example of a reader's identifying with Mrs. Drover in this passage?

As a woman whose utter dependability was the keystone of her family life she was not willing to return to the country, to her husband, her little boys and her sister, without the objects she had come up to fetch. Resuming work at the chest she set about making up a number of parcels in a rapid, fumbling-decisive way. These, with her shopping parcels, would be too much to carry: these meant a taxi—at the thought of the taxi her heart went up and her normal breathing resumed.

   A. I remember I had to call a taxi once.
   B. I understand "fumbling-decisive"; I think that's how I act when I'm nervous or upset.
   C. I don't think I'm very dependable.
   D. I have a sister, but not a husband or little boys.

_____ 12. What is the theme of this story?
   A. the disorientation caused by war
   B. the effect of fatigue
   C. the inevitability of destiny
   D. the tragedy of not knowing oneself

Vocabulary and Grammar

____ 13. Mrs. Drover is able to see the taxi driver because of the *aperture*, or
  A. mirror.
  B. opening.
  C. picture.
  D. inner sight.

____ 14. Which correctly identifies the participial phrase in this sentence?
    She stopped dead, startled by the letter, then moved to pick it up.

  A. She stopped dead
  B. startled by the letter
  C. then moved
  D. to pick it up

Essay

15. Elizabeth Bowen uses World War II as a backdrop for a number of her stories, including "The Demon Lover." Yet she never talks about the Germans or other circumstances of the war directly. Is this a sign of passivity or acceptance? Or do other details in her story express antiwar attitudes? In an essay, take a stand and support it with ideas and details from the story.

16. "The Demon Lover" contains elements of the unnatural and supernatural throughout. In an essay, trace those elements as they appear throughout the story. Indicate why each element is unnatural. Then explain how these elements prepare readers for the final paragraph and the ending of the story.

Unit 6: A Time of Rapid Change
Benchmark Test 10

MULTIPLE CHOICE

Literary Analysis and Reading Strategy *Read the selection. Then, answer the questions that follow.*

> The cheese-mites asked how the cheese got there,
> And warmly debated the matter;
> The Orthodox said that it came from the air,
> And the Heretics said from the platter.
> They argued it long and they argued it strong,
> And I hear they are arguing now;
> But of all the choice spirits who lived in the cheese,
> Not one of them thought of a cow.

> "A Parable" by Arthur Conan Doyle

1. Which of the following helps define the Modernist movement in poetry?
   A. the use of imagery in poems
   B. the revelation of intensely personal details in poetry
   C. the use of traditional verse forms, such as the sonnet
   D. the depiction of experience in disconnected glimpses or fragments

2. In the early twentieth century, what were Modernist poems a reaction to?
   A. changing opinions about education
   B. a confusing, fragmented world
   C. a return to simpler ways of life
   D. the rise of the middle class

3. Which of these does the *cheese* in this selection likely symbolize?
   A. religious faith
   B. the world
   C. food
   D. ideas

4. Which lines from the selection best help you interpret the poem's theme?
   A. lines 1 and 2
   B. lines 3 and 4
   C. lines 5 and 6
   D. lines 7 and 8

5. Which of these best defines *theme* in a literary work?
   A. the central concern of the work
   B. the author's attitude toward the subject
   C. a reader's response to the work
   D. the overall mood of a work

Name _____ Date _____

Read the selection. Then, answer the questions that follow.

> Fish (fly-replete [full] in depth of June,
> Dawdling away their wat'ry noon)
> Ponder deep wisdom, dark or clear,
> Each secret fishy hope or fear,
> Fish say, they have their Stream and Pond;
> But is there anything Beyond?
> This life cannot be All, they swear,
> For how unpleasant if it were!
> One may not doubt that, somehow, Good
> Shall come of Water and of Mud;
> And, sure, the reverent eye must see
> A Purpose in Liquidity.

> from "Heaven" by Rupert Brooke

6. In this selection, what does "a purpose in Liquidity" most likely stand for?
   A. the whims of nature
   B. spiritual rebirth
   C. the triumph of good over evil
   D. the meaning of life

7. The poet of this selection also wrote many poems about war. How does this background information help the reader better understand the selection?
   A. It helps explain the poet's concern with life and death.
   B. It helps the reader understand the symbolism in the poem.
   C. It helps the reader understand the irony in the poem.
   D. It helps explain the poet's references to hope and fear.

8. Which of these best states the theme of this selection?
   A. All creatures share hopes and fears.
   B. Most of daily life is unpleasant.
   C. There must be a larger purpose to life.
   D. Most lives are lived without purpose.

9. Which of these is the best paraphrase of lines 7 and 8?
   A. Life would be boring if there were only one way to live it.
   B. Life should not be lived by others' rules and expectations.
   C. There are some things in life that cannot be understood.
   D. There must be more to life than meets the eye.

10. For which of the following is paraphrasing especially helpful?
    A. figuring out the meanings of words
    B. understanding difficult passages
    C. determining the author's purpose
    D. drawing conclusions from reading

11. Which of these helps shape a writer's works?
    A. the form of each work
    B. critical reviews of the works
    C. the writer's beliefs
    D. the rules of grammar

12. Which of these is helpful in interpreting the theme of a literary work?
    A. finding patterns in the work from which conclusions can be drawn
    B. understanding the writer's background
    C. reading other works by the author to understand his or her other topics
    D. connecting the work to similar works

Read the selection. Then, answer the questions that follow.

Among the rich you will never find a really generous man even by accident. They may give their money away, but they will never give themselves away; they are egotistic, secretive, dry as old bones. To be smart enough to get all that money you must be dull enough to want it.

from *A Miscellany of Men* by G. K. Chesterton

13. According to the author of the selection, what is ironic about the rich?
    A. They are smart in some ways but dull in others.
    B. They are very involved in their own lives and goals.
    C. They are generous with everything except money.
    D. They would give themselves away before parting with money.

14. Which term describes the last sentence of the selection?
    A. symbolism
    B. figurative language
    C. irony of situation
    D. ambiguity

15. Which of these best describes the writer's attitude toward the rich?
    A. amused
    B. scornful
    C. sympathetic
    D. patient

16. Which of these is most useful in recognizing a writer's attitude in a literary work?
    A. the historical period of the work
    B. the main ideas of the work
    C. the title of the work
    D. the tone of the work

17. Which of these is usually the first step in understanding a literary work?
    A. responding as you read
    B. learning about the author
    C. identifying the literary form
    D. making notes of the main ideas

18. Which of these is characteristic of a ghost story?
    A. a resolution that gives a logical explanation for events
    B. an exploration of the natural events that occur in the world
    C. a clear distinction between the familiar and the unfamiliar
    D. the suggestion of supernatural forces at work

19. Which of these would a reader learn from a well-written mission statement provided by an organization?
    A. names of the board of directors
    B. the guiding purpose
    C. the history of the organization
    D. financial information

Vocabulary

20. Based on your knowledge of the root -ques-, what is the meaning of *quest* in the following sentence: "The knights in the story were on a quest for the Holy Grail"?
    A. battle
    B. errand
    C. search
    D. ship

21. What is the meaning of *fractured* in the following sentence, based on your knowledge of the root -fract-?

    The fractured marriage of the two celebrities came as no surprise to the public.

    A. secret
    B. sudden
    C. broken
    D. unlikely

22. Based on your knowledge of the root -top-, what is the meaning of *topographical* in the following sentence?

    From a desk drawer, Ted withdrew topographical maps of New Zealand.

    A. describing political groups
    B. showing surface features
    C. showing major cities
    D. covering various subjects

23. With which of these is the word *dominion* in the following sentence most likely connected?

The villagers feared dominion by the king, who was said to be cruel.

A. politics
B. science
C. mathematics
D. philosophy

24. Based on your knowledge of the root *-loc-*, what is the meaning of *locale* in the following sentence?

Jade figured that a college campus was the perfect locale for a climbing gym?

A. excuse
B. plan
C. reason
D. place

Grammar

25. Which of the following sentences contains a noun clause?
A. Who taught you the excellent French you speak?
B. What is the movie for which Morgan Freeman won an award?
C. Which bird of flight has the largest wingspan?
D. Alex left fresh water for whoever might need it next.

26. Which sentence contains an adjectival modifier?
A. I am not permitted to give refunds.
B. Writing a poem can be very difficult.
C. The father of my friend writes novels.
D. Please park the car outside the garage.

27. What word does the adjectival modifier in this sentence modify?

The owner of a scruffy-looking dog appeared on the rocky beach.

A. dog
B. appeared
C. owner
D. beach

28. Which sentence has correct parallel structure?
A. The children are occupied with drawing pictures and the creation of collages.
B. Doing a job right the first time is easier than to correct a sloppy job later.
C. To be faster, stronger, and getting more flexible are my goals this year.
D. Winter is a time for reading books, making cocoa, and building fires.

29. Which sentence contains a restrictive participial phrase?
   A. The teacher was leading the children across the street.
   B. Jaime tried swimming without kicking his legs.
   C. The runner speeding toward the finish line is my brother.
   D. The thundering waterfall amazed Cecilia and her friends.

30. Which sentence contains a nonrestrictive participial phrase?
   A. The setting sun dazzled our eyes with its reds, pinks, and oranges.
   B. Some children played happily in the park, running through the grass.
   C. To meet the deadline, Allie wrote for ten hours without taking a break.
   D. The man wearing the baseball cap is selling the extra tickets.

31. Which word does the participial phrase in the following sentence modify?

   The sheets, flapping crisply in the summer breeze, reminded me of my childhood.

   A. breeze
   B. sheets
   C. childhood
   D. summer

32. What is the meaning of *relocate* in the following sentence, based on your knowledge of the root *-loc-*?

   The computer company announced that it will relocate its headquarters to Atlanta.

   A. move
   B. expand
   C. remodel
   D. shut down

ESSAY

33. Choose one of the selections from this test. On a separate sheet of paper, write a sentence of either positive or negative criticism that someone might write about the selection. Then, think about a possible response to the criticism. Write one sentence in which you state the main point of your response. Then, jot down two details or examples from the selection that support your point.

34. Suppose that you have decided to earn money by writing one-minute poems (rhyming or nonrhyming) for $5 each at a shopping mall. Pretend that a customer has asked you to write a poem about a water fountain. Picture the fountain in your mind. Then, use a watch or clock—or estimate the time—as you quick-write a one-minute poem about the fountain.

35. What book, story, or movie has made a deep impression on you lately? Suppose that you have been asked to write a sequel, or an additional chapter, for the work. On a separate sheet of paper, write the name of the book, story, or movie that affected you. Then, give a brief overview of events in your sequel.

Unit 6: A Time of Rapid Change
Diagnostic Test 11

MULTIPLE CHOICE

Read the selection. Then, answer the questions that follow.

For centuries, people around the world have enjoyed versions of the story Cinderella or Ashputtle. The basic story revolves around a young girl whose mother dies and whose father remarries. The evil step-mother and one or two stepsisters treat the heroine cruelly, forcing her to do menial tasks. Yet the hero-ine works dutifully and shows her natural goodness. In many versions, the king makes a decree that all the young women of the kingdom should come to a festival, where the heroine's life changes.

In the oldest version of the story, which comes from China, Yeh-Shen's mother and father both die, and she is with her stepmother, who hates her. A fish befriends her, but Yeh-Shen's stepmother kills the fish. An old man instructs Yeh-Shen to bury the fish's bones, and to go to the burial spot when she needs help. When a festival takes place in town, Yeh-Shen goes to the burial spot and requests a beautiful dress. She receives the dress and a pair of golden shoes. When she loses one of the shoes, the king looks for the person whom it fits. When Yeh-Shen tries on the shoe, she is transformed, and the king and Yeh-Shen marry and live happily ever after, while her stepmother and stepsister die in a shower of flying stones.

1. Around which basic characters do the stories of Cinderella or Ashputtle revolve?
   A. mother, father, daughter
   B. mother, father, wicked stepsisters
   C. stepmother, father, daughter
   D. daughter, stepmother, stepsisters

2. Which of the following best describes Cinderella?
   A. resentful, but dutiful
   B. dutiful and good
   C. weak and dutiful
   D. angry, but good

3. Which of the following is a frequent element in Cinderella tales?
   A. an enchanted forest
   B. a festive occasion for young women
   C. a unicorn
   D. a glass slipper

4. Where did the oldest version of the Cinderella tale originate?
   A. an ancient kingdom
   B. Europe
   C. China
   D. Africa

5. Who befriends Yeh-Shen and grants her wish?
   A. her stepmother
   B. the king
   C. an old man
   D. a fish

6. How does Yeh-Shen get her beautiful dress and golden shoes?
   A. She asks the bones of the fish for them.
   B. The king gives them to her.
   C. She asks the old man for them.
   D. Her stepmother gives them to her.

7. What element of the Yeh-Shen story is similar to the modern Cinderella story?
   A. the king
   B. the death of the fish
   C. the death of her stepmother and stepsister
   D. the search for the owner of the lost shoe

8. Which best describes how the story of Yeh-Shen ends?
   A. She is transformed into a beautiful fish and comes to live in the castle.
   B. She saves her stepmother and step-sister from death by falling stones.
   C. She marries the king and lives happily ever after.
   D. She forgives her stepmother and step-sister and lets them live in the castle.

Read the selection. Then, answer the questions that follow.

Many folk tales center around a heroine, who shows her worth by coping with a multitude of trials and tribulations. In many stories, a young girl is left in the care of an unloving stepmother. The stepmother often has a haughty, arrogant daughter who treats the young girl badly.

In many of these tales, the young girl is promised a favor of some kind if she can perform a difficult, demeaning task. In some stories she must separate lentils from ashes or good seeds from bad. The step-mother often designs a task that is impossible to complete, but the young girl receives assistance from an unlikely source, such as birds.

In "Pepelyouga," a young girl named Marra sits on a high mountain spinning yarn when a man warns her that if she drops her spindle over the precipice, her mother will turn into a cow. When Marra acciden-tally drops her spindle over the cliff, her mother is transformed and her father soon remarries. Marra's stepmother gives her hemp and tells her that she must spin a shirt by that very evening or she will be killed. Marra is distraught as she realizes that the task is an impossible one. Marra's mother (the cow) arrives, however, and chews the hemp. The hemp then comes out of her ear as thread, enabling Marra to make the shirt.

9. Which best explains the purpose of the difficult tests the heroine must endure in folk tales?
   A. to test her wit
   B. to test her strength
   C. to show her worthiness
   D. to show she can endure suffering

10. Which of the following best describes the impossible task the cruel stepmother sets for the young girl in some folk tales?
    A. separating lentils from ashes
    B. scouring the floors
    C. separating bird seed
    D. cleaning up ash pits

11. In the tale "Pepelyouga," who is Marra?
    A. Cinderella
    B. a wicked stepmother
    C. a woman who became a cow
    D. the heroine

12. What is Marra doing as the story "Pepelyouga" opens?
    A. walking in the mountains
    B. visiting her mother
    C. spinning
    D. making a shirt

13. What does the man warn Marra about?

    A. If she does not finish her spinning, she will be killed.

    B. If she drops her spindle over the cliff, her mother will turn into a cow.

    C. If her mother becomes a cow, she will have a wicked stepmother.

    D. If she drops her spindle over the cliff, her mother will die.

14. What task does the wicked stepmother set for Marra?

    A. to separate lentils from ashes

    B. to spin yarn all day

    C. to recover her spindle that she dropped

    D. to spin a shirt from hemp by evening

15. How does Marra's mother save Marra's life?

    A. by chewing the hemp and turning it into thread

    B. by killing the wicked stepmother

    C. by turning into a cow

    D. by recovering the lost spindle

Vocabulary Warm-up Word Lists

Study these words from the selections. Then, complete the activities that follow.

Word List A

artillery [ahr TIL uh ree] *n.* large mounted guns; cannon
   The attack by the <u>artillery</u> caused considerable damage.

battlefield [BAT uhl feeld] *n.* the land on which a battle is fought
   The <u>battlefield</u> was an open meadow with not many places to hide.

clods [KLAHDZ] *n.* lumps, especially of earth or clay
   Robert threw dirt <u>clods</u> against the fence to see what would happen.

doubtless [DOUT lis] *adv.* certainly
   Anna will <u>doubtless</u> be late for the party as usual.

indulge [in DULJ] *v.* to permit oneself to take pleasure in something
   Cole and Stephanie <u>indulge</u> themselves every Saturday with an ice cream.

probably [PRAHB uh blee] *adv.* very likely
   Sharon will <u>probably</u> buy a new digital camera soon.

solitary [SAHL uh ter ee] *adj.* living, being, or going alone
   Lydia led a fairly <u>solitary</u> life in her remote beachfront cottage.

wary [WAIR ee] *adj.* watchful and suspicious; cautious
   Thomas has always been <u>wary</u> of strangers.

Word List B

accommodation [uh kahm uh DAY shuhn] *n.* lodging; room and board
   As for <u>accommodation</u> for the weekend, we stayed at a lovely inn.

consequently [KAHN suh kwent lee] *adv.* as a result; therefore
   Michael did not buy a ticket; <u>consequently</u>, he did not see the show.

cope [KOHP] *v.* to deal successfully; handle
   Rich is able to <u>cope</u> with all sorts of bad weather.

deterred [di TERD] *v.* prevented from doing something; discouraged
   Her fear of failure <u>deterred</u> Madison from trying out for the school play.

locality [loh KAL uh tee] *n.* a certain place, area, region, or the like
   George prefers to live in a desert <u>locality</u> like Palm Springs.

restricted [ri STRIK tid] *adj.* limited; confined
   The injury to her arm has caused Amy to have <u>restricted</u> mobility.

sensitive [SEN suh tiv] *adj.* capable of reacting quickly or easily
   Morgan is <u>sensitive</u> to his dog's moods.

tranquil [TRANG kwuhl] *adj.* calm; serene
   Wanda enjoyed the chirping of the crickets that <u>tranquil</u> summer evening.

Name _____ Date _____

Poetry of Rupert Brooke, Siegfried Sassoon, and Wilfred Owen
"Birds on the Western Front" by Saki
Vocabulary Warm-up Exercises

Exercise A *Fill in the blanks, using each word from Word List A only once.*

While vacationing in Virginia, Paul decided to [1] _____ in his hobby of visiting historic sites. He visited a Civil War [2] _____. He thought that heavy [3] _____ had [4] _____ been used there, and he wondered if he would see any evidence of it. As he walked across the grass, he noticed some [5] _____ of dirt, out of place on the green background. Approaching the spot, he saw a [6] _____ dog nearby. [7] _____, the dog had dug up the field in order to bury something. The dog, [8] _____ of any strangers, was hanging back, near some trees. "What could he have buried?" Paul wondered.

Exercise B *Write two different sentences for each word from Word List B. You may use different forms of the vocabulary word for your second sentence.*

Example: Women fought for a long time for equality and <u>consequently</u> the right to vote. *Mozart's fame is a <u>consequence</u> of his genius.*

1. accommodation: _____
   _____

2. cope: _____
   _____

3. deterred: _____
   _____

4. locality: _____
   _____

5. restricted: _____
   _____

6. sensitive: _____
   _____

7. tranquil: _____
   _____

Poetry of Rupert Brooke, Siegfried Sassoon, and Wilfred Owen
"Birds on the Western Front" by Saki
Reading Warm-up A

Read the following passage. Pay special attention to the underlined words. Then, read it again, and complete the activities. Use a separate sheet of paper for your written answers.

Five months into the First World War, an extraordinary event occurred—a spontaneous truce in the trenches of France. The participants were mostly British and German soldiers, all of them <u>doubtless</u> missing their loved ones and longing for the comforts of home. It all began on Christmas Eve, 1914. Looking across the <u>battlefield</u>, the British soldiers could see small Christmas trees above the German trenches, complete with candles as decorations. According to reports of men who were there, one <u>solitary</u> German soldier, followed shortly afterwards by a few others, stood up outside the trench. Facing the enemy unarmed, they wished them a Merry Christmas and proposed a truce.

The truce was not to begin officially until the following morning. At about 8:00 A.M., a British captain met with a German officer in No-Man's Land, the area between the trenches that was strung with barbed wire. They agreed on the terms of the truce—neither side was to fire a shot on Christmas Day. Within moments, men on both sides were climbing out of the trenches and approaching one another. At first they were a bit <u>wary</u> of shaking hands with men they had been trying to kill just the day before. Nevertheless, they met, shook hands, exchanged small gifts, and shared family photographs. Some of them even decided to <u>indulge</u> in a game of football, kicking up <u>clods</u> of the nearly frozen ground on that cold December day.

Both sides took advantage of this time to retrieve and bury their dead and to drain and repair their trenches. By about 8:30 A.M. on December 26, the truce was officially over. Officers on both sides bowed to each other, saluted, and fired three shots in the air. The war was officially back on. Soon the sound of <u>artillery</u> fire would <u>probably</u> fill the air once again.

1. Underline the words that tell what the British and German soldiers were <u>doubtless</u> doing. Describe something that you will **doubtless** be doing this weekend.

2. Circle the word that describes part of the <u>battlefield</u>. Use **battlefield** in a sentence.

3. Underline the word that means about the same as <u>solitary</u>. Tell about a **solitary** experience you once enjoyed.

4. Underline the words that tell why the men on both sides were <u>wary</u>. Describe how a dog might act if it were **wary** of you.

5. Circle the words that describe what the men decided to <u>indulge</u> in. What do you like to **indulge** in whenever you get the chance?

6. Circle the words that tell the source of the <u>clods</u>. What are **clods**?

7. Underline the word that describes a result of <u>artillery</u> fire. What does **artillery** mean?

8. Underline the words that tell what would <u>probably</u> happen soon. What is one thing you will **probably** do after school today?

Poetry of Rupert Brooke, Siegfried Sassoon, and Wilfred Owen
"Birds on the Western Front" by Saki
Reading Warm-up B

Read the following passage. Pay special attention to the underlined words. Then, read it again, and complete the activities. Use a separate sheet of paper for your written answers.

Owls are not <u>restricted</u> to any one type of area; they can be found in rainforests, grasslands, wooded areas, and tundras. No matter what area owls inhabit, they can find <u>accommodation</u>, for they make their homes in mixed wooded areas, evergreen thickets, wooded swamps, isolated pine trees, or even in a residential <u>locality</u> with lots of trees. Not to be <u>deterred</u> from finding a place to roost, some owls even live in barns or birdhouses.

During the day, owls are calm and <u>tranquil</u>, for they spend most of the day resting. Owls are nocturnal, hunting for prey—rodents, insects, frogs, and other birds—at night. To help owls <u>cope</u> with the difficulties of night-hunting, nature has equipped them with special adaptations; for example, their keen sense of sight helps them deal with the problem of seeing prey in the dark, and their sense of hearing is so acute that an owl sitting in a tall tree can hear a mouse or a cricket on the ground. Owls' wings have downy fringes that muffle the sound as they fly; <u>consequently</u>, owls can easily sneak up on their prey.

The eyes of owls are especially interesting. Unlike other birds, whose eyes are on the sides of their heads, owls have large eyes located on the front of their faces. Compared to human eyes, the owls' eyes are ten times more <u>sensitive</u> to light. They have fine depth perception, but they see mostly in black and white. Because their eyes are so large, there is not enough room in their skulls for eye muscles. Therefore, the owl cannot move its eyes within its sockets. Instead, it must turn its head, rather than its eyes, to look at moving objects. The owl can turn its head as much as 270 degrees.

1. Underline the words that explain why owls are not <u>restricted</u> to any one type of area. What does *restricted* mean?

2. Circle the word that means about the same as <u>accommodation</u>. Describe the *accommodation* a family might offer guests who visit their home for a few days.

3. Underline a word that means about the same as <u>locality</u>. Use *locality* in a sentence.

4. What does <u>deterred</u> mean?

5. Circle the word that means about the same as <u>tranquil</u>. If you are in a *tranquil* mood, what do you like to do?

6. Underline the words that mean about the same as <u>cope</u>. What is an antonym for *cope*?

7. Circle the cause and underline the effect that are joined by the word <u>consequently</u>. What does *consequently* mean?

8. What kind of job would probably be best for a person with very <u>sensitive</u> taste buds?

Name _____ Date _____

"The Soldier" by Rupert Brooke
"Wirers" by Siegfried Sassoon
"Anthem for Doomed Youth" by Wilfred Owen
"Birds on the Western Front" by Saki (H. H. Munro)
Literary Analysis: Tone

The **tone** of language conveys an attitude toward the audience or the subject. We recognize tone in spoken language quickly. The way in which words are spoken, as well as the speaker's volume and facial expressions help us sort out his or her attitude. Some of these advantages aren't available to the writer, who must create tone with language alone. In literature, tone is transmitted primarily through choice of words and details.

Details selected may imply an attitude about the subject. In "The Soldier," Rupert Brooke represents England with "her flowers to love" and "the suns of home." Apart from descriptive language, these choices tell us part of what Brooke feels for his country.

The particular words selected matter greatly. When Wilfred Owen writes of "shrill, demented choirs of wailing shells," we get a clear sense of his attitude toward war. A writer's manner of speaking, or voice, conveys tone, too. Is it formal or informal? Serious or light? Lofty or low? How does the language help you make these decisions?

DIRECTIONS: *Analyze the tone of each of the following passages. For each one, explain what impression details, word choices, and voice make. Then describe the overall tone of the passage.*

"Wirers"		
. . . I heard him carried away, / Moaning at every lurch; no doubt he'll die today. / But *we* can say the front-line wire's been safely mended.		
Details:	Word Choice:	Voice:
Tone:		

"Birds on the Western Front"		
. . . once, having occasion to throw myself down with some abruptness on my face, I found myself nearly on the top of a brood of young larks. Two of them had already been hit by something and were in rather a battered condition, but the survivors seemed as tranquil and comfortable as the average nestling.		
Details:	Word Choice:	Voice:
Tone:		

"The Soldier" by Rupert Brooke
"Wirers" by Siegfried Sassoon
"Anthem for Doomed Youth" by Wilfred Owen
"Birds on the Western Front" by Saki (H. H. Munro)

Reading Strategy: Make Inferences

An **inference** is a conclusion drawn by reasoning. We make inferences all the time in daily life. Someone stands in the hall with wet hair and a dripping umbrella, and we conclude that it has been raining outside. If the sprinkler system had gone off in the building ten minutes ago, however, we might make a different inference. In short, we infer based on all available evidence. In daily life, we do this quickly, almost automatically.

In literature, we may have to make inferences more consciously. Writers engage readers by portraying a world of details or evidence and understand that readers will draw conclusions from clues they read.

Much in literature is implied, especially in poetry, so picking up quickly on setting, images, language, tone, and theme is a valuable skill for a reader. What do you know about the setting and speaker? How do you know it? What's going on? How soon do you find out? What clues do you use? What is the tone and message of the work? What language lets you make the inference?

Use the following chart to practice making inferences.

DIRECTIONS: *Write down the inference you make about each element of "Birds on the Western Front." In the Clues column, identify specifically the evidence that you used to make the inference.*

Element	Inference	Clues
Setting (Where?)		
Speaker (Who?)		
Action/Topic (What?)		
Tone (Attitude)		
Theme (Message)		

"The Soldier" by Rupert Brooke
"Wirers" by Siegfried Sassoon
"Anthem for Doomed Youth" by Wilfred Owen
"Birds on the Western Front" by Saki (H. H. Munro)
Vocabulary Builder

Using the Root -*laud*-

The word *laudable*, which means "praiseworthy," originates from the Latin verb *laudere*, which means "to praise." Other related words are *laud, laudatory,* and *laudation.*

A. DIRECTIONS: *Complete the following sentences with one of the words in the preceding paragraph that use the -laud- root.*

1. Wilfred Owen's poem is powerful enough to _____ young soldiers and say that they "die like cattle" at the same time.

2. Is Brooke's _____ of England different in tone from one a homesick German might imagine for his country?

3. Saki's _____ remarks about birds gloss an ironic view of human beings.

Using the Word List

stealthy	desolate	mockeries	pallor
laudable	requisitioned	disconcerted	

B. DIRECTIONS: *Each item consists of a word from the Word List followed by four lettered words or phrases. Choose the word or phrase most nearly similar in meaning to the Word List word. Circle the letter of your choice.*

1. stealthy
   A. furtive
   B. luxurious
   C. pilfered
   D. invisible

2. desolate
   A. absent
   B. disconnected
   C. selected
   D. deserted

3. mockeries
   A. imitations
   B. farces
   C. symbols
   D. vanities

4. pallor
   A. salon
   B. friendship
   C. gloom
   D. paleness

5. laudable
   A. humorous
   B. flexible
   C. praiseworthy
   D. clamorous

6. requisitioned
   A. relocated
   B. investigated
   C. ordered
   D. recovered

7. disconcerted
   A. silenced
   B. confused
   C. detached
   D. failed

"**The Soldier**" by Rupert Brooke
"**Wirers**" by Siegfried Sassoon
"**Anthem for Doomed Youth**" by Wilfred Owen
"**Birds on the Western Front**" by Saki (H. H. Munro)

Grammar and Style: Using *Who* and *Whom* in Adjective Clauses

The pronouns *who* and *whom* sometimes cause confusion when they occur in clauses. A clause has both a subject and predicate and serves as a sentence element. In a sentence with an **adjective clause,** the entire clause modifies a noun or pronoun.

Determine which pronoun to use by what the pronoun is doing *within the clause.* If the pronoun serves as a subject, appositive, or complement in the clause, use *who*, the nominative form. If the pronoun serves as an object, indirect object, or object of a preposition in a clause, use *whom*, the objective form, regardless of how the entire clause functions. For example:

Sassoon, *whom* Owen met, published Owen's poetry after the war.

The pronoun *whom* serves as the object of *met*, the verb within the adjective clause. Because it is the object of a verb, *whom* is the correct pronoun, even though the clause is part of the subject.

A. PRACTICE: *Write either* who *or* whom *on the line to complete each of the following sentences.*

1. In World War I, the killing efficiency of modern machine guns shocked those _____ had romantic notions of the glory of war.

2. Brave soldiers, _____ unprepared generals thought would attack as they always had, were mown like grass.

3. Tanks and airplanes were dismissed as interesting novelties by strategists _____ four years of slaughter taught little.

B. Writing Application: *Write sentences with adjective clauses using* who *or* whom. *Follow the prompts provided.*

1. Write a sentence using *who* about Rupert Brooke and talented writers dying in World War I.

_____

_____

2. Write a sentence using *whom* about Siegfried Sassoon. The world discovered him in war and he wrote about peace in later life.

_____

_____

3. Write a sentence using *whom* about families that soldiers left behind—a subject on Wilfred Owen's mind as he writes his poem.

_____

_____

Name _____ Date _____

"The Soldier" by Rupert Brooke
"Wirers" by Siegfried Sassoon
"Anthem for Doomed Youth" by Wilfred Owen
"Birds on the Western Front" by Saki (H. H. Munro)

Support for Writing

Before writing your critical response, reread "The Soldier" and "Wirers." Record in the diagrams below which details about patriotism are sentimental and unsentimental. You may not fill every row.

Sentimental		Unsentimental
	"The Soldier"	

Sentimental		Unsentimental
	"Wirers"	

On a separate page, use the details you gather to analyze the two poems. Write a thesis statement that expresses your opinion about whether the poems are sentimental or unsentimental. Support your position as you write your critical response.

"The Soldier" by Rupert Brooke
"Wirers" by Siegfried Sassoon
"Anthem for Doomed Youth" by Wilfred Owen
"Birds on the Western Front" by Saki (H. H. Munro)

Support for Extend Your Learning

Listening and Speaking

Use the chart to collect and organize ideas for a **debate** on the costs and benefits of war.

Resolution: There are occasions when war is necessary.	
Arguments For	**Arguments Against**

Research and Technology

Use the graphic organizer below to gather information on trench warfare in World War I. First, decide on a focus for your report, and write it in the center circle. Then, collect details about your focus and write them in the linked boxes.

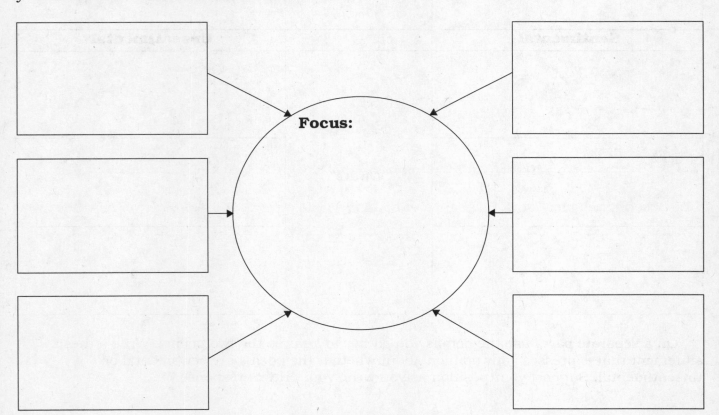

Focus:

"The Soldier" by Rupert Brooke
"Wirers" by Siegfried Sassoon
"Anthem for Doomed Youth" by Wilfred Owen
"Birds on the Western Front" by Saki (H. H. Munro)

Enrichment: Social Studies

European Boundaries Before and After World War I

In early 1918, Germany nearly won the war, but fresh American troops and dawning tank warfare turned the tide. Germany sought peace, and with the armistice of November 11, the slaughter ended. The Treaty of Versailles (1919) compelled Germany to accept terms it found hard to accept. Forced to admit guilt for the war and pay harsh damages, Germany lost all colonies and its territory was reduced and reorganized. The "guilt clause" and war reparations were especially resented by Germans, prolonging hatred and sowing the seeds of World War II.

DIRECTIONS: *Study the following maps. Map A represents the boundaries of continental Europe in 1914. Map B represents the redrawn boundaries resulting from the treaty of Versailles in 1919. Then answer the following questions about the maps.*

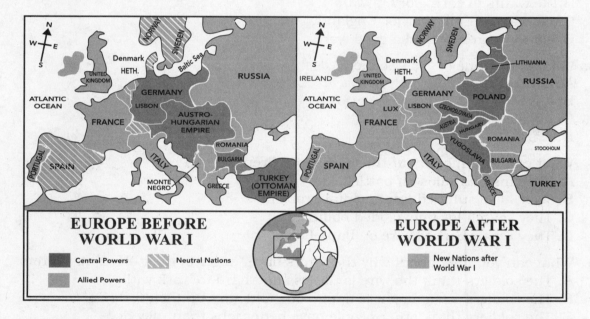

1. Describe the most obvious change in boundaries as a result of the Treaty of Versailles.

   _____

2. What losses of German territory resulted from the Treaty?

   _____

3. What changes in Russian territory occurred?

   _____

4. Italy was an ally of the British and Americans. How did Italy's boundaries change?

   _____

"The Soldier" by Rupert Brooke
"Wirers" by Siegfried Sassoon
"Anthem for Doomed Youth" by Wilfred Owen
"Birds on the Western Front" by Saki (H. H. Munro)

Selection Test A

Critical Reading *Identify the letter of the choice that best answers the question.*

____ 1. What does Rupert Brooke mean when he says in "The Soldier" that "some corner of a foreign field" will be "forever England" if he dies there?
A. He is not afraid to die fighting in another country for England.
B. If he dies, the earth where he is buried will contain a bit of England.
C. No matter how bad the war is, the English people will never give up.
D. Sooner or later the English will win the war and conquer their enemies.

____ 2. What can you infer about the speaker's attitude toward war in "The Soldier"?
A. He fears war above everything.
B. He wants to earn glory in war.
C. He will fight any war for England.
D. No war can be called a good war.

____ 3. What is the tone of "The Soldier"?
A. hopefulness
B. anger
C. hopelessness
D. fear

____ 4. What can you infer about the wirers in "Wirers"?
A. They install radios on battlefields.
B. They have suffered from mental problems.
C. They search for unexploded bombs.
D. They repair barbed wire on battlefields.

____ 5. What can you infer about why the wirers have "anger in their blood" in "Wirers"?
A. The soldiers think the wire is useless and hard to work with.
B. The soldiers' assignment is dangerous and stirs up their feelings.
C. The soldiers think other people have better jobs than they do.
D. The soldiers are afraid that they will cut themselves on the wire.

____ 6. The final lines from "Wirers" describe a young soldier who has been shot. Then the poet remarks, "But *we* can say the front-line wire's been safely mended." Why is the speaker's tone so bitter?
A. because the wirers had to leave home
B. because the wires are not always fixed
C. because the wirers' lives are not valued
D. because the wirers are lonely

_____ 7. Who are the doomed youth in "Anthem for Doomed Youth"?
   A. any person who dies young
   B. young people whose lives lack meaning
   C. any person who fights in wars
   D. young people who die in battle

_____ 8. What is the theme of "Anthem for Doomed Youth"?
   A. War is difficult for everyone.
   B. Mourning does not take place on the battlefield.
   C. The loss of soldiers is hardest on women.
   D. No one but soldiers notice one another's deaths.

_____ 9. Why does the speaker refer to soldiers as "those who die as cattle" in "Anthem for Doomed Youth"?
   A. The speaker thinks soldiers' deaths are not honored.
   B. The speaker thinks cattle are well-treated.
   C. The speaker thinks all soldiers are heroes.
   D. The speaker thinks soldiers who die in battle are heroes.

_____ 10. Who can you infer is the narrator in "Birds on the Western Front"?
   A. a zookeeper
   B. a soldier
   C. a biologist
   D. a doctor

_____ 11. What is the Western Front in Saki's poem "Birds on the Western Front"?
   A. the great plains of the United States
   B. places in Russia where battles were fought
   C. parts of Great Britain
   D. the battle lines in Western Europe

_____ 12. What does the narrator conclude about birds in "Birds on the Western Front"?
   A. Some birds are frightened by battle, but many seem to go on as usual.
   B. The sounds of battle have frightened away all but a few birds.
   C. The emotional state of soldiers is influenced by the lack of birds nearby.
   D. War has resulted in the needless slaughter of most birds.

Vocabulary and Grammar

_____ 13. Which word best replaces _desolate_ in this sentence: "The _desolate_ landscape had no hint of growth"?
   A. rainy
   B. empty
   C. proud
   D. confused

____ **14.** Which sentence **correctly** uses an adjective clause as a subject with *who*?

    A. The soldier who was sent to repair the wire returned safely.

    B. The soldiers to who medals were given were proud.

    C. The soldiers at who the bullets were shot died immediately.

    D. The soldiers without who the war was lost were never thanked.

Essay

15. Young men looked forward to combat and the opportunity it gave them to have adventure and become heroes in World War I. Brooke, Sassoon, Owen, and Saki were among these men. Choose one of the selections in this group and write an essay in which you discuss how the writer's attitude and opinion of the war changed. Give examples from the selection to support your response.

16. War remains a part of the world. Which of the poems—"The Soldier," "Wirers," or "Anthem for Doomed Youth"—expresses the modern view of warfare? With which poem do you think most Americans today would agree? Give reasons for your choice and cite examples from the poem.

"The Soldier" by Rupert Brooke
"Wirers" by Siegfried Sassoon
"Anthem for Doomed Youth" by Wilfred Owen
"Birds on the Western Front" by Saki (H. H. Munro)
Selection Test B

Critical Reading *Identify the letter of the choice that best completes the statement or answers the question.*

_____ 1. In Rupert Brooke's poem "The Soldier," how is it possible that there could be "some corner of a foreign field / That is forever England"?
   A. Brooke believes totally in England's eventual victory.
   B. England will never yield ground gained at a high price.
   C. The sacrifice of English soldiers lays claim to the land.
   D. His English body will always occupy a part of the earth.

_____ 2. In "The Soldier," the speaker suggests the strength of his patriotism when he
   A. feels blessed by the sun in England.
   B. dreams of exerting an English influence in his afterlife.
   C. assumes his corpse will make richer the soil in which it is buried.
   D. says he wants to die for his country.

_____ 3. Brooke implies in "The Soldier" that he associates England with
   A. ambition.
   B. gentleness.
   C. morbidity.
   D. warfare.

_____ 4. Which word best summarizes Brooke's tone in "The Soldier"?
   A. uncertain
   B. determined
   C. guarded
   D. idealistic

_____ 5. "Wirers" by Siegfried Sassoon is about
   A. men who strung barbed-wire fences on the battlefield.
   B. demolition experts working behind the lines.
   C. the contribution of scientists to munitions work.
   D. bomb-disposal crews defusing unexploded bombs.

_____ 6. What is the theme of "Wirers"?
   A. War is dreadful and meaningless.
   B. Soldiers in wartime think only of survival.
   C. Friendship is impossible in the face of death.
   D. Dying is better than confronting horror day after day.

_____ 7. In "Anthem for Doomed Youth," the "holy glimmers of good-byes" refers to
    A. candles.
    B. prayers.
    C. waves.
    D. tears.

_____ 8. In "Anthem for Doomed Youth," what can you infer from this line?
    The pallor of girls' brows shall be their pall;
    A. Families will never know what happened to their loved ones.
    B. The grief of lovers will be the sole memorial service.
    C. There will be no way of honoring those lost.
    D. Memorial services are not held at home for the dead.

_____ 9. The theme of "Anthem for Doomed Youth" is
    A. Civilians mourn dead soldiers more than other soldiers do.
    B. The horrors of war do not allow for customary mourning.
    C. Battles do not stop for funeral ceremonies.
    D. Soldiers don't want to be buried in foreign soil.

_____ 10. The speaker in Saki's "Birds on the Western Front" is a
    A. minister.
    B. pilot.
    C. soldier.
    D. biologist.

_____ 11. The tone of "Birds on the Western Front"
    A. honors the persistence of natural life in a hazardous environment.
    B. defends the value of understatement and reserve in English patriotism.
    C. satirizes the foolishness of natural instinct in wartime.
    D. contrasts natural life and the absurdity of war.

_____ 12. In "Birds on the Western Front," when the narrator notes that "there are always sufficient mice left over to populate one's dugout and make a race course of one's face at
night," he is
    A. commenting upon the conditions of life in the trenches.
    B. explaining the war's effect on the balance of nature.
    C. suggesting a decline in the number or efficiency of owls.
    D. accounting for the mice because of the destruction of grain fields.

Vocabulary and Grammar

_____ 13. Someone who is *stealthy* is
    A. evil.
    B. peculiar.
    C. secretive.
    D. determined.

____ 14. A *laudable* behavior is
  A. shameful.
  B. comic.
  C. praiseworthy.
  D. wasted.

____ 15. Which sentence uses the pronoun *who* or *whom* correctly?
  A. Few soldiers still survive whom were in World War I.
  B. Few soldiers who fought in World War I still survive.
  C. Few soldiers who we know of from World War I survive.
  D. Few soldiers fought in World War I whom still survive.

____ 16. The correct case for *who* or *whom* in an adjective clause is determined by the
  A. function of the clause in the sentence.
  B. function of the noun modified by the adjective clause.
  C. position of the clause in the subject or predicate.
  D. function of the pronoun within the clause.

Essay

17. In "The Soldier" and "Wirers," Rupert Brooke and Siegfried Sassoon offer two visions of a soldier's life and death. What views do they express? In an essay, compare and contrast the two poets' visions as shown in their poems. Use examples from the poems to illustrate your points.

18. Saki's "Birds on the Western Front" doesn't say a great deal about the life of a soldier, preferring to talk about bird life instead. How does the tone of the piece carry the message that the essay is not really about birds? Write an essay in which you explain how Saki uses tone to turn an article about birds into a commentary on the human endeavor of war. Use examples from the essay to support your ideas.

"Wartime Speech" by Sir Winston Churchill
"Defending Nonviolent Resistance" by Mohandas K. Gandhi
Vocabulary Warm-up Word Lists

Study these words from the selections. Then, complete the activities that follow.

Word List A

agricultural [ag ri KUL churh uhl] *adj.* relating to the science of farming
David's <u>agricultural</u> knowledge contributed to the success of his farm.

contribution [kahn truh BYOO shuhn] *n.* something given to a cause
Alan's <u>contribution</u> to the pot-luck supper was a salad.

exertions [eg ZER shuhnz] *n.* great efforts
Heather's <u>exertions</u> during the aerobics class left her gasping for breath.

fulfilled [fool FILD] *v.* carried out, as a promise or prediction
Chuck <u>fulfilled</u> his obligation to babysit the twins on Saturday.

similarly [SIM uh luhr lee] *adv.* in a manner that is alike
Crystal wore a shawl; <u>similarly</u>, Claire wore a cape.

supplement [SUP luh muhnt] *n.* something added, often to fill a lack
The doctor recommended a daily <u>supplement</u> of vitamins and minerals.

totality [toh TAL uh tee] *n.* the whole sum or quantity
The <u>totality</u> of the team's effort was not enough to win the game.

voluntary [VAHL uhn ter ee] *adj.* given or done by one's own choice
Melissa's participation in the clean-up effort was <u>voluntary</u>.

Word List B

agitation [aj uh TAY shuhn] *n.* arousing interest in order to cause change
<u>Agitation</u> against the injustices led to the Civil Rights Act.

inadequate [in AD i kwit] *adj.* less than is needed or required
<u>Inadequate</u> amounts of food lead to malnutrition and starvation.

occurrences [uh KER uhn siz] *n.* events; incidents; happenings
Several <u>occurrences</u> of disturbance led to a police investigation.

onslaught [AHN slawt] *n.* a very violent attack
The <u>onslaught</u> caused many serious injuries.

penalty [PEN uhl tee] *n.* the legal punishment for having broken a law
The <u>penalty</u> for grand theft is imprisonment.

resources [REE sawr siz] *n.* supplies that can be used or drawn on
The army used all its available <u>resources</u> in the long years of war.

utmost [UT mohst] *adj.* greatest or highest in amount, degree, or number
Todd gave his <u>utmost</u> effort in running the marathon.

wholly [HOH lee] *adv.* completely; totally
Isabel did not <u>wholly</u> agree with Anna.

Name _____ Date _____

Vocabulary Warm-up Exercises

Exercise A *Fill in each blank below with the appropriate word from Word List A.*

The Future Farmers of America, a club at Wilson High School, is dedicated to providing

[1] _____ experience to its members. The [2] _____ of its

activities centers on growing crops. An interesting project last year required serious

[3] _____ from all members. They wanted to establish a vegetable garden

that could provide some [4] _____ to the diets of those in need in their

city. Each member made more than one [5] _____ of time and energy to

this [6] _____ effort. Within one growing season, they had

[7] _____ their promise to feed the hungry. [8] _____, they

vowed to do the same thing next year—but with different crops.

Exercise B *Write two different sentences for each word from Word List B. You may use
different forms of the vocabulary word for your second sentence.*

Example: I think he is dangerously inexperienced, and I am <u>wholly</u> opposed to his candidacy.
In this recipe, you use the <u>whole</u> lemon, peel and all.

1. agitation: _____

    _____

2. inadequate: _____

    _____

3. occurrences: _____

    _____

4. onslaught: _____

    _____

5. penalty: _____

    _____

6. resources: _____

    _____

7. utmost: _____

    _____

"Wartime Speech" by Sir Winston Churchill
"Defending Nonviolent Resistance" by Mohandas K. Gandhi
Reading Warm-up A

Read the following passage. Pay special attention to the underlined words. Then, read it again, and complete the activities. Use a separate sheet of paper for your written answers.

In 1930, Mohandas Gandhi made his most important <u>contribution</u> to the struggle against British rule in India, he began his famous "march to the sea." For some time, Gandhi had been campaigning quite publicly and vocally for an end to British rule, but he began to see that these <u>exertions</u> were not enough. He knew that he needed to do something more dramatic. He decided to march across India, through cities and rural <u>agricultural</u> areas, until he came to the sea. There, he would pick up salt in a symbolic gesture.

The march to the sea had a definite objective: to defy the British law that made the government entirely responsible for the <u>totality</u> of salt production in India. According to the Salt Tax, it was illegal for any entity but the government to sell or produce salt. Since salt is a necessary <u>supplement</u> in everyone's diet, this law affected everyone in India. It forced them to buy salt at high prices.

At the first stop of his famous march, Gandhi told his followers to be ready for "the worst, even death, for defiance of the salt tax." His words of warning did not stop the 78 <u>voluntary</u> fellow marchers who walked with him for 23 days and over 240 miles to the Indian coast. There, he <u>fulfilled</u> his promise and picked up a handful of mud and salt at the beach. Within moments, his followers <u>similarly</u> began picking up salt everywhere along the coast. In a matter of a few days, thousands of people were in jail, and Gandhi himself was arrested a month later. The Salt March led to other demonstrations and violence against the nonviolent protestors. It was a slow and difficult process, but eventually India gained its freedom from British rule.

1. Underline the words that tell what Gandhi's <u>contribution</u> was. What **contribution** have you made to a cause or a project recently?

2. Circle the words that describe the <u>exertions</u> Gandhi had made earlier. Then, use **exertions** in a sentence.

3. Underline the word that offers a clue to the meaning of <u>agricultural</u>. What does **agricultural** mean?

4. Circle the word that offers a clue to the meaning of <u>totality</u>. What is an antonym of **totality**?

5. Underline the word that names an important dietary <u>supplement</u>. What is one **supplement** a person might add to their diet on a daily basis?

6. Underline the words that tell what the <u>voluntary</u> marchers did with Gandhi. Tell about a time you participated in a project on a **voluntary** basis.

7. Underline the words that tell what Gandhi <u>fulfilled</u>. What does **fulfilled** mean?

8. Circle the words that tell what the followers <u>similarly</u> began to do. Then, use **similarly** in a sentence.

Name _____   Date _____

"Wartime Speech" by Sir Winston Churchill
"Defending Nonviolent Resistance" by Mohandas K. Gandhi
Reading Warm-up B

Read the following passage. Pay special attention to the underlined words. Then, read it again, and complete the activities. Use a separate sheet of paper for your written answers.

The spring of 1940 was a time of great <u>agitation</u> for the British forces during World War II. Hitler's armies had already invaded Holland, Belgium, and the northern areas of France. As the <u>onslaught</u> of the German "Blitzkrieg" moved into the west and south of France, it split the British and French forces fighting there. One of the major <u>occurrences</u> of this phase of the war was when the German army trapped the British forces at Dunkirk. This forced the British to evacuate all their <u>resources</u>. By June 14, the Germans entered Paris, forcing the surrender of France eight days later. Without France as an ally, England was now <u>wholly</u> on its own, facing the seemingly inevitable invasion by Germany completely by itself.

This was a dark time for England. The soldiers who had been rescued at Dunkirk had already put forth their <u>utmost</u> efforts and were exhausted. The Germans began to attack England by air in the early summer. The only hope for England lay with a small group of Royal Air Force pilots who were outnumbered by German pilots four to one. It certainly seemed as if England's strength was <u>inadequate</u> for the task, but it would be a mistake to dismiss those brave pilots as lacking. For months, the pilots took to the sky to do battle, often several times a day. Many paid the supreme <u>penalty</u>, losing their lives in air battles, but by September, the Germans gave up. Hitler canceled his plans to invade England, and turned instead to the defeat of Russia. In praise of the heroism of the British pilots, Winston Churchill said, "Never before in human history was so much owed by so many to so few."

1. Underline the words that explain what caused <u>agitation</u>. Then, use *agitation* in a sentence.

2. Circle the words that tell the result of the German <u>onslaught</u>. What does *onslaught* mean?

3. Underline the words that describe one of the major <u>occurrences</u> at this time. Name two *occurrences* in the past week that you enjoyed.

4. Name a goal that you have, and tell what <u>resources</u> you would have to use in order to accomplish it.

5. Circle a synonym for <u>wholly</u>. What is an antonym of *wholly*?

6. Underline the words that describe the result of using their <u>utmost</u> efforts. Describe the last time you put forth your *utmost* effort.

7. Underline the word that is a synonym for <u>inadequate</u>. Use *inadequate* in a sentence.

8. Circle the words that describe the supreme <u>penalty</u>. What do you think is a fair *penalty* for failing to pay a debt in time?

"Wartime Speech" by Winston Churchill
"Defending Nonviolent Resistance" by Mohandas K. Gandhi
Literary Analysis: Speech

Although different in rhetorical style, Churchill and Gandhi were excellent persuasive speakers. Both understood that the audience for a **speech** has needs different from the audience for a written work, and developed speaking styles to meet those needs.

The purpose of a speech may be to entertain, inform, or persuade, but to do any of these, it must capture and hold the attention of its audience. Features of an effective speech include:

An engaging introduction Depending on its purpose, a speech may begin with an announcement, brief statement of purpose, entertaining anecdote, or surprising declaration. The introduction serves as a "hook" to capture the interest of the audience. Churchill knows his audience is worried about war news, and begins there. Gandhi begins a "defense" by admitting guilt.

Clear organization The audience for a speech cannot stop and reread for information, so clarity and organization are especially important in a speech. Churchill uses simple statements followed by explanations and Gandhi addresses his points chronologically, but neither is hard to follow.

Concrete language and vivid images Although Churchill uses more formal rhetoric, his terms are familiar, and when he speaks of "gashed" Holland, or when Gandhi refers to "skeletons in many villages", the words have impact.

Examples Churchill gives specific examples of British heroism in the air and service at home, and Gandhi traces precisely the causes of his disaffection with British rule.

A strong conclusion In many speeches, the conclusion summarizes main points in an appealing way. In a persuasive speech, appeals to high ideals may be made. Gandhi and Churchill do both.

DIRECTIONS: *Cite specific examples or passages from each selection that correspond to features of an effective speech.*

1. Engaging Introduction: _____

    _____

2. Clear Organization: _____

    _____

3. Concrete Language/Vivid Images: _____

    _____

4. Examples: _____

    _____

5. Strong Conclusion: _____

    _____

122

Name _____ Date _____

"Wartime Speech" by Winston Churchill
"Defending Nonviolent Resistance" by Mohandas K. Gandhi
Reading Strategy: Identify Main Points and Support

One of the most important reading skills is the ability to recognize **main points** and supporting details. Readers and listeners look for main ideas and supporting details almost intuitively. You can see the principle operating in even a single sentence:

Churchill was a great wartime leader who refused to quit and inspired his people.

The main idea is that Churchill was a great wartime leader. The rest of the sentence gives evidence for the idea. Here is a graphic representation of the idea and support:

Main Idea	Churchill was a great wartime leader
Support 1	He refused to quit.
Support 2	He inspired his people.

The same principles of analysis work in paragraphs. In most paragraphs, a topic sentence near the beginning identifies the main idea. Other sentences provide support.

You can extend this type of analysis even to whole documents. The main idea of the Declaration of Independence, for example, is that the bonds of government between the King and the colonies must be broken. Thomas Jefferson gives about twenty-five reasons.

DIRECTIONS: *Use the grid below to list the main idea and supporting features for the following paragraph. Label the supporting features S1, S2, and so on.*

We must not allow ourselves to be intimidated by the presence of these armored vehicles behind our lines. If they are behind our Front, the French are also at many points fighting actively behind theirs. Both sides are therefore in an extremely dangerous position. If the French Army, and our own Army are well handled, as I believe they will be; if the French retain that genius for recovery and counter-attack for which they have so long been famous; and if the British Army shows the dogged endurance and solid fighting power of which there have been so many examples in the past—then a sudden transformation of the scene might spring into being.

Main Idea	
S1	

"Wartime Speech" by Winston Churchill
"Defending Nonviolent Resistance" by Mohandas K. Gandhi
Vocabulary Builder

Using the Root -dur-

The Latin word *durus* is an adjective meaning "hard." It is an ancestor of the Word Bank word *endurance,* which means "stamina" or "resistance to wear." Most words with a *-dur-* root carry this connotation of toughness.

A. DIRECTIONS: *For each of the sentences, write the word from among the following that can replace the underlined words:*

duration   endured   obdurate

1. For the <u>time</u> the war wore on, Churchill never let show his fear. _____
2. Gandhi was <u>hard and unyielding</u> in not compromising his position. _____
3. Though they differed on the role of the British Empire, the resistance to corruption of their reputations has <u>lived</u> beyond both the men and the issues that divided them. _____

Using the Word List

intimidated	diabolical	retaliate	formidable	excrescence
invincible	endurance	extenuating	disaffection	

B. DIRECTIONS: *Complete each sentence with the best choice from the Word List.*

After the Germans tore through France early in World War II, there appeared no way to defeat them. The Nazi war machine looked (1) _____. Hitler, however, feared crossing water for military action, and the British Navy was still (2) _____. German planes began to bomb England in an effort to terrorize Britons. The British, however, were unafraid and not (3) _____. Churchill chose to bomb Berlin. Hitler was shocked that the English had the means to (4) _____. Bombing raids struck at civilians, an evil development in the (5) _____ history of war. This horrible tactic, an (6) _____ of previous military strategy, became common. With unbelievable stamina, civilians went about daily life with incredible (7) _____. In spite of their suffering, British citizens showed little (8) _____ with the war effort. The recognition that this was total war for both sides may be an (9) _____ factor in the decision to bomb civilians, but it doesn't make less terrible the death of innocent millions.

Name _____ Date _____

Grammar and Style: Parallel Structure

Parallel structure is the use of matching grammatical forms or patterns to express related ideas. Parallel structure adds rhetorical power through rhythm, repetition, and balance. Writers may repeat single words, phrases, or clauses in parallel structure. In a parallel structure, each part of the coordinating structure must be of the same grammatical form.

A. PRACTICE: *Underline parallel structures in the following passages and identify the grammatical element of each.*

"Wartime Speech"

1. And if the French Army, and our own Army, are well handled, as I believe they will be; if the French retain that genius for recovery and counter-attack for which they have so long been famous; and if the British Army shows the dogged endurance . . . of which there have been so many examples in the past—then a sudden transformation might spring into being.

2. Only a very small part of that splendid army has yet been heavily engaged; and only a very small part of France has yet been invaded.

3. After this battle in France abates its force, there will come the battle for our island—for all that Britain is, and all that Britain means.

"Defending Nonviolent Resistance"

4. Nonviolence is the first article of my faith. It is also the last article of my creed.

5. No sophistry, no jugglery in figures can explain away the evidence that the skeletons in many villages present to the naked eye.

B. Writing Application: *Rewrite each of the following items to use parallel structure.*

1. Churchill wanted to explain the situation so he could encourage the Army and reassure the people. He also wanted to prepare both Army and people and inspire them for the long struggle he foresaw.

_____

_____

_____

2. Gandhi did not dispute the British charges. He disputed the British right of administration. He objected to their application of the law and imposition of justice. He opposed British rule of India.

_____

_____

_____

125

Name _____ Date _____

"Wartime Speech" by Winston Churchill
"Defending Nonviolent Resistance" by Mohandas K. Gandhi
Support for Writing

Use the graphic organizer that follows to gather and organize ideas for your persuasive speech.

Issue: _____

Audience: _____

What questions will my audience have?

_____

_____

_____

Main Points	**Supporting Facts, Reasons, and Examples**
←	
←	
←	

On a separate page, use information from the organizer to draft your speech. Keep in mind your audience and the questions they will have. Strengthen your main points with examples.

Name _____ Date _____

"Wartime Speech" by Winston Churchill
"Defending Nonviolent Resistance" by Mohandas K. Gandhi
Support for Extend Your Learning

Listening and Speaking

Prepare for the **panel discussion** by thinking about the situation Churchill faced with the Nazis and how Gandhi's philosophy might be used in the same situation. Use the chart to organize your thoughts.

Details of Churchill's Situation	Gandhi's Response

Research and Technology

Use the first column of the chart to record details from the film on Gandhi or Churchill. Then, check the information in a print source and record your findings. Use the information to write your critique of the film.

The Film: _____	Print Source: _____
Details:	Details:
Differences Between Information in Film and Print Source:	

"Wartime Speech" by Winston Churchill
"Defending Nonviolent Resistance" by Mohandas K. Gandhi
Enrichment: Community Action

Remembered for his use of nonviolent resistance against the British, Mohandas K. Gandhi was an advocate of fundamental social reform. He fought against India's caste system, and began basic literacy programs and other social services for the poor.

What local community action program might you advocate? How would you explain or persuade others of its value? What would you say in a speech to acquire funding for your plan?

DIRECTIONS: Select a topic for a speech on community action. Fill out this worksheet to plan your speech.

1. **Topic:** Pick a local problem you think you could help solve.
   _____

2. **Introduction:** Engage the audience with the topic. Plan a "hook" to draw in listeners.
   _____
   _____

3. **Clear Organization:** List the main idea and supporting ideas.

Main Idea	
S1	_____
S2	_____
S3	_____
S4	_____

4. **Concrete language, vivid images, and specific examples:** Use these in your support features. Provide transitions between ideas.
   _____
   _____
   _____

5. **Conclusion:** Plan an ending that summarizes your points in an appealing way. What would you like your audience to think or do?
   _____
   _____

"Wartime Speech" by Winston Churchill
"Defending Nonviolent Resistance" by Mohandas K. Gandhi
Selection Test A

Critical Reading *Identify the letter of the choice that best answers the question.*

_____ 1. Where did Churchill deliver his "Wartime Speech"?
  A. on television
  B. in the United States
  C. on radio
  D. from an airplane

_____ 2. What was the purpose of Churchill's "Wartime Speech"?
  A. to encourage the British people to support the war effort
  B. to tell the French that the British would soon surrender
  C. to ask young men to join the British armed forces
  D. to urge the United States to join the war and support Britain

_____ 3. In Churchill's "Wartime Speech," why is the phrase "we are ready to face it; to endure it; and to retaliate against it" called parallelism?
  A. It repeats the same key words again and again.
  B. It sets up similar ideas using similar grammar.
  C. It refers to well-known people, places, and events.
  D. It offers choices that are very different from one another.

_____ 4. Which detail supports Churchill's point in "Wartime Speech" that England and France can together defeat Germany?
  A. German tanks have broken through French defenses.
  B. Many of Germany's tanks and planes are in use.
  C. Germany's army numbers three or four millions and is well equipped.
  D. For every warplane Britain has lost, Germany has lost three or four.

_____ 5. Why does Churchill end his "Wartime Speech" by asking listeners to "be in readiness for the conflict"?
  A. to show that Germany does not believe in God
  B. to convince British people that God is on their side
  C. to ask for God's help in defeating Germany and saving Europe
  D. to urge the British to commit themselves to winning the war

_____ 6. What was Gandhi's purpose in "Defending Nonviolent Resistance"?
  A. to explain to listeners how he would achieve his goals
  B. to convince the judge to reduce his jail sentence
  C. to describe his years of service to the British Empire
  D. to explain why he became a protester

_____ 7. How does Gandhi respond to the charges against him in "Defending Nonviolent Resistance"?
A. He ignores them.
B. He says they are wrong.
C. He agrees with them.
D. He claims the witnesses lied.

_____ 8. In "Defending Nonviolent Resistance," why does Gandhi consider it an honor to be charged as someone who is "promoting disaffection"?
A. It will make him famous as one of India's nonviolent leaders.
B. He knows he is innocent of breaking that law and will be freed.
C. No one has ever been charged with breaking that law before.
D. He considers it to be a mark of his true patriotism.

_____ 9. In "Defending Nonviolent Resistance," why does Gandhi claim that Britain "made India more helpless than she ever was before"?
A. Early in life Gandhi discovered that he had no rights because he was an Indian.
B. British rule ruined the small weaving industry that once supported India.
C. Gandhi organized several volunteer ambulance corps to support British troops.
D. Gandhi has made nonviolence the first and most important part of his personal creed.

_____ 10. Why does Gandhi insist in "Defending Nonviolent Resistance" that nonviolence is the only way to bring political change?
A. Britain cannot be defeated by violence.
B. Nonviolence is safer than violence.
C. Violence only creates more evil.
D. Nonviolent acts are legal everywhere.

Vocabulary and Grammar

_____ 11. Which word best replaces *formidable* in this sentence: "The *formidable* army conquered Europe"?
A. strong
B. remembered
C. frightened
D. cooperative

_____ 12. Which sentence uses parallel structure, or the same grammatical form to express like ideas?
A. The Germans have broken through the French defenses.
B. It would be foolish, however, to pretend this is not serious.
C. Our task is not only to win the battle—but to win the War.
D. I have every confidence in our ability to fight and win this War.

Essay

13. Near the end of his "Wartime Speech," Winston Churchill says that war with Germany "is one of the most awe-striking periods . . . It is also beyond doubt the most sublime [inspiring]." In an essay, explain why Churchill sees the war as both a challenge and an opportunity for France and Britain. Use details from the speech to support his position.

14. While still a young man, Mohandas Gandhi thought at first that the British government system was basically a good one and only needed to be adjusted. Later, he changed his mind and decided that the system was corrupt. In an essay, explain what he learned that caused him to change his attitude toward the British Imperial government, as expressed in "Defending Nonviolent Resistance."

Name _____ Date _____

"Wartime Speech" by Winston Churchill
"Defending Nonviolent Resistance" by Mohandas K. Gandhi
Selection Test B

Critical Reading *Identify the letter of the choice that best completes the statement or answers the question.*

_____ 1. Churchill's "Wartime Speech" was delivered
   A. on radio.
   B. on television.
   C. to the king.
   D. to Parliament.

_____ 2. What "solemn hour" was Churchill referring to in the opening of his "Wartime Speech"?
   A. the declaration of war
   B. an attack on London
   C. the imminent defeat of France
   D. the transfer of power

_____ 3. The audience for Churchill's "Wartime Speech" speech is the people of
   A. America.
   B. France.
   C. Great Britain.
   D. Germany.

_____ 4. Which point in "Wartime Speech" supports Churchill's claim that all might not be lost?
   A. the size of the German Air Force
   B. the French gift for counterattack
   C. the unexpected tactics of the Germans
   D. the columns of armor followed by infantry

_____ 5. What is Churchill trying to do for his audience as he first describes the situation in his "Wartime Speech"?
   A. eliminate alarm and confusion
   B. explain the cause of defeat
   C. establish his military authority
   D. deceive the Germans

_____ 6. In "Wartime Speech," why does Churchill say it would be "foolish to disguise the gravity of the hour"?
   A. Overconfidence at this time might be disastrous.
   B. Despite some hope, the situation does not look good.
   C. The High Command must be persuaded to undertake a "furious and unrelenting assault."
   D. Only a very small part of the French Army has been engaged.

_____ 7. In Churchill's "Wartime Speech," what does he say will happen as soon as "stability is reached on the Western Front"?
A. The battle and the war will have been won.
B. The oil refineries on which the Germans depend will be damaged.
C. Holland will be ruined and enslaved within days.
D. The assault will be turned upon Britain.

_____ 8. When Churchill says in "Wartime Speech" that many will feel a pride in "sharing the perils of the Lads at the front," he is preparing his audience for
A. possible warfare in England itself.
B. increased efforts to supply munitions.
C. the need for less waste and more reserves.
D. an end "bitter or glorious" in France.

_____ 9. Why does Churchill conclude his "Wartime Speech" with a passage written long ago for Trinity Sunday?
A. to demonstrate the Germans' disrespect for religious values
B. to encourage Britons to make a fateful effort as in historic times
C. to ask for divine help to defeat Nazi Germany
D. to assure the people that God will not fail them

_____ 10. What is the primary purpose of Gandhi's "Defending Nonviolent Resistance"?
A. to persuade the judges to resign
B. to trace the history of British rule in India
C. to explain why he has become a noncooperator
D. to force the judges to lighten his sentence

_____ 11. Why does Gandhi recount his service to the British Empire in "Defending Nonviolent Resistance"?
A. to establish himself as a reasonable and credible speaker
B. to gain the sympathy of the audience for the discrimination he faced
C. to gain the sympathy of the judge for his efforts
D. to express his regret at ever having helped the British

_____ 12. Which point is *not* support for Gandhi's assertion in "Defending Nonviolent Resistance" that the "British connection had made India more helpless . . ."?
A. A disarmed India has no power against an aggressor.
B. Affection cannot be manufactured or regulated by law.
C. India is so poor that it cannot resist famines.
D. The cottage industries have been ruined by British policies.

Vocabulary and Grammar

_____ 13. Parallel structure is the
A. use of sentences all more or less the same length.
B. dispersal of thematic elements evenly throughout a work.
C. balanced arrangement of main points in a speech or essay.
D. repetition of words, phrases, or grammatical forms.

___ **14.** A *formidable* opponent would be one who is
  A. reconciled.
  B. powerful.
  C. reasonable.
  D. deceitful.

___ **15.** Circumstances that are *extenuating* are
  A. improving.
  B. protracted.
  C. intolerable.
  D. mitigating.

Essay

16. Gandhi tells the Court that it must either sentence him to a maximum sentence or agree with him that British rule is bad for India, and resign. The audience for the speech was a packed courtroom and the judges who were about to sentence him. Write an essay in which you explain what the purpose of the speech was and how Gandhi suited the contents of the speech to his purpose. Use examples from the speech to support your ideas.

17. Early in his May 19 speech, Churchill points out that if things went well "a sudden transformation of the scene" might occur. He was wrong, and he likely knew it at the time. Within a week the Germans would trap the British on the beaches of Dunkirk, and in a month, all France would be occupied by the Nazis. If Churchill knows France is lost, why give this speech? What is his purpose? Write an essay in which you explain what Churchill's purpose is in this speech, and how he accomplishes it. Use examples from the speech to support your points.

Vocabulary Warm-up Word Lists

Study these words from the selections. Then, complete the activities that follow.

Word List A

angled [ANG uhld] *v.* moved or turned at a slant
   The football player <u>angled</u> his way down the field.

conceit [kuhn SEET] *n.* too high an opinion of oneself
   Paula's <u>conceit</u> about her intelligence is almost comical.

expert [EK spert] *n.* a person who has special skill or knowledge
   Tiffany is such an <u>expert</u> at knitting that she should give lessons.

heft [HEFT] *v.* to lift up; heave
   Two strong men will <u>heft</u> the heavy container onto the loading dock.

ordeal [awr DEEL] *n.* a very difficult or trying experience
   The long <u>ordeal</u> left Jeffrey exhausted.

pluck [PLUK] *n.* a quick or sudden pull
   With a <u>pluck</u> on the cord, Michelle signaled to the bus driver to stop.

reins [RAYNZ] *n.* straps used to control a horse being ridden or driven
   Latonya pulled back on the <u>reins</u> to get the horse to stop.

strained [STRAYND] *v.* made a great effort
   Bruno <u>strained</u> against the current but made no progress in the canoe.

Word List B

flurry [FLER ee] *n.* a sudden commotion; stir
   In a <u>flurry</u> of excitement, the children chased the balloons.

myth [MITH] *n.* a traditional story, often about gods and heroes
   Andrew's favorite <u>myth</u> is the one about Hercules.

furrow [FER oh] *n.* a long, deep groove made in the ground by a plow
   It was difficult to plow a <u>furrow</u> in the rocky soil.

nuisance [NOO suhns] *n.* anything that annoys or bothers
   This mosquito is such a <u>nuisance</u>!

shafts [SHAFTS] *n.* the two poles harnessing a horse, as to a wagon
   The horse owner bought three sets of <u>shafts</u> to replace the old ones.

sod [SAHD] *n.* the top layer of earth, especially when covered with grass
   Our lawn died during the drought, so we put in <u>sod</u> to make it green again.

stumbled [STUHM buhld] *v.* missed a step; tripped
   The toddler <u>stumbled</u> and skinned her knee.

tally [TAL ee] *v.* to add
   The boss will <u>tally</u> the number of strawberry baskets each worker filled.

Poetry of Seamus Heaney and Eavan Boland
Vocabulary Warm-up Exercises

Exercise A *Fill in each blank below using the appropriate word from Word List A.*

Tyler wished he had brought an [1] _____ with him to pick out
equipment for his new horse. He thought he knew everything, so his own foolish
[2] _____ had prevented him from realizing he needed help. He knew
he needed [3] _____, but what else? If he got the wrong things, he
knew it would be such an [4] _____ to return them. With a gentle
[5] _____ at the salesperson's sleeve, Tyler got his attention. Soon they had
selected all the necessary equipment, and they [6] _____ to get it all in
Tyler's truck. It took the two of them to [7] _____ the bigger pieces into the
truck. Some of the equipment barely fit, so they [8] _____ it in sideways.

Exercise B *Write a complete sentence to answer each question. For each item, use a word
from Word List B to replace each underlined word or phrase without changing its meaning.*

1. What two colors are you likely to find in a piece of <u>grass-covered earth</u>?
   _____

2. If you <u>tripped</u> and fell in front of an audience, how would you feel?
   _____

3. Which <u>traditional story</u> about gods and heroes is your favorite?
   _____

4. Where would you go to buy <u>two poles used for harnessing horses</u>?
   _____

5. What might cause you to go into a <u>sudden commotion</u> of house-cleaning?
   _____

6. Why might you plow a <u>deep groove in the ground</u>?
   _____

7. If you were to <u>add up</u> the times you brushed your teeth this week, what would the
   final number be?
   _____

8. What is one great <u>annoyance</u> in your life?
   _____

Poetry of Seamus Heaney and Eavan Boland
Reading Warm-up A

Read the following passage. Pay special attention to the underlined words. Then, read it again, and complete the activities. Use a separate sheet of paper for your written answers.

You don't have to be an <u>expert</u> to saddle a horse correctly, but it might help if you took a lesson from a person who knows. And don't let one little lesson cause you to feel <u>conceit</u> about your skill—you'll likely need a demonstration, too.

The first thing to do is groom the horse. The reason for this is to remove dirt and mud from the horse's body in order to prevent sores; if a horse gets sores, every time you ride, it will be an <u>ordeal</u> for the animal.

Put a clean saddle blanket on the horse's back. A quick <u>pluck</u> at any dirt clods should pull them off easily. Put the blanket forward on the horse's withers (the highest part of its back), and then slide it back, placing the front edge four to six inches in front of the withers. This assures that the hairs will be running in the correct direction. If the hairs are <u>angled</u>, or slanted, incorrectly, the horse will be uncomfortable. Also, make sure that the <u>reins</u> don't get caught under the blanket—you'll need them later to control the horse!

Lift the saddle and bring it to the left side of the horse. Gently <u>heft</u> it onto the horse's back, leaving four inches of blanket in front. Move to the right side of the horse and secure the cinches properly—not too tight and not too loose. If you have <u>strained</u> yourself too much while tightening the cinches, they will no doubt be hurting the horse. It doesn't take too much effort to do this properly. You will probably need an actual demonstration of the entire process in order to do it properly yourself.

1. Underline the words that tell what an <u>expert</u> is. In what field do you think you might like to become an **expert**?

2. Circle the word that tells what might cause a person to feel <u>conceit</u>. Use **conceit** in a sentence.

3. Underline the words that explain why a ride might be an <u>ordeal</u> for a horse. What does **ordeal** mean?

4. Circle the words that explain the result of a quick <u>pluck</u> at any dirt clods on the horse. Why might a rider give a **pluck** to a horse's reins?

5. Circle the word that means about the same as <u>angled</u>. What is one reason a person might have **angled** a car while driving?

6. Underline the words that tell why a rider would need <u>reins</u>. What might happen if a rider lost the **reins** while riding?

7. Underline the word in a nearby sentence that means about the same as <u>heft</u>. Use **heft** in a sentence.

8. Circle the words in a nearby sentence that mean about the same as <u>strained</u>. Tell about a time you **strained** yourself when performing a task.

Poetry of Seamus Heaney and Eavan Boland
Reading Warm-up B

Read the following passage. Pay special attention to the underlined words. Then, read it again, and complete the activities. Use a separate sheet of paper for your written answers.

Colleen had been born in Chicago, but she always wanted to go to Ireland, the home of her ancestors. Having heard nothing but good stories about the "old <u>sod</u>," she wanted to see Irish green earth for herself. In a <u>flurry</u> of activity, she planned the trip, packed, got a passport, bought a plane ticket, and was off.

The first thing she did upon landing was get in touch with the company that would guide her on her "escorted walking holiday." Colleen's plan was to walk from town to town, enjoying the countryside in between, while the touring company dealt with the <u>nuisance</u> of transporting her luggage from one inn to the next. All Colleen had to do was put on her hiking boots in the morning and get ready to walk.

Colleen was astonished by the beauty of the countryside. Coastal views were spectacular, and the fields were lush and green. One day the group came upon a farmer plowing his field. Each <u>furrow</u> plowed into the earth by the horse was long and straight. The <u>shafts</u> used to harness the horse to the plow were shiny and new, in stark contrast to the wrinkled old face of the farmer.

The one thing Colleen wanted to be sure to do was kiss the Blarney Stone. She had heard the <u>myth</u> that doing so would give a person the gift of eloquence. On her way to do so, she <u>stumbled</u> and nearly fell, but her tour guide caught her. "If I'd tripped closer to the edge, I'd have been in trouble," she thought.

Colleen made many new friends on her trip. And when it came time to <u>tally</u> the costs of her vacation, she found that it didn't add up to any more than a vacation closer to home.

1. Underline the words that mean about the same as <u>sod</u>. Use **sod** in a sentence.

2. Circle the words that describe Colleen's <u>flurry</u> of activity. What does **flurry** mean?

3. Underline the words that describe one <u>nuisance</u> with which Colleen did not have to deal. Describe something in your life that you consider a **nuisance**.

4. Circle the words that describe each <u>furrow</u> plowed by the horse. When would a farmer plow a **furrow**?

5. Underline the words that tell the purpose of <u>shafts</u>. Name another piece of equipment besides **shafts** that a horse-owner might have to buy.

6. Circle the words that explain the <u>myth</u> about kissing the Blarney Stone. Name one god or goddess from a Greek or Roman **myth**.

7. Underline the word in a nearby sentence that means about the same as <u>stumbled</u>. Tell what might happen if you **stumbled** while jogging.

8. Circle the words that mean about the same as <u>tally</u>. Use **tally** in a sentence.

Name _____ Date _____

"Follower" and "Two Lorries" by Seamus Heaney
"Outside History" by Eavan Boland
Literary Analysis: Diction and Style

Style refers to these poetic elements: **diction,** or word choice; imagery; rhythms; poetic form; and theme. How each poet *uses* these elements is that poet's style. The style of a poem adds meaning to the poem and affects how a reader responds to that poem. Though generalizations can be made, a poet's style varies from poem to poem.

Following is the first stanza of "Follower." Read it and then refer to the table for an explanation of Heaney's style.

> My father worked with a horse plow,
> His shoulders globed like a full sail strung
> Between the shafts and the furrow.
> The horses strained at his clicking tongue.

Elements of Style	Examples
Diction—Is the poet's word choice formal or informal, conversational or stilted, concrete or abstract?	Diction is informal and easy to read, just as if a boy were talking to the reader. Poet uses many concrete words.
Imagery—Is the imagery easily perceived by the senses? Or does it create unusual or abstract pictures? Do the images tell a story, or do they just stand next to each other?	The imagery appeals to the senses of sight and hearing. Poet creates a vivid image of the father's strong shoulders.
Rhythm—Does the poet use rhyme? Does the poet use rhythm? How much? Are they conventional or irregular?	Poet uses a traditional *abab* rhyme scheme.
Form—Are there stanzas? Are they regular or irregular? Does the poet write in free verse?	Poet uses regular, four-line stanzas.

DIRECTIONS: *Using the table on this page as a model, examine the first stanza of "Two Lorries" for style. Write your evaluation of each element of style in the space provided.*

Diction: _____

_____

Imagery: _____

_____

Rhythm: _____

_____

Form: _____

_____

"Follower" and **"Two Lorries"** by Seamus Heaney
"Outside History" by Eavan Boland
Reading Strategy: Summarize

A summary is a restatement of main ideas in a condensed, or shortened, form. Creating a summary is a useful study tool because it makes you think critically about material you've read, identifying main ideas and pushing aside unnecessary details or examples. When you **summarize** a poem you will do the same thing—identify and restate the main ideas aside from the poem's images.

For poetry, it may be helpful to note the main points of each stanza and then build a complete summary from there. Here is a portion of "Outside History" (lines 7–12), accompanied by notes about the main ideas of these two stanzas.

They keep their distance. Under them remains   discovery of humanness—being alive
a place where you found
you were human, and

a landscape in which you know you are mortal.   discovery of mortality; must choose
And a time to choose between them.
I have chosen:

DIRECTIONS: *Use the space on this page to note the main idea of each stanza of "Two Lorries" as you read. Then use your notes to summarize the essence of the whole poem.*

"Two Lorries"

Stanza 1: _____

Stanza 2: _____

Stanza 3: _____

Stanza 4: _____

Stanza 5: _____

Stanza 6: _____

Stanza 7: _____

Summary of "Two Lorries":

_____

_____

_____

_____

"Follower" and **"Two Lorries"** by Seamus Heaney
"Outside History" by Eavan Boland
Vocabulary Builder

Using the Root *-mort-*

A. DIRECTIONS: *Each of the following words contains the root -mort-, meaning "dead" or "death." Match each word with its definition. Write the letter of the definition on the line next to the word it defines.*

___ 1. mortify   A. in a deadly or fatal manner
___ 2. mortally   B. to subject to severe embarrassment
___ 3. postmortem   C. after death

Using the Word List

furrow	nuisance	inklings
mortal	ordeal	

B. DIRECTIONS: *Choose the lettered word or phrase that is most similar in meaning to the numbered word. Circle the letter of your choice.*

1. furrow
   A. groove
   B. mold
   C. measurement
   D. ditch

2. inklings
   A. notes
   B. blotches
   C. suggestions
   D. ideas

3. mortal
   A. impermanent
   B. prone to error
   C. inexact
   D. everlasting

4. nuisance
   A. boredom
   B. excitement
   C. distress
   D. annoyance

5. ordeal
   A. comedy club
   B. severe test
   C. new freeway
   D. light supper

"Follower" and **"Two Lorries"** by Seamus Heaney
"Outside History" by Eavan Boland

Grammar and Style: Concrete and Abstract Nouns

You already know that a noun names a person, place, thing, or idea. More specifically, a **concrete** noun names something that can be perceived by the senses. An **abstract** noun names an idea, a quality, or a characteristic. Following are some examples:

Concrete: salt, fire, field, clang, sunset

Abstract: ability, ego, wit, cleverness, certainty

The kinds of nouns you use in your writing affect the impact your writing has on your readers. Concrete nouns tend to create vivid pictures because readers can perceive with their senses the objects being named. The use of abstract nouns tends to create impressions rather than images, and readers have to grasp the meaning with something other than their senses.

A. PRACTICE: *Following are lines from the poems in this section. Above each italicized noun, write C if the noun is concrete or A if the noun is abstract.*

1. An *expert.* He would set the *wing*
   And fit the bright steel-pointed sock.
   The *sod* rolled over without breaking.
   At the *headrig*, with a single pluck

   Of *reins*, the sweating *team* turned round
   And back into the *land.*
      ("Follower," ll. 5–10)

2. And *films* no less! The *conceit* of a coalman . . .
   She goes back in and gets out the black lead
   And emery paper, this nineteen-forties *mother,*
   All *business* round her stove, half-wiping *ashes*
   With a backhand from her *cheek* as the bolted *lorry*
   Gets revved and turned and heads for *Magherafelt*
      ("Two Lorries," ll. 13–18)

B. Writing Application: *Write sentences using concrete and abstract nouns according to the instructions that follow.*

1. Describe the farmer in "Follower" using only concrete nouns.

   _____

2. Now describe the farmer using at least two abstract nouns.

   _____

3. Write a sentence about what the boy in "Follower" does, using only concrete nouns.

   _____

Name _____ Date _____

Support for Writing

Use the cluster diagram to gather details for your poem. First, write your central image or topic in the center circle. Then, write thoughts, feelings, sensory images, and other details that remind you of the central image in the surrounding circles.

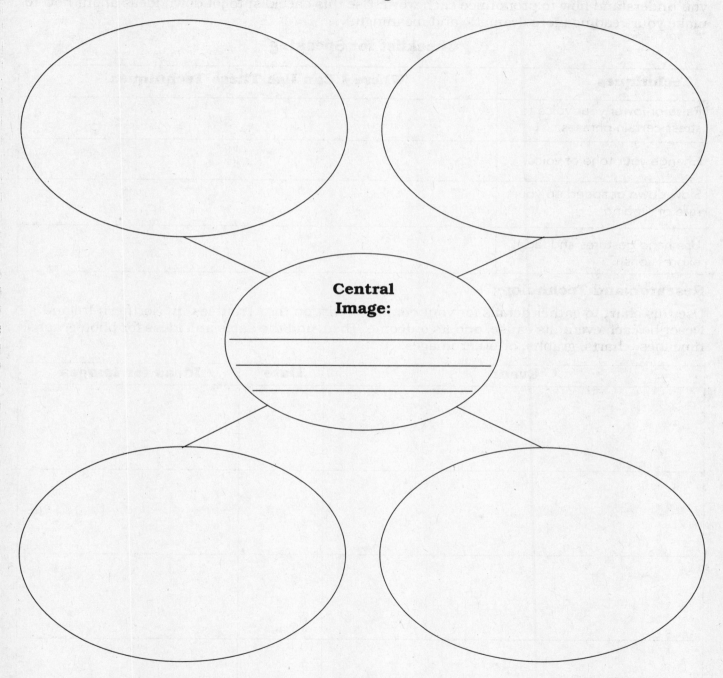

Central Image:

Use the information in your cluster diagram as you write your poem on a separate page. Remember your central image as you write.

"Follower" and **"Two Lorries"** by Seamus Heaney
"Outside History" by Eavan Boland
Support for Extend Your Learning

Listening and Speaking

As you prepare for an **interpretive reading** of your poem, think about its meaning. Make sure you understand how to pronounce each word. Use this checklist to jot down ideas about how to make your reading more dramatic and meaningful.

Checklist for Speaking

Techniques	Where I Can Use These Techniques
Raise or lower your voice to stress certain phrases.	
Change your tone of voice.	
Slow down or speed up your rate of reading	
Use hand gestures and facial expressions	

Research and Technology

Use this chart to gather details for your conflict report on the "Troubles" in Northern Ireland. Describe each event, its cause, and its outcome. Then, add the dates and ideas for photographs, timelines, charts, graphs, or other images.

Event	Date	Ideas for Images

Name _____ Date _____

"**Follower**" and "**Two Lorries**" by Seamus Heaney
"**Outside History**" by Eavan Boland
Enrichment: Contemporary Farmer

In 1977, the U.S. Census Bureau revised the definition of "farm" to distinguish it from merely rural property. Under the new definition, a landowner who earns more than $1,000 annually from selling agricultural products is a farmer. In the United States, there are about two million farms so defined.

The nature of farming has changed much in recent history. Farm technology, farm markets (what products are needed and how much they sell for), and the business of running a farm have all become complex issues.

Consider the following statistics and what they mean in terms of being a farmer.

	1935	**1992**
Number of farms in U.S.	6.8 million	1.9 million
Acreage devoted to farming	982 million acres	126 million acres
Average farm size	155 acres	467 acres

The change in farm size reflects the changing nature of farming in general. The family-owned farm is becoming harder to find. Instead there are farmers or landowners who hire farm managers to make decisions about hundreds and hundreds of acres of land or perhaps thousands of head of livestock. Large farming corporations also operate farms.

Economic influences have brought about a radical change in farming. A single crop failure, or one year of low wheat prices, for example, can ruin a small farmer who has invested everything in that one crop. A large-scale farmer or corporation can afford to raise larger crops or more than one crop to ensure protection from crop failure or low prices.

DIRECTIONS: *Refer to details in Seamus Heaney's poem "Follower," as well as to information on this page, to answer the following questions.*

1. The subject of Heaney's poem is probably a small farmer working his own farm in the 1940s. List the tools and equipment that are apparently in use by the farmer in "Follower."

   _____

   _____

2. What might the farmer in "Follower" need to know about "farm management?"

   _____

   _____

3. What do you think a contemporary farmer needs to know about farm management? List as many areas of knowledge as you can.

   _____

   _____

"Follower" and **"Two Lorries"** by Seamus Heaney
"Outside History" by Eavan Boland
Selection Test A

Critical Reading *Identify the letter of the choice that best answers the question.*

_____ 1. What does the speaker in "Follower" do as his father plows?
   A. follows behind
   B. watches from nearby
   C. leads the horses
   D. goes to school

_____ 2. What is the best summary of the speaker in "Follower," a "nuisance, tripping, [and] falling, / Yapping always"?
   A. He was like a young farmer.
   B. He was always in the way.
   C. He was a clumsy, talkative young child.
   D. He was a child who got into trouble.

_____ 3. What does the speaker in "Follower" admire about his father?
   A. his physical strength
   B. his expert plowing
   C. his firmness and leadership
   D. his gentleness

_____ 4. In the final line of "Two Lorries," the speaker describes the lorry driver "filmed in silk-white ashes." What does this coalman represent?
   A. peace
   B. love
   C. Ireland
   D. death

_____ 5. Which answer best summarizes this line from "Two Lorries":
   ". . . a different lorry Groans into shot, up Broad Street, with a payload / That will blow the bus station to dust and ashes"?
   A. The coalman makes his last delivery in Broad Street.
   B. A truck carrying plenty of money goes to the bus station.
   C. Another truck carries a bomb that destroys a bus station.
   D. The coalman drives up Broad Street while the bus station blows up.

____ 6. What is the main idea of "Two Lorries"?

    A. Everyday sights, such as coal delivery, remain the same in Ireland.

    B. Violence in Ireland is everywhere and is destroys everything.

    C. Memories of our mothers remain with us as long as we live.

    D. Our minds do not separate the good memories from the bad ones.

____ 7. In "Outside History," the speaker says that the stars are outside history. What does she mean?

    A. There is no life in outer space to observe earth.

    B. Life in outer space does not care about events on earth.

    C. Earth is too far away to be seen from the stars.

    D. The stars' light happened thousands of years before us.

____ 8. In "Outside History," what is the best summary of the image of "a place where you found / you were human"?

    A. People are always finding out new things.

    B. Everyone who lives on earth can see the stars.

    C. By living, people learn they are human.

    D. The people of earth formed long after the stars.

____ 9. Which word best describes the word choices used in Boland's poem "Outside History"?

    A. formal

    B. casual

    C. homespun

    D. humorous

____ 10. What is the "ordeal" that faces her country that Boland refers to in "Outside History"?

    A. World War II

    B. the Irish conflict

    C. being human

    D. a search for religious faith

Vocabulary and Grammar

____ 11. Which word best replaces the word *inklings* in this sentence: "After one reading, readers only have a few *inklings* about the meaning of this poem"?

    A. grooves

    B. deliveries

    C. hints

    D. problems

___ **12.** Which line from "Two Lorries" contains an abstract noun that names a general idea?

    A. "In a time beyond her time"

    B. "black coal and warm wet ashes"

    C. "the lode our coal came from was silk-black"

    D. "With its emptied, folded coal-bags"

Essay

13. "Follower" closes by saying that the speaker was once "a nuisance, tripping, falling, / Yapping always. But today / It is my father who keeps stumbling / Behind me, and will not go away." In an essay, explain the meaning of this change in the roles of father and son. Why and how does this change happen? Use information from your experience or the poem to help you respond.

14. A summary is a brief restatement of the main ideas of a piece of literature. Choose one of the poems in this selection: "Follower," "Two Lorries," or "Outside History." In an essay, write a summary of the poem.

Name _____ Date _____

"Follower" and "Two Lorries" by Seamus Heaney
"Outside History" by Eavan Boland
Selection Test B

Critical Reading *Identify the letter of the choice that best completes the statement or answers the question.*

____ 1. What does the speaker of "Follower" do while the father works with the horse plow?
A. He walks at the front, with the horses.
B. He sits at the edge of the field and watches.
C. He waits at home for the father to return.
D. He follows along behind, stumbling in the furrows.

____ 2. In "Follower," the line "His shoulders globed like a full sail strung" suggests that the father is
A. bent and aging.
B. expansive and powerful.
C. angry and unpredictable.
D. loud and threatening.

____ 3. How does the speaker of "Follower" imply how he felt in these lines?
    All I ever did was follow / In his broad shadow . . .

A. frustrated
B. neglected
C. lazy
D. useless

____ 4. How does the diction of this stanza from "Follower" add to the meaning of the stanza?
    I stumbled in his hobnailed wake,
    Fell sometimes on the polished sod;
    Sometimes he rode me on his back
    Dipping and rising to his plod.

A. The word *hobnailed* is an especially effective farming term.
B. The repetition of *sometimes* emphasizes the occasional nature of the boy's being in the field with his father.
C. The rhythm of the short, ordinary words creates a sense of the boy's difficulty walking on the uneven ground.
D. The word *plod* brings up images of a horse plodding.

____ 5. Which is the best summary of "Follower"?
A. I was the follower as a child; now my father follows me.
B. Sometimes I stumbled when I was young; sometimes I rode on my father's back.
C. I could never handle a plow like my father.
D. Sometimes I helped my father when he worked.

___ 6. In this line from "Follower," what image is the poet invoking?

"I was a nuisance, tripping, falling, / Yapping always"

A. the image of a puppy
B. the image of a clumsy young child
C. the image of a very bothersome child
D. the image of a parent who puts up with a talkative child

___ 7. In "Two Lorries," what does the first lorry driver do?
A. He dumps his coal in the speaker's yard.
B. He sweet-talks the speaker's mother, inviting her to a film.
C. He helps the speaker's mother clean the stove.
D. He carries explosives in his lorry to deliver to Magherafelt.

___ 8. What does the coalman represent, or symbolize, at the end of "Two Lorries"?
A. the mother's flirtations
B. death
C. the explosion
D. Ireland itself

___ 9. Considering the poet's word choices in "Two Lorries," which statement foreshadows what eventually happens?
A. The mother being "moved" foreshadows her involvement in the explosion.
B. The "leather-aproned coalman" foreshadows the other lorry driver.
C. The ashes, the bus, and the empty bags foreshadow the aftermath of the bus station explosion.
D. The phrase "To deliver farther on" foreshadows the lorry driver's next delivery.

___ 10. The imagery in "Outside History"
A. is completely abstract.
B. is concrete only when the speaker mentions the stars.
C. is almost nonexistent as the poet speaks in philosophical terms.
D. becomes more concrete as the speaker gets involved with the "ordeal."

___ 11. Which is the best summary of "Outside History"?
A. The stars witness everything that happens.
B. The stars have given us light for thousands of years, but eventually they die.
C. Some choose to keep their distance. I chose to become involved, but I am too late.
D. There is nothing we can do to save dying people out in the fields and roads.

Vocabulary and Grammar

___ 12. The boy was a *nuisance* because he
A. caused trouble.
B. wasn't able to be helpful.
C. followed his father instead of walking beside him.
D. was just learning how to plow.

____ **13.** All people are *mortal* because they
  A. are born.
  B. eventually die.
  C. make mistakes.
  D. have feelings and emotions.

____ **14.** Choose the item that contains only concrete nouns.
  A. cord, signature, generosity
  B. margin, photograph, mask
  C. attitude, blanket, lake
  D. echo, fear, splash

____ **15.** Which line contains an abstract noun?
  A. "It's raining on black coal and warm wet ashes."
  B. "And films no less! The conceit of a coalman . . ."
  C. "I stumbled in his hobnailed wake,"
  D. "That will blow the bus station to dust and ashes . . ."

Essay

16. In an essay, discuss the style Seamus Heaney uses in "Follower." Include diction, imagery, rhythm, and form in your discussion. Consider, also, the effect of the style on the meaning of the poem. Cite examples whenever you can to support your observations about style.

17. Heaney and Boland express some of their views, at least about Ireland and its "troubles," in the poems "Two Lorries" and "Outside History." In an essay, explain what each poet's views are, using evidence from the respective poems. Then compare their views.

Vocabulary Warm-up Word Lists

Study these words from the selections. Then, complete the activities that follow.

Word List A

chinks [CHINGKS] *n.* breaks that show as narrow openings
  Alberto filled the <u>chinks</u> in the stone fence with cement.

commotion [kuh MOH shuhn] *n.* great confusion; disturbance
  The <u>commotion</u> in the yard was increased by the barking dogs.

exaggerated [eg ZAJ uh ray tid] *v.* overstated; made seem greater
  Sally <u>exaggerated</u> the size of the fish she caught.

hundredth [HUN dridth] *adj.* next after ninety-nine others
  Sanjay was the <u>hundredth</u> person in line.

inevitable [in EV uh tuh buhl] *adj.* unavoidable; certain
  Jeff braced himself for the <u>inevitable</u> coldness of winter in Alaska.

punctures [PUNGT chuhrz] *n.* holes made by piercing
  The <u>punctures</u> in the tire caused it to go flat.

unreasonable [un REE zuhn uh buhl] *adj.* not sensible
  Kate quit her job after her employer made <u>unreasonable</u> demands.

vigorously [VIG uh ruhs lee] *adv.* in an energetic manner
  Sylvia <u>vigorously</u> shook the rug to get all the dust out.

Word List B

discomfort [dis KUM fuhrt] *n.* distress; an uncomfortable condition
  Angelina experienced some <u>discomfort</u> as a result of her allergies.

distasteful [dis TAYST fuhl] *adj.* unpleasant; disagreeable
  Janet had the <u>distasteful</u> job of cleaning up after the sick dog.

distorted [dis TAWRT uhd] *adj.* twisted out of the normal shape
  The grieving survivor's face was <u>distorted</u> with sorrow.

flustered [FLUHS tuhrd] *adj.* confused or upset
  The young actress was <u>flustered</u> by all the screaming fans.

hereditary [huh RED uh tehr ee] *adj.* passed on from parents to offspring
  One of Sara's <u>hereditary</u> characteristics is blue eyes.

irritated [EER uh tay tuhd] *adj.* annoyed or bothered
  The <u>irritated</u> dogs continued to whine.

scorching [SKAWR ching] *v.* burning just a little on the surface
  The hot iron was <u>scorching</u> the cloth.

writhing [RY<u>TH</u> ing] *adj.* twisting or distorting the body, as in pain
  The doctor had to restrain the <u>writhing</u> patient in order to treat him.

Name _____ Date _____

Vocabulary Warm-up Exercises

Exercise A *Fill in each blank below using the appropriate word from Word List A.*

For about the [1] _____ time that month, the black horse peeked through the [2] _____ in the stone wall surrounding the pasture. No matter how [3] _____ he kicked at these cracks, he could not make them any larger. Although he could not say the words, he felt that it was [4] _____ for his owners to keep him confined this way. To his way of thinking, the benefits of being tamed and taken care of by humans were [5] _____ by the other horses. He would much rather take his chances in the wild, even risking the [6] _____ a snake or other creature might make in his hide. The other horses in the pasture were puzzled by the [7] _____ the black horse always made in his attempts at escape. They felt that loss of freedom was an [8] _____ result of being cared for by humans.

Exercise B *Revise each sentence so that the underlined vocabulary is used in a logical way. Be sure to keep the vocabulary word in your revision.*

Example: The boy, <u>writhing</u> with pain, slept peacefully for ten hours.
The boy, <u>writhing</u> in pain, could not sleep at all that night.

1. The <u>scorching</u> ground chilled Amy's feet.

   _____

2. Danielle was <u>irritated</u> by the soothing sound of the ocean waves.

   _____

3. The identical twin brothers shared no <u>hereditary</u> traits.

   _____

4. The <u>flustered</u> speaker calmly delivered his speech.

   _____

5. Percy's face, <u>distorted</u> by puffiness and pain, looked the same as ever.

   _____

6. <u>Discomfort</u> from the flu made Carla's afternoon even more pleasant.

   _____

7. Pat's <u>distasteful</u> duty was to hire his friend for a high-paying job.

   _____

Name _____ Date _____

"No Witchcraft for Sale" by Doris Lessing
Reading Warm-up A

Read the following passage. Pay special attention to the underlined words. Then, read it again, and complete the activities. Use a separate sheet of paper for your written answers.

Snakes are fascinating creatures that can be quite tame when handled properly. It would certainly be an <u>exaggerated</u> claim to say that a snake can be as friendly as a dog or cat. However, for the pet owner who prefers a quiet pet, it is clear that a snake wouldn't make the same kind of <u>commotion</u> that a dog or cat might. Obviously, a snake is not the ideal pet for everyone. Some people, in fact, would be <u>vigorously</u> and energetically opposed to the idea. It is not <u>unreasonable</u> to expect that anyone interested in having a snake as a pet will take time to research its needs.

Corn snakes, king snakes, and ball pythons make particularly good pets. These snakes are gentler than other species, and they are comparatively easy to care for. It is <u>inevitable</u> that they will grow—it cannot be avoided—but these three species are relatively small. Corn snakes and ball pythons reach adult lengths of four or five feet, and king snakes can grow to seven feet.

No matter what kind of snake you choose, you must have an escape-proof cage for it. It must close tightly and have no <u>chinks</u> or holes or other openings from which the snake can escape.

All snakes are meat-eaters, so they prefer mice or rats as food. It is not a good idea to give live prey to a snake. A live rodent might inflict <u>punctures</u> or other injuries in the snake's skin in self defense.

Be patient when looking for the ideal snake for you. You might look at ninety-nine snakes before you find that the <u>hundredth</u> one is perfect! The best place to get a pet snake is from a reputable breeder. Snakes bred in captivity are greatly preferable to captured wild snakes.

1. Underline the words that tell what would be an <u>exaggerated</u> claim. What is an *exaggerated* claim you have heard about an advertised product?

2. Circle the words that tell who might make a <u>commotion</u>. What would you do if you heard an unusual *commotion* outside your home at night?

3. Circle the word that means about the same as <u>vigorously</u>. Describe a housecleaning job that you might do *vigorously*.

4. Underline the words that tell what is not <u>unreasonable</u>. Define *unreasonable*.

5. Underline the words that tell what <u>inevitable</u> means. What is one thing in life that is *inevitable*?

6. Circle the word that means about the same as <u>chinks</u>. How could you patch *chinks* in a wall?

7. Underline the word that describes what <u>punctures</u> would be in a snake's skin. Use *punctures* in a sentence.

8. Circle the word that tells what number comes before the <u>hundredth</u> one. What activity of yours would not bore you, even after the *hundredth* time you did it?

"No Witchcraft for Sale" by Doris Lessing
Reading Warm-up B

Read the following passage. Pay special attention to the underlined words. Then, read it again, and complete the activities. Use a separate sheet of paper for your written answers.

Imagine being out for a hike on a <u>scorching</u> summer day, and you encounter a snake sunning itself in the path. What is the best course of action? You should go back the way you came. However, some people—those suffering from <u>hereditary</u> stupidity, no doubt—might decide to throw a rock at it or otherwise threaten the snake. This is probably the worst thing they could do, for snakes are defensive animals. Snakes would prefer being left alone and will do their best to avoid contact with humans; however, if they are provoked, <u>irritated</u>, or startled, they will defend themselves.

What should you do if you or your companion is bitten by a snake? Try not to get <u>flustered</u> to the point of panic—stay calm; too much excitement or activity can hasten the spread of the poison. If you have a suction device in your first-aid kit, use it within the first fifteen minutes. Most experts advise against the <u>distasteful</u> alternative of cutting the skin and trying to suck out the venom, which may actually increase the spread of the toxins throughout the body and almost invariably leads to an infection and a scar.

Remember that most snakebites, even by venomous snakes, are not fatal—in fact, the U.S. Food and Drug Administration reports that of the 8,000 people a year who are bitten by poisonous snakes, only 9 to 15 die. Even so, the aftermath of a bite can cause more than just a little <u>discomfort</u>—the pain can be quite great. No one wants to see a friend <u>writhing</u> in pain, face <u>distorted</u> in agony from the pain caused by the venom. To prevent this, the best thing to do is to get the victim to the nearest medical facility for the administration of antivenom.

1. Underline the word that tells what kind of day is likely to be <u>scorching</u>. What is your favorite activity on a *scorching* day?

2. Circle the word that tells what characteristic is sometimes <u>hereditary</u>. What does *hereditary* mean?

3. Underline the word that means about the same as <u>irritated</u>. Name something a friend once did that *irritated* you.

4. Circle the word that describes an extreme form of being <u>flustered</u>. Describe a time you got *flustered*.

5. Underline the words that describe a <u>distasteful</u> alternative to using a suction device. What is another word for *distasteful*?

6. Underline the word that describes a greater degree of <u>discomfort</u>. Use *discomfort* in a sentence.

7. Underline the word that tells what might cause a person to be <u>writhing</u>. What does *writhing* mean?

8. Circle the word that tells what might cause a person's face to become <u>distorted</u>. Describe a scene in a movie in which a character's face is *distorted* in some way.

Name _____ Date _____

"No Witchcraft for Sale" by Doris Lessing
Literary Analysis: Cultural Conflict

Doris Lessing's story is based on the premise that Gideon's culture and the Farquars' culture are in conflict. In spite of the fact that the characters seem accepting of their roles and live relatively compatibly, they possess different customs, ideas, and values.

Perhaps, in the workings of everyday life, the cultural differences between the Farquars and Gideon were invisible. In the aftermath of Teddy's accident, however, differing ideas revealed themselves. In fact, Lessing even introduces a third culture in the form of the scientist who comes to learn about the cure Gideon used for Teddy's eyes. His added ideas from the scientific and commercial world serve to emphasize the conflict between the Farquars and Gideon, who otherwise live harmoniously.

DIRECTIONS: *List below the viewpoints represented by members of each of the three cultures over the issue of the medicine. Then answer the questions that follow.*

The Farquars' Attitudes	The Scientists's Attitudes	Gideon's Attitudes
_____	_____	_____
_____	_____	_____
_____	_____	_____
_____	_____	_____
_____	_____	_____
_____	_____	_____
_____	_____	_____
_____	_____	_____
_____	_____	_____

1. How do the attitudes of the Farquars bring them into conflict with the scientist?

   _____

2. How do the Farquars' attitudes bring them into conflict with Gideon?

   _____

   _____

3. How do the scientist's attitudes cause him to conflict with Gideon?

   _____

   _____

   _____

*"**No Witchcraft for Sale**" by Doris Lessing*
Reading Strategy: Analyze Cultural Differences

All short stories contain a conflict of some sort. Often the conflict is between two individuals or between an individual and nature. Sometimes, as is the case in "No Witchcraft for Sale," the conflict is between the characters' cultures. For the most part, the characters themselves are not in conflict. Differences in their cultures, however, lead to misunderstandings or actions that cause conflict.

Analyzing the cultural differences among characters can increase your understanding of the characters themselves as well as of the story as a whole. When comparing the similarities and differences of two things, it is helpful to do so in chart form.

A. DIRECTIONS: *In the Venn diagram, note details about the Farquars that are unique to them and their way of thinking in the circle labeled "Farquars." In the circle labeled "Gideon," note details that are unique to Gideon's culture and way of thinking. In the center, where the circles intersect, write ideas or attitudes that the Farquars and Gideon share.*

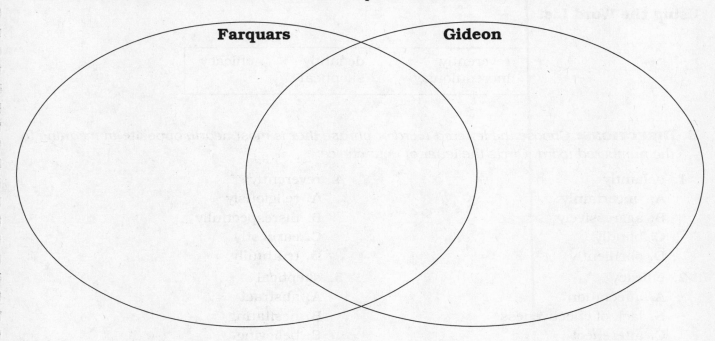

Farquars   **Gideon**

B. DIRECTIONS: *Now that you have analyzed the cultural differences in the story, answer this question.*

1. If the characters' cultural differences—that is, the cultural conflict—did not exist, what would be left of the plot? Describe what this story would be without the cultural differences. Would it still be an engaging story? Why or why not?

_____

_____

_____

_____

_____

"No Witchcraft for Sale" by Doris Lessing
Vocabulary Builder

Using Forms of *Skeptical*

A. DIRECTIONS: *The word* skeptical *means "doubting" or "not easily persuaded." Use one of the following words related to* skeptical *to complete each sentence correctly.*

skeptically   skeptic   skepticism

1. The pleasure of the circus may be somewhat deflated for an audience member who is a _____.

2. The child looked at the circus performer _____ after the clown had apparently pulled an egg out of the child's ear.

3. There was even more _____ on the part of the child's parents, whose eyes told them one thing, but whose minds told them another.

Using the Word List

reverently	defiantly	efficacy
incredulously	skeptical	

B. DIRECTIONS: *Choose the lettered word or phrase that is most nearly* opposite *in meaning to the numbered word. Circle the letter of your choice.*

1. defiantly
   A. uncertainly
   B. aggressively
   C. blindly
   D. obediently

2. efficacy
   A. affectation
   B. lack of effectiveness
   C. aftereffect
   D. self-sufficiency

3. incredulously
   A. trustingly
   B. curiously
   C. childishly
   D. massively

4. reverently
   A. religiously
   B. disrespectfully
   C. earnestly
   D. truthfully

5. skeptical
   A. abstract
   B. hesitating
   C. believing
   D. artificial

"No Witchcraft for Sale" by Doris Lessing

Grammar and Style: Correct Use of *Like* and *As*

The words *like* and *as* have become almost interchangeable in casual conversation. This informal usage can lead to errors in formal speaking or writing. Sometimes *like* is a verb meaning "to prefer." When used for comparisons, however, *like* is always a preposition. Remember that a prepositional phrase consists of a preposition followed by a noun or pronoun and any related words.

Gideon, *like the Farquars,* dotes on Teddy.

In casual speech, we often use *like* as a conjunction to introduce a subordinate clause. (Remember that a subordinate clause contains a subject and a verb, but does not express a complete thought and cannot stand alone.) In formal speaking or writing, use *as* in such situations.

As the scientist suspects, Gideon will not reveal the source of his medicine.

In general, use *like* to compare people or things. Use *as* to compare or demonstrate actions or states. If you are unsure about which word to use, look for a verb form. If the phrase in question contains a verb, use *as* to complete your subordinate clause.

A. PRACTICE: *Each of the following sentences uses* like *or* as. *Write C if a sentence is correct. Write I if a sentence is incorrect.*

_____ 1. As the other servants, Gideon calls Teddy "Little Yellow Head."

_____ 2. The Farquars, as many colonials, kept a number of servants to run their household.

_____ 3. Gideon, like many other Africans, had been educated in a mission school.

_____ 4. Later, Gideon was unable to be as comfortable with Teddy as he once had been.

_____ 5. As Teddy, Gideon's youngest son was fascinated with the scooter.

B. Writing Application: *Write comparative constructions using* like *and* as *according to the instructions that follow.*

1. Use *like* to compare Teddy with other young children.

   _____

2. Use *as* to compare Mrs. Farquar with other mothers.

   _____

3. Describe Teddy's treatment of Gideon's son, using a subordinate clause that begins with *as*.

   _____

4. Compare Mrs. Farquar's and Gideon's reactions to Teddy's accident, using the preposition *like*.

   _____

Name _____ Date _____

Use the graphic organizer below to collect and organize ideas for your problem-and-solution essay. First describe the problem between the Farquars and Gideon. Then, brainstorm for solutions to the problem and list them in the first column of the chart. In the second column, state the conditions needed to implement them. In the third column, list the steps that must be taken.

Problem:

	Conditions that would have to exist for the solution to happen	*Steps* that people could take to make the solution happen
Solution 1:		
Solution 2:		
Solution 3:		

Use the details from you chart as you write your essay on a separate page. Add details such as *why, for how long, what kind,* and so on to elaborate on your ideas and to clarify the steps in your solution.

"No Witchcraft for Sale" by Doris Lessing
Support for Extend Your Learning

Listening and Speaking

Use details to build ideas for your **debate on colonialism** by completing the pro-and-con chart below. In your debate, be sure to respond to opposing arguments as well as presenting your own views.

| Proposition: The benefits of colonialism outweigh the injustices it causes. ||
Pro (For)	Con (Against)
1.	1.
2.	2.
3.	3.

Research and Technology

Use the chart below to record details for your **oral report on medical botany.** Use sources such as Web sites, books, and magazines to gather information.

Medicine	Name and Description of Plant	Disease Name and Description

"No Witchcraft for Sale" by Doris Lessing
Enrichment: Science

Alternative Medicine

Alternative therapies for pain management, chronic illness, and prevention of illness have been getting a new and analytical look from the medical establishment. Originally part of a consumer rebellion against high medical costs and intrusive drugs or surgery, alternative medicine employs a variety of approaches, some with techniques thousands of years old.

Pain management. Traditional Western medicine is very good at emergency care, but not as successful with long-term problems such as chronic back pain or arthritis. Ancient techniques such as acupuncture, which seems somehow to relieve pressure on nerves, have been shown to be effective in many cases. Diet, exercise, and nondrug therapies also play a role in alternative treatments for chronic health problems.

Alternative medications. The side effects of many drugs have led some people to consider naturally occurring substances that provide relief. Bee pollen, various vitamin regimens, and herbs have been used for relief of pain. Effectiveness and safety are issues for many people who choose alternative medications.

Holistic medicine. Traditional medicine often treats one problem at a time. For example, cancer is treated with chemicals, and then other drugs ease symptoms brought on by those chemicals. Holistic medicine claims to treat the entire body and mind, using such techniques as biofeedback, massage, and relaxation therapy.

Prevention. The tremendous cost of modern medical care has placed a new emphasis on prevention as a medical therapy equal to correction. Diet, exercise, and stress relief all play a role in health, and alternative approaches to foods, recreation, and work are the least controversial aspects of alternative medicine.

DIRECTIONS: *Consider the issues raised in "No Witchcraft for Sale" and the recent trend toward alternative therapies as you answer the following questions.*

1. What are the risks involved in using alternative medicine?

   _____

   _____

2. What might be an effective way to evaluate the worth of alternative medicine?

   _____

   _____

3. Should insurance companies pay for alternative therapies like massage or acupuncture? Why or why not?

   _____

   _____

   _____

"No Witchcraft for Sale" by Doris Lessing
Selection Test A

Critical Reading *Identify the letter of the choice that best answers the question*

1. What is Gideon's job in Lessing's "No Witchcraft for Sale"?
   A. driver
   B. farmer.
   C. cook
   D. teacher.

2. In "No Witchcraft for Sale," how does Gideon treat Teddy when he is a child?
   A. affectionately
   B. humorously
   C. impatiently
   D. angrily

3. From what point of view does Lessing tell the story "No Witchcraft for Sale"?
   A. first person point of view
   B. second person point of view
   C. limited third-person point of view
   D. omniscient third-person point of view

4. In "No Witchcraft for Sale," why does Mrs. Farquar like Gideon?
   A. He is a good cook and servant.
   B. He treats Teddy with affection.
   C. He helped her feel welcome in the area.
   D. He shares his knowledge of native ways.

5. In "No Witchcraft for Sale," Gideon becomes more distant with Teddy. Why?
   A. Teddy insults Gideon.
   B. Teddy makes Gideon take an orange.
   C. Teddy laughs at Gideon.
   D. Teddy is growing into a young man.

6. How are Teddy's eyes injured in "No Witchcraft for Sale"?
   A. A snake spits venom into them.
   B. A branch hits him in the eyes.
   C. He gets into a fight with another boy.
   D. He gets sap from a plant in them.

____ 7. In "No Witchcraft for Sale," what does Gideon do to save Teddy's eyes?
   A. He gets a witch doctor to say magic words over Teddy.
   B. He washes Teddy's eyes out with water from a nearby spring.
   C. He chews the root of a plant and spits the juice in Teddy's eyes.
   D. He has Teddy chew the leaves of a local tree.

____ 8. In "No Witchcraft for Sale," why does Gideon's cure save Teddy's eyes?
   A. Teddy believed it would work.
   B. Gideon believed it would work.
   C. It came from a witch doctor.
   D. It was a native herbal treatment.

____ 9. How do the Farquars respond to Gideon's effort to save Teddy's eyes in "No Witchcraft for Sale"?
   A. with confusion
   B. with extreme gratitude
   C. with anger
   D. with embarrassment

____ 10. What can you conclude about cures such as Gideon's from "No Witchcraft for Sale"?
   A. They are used often.
   B. They have no scientific basis.
   C. They do not really occur.
   D. They are based entirely on faith.

____ 11. In "No Witchcraft for Sale," how does Gideon respond when the scientist asks him to explain his cure?
   A. by asking him to buy the cure
   B. be being ashamed that he cured Teddy
   C. by saying he cannot remember the cure
   D. by telling him how to make the cure

____ 12. How does the relationship between the Farquars and Gideon conclude in "No Witchcraft for Sale"?
   A. Gideon is forced to leave.
   B. The relationship remains awkward.
   C. The Farquars reward Gideon for his values and loyalty.
   D. The relationship returns to one of warmth and respect.

Name _____ Date _____

Vocabulary and Grammar

___ **13.** Which word best replaces *skeptical* in this sentence: "The *skeptical* doctor laughed at the native cure"?
   A. friendly
   B. relaxed
   C. anxious
   D. doubtful

___ **14.** Which sentence uses *like, as, as if,* or *as though* correctly?
   A. Teddy spoke to Gideon *like* a servant.
   B. Gideon played with Teddy *as if* he were his own child.
   C. Gideon's cure worked *like* a miracle in saving Teddy's eyes.
   D. The scientist looked *as* an intelligent person.

Essay

15. In an essay, explain the meaning of the title of the short story "No Witchcraft for Sale." Answer these questions: What events in the story illustrate this title? Why do you think Gideon refuses to share his secret? Use details from the story to support your response.

16. In "No Witchcraft for Sale," Gideon's cure is widely talked about in the white community. A scientist is then sent to investigate. Why was the scientist interested in this story? What do you think the scientist thought of the cure? Write an essay in which you answer these questions. Give examples from the story to explain your response.

"No Witchcraft for Sale" by Doris Lessing
Selection Test B

Critical Reading *Identify the letter of the choice that best completes the statement or answers the question.*

_____ 1. In Doris Lessing's "No Witchcraft for Sale," Gideon is
   A. a herder.
   B. a local medicine man.
   C. the Farquars' cook.
   D. a scientist.

_____ 2. Gideon's attitude toward Teddy as a young child could best be described as
   A. kind but distant.
   B. fond and indulgent.
   C. patient and indifferent.
   D. polite but hostile.

_____ 3. Why was Mrs. Farquar fond of Gideon?
   A. He was affectionate toward Teddy.
   B. He had helped others in the area accept them.
   C. He had a knowledge of native ways.
   D. He was wiser than she.

_____ 4. How did Gideon change after Teddy used his scooter to terrorize Gideon's son?
   A. He became distant and formal.
   B. He tried harder to teach Teddy right from wrong.
   C. He became angry and restrained.
   D. He became sad and silent.

_____ 5. How did Teddy respond to Gideon's change after the scooter incident?
   A. He was unaware of the change, not understanding Gideon's words.
   B. He missed Gideon's closeness but began to assume the role of master.
   C. He was determined to receive a full explanation of Gideon's attitude.
   D. He turned to his parents as interpreters of the event.

_____ 6. Teddy's eyes were injured by
   A. a scooter accident.
   B. a venomous insect.
   C. a spitting snake.
   D. sap from a potted plant.

_____ 7. Gideon's remedy for Teddy's eyes
   A. worked because he believed it would.
   B. supplemented the permanganate.
   C. came from a witch doctor.
   D. was a form of native herbal treatment.

_____ 8. The Farquars' response to Gideon after the incident with Teddy's eyes was
    A. to take Gideon's effort for granted.
    B. profound respect.
    C. inexpressible gratitude.
    D. to attempt to profit from the cure.

_____ 9. These sorts of cures
    A. had no scientific validity.
    B. were commonly reported.
    C. were mere legends before this incident.
    D. were usually hoaxes.

_____ 10. The general attitude of the white community toward these cures was
    A. outright disbelief.
    B. shocked discovery.
    C. bemused amazement.
    D. neutrality.

_____ 11. When the Farquars called Gideon to talk to the scientist, his response was
    A. a clever deceit.
    B. embarrassed humility.
    C. grudging cooperation.
    D. stubborn defiance.

_____ 12. Gideon ultimately gave no help to the Farquars and the scientist about the cure because
    A. he wished to protect the cure and his culture.
    B. he believed his knowledge would be of no value in another culture.
    C. he was interested only in curing people, not in how or why it worked.
    D. he was offended at being embarrassed in front of the scientist.

Vocabulary and Grammar

_____ 13. The word *skeptical* means
    A. careless.
    B. unbelieving.
    C. secretive.
    D. hostile.

_____ 14. Considering the *efficacy* of an action is evaluating its
    A. goal.
    B. history.
    C. cost.
    D. effectiveness.

_____ 15. Which sentence is grammatically *correct*?
    A. Like he had suspected, Gideon learned the Farquars didn't understand him.
    B. Mrs. Farquar could just not think like Gideon did.
    C. Gideon could no longer treat Teddy like an innocent child.
    D. Neither could Gideon accept being treated like the scientist would treat him.

_____ **16.** In the sentence, "He spoke to Mr. Farquar like an unwilling servant," the word *like* is a
   A. preposition.
   B. verb.
   C. subordinate conjunction.
   D. coordinating conjunction.

Essay

17. In "No Witchcraft for Sale," Gideon seems to like and respect the Farquars, and the Farquars like and respect Gideon. Why can't they communicate on some fundamental issues? Write an essay in which you describe and explain the basic conflict, discussing the points of view of the Farquars and Gideon on the events in the story. Use examples from the story to illustrate your ideas.

18. In spite of basic differences between cultures, it's clear that Gideon has great affection for the young Teddy. If Gideon is willing to help the colonists by saving the boy, why won't he help them by sharing information about the cure? Write an essay in which you explain the difference between these two actions. Use examples from the story to support your ideas.

"The Lagoon" by Joseph Conrad
"Araby" by James Joyce
Vocabulary Warm-up Word Lists

Study these words from the selections. Then, complete the activities that follow.

Word List A

discreetly [dis KREET lee] *adv.* in a tactful, cautious, and wise manner
   Very <u>discreetly</u>, Franklin asked questions about Ryan's character.

enchantment [in CHANT muhnt] *n.* the use or effect of charms or spells
   As if under <u>enchantment</u>, Gregory stared at Isabella without blinking.

fascination [fas uh NAY shuhn] *n.* great interest
   Our <u>fascination</u> with the magician's tricks kept us interested for hours.

fringing [FRINJ ing] *adj.* bordered with or as if with an ornamental trim
   The <u>fringing</u> flowers surrounded the scene like a frame.

noiselessly [NOYZ lis lee] *adv.* quietly; silently
   The little spider <u>noiselessly</u> crept up the wall.

offensive [uh FEN siv] *adj.* unpleasant or disagreeable
   An <u>offensive</u> odor hung over the swamp.

somber [SAHM buhr] *adj.* having little light or color; dark
   For some reason, Rachel always wears dark, <u>somber</u> colors.

withstand [with STAND] *v.* to oppose; to resist
   This well-made broom can <u>withstand</u> hard use.

Word List B

calamity [kuh LAM uh tee] *n.* any happening that causes great distress
   The hurricane was a <u>calamity</u> for the coastal town.

ceaseless [SEES lis] *adj.* going on without pause; continual
   The <u>ceaseless</u> breaking of the waves on shore was soothing to Samuel.

energetically [en uhr JET ik lee] *adv.* vigorously; in a forceful manner
   Estelle danced <u>energetically</u>, making all of us tired just watching her.

jasmine [JAZ min] *n.* a shrub with fragrant white, yellow, or red flowers
   The <u>jasmine</u> filled the air with a fragrant scent.

monotonous [muh NAHT uh nuhs] *adj.* boring because of lack of variety
   The <u>monotonous</u>, repetitive song was putting us all to sleep.

periodic [peer ee AHD ik] *adj.* recurring at regular intervals
   Dan is due for one of his <u>periodic</u> dental checkups.

placid [PLAS id] *adj.* calm; peaceful
   The lake is so <u>placid</u> that the sailboats cannot move.

strife [STRYF] *n.* any bitter or angry fight, conflict, or quarrel
   The <u>strife</u> between the two sisters has been going on for years.

"The Lagoon" by Joseph Conrad
"Araby" by James Joyce
Vocabulary Warm-up Exercises

Exercise A *Fill in each blank below with the appropriate word from Word List A.*

Nathan had always felt a great [1] _____ for magic. He watched every

magic show he could, [2] _____ keeping his eyes on the magician's hands

at all times. Most of the time, he could not figure out the trick. Once, trying not to make

any sound, he [3] _____ crept behind the stage to see what he could see,

but the annoyed magician's assistant noticed this [4] _____ behavior and

shooed him away. Another time he dressed in especially [5] _____ cloth-

ing, hoping to avoid being noticed in the dark. At intermission, he sneaked past the cur-

tains [6] _____ the stage, hoping to get some insight. No one bothered to

[7] _____ this intrusion—perhaps the magician understood what Nathan

was going through. He actually did find out how one trick was done. After that, all the

[8] _____ seemed to be over for him.

Exercise B *Write a complete sentence to answer each question.*

1. If you had two <u>placid</u> cats, do you think they would fight all the time?

   _____

2. Which two of the five senses would be most stimulated by <u>jasmine</u>?

   _____

3. Would a <u>monotonous</u> song be likely to make it to number one on the charts?

   _____

4. Would a <u>ceaseless</u> buzzing in your ears be a good reason to see a doctor?

   _____

5. Would you expect people in the middle of <u>strife</u> to have dinner together?

   _____

6. If you swam <u>energetically</u>, would you burn many calories?

   _____

7. With which member of your family do you like to have <u>periodic</u> visits?

   _____

8. What is one recent <u>calamity</u> you heard about in the news?

   _____

Name _____ Date _____

"The Lagoon" by Joseph Conrad
"Araby" by James Joyce
Reading Warm-up A

Read the following passage. Pay special attention to the underlined words. Then, read it again, and complete the activities. Use a separate sheet of paper for your written answers.

The bazaar in Chinatown had always been a source of great <u>fascination</u> and interest for Polly, luring her with its charm. She tried to get over there every Saturday so she could browse among the stalls and shops along the main street. She would stroll along in a daze, as if under some mysterious <u>enchantment</u>, and marvel at the interesting toys, gadgets, foods, tablecloths, scarves, bangles, soaps, incense, and such.

Once she found a scarf with a <u>fringing</u> border of strung beads. She just had to have it. She knew it would brighten up any dark, <u>somber</u> outfit that she or her mother might wear. It would make a perfect gift for her mother—one that Polly could borrow anytime.

Another time she saw a small jade sculpture of an elephant. The owner of the shop told her it would <u>withstand</u> any kind of abuse. Even if Polly dropped it on a hard tile floor, she said, it would not break. Polly didn't believe the owner. In fact, she thought it rather <u>offensive</u> that she would tell such an obvious lie to make a sale. Even so, Polly wanted to buy the jade elephant. She just couldn't afford it right now.

One particular Saturday, as Polly was <u>noiselessly</u> poking her way along the street, she noticed another girl about her age, also silently examining every trinket that caught her eye. Then she saw the girl pick up the jade elephant. Polly held her breath for what seemed like a full five minutes until the girl put it back down. That evening, Polly vowed, she would have to <u>discreetly</u> approach her mother and ask for a loan. If she asked tactfully, promising to pay it back soon, perhaps she could come back tomorrow and buy the elephant.

1. Underline the word that means about the same as <u>fascination</u>. What holds great *fascination* for you?

2. Circle what made Polly seem like she was under an <u>enchantment</u>. Tell about a story you have read that includes *enchantment*.

3. Underline the words that describe the <u>fringing</u> border on the scarf.

4. Circle the word that is close to <u>somber</u>. When would you wear a *somber* outfit?

5. Circle the words that describe an example of the abuse the jade sculpture might be able to <u>withstand</u>. What is the worst weather your town has had to *withstand*?

6. Underline the words that explain what Polly thought was so <u>offensive</u>. How do people usually react when something is *offensive*?

7. Underline the word that means the same as <u>noiselessly</u>. Where would it be important to move *noiselessly*?

8. Circle the word in a nearby sentence that means about the same as <u>discreetly</u>. Tell about a time you had to act *discreetly*.

"The Lagoon" by Joseph Conad
"Araby" by James Joyce
Reading Warm-up B

Read the following passage. Pay special attention to the underlined words. Then, read it again, and complete the activities. Use a separate sheet of paper for your written answers.

The Malay Archipelago, sometimes called the East Indies, is an area of unsurpassed natural beauty. This vast group of islands is located between mainland Southeast Asia (Indochina) and Australia. It includes Indonesia, the Philippines, Brunei, East Timor, and Papua New Guinea. (Some experts say that Papua New Guinea should not be included, as it is so different, culturally). From east to west, the area stretches 4,000 miles. From north to south, it stretches 1,300 miles. From calm, <u>placid</u> lakes to raging rivers to teeming rain forests, nature's abundance and <u>ceaseless</u>, continual energy is in evidence on these numerous islands.

A traveler wishing to get away from a <u>monotonous</u>, boring job might consider a trip to this area. He or she could relax in a comfortable hotel. Perhaps the scent of fragrant <u>jasmine</u> growing outside the hotel window would perfume the air. That same traveler might decide to hike <u>energetically</u> in the rain forests, searching out rare orchids, butterflies, and other interesting tropical species. It is entirely possible that even an amateur botanist or entomologist could find a new species of plant or insect.

The traveler to the Malay Archipelago should be aware that the area has frequent volcanic eruptions and earthquake activity. In fact, these <u>periodic</u> events have been the cause of great grief in the area because they happen with some regularity. Thousands of people have suffered each time a disaster like this has occurred. Visitors to the area should try to be prepared for such a <u>calamity</u> without letting such a possibility ruin their vacation.

Certain parts of this area sometimes experience political <u>strife</u>, so the traveler should avoid those areas where conflict might be occurring.

1. Underline the word that means about the same as <u>placid</u>. Use *placid* in a sentence.

2. Circle the word that means about the same as <u>ceaseless</u>. Describe something else that goes on in a *ceaseless* fashion.

3. Underline the word that means about the same as <u>monotonous</u>. How might you pep up an exercise routine that is beginning to get *monotonous*?

4. Circle the words that suggest what <u>jasmine</u> is. Why do you think hotel owners would want to have *jasmine* around?

5. Circle the word that tells what a traveler might do <u>energetically</u>. What is one school activity that people usually do *energetically*?

6. Circle the words that tell what <u>periodic</u> means. What is one *periodic* event that families in your community often celebrate together?

7. Underline the word in a nearby sentence that means about the same as <u>calamity</u>. How can you help people who have suffered from a natural *calamity*?

8. Circle the word that means about the same as <u>strife</u>. Use *strife* in a sentence.

Name _____ Date _____

"The Lagoon" by Joseph Conrad
"Araby" by James Joyce
Literary Analysis: Plot Devices

In "The Lagoon," Conrad uses a **story within a story,** a plot device in which a character in a fictional narrative tells a story. Conrad's plot device focuses attention on Arsat's story by framing it with another narrative. In "Araby," Joyce uses an **epiphany,** a plot device in which a character has a sudden and profound revelation in an ordinary moment, to heighten the story's climax.

DIRECTIONS: *Write your answers to the following questions.*

1. As you read "The Lagoon," what clues signal the beginning and the end of the story within the story?

   _____

   _____

   _____

2. In "The Lagoon," is Arsat's story ever interrupted by the outside narrative? If so, what is the effect?

   _____

   _____

   _____

3. Would Arsat's story in "The Lagoon" have the same effect if it had been told on its own? Explain.

   _____

   _____

   _____

4. What is the epiphany in "Araby"?

   _____

   _____

   _____

5. In "Araby," what is the boy doing or looking at when he has an epiphany?

   _____

   _____

   _____

Name _____ Date _____

Reading Strategy: Picture the Action and Situation

Conrad and Joyce place great importance on the psychological states of their characters. As you read modernist fiction, pause to picture the action and situation. Pay particular attention to the characters' internal responses to what is happening. For example, in "The Lagoon," as the narrator details the crew's thoughts about Arsat, try to picture the physical scene and imagine what the white man might be thinking at the same moment.

DIRECTIONS: *Read the following passages from the stories. For each, write a few sentences describing what the characters do and see as well as what they might think or feel.*

1. The white man . . . murmured sadly without lifting his head—
   "We all love our brothers."
   Arsat burst out with an intense whispering violence—
   "What did I care who died? I wanted peace in my own heart."

   _____

   _____

   _____

   _____

2. At nine o'clock I heard my uncle's latchkey in the hall door. I heard him talking to himself and heard the hallstand rocking when it had received the weight of his overcoat. I could interpret these signs. When he was midway through his dinner I asked him to give me the money to go to the bazaar. He had forgotten.

   _____

   _____

   _____

   _____

3. Nearly all the stalls were closed and the greater part of the hall was in darkness. I recognized a silence like that which pervades a church after a service. I walked into the center of the bazaar timidly.

   _____

   _____

   _____

   _____

"The Lagoon" by Joseph Conrad
"Araby" by James Joyce
Vocabulary Builder

Using the Root *-vinc-*

A. DIRECTIONS: *In each sentence, cross out the italicized word or phrase and replace it with one of the following words:* convince, evince, invincibility.

1. I have doubts about this alarm system's *unconquerable quality*.
2. What can you do to *conquer the doubt in* me?
3. If you *show* clear, overwhelming evidence of the system's performance, perhaps I'll buy it.

Using the Word List

portals	invincible	propitiate	conflagration	august
imperturbable	litanies	garrulous	derided	

B. DIRECTIONS: *For each related pair of words in CAPITAL LETTERS, choose the lettered pair that best expresses a* similar *relationship. Circle the letter of your choice.*

1. PORTALS : ENTRANCES ::
   A. gates : iron   B. locks : keys   C. roads : pathways
2. INVINCIBLE : VICTORY ::
   A. strong : muscula   B. confident : success   C. fear : doubt
3. PROPITIATE : VICTORY ::
   A. welcome : greet   B. confident : success   C. hasten : hurry
4. CONFLAGRATION : SPARK ::
   A. flood : droplet   B. burn : destroy   C. thunder : lightning
5. AUGUST : REVERE ::
   A. November : spring   B. authoritative : obey C. powerful : weak
6. IMPERTURBABLE : DISRUPT ::
   A. anger : hatred   B. wealthy : inherit   C. contented : dismay
7. LITANIES : PRAYER :
   A. clery : congregation B. songs : music   C. snow : sleet
8. GARRULOUS : TALKATIVE ::
   A. sickly : healthy   B. yawning : tired   C. energetic : lively
9. DERIDED :TEASE ::
   A. ran : sprint   B. stretched : squeeze   C. grasped : release

Name _____ Date _____

"The Lagoon" by Joseph Conrad
"Araby" by James Joyce

Grammar and Style: Adverb Clauses

Adverb clauses are subordinate clauses that modify verbs, adjectives, and adverbs. As modifiers, adverb clauses add specificity and vivid detail to writing. In the following sentence from "The Lagoon," the adverb clause shown in italics modifies the adverb *paler:*

The stars shone paler *as if they had retreated into the frozen depths of immense space.*

A. PRACTICE: *Underline the adverb clauses in the following sentences. Circle the word each adverb clause modifies.*

1. ". . . his voice and demeanor were composed as he asked, without any words of greeting— 'Have you medicine, Tuan?'"

2. "She lay still, as if dead; but her big eyes, wide open, glittered in the gloom. . . ."

3. "But since the sun of today rose she hears nothing—she hears not me."

4. "He had known Arsat years ago, in a far country in times of trouble and danger, when no friendship is to be despised."

5. "When we returned to the street, light from the kitchen windows had filled the areas."

6. "She could not go, she said, because there would be a retreat that week in her convent."

7. "When he was midway through his dinner I asked him to give me the money to go to the bazaar."

B. Writing Application: *For each of the following, write a sentence containing an adverb clause that answers the question.*

1. Why does the white man stay with Arsat in "The Lagoon"?

_____

_____

2. In "The Lagoon" when do Arsat and his brother kidnap the young woman?

_____

_____

3. How does the boy in "Araby" feel about Mangan's sister?

_____

_____

4. In "Araby," what circumstance prevents the boy from going to the bazaar when he wants?

_____

_____

Name _____   Date _____

"The Lagoon" by Joseph Conrad
"Araby" by James Joyce

Support for Writing

Use the graphic organizer below to develop ideas for your literary essay on the concept of *nothing* in Arsat's tale and in "The Lagoon." Write details about images of silence and nothing in the left column. In the right column, jot down notes about the events surrounding each image.

Images of Silence and Nothing　　　　　　**Events Connected to the Images**

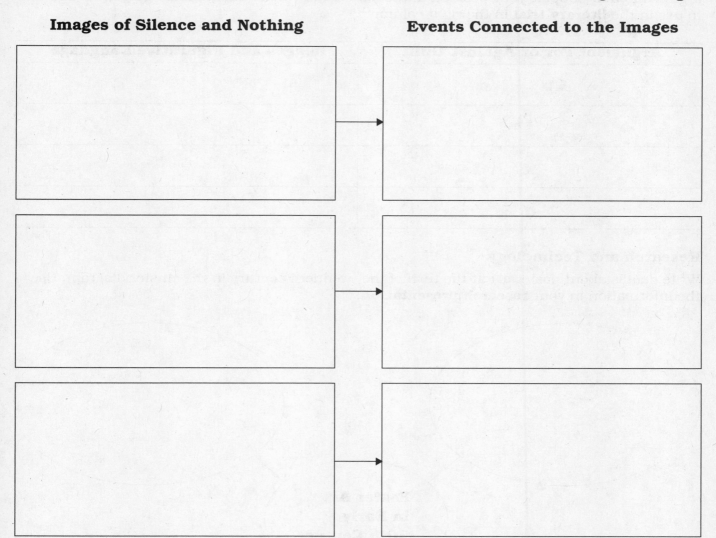

Draw on details and ideas from your graphic organizer as you draft your essay on a separate page. Present your ideas in a logical order, and make sure that the details you have selected support the points you wish to make.

"The Lagoon" by Joseph Conrad
"Araby" by James Joyce
Support for Extend Your Learning

Listening and Speaking

Think about your role in Arsat's trial—defense lawyer, prosecuting lawyer, or judge. List arguments that support your position in the left column. Write images and figurative language to use in the **literary trial** in the right column.

Argument For or Against Guilt	Images and Figurative Language

Research and Technology

Write details about poster art at the turn of the twentieth century in the cluster diagram. Use the information in your **research presentation.**

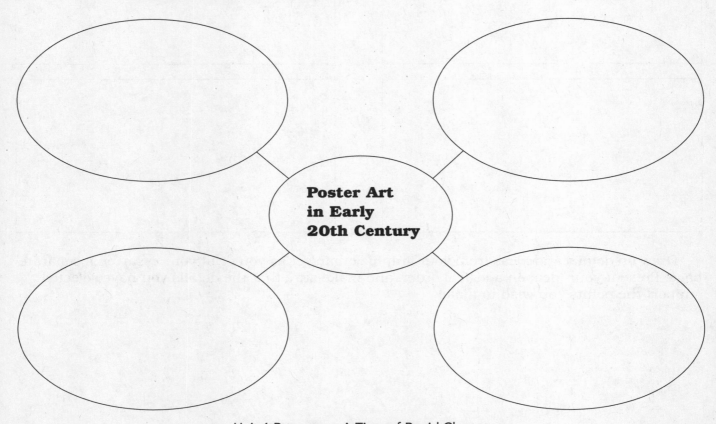

Poster Art
in Early
20th Century

Name _____ Date _____

"The Lagoon" by Joseph Conrad
"Araby" by James Joyce
Enrichment: Fine Art

In their stories, Conrad and Joyce create an exterior world that suggests the inner world of their characters. Fine art that accompanies a literary work can either depict characters or setting or go beyond the literal to suggest a deeper meaning in the story. Artists can use techniques to suggest mood and atmosphere. For example, the perspective, or the perceived distance between the viewer and the subject of the painting, can create feelings of either isolation or inclusion. A palette with bright, soft colors might create a warm and inviting atmosphere, while dark colors might convey a depressing or oppressive mood.

DIRECTIONS: *Complete the following chart by listing details about the art that accompanies each story.*

Questions	Photographs	*St. Patrick's Close* by Walter Osborne
1. What is depicted?		
2. What is the center of interest in the work?		
3. What effect does the perspective create?		
4. What colors or play between light and shadow is used?		
5. What mood or atmosphere does the work create?		
6. Which artistic techniques have the greatest effect on mood or atmosphere?		

Name _____ Date _____

"The Lagoon" by Joseph Conrad
"Araby" by James Joyce

Selection Test A

Critical Reading *Identify the letter of the choice that best answers the question.*

___ 1. In "The Lagoon," what words best describe the relationship between the white man and Arsat?
   A. distrustful and competitive
   B. friendly and trusting
   C. angry and jealous
   D. unequal but respectful

___ 2. In "The Lagoon," picture the narrator of the story within a story. Who would it most likely be?
   A. the white man
   B. Arsat
   C. the steersman
   D. the author

___ 3. What happens to Arsat's brother in "The Lagoon"?
   A. He runs away with a girl he loves.
   B. He is left on a lonely island.
   C. He is killed as Arsat leaves.
   D. He breaks contact with Arsat.

___ 4. What is the effect of the story within a story in "The Lagoon"?
   A. It explains why the steersman does not like Arsat.
   B. It tells why the white man and Arsat are friends.
   C. It tells Arsat's story and gives insights into his feelings.
   D. It describes the white man's personal struggle and goals.

___ 5. What becomes of Diamelen, the woman Arsat loves in "The Lagoon"?
   A. She remains with the ruler.
   B. She dies.
   C. She hides with Arsat's brother.
   D. She runs away with the white man.

___ 6. What is the theme of the story within a story in "The Lagoon"?
   A. People cannot escape the results of their past actions.
   B. Love is the greatest human need.
   C. Bridging cultural differences is worth great effort.
   D. People can never understand the depths of others' love.

7. What is Joyce's attitude toward the narrator in "Araby"?
   A. sympathetic
   B. bitter
   C. disapproving
   D. annoyed

8. In "Araby," why is the narrator late in reaching Araby?
   A. The train to Araby has been delayed.
   B. His uncle has forgotten and gets home late.
   C. His friends cannot join him until late.
   D. His aunt does not want him to go alone.

9. In "Araby," why does the narrator want to go to Araby?
   A. to buy a gift for a girl
   B. to buy a gift for his uncle
   C. to see a bazaar
   D. to be with his friends

10. Picture the narrator of "Araby" as he waits. When he finally gets to Araby, how does he feel?
    A. relieved
    B. discouraged
    C. satisfied
    D. excited

11. What does Araby symbolize in "Araby"?
    A. love
    B. religious faith
    C. home
    D. dreams

12. How do the narrator's feelings change from the beginning to the end of "Araby"?
    A. angry to satisfied
    B. romantic to joyful
    C. hopeful to depressed
    D. lonely to hopeful

Vocabulary and Grammar

____ 13. Which word best replaces *portals* in this sentence: "The man entered the *portals* that led to the castle"?
  A. prayers
  B. rivers
  C. doors
  D. mountains

____ 14. Which line from "Araby" contains an adverb clause that shows *when* something happens?
  A. "At night in my bedroom . . . her image came between me and the page."
  B. "I went into the back drawing room in which the priest had died."
  C. "It would be a splendid bazaar, she said; she would love to go."
  D. "Every morning I lay on the floor in the front parlor watching her door."

Essay

15. In the final line of "The Lagoon," the narrator describes Arsat staring into the sun: "He looked beyond the great light of a cloudless day into the darkness of a world of illusions [dreams]." This line is a statement of the main idea of the story. In an essay, explain how the final line describes Arsat's experiences with his brother and with Diamelen.

16. At the end of "Araby," the narrator realizes that dreams do not always come true, and it is foolish to put all of one's hopes in them. In an essay, tell what the narrator has learned in this story. Consider the feelings and attitude he expresses in the opening description of playing with his friends. What causes him to change? What does he realize? Use details from the story to support your response.

"The Lagoon" by Joseph Conrad
"Araby" by James Joyce
Selection Test B

Critical Reading *Identify the letter of the choice that best completes the statement or answers the question.*

____ 1. In "The Lagoon," which description of setting symbolically reflects the meaning of the story?
   A. "The churned-up water frothed alongside with a confused murmur."
   B. ". . . tortuous, fabulously deep; filled with gloom under the thin strip of pure and shining blue of the heaven."
   C. "Nothing moved on the river but the eight paddles that rose flashing regularly . . ."
   D. ". . . the slanting beams of sunset touched the broadside of the canoe with a fiery glow . . ."

____ 2. Why does Conrad fail to characterize the white man fully?
   A. to focus on Arsat and the Malays
   B. to show that the man's life is uninteresting
   C. to reflect the man's rootlessness and detachment
   D. to symbolize human hollowness

____ 3. Which words best describe the relationship between the white man and Arsat in "The Lagoon"?
   A. unequal but respectful
   B. tender but uncaring
   C. distant but envious
   D. wary but jovial

____ 4. At several points in "The Lagoon," when Arsat is telling his story, he pauses, listens toward the hut, and continues. At these moments, Arsat is probably
   A. thinking that the white man is bored.
   B. worrying if Diamelen is still breathing.
   C. trying to remember what happens next in his story.
   D. wanting to be alone.

____ 5. At the end of "The Lagoon," when the white man resumes his posture from the opening scene, Conrad suggests that the man
   A. is unaffected by his experience.
   B. seeks comfort in habit.
   C. is perpetually restless.
   D. fears his steersman.

____ 6. In "The Lagoon," what is the primary effect of the story within a story?
   A. It illuminates the white man's inner struggle.
   B. It intensifies Arsat's experience.
   C. It explains why the steersman is afraid of Arsat.
   D. It makes Arsat's story seem unreal.

_____ 7. What is the theme of "The Lagoon"?
   A. Cultural differences can be bridged, with enough good will.
   B. People have no business meddling in foreign affairs.
   C. We are ultimately alone with our own consciences.
   D. Western culture offers nothing of value.

_____ 8. What does the boy in "Araby" feel when he hears his uncle talking to himself?
   A. regret
   B. fear
   C. anxiety
   D. rage

_____ 9. Which word best describes Joyce's attitude toward the boy in "Araby"?
   A. understanding
   B. respectful
   C. superior
   D. indulgent

_____ 10. Which detail in this passage from "Araby" is the strongest indicator of the boy's inner feelings?

   I found myself in a big hall girdled at half its height by a gallery. Nearly all the stalls were closed and the greater part of the hall was in darkness.

   A. the hall's height
   B. the gallery that girdles the hall
   C. the stalls
   D. the hall's darkness

_____ 11. At the end of "Araby," the boy experiences anger and sadness because his epiphany reveals that
   A. he will never be able to satisfy his desires.
   B. he will have to disappoint Mangan's sister.
   C. he cannot buy someone's love.
   D. he will always fall short of his goals.

_____ 12. In a broad sense, the boy's epiphany in "Araby" reveals the
   A. futility of human pursuits.
   B. indifference of society to individuals.
   C. pervasiveness of self-deception.
   D. pointlessness of religious ceremony.

Vocabulary and Grammar

_____ 13. In "The Lagoon," Arsat discovers that his brother, who is overcome by his pursuers, is not _____.
   A. invincible
   B. august
   C. garrulous
   D. derided

____ 14. The _____ white man shows very little emotion as he listens to Arsat's story.
   A. invincible
   B. propitiate
   C. imperturbable
   D. garrulous

____ 15. Which sentence contains an adverb clause?
   A. "The white man . . . looked back at the shining ripple of the boat's wake."
   B. "Before the sampan passed out of the lagoon into the creek he lifted his eyes."
   C. "Arsat had not moved."
   D. "He stood lonely in the searching sunshine. . . ."

____ 16. In which item is the adverb clause underlined?
   A. <u>She lay still,</u> as if dead; but her big eyes, wide open, glittered in the gloom . . .
   B. She lay still, <u>as if dead;</u> but her big eyes, wide open, glittered in the gloom . . .
   C. She lay still, as if dead; but her big eyes, <u>wide open,</u> glittered in the gloom . . .
   D. She lay still, as if dead; but her big eyes, wide open, <u>glittered in the gloom</u> . . .

Essay

17. In both stories, the exterior setting provides clues to the interior lives of the characters. In an essay, explain how envisioning the physical setting and action in either "The Lagoon" or "Araby" leads to revelations about the characters' inner reactions.

18. Conrad and Joyce use different plot devices to strengthen the underlying meaning of their stories. Write an essay in which you analyze each writer's use of a plot device, and explain how its use affects the story. Support your main points with evidence from the stories.

Vocabulary Warm-up Word Lists

Study these words from the selections. Then, complete the activities that follow.

Word List A

barricade [BAR uh kayd] *n.* something that blocks passage; barrier
   The car could not proceed past the <u>barricade</u> at the bridge.

bowels [BOW uhlz] *n.* intestines, the part of the digestive system after the stomach.
   Eating fiber helps maintain healthy <u>bowels</u>.

cleansed [KLENZD] *v.* made clean and pure
   Her long meditation made Helen feel <u>cleansed</u> in spirit.

intimacy [IN tuh muh see] *n.* the condition of being very close or friendly
   Gathered around the campfire, we had a feeling of <u>intimacy</u>.

Oriental [awr ee EN tuhl] *adj.* of or from Asia, especially eastern Asia
   Jackie's new dresser has an <u>Oriental</u> design.

pitiless [PIT i lis] *adj.* without pity; cruel; ruthless
   The <u>pitiless</u> king refused to lower the peasants' taxes.

rendezvous [RAHN day voo] *n.* a planned meeting
   Max and Jean's <u>rendezvous</u> was at four o'clock in the park.

sayings [SAY ingz] *n.* phrases or proverbs much repeated
   Macy's grandmother is fond of repeating old <u>sayings</u>.

Word List B

authenticity [aw then TIS uh tee] *n.* the condition of being genuine or true
   The <u>authenticity</u> of the painting bought by the museum is in question.

comprehension [kahm pree HEN shuhn] *n.* the act of understanding
   Tyler's reading <u>comprehension</u> has improved this year.

exquisite [ek SKWIZ it] *adj.* having an unusually fine or delicate beauty
   The ring Todd gave Carla was just <u>exquisite</u>.

flexible [FLEK suh buhl] *adj.* easily changed; adaptable
   The plans for the party are <u>flexible</u>.

hectic [HEK tik] *adj.* marked by or full of excitement, confusion, or haste
   Matt's <u>hectic</u> trip from California to New York was tiring.

immortality [im awr TAL uh tee] *n.* life or fame lasting forever
   Great, brave deeds brought Alexander a kind of <u>immortality</u>.

infinite [IN fuh nit] *adj.* having no limits; endless or boundless
   George spends money as if he has an <u>infinite</u> supply.

subtlest [SUT uh list] *adj.* hardest to see or understand; least obvious
   The two colors had the <u>subtlest</u> of differences in shade.

Name _____ Date _____

"The Lady in the Looking Glass" by Virginia Woolf
"The First Year of My Life" by Muriel Spark
Vocabulary Warm-up Exercises

Exercise A *Fill in the blanks, using each word from Word List A only once.*

With a feeling of friendly [1] _____, Glenn invited Gloria to take a walk.
He wanted to show her the lovely [2] _____ gardens near his house. He
told her that his own spirit always felt renewed and [3] _____ after visiting the gardens. Gloria said yes, and they set up their [4] _____ for three
o'clock the next afternoon. The next day, Gloria's mom uttered one of her favorite
[5] _____ before Gloria left: "Put on some sunscreen, honey, to guard
against the [6] _____ sun." At the ticket counter, Glenn paid for their
admission, and the [7] _____ blocking the entrance was opened. As they
entered the garden, Gloria felt a surge of excitement all through her body—from her
heart to her [8] _____ and even down to her toes. The garden was as
beautiful as Glenn had said.

Exercise B *Find a synonym for each word in the following vocabulary list. Use each synonym
in a sentence that makes the meaning of the word clear.*

Example: Vocabulary Word: *hectic*   Synonym: *frantic*
   Sample sentence: *After a long, <u>frantic</u> day, I need to relax.*

1. Vocabulary word: <u>infinite</u>   Synonym: _____
   _____

2. Vocabulary word: <u>authenticity</u>   Synonym: _____
   _____

3. Vocabulary word: <u>subtlest</u>   Synonym: _____
   _____

4. Vocabulary word: <u>flexible</u>   Synonym: _____
   _____

5. Vocabulary word: <u>immortality</u>   Synonym: _____
   _____

6. Vocabulary word: <u>comprehension</u>   Synonym: _____
   _____

7. Vocabulary word: <u>exquisite</u>   Synonym: _____
   _____

"The Lady in the Looking Glass" by Virginia Woolf
"The First Year of My Life" by Muriel Spark
Reading Warm-up A

Read the following passage. Pay special attention to the underlined words. Then, read it again, and complete the activities. Use a separate sheet of paper for your written answers.

Among all the <u>sayings</u> applied to children, one of the most ridiculous is that children should be seen and not heard. During the first year of life, children make their needs known by making noise of some kind. This noise might be in the form of fussing, crying, or even saying a few syllables. Some parents even claim that the sound of the child's fussing tells them whether the child needs to be changed or fed. A child's needs are really quite basic and easy to understand. He or she wants to be fed, clothed, <u>cleansed</u>, and loved. Only the most <u>pitiless</u> adults would let a child cry for any length of time without trying to make the child clean, comfortable, and happy.

The first year of life is perhaps the most eventful in a person's life. He or she is helpless at birth, unable to control bladder or <u>bowels</u>, and totally dependent on others for survival. Within one year, the child learns to communicate needs, wants, and affection. By age one, a child can crawl on hands and knees and walk around furniture by holding on. He or she may even be able to walk alone.

How can an adult keep a one-year-old safe? One way is to set up a play area with a <u>barricade</u> of some kind so the child cannot leave the area. Some people think a nice, thick <u>Oriental</u> rug is a perfect floor covering for a child's play area because of the intricate patterns that tend to hide stains. Other people prefer bright, cheerful colors for children's play areas.

A <u>rendezvous</u> or meeting with other children is not a high priority for one-year-olds. At age one, they still prefer the company of familiar adults to whom they can communicate feelings of affection and <u>intimacy</u>.

1. Underline the words that tell one of the <u>sayings</u> applied to children. What is one of your favorite old *sayings*?

2. Circle the word in a nearby sentence that means about the same as <u>cleansed</u>. Then, use *cleansed* in a sentence.

3. Underline the words that tell what a <u>pitiless</u> adult might do. Then, tell what *pitiless* means.

4. Circle the word that tells what a one-year-old cannot control, in addition to <u>bowels</u>. Then, use *bowels* in a sentence.

5. Underline the words that tell the purpose of a <u>barricade</u> around a play area. What kind of *barricade* might you use to keep a dog inside a yard?

6. Circle the words that tell something about the design in an <u>Oriental</u> rug. What is your favorite type of *Oriental* food?

7. Underline the word that means about the same as <u>rendezvous</u>. Then, tell about a recent *rendezvous* you had.

8. Circle the word that means about the same as <u>intimacy</u>. Then, use *intimacy* in a sentence.

"The Lady in the Looking Glass" by Virginia Woolf
"The First Year of My Life" by Muriel Spark
Reading Warm-up B

Read the following passage. Pay special attention to the underlined words. Then, read it again, and complete the activities. Use a separate sheet of paper for your written answers.

Many people who are looking for some kind of escape from their busy and <u>hectic</u> lives turn to gardening as a hobby. For some of these people, tending to their roses is one of the most relaxing times of their day. Your gardening schedule can be somewhat <u>flexible</u>, for roses are not exactly delicate plants. They are hardy and easy to care for. However, to be a successful rose gardener, you must have <u>comprehension</u> and understanding of a few basic guidelines:

1. Select varieties that will grow well in your climate.
2. Buy the best-quality plants that are available.
3. Plant them properly, in suitable locations.
4. Take care of their basic needs of water, nutrients, pest control, and pruning.
5. Provide winter protection if necessary.

For the beginning gardener, the great variety of roses comes as a pleasant surprise. You can choose from a rainbow of colors, ranging from the darkest of purples and reds to the palest of pinks and yellows. You might even choose from whites with the <u>subtlest</u>, barely noticeable differences in their shades. You can choose plants that produce large or small flowers, many or few flowers, long-stemmed or short-stemmed flowers. The choices are so numerous as to seem almost <u>infinite</u>. For the gardener who wants to be assured of high quality when buying roses, the American Rose Society offers guarantees of <u>authenticity</u> for certain varieties.

The serious gardener might even develop a new variety of rose—some <u>exquisite</u> specimen, extremely beautiful and highly desirable. In doing this, such a gardener could even achieve a kind of <u>immortality</u>, being remembered forever for this new rose. Imagine having a rose named after yourself! What kind of rose would you design?

1. Underline the word that means about the same as <u>hectic</u>. Then, tell what you do to relax after a *hectic* day.

2. Circle the words that tell what can be somewhat <u>flexible</u>. Then, explain why a *flexible* schedule is easier to live with than a rigid schedule.

3. Underline the word that means about the same as <u>comprehension</u>. Then, describe one way to study that aids in *comprehension*.

4. Circle the words that mean about the same as <u>subtlest</u>. Then, use *subtlest* in a sentence.

5. Underline the words that tell why the choices seem almost <u>infinite</u>. Define *infinite*.

6. Underline the words that tell what a person wants when seeking a guarantee of <u>authenticity</u>. If you doubted the *authenticity* of a signature, how might you check it?

7. Circle the words that mean about the same as <u>exquisite</u>. Name a piece of jewelry that you think is *exquisite*.

8. Circle the word that tells how long a being who has <u>immortality</u> would live. Use *immortality* in a sentence.

"The Lady in the Looking Glass: A Reflection" by Virginia Woolf
"The First Year of My Life" by Muriel Spark
Literary Analysis: Point of View: Modern Experiments

Point of view is the perspective from which a writer tells a story. Many writers, including Woolf and Spark, have experimented with point of view to reflect the state of modern life. Woolf uses **stream-of-consciousness narration,** which attempts to convey the random flow of thoughts in a character's mind. Spark experiments with the **omniscient narrator,** who knows every character's thoughts. Spark's narrator displays omniscience in an extreme sense—she knows everything that is going on everywhere in the world.

DIRECTIONS: *Write your answers to the following questions.*

1. Identify a stream-of-consciousness passage in Woolf's story. Explain what elements of stream of consciousness it demonstrates.

_____

_____

_____

2. Does the narrator in "The Lady in the Looking Glass" convey reliable information about Isabella? Why or why not?

_____

_____

_____

3. Why might Woolf have chosen this type of narrator?

_____

_____

_____

4. How is the narrator of "The First Year of My Life" unusual?

_____

_____

5. How does Spark's omniscient narrator affect her story's tone?

_____

_____

6. Why might Spark have chosen this type of narrator?

_____

_____

_____

"The Lady in the Looking Glass: A Reflection" by Virginia Woolf
"The First Year of My Life" by Muriel Spark
Reading Strategy: Question

When reading experimental works, like those of Virginia Woolf and Muriel Spark, you must continually ask **questions** to find your way through each story and determine its meaning. Two areas of focus are *who* is narrating and *why* the narrator emphasizes an incident. For example, as you begin "The Lady in the Looking Glass," you must ask who the narrator is. Questioning and suggesting possible answers can help you determine the story's meaning.

DIRECTIONS: *Write a question and answer for each of the following passages.*

"The Lady in the Looking Glass: A Reflection"

1. As for facts, it was a fact that she was a spinster; that she was rich; that she had bought this house and collected with her own hands . . . the rugs, the chairs, the cabinets, which now lived their nocturnal life before one's eyes. Sometimes it seemed as if they knew more about her than we, who sat on them, wrote at them, and trod on them so carefully, were allowed to know.

    Question: _____

    Answer: _____

2. At last there she was, in the hall. She stopped dead. She stood by the table. She stood perfectly still. At once the looking glass began to pour over her a light that seemed to fix her; that seemed like some acid to bite off the unessential and superficial and to leave only the truth. It was an enthralling spectacle.

    Question: _____

    Answer: _____

"The First Year of My Life"

3. I wailed for my feed. . . . They rocked the cradle. I never heard a sillier song. Over in Berlin and Vienna the people were starving, freezing, striking, rioting and yelling in the streets. In London everyone was bustling to work and muttering that it was time the whole . . . business was over.

    Question: _____

    Answer: _____

4. . . . occasionally I beamed over to the House of Commons which made me drop off gently to sleep. Generally, I preferred the Western Front where one got the true state of affairs. It was essential to know the worst, blood and explosions and all, for one had to be prepared, as the boy scouts said.

    Question: _____

    Answer: _____

"The Lady in the Looking Glass: A Reflection" by Virginia Woolf
"The First Year of My Life" by Muriel Spark
Vocabulary Builder

Using the Prefix *trans-*

A. DIRECTIONS: *Knowing that* trans- *means "through" or "across," use the following words to complete the sentences.*

transatlantic   translucent   transom   transmutation

1. The glass panel is _____, allowing light to shine through it.

2. Opening the _____ above the door allowed the breeze to pass through.

3. The scientific experiment caused a _____ of the chemical substance.

4. During World War I, how many days did a _____ crossing require?

Using the Word List

suffused	transient	upbraidings	evanescence
reticent	omniscient	authenticity	discerned

B. DIRECTIONS: *Match each word in the left column with its definition in the right column. Write the letter of the definition on the line next to the word it defines.*

___ 1. suffused
___ 2. transient
___ 3. upbraidings
___ 4. evanescence
___ 5. reticent
___ 6. omniscient
___ 7. authenticity
___ 8. discerned

A. temporary; passing through quickly
B. gradual disappearance, especially from sight
C. silent; reserved
D. recognized as separate or different
E. filled
F. quality or state of being genuine
G. stern words of disapproval for an action
H. having infinite knowledge; knowing all things

Name _____ Date _____

"The Lady in the Looking Glass: A Reflection" by Virginia Woolf
"The First Year of My Life" by Muriel Spark

Grammar and Style: Subject-Verb Agreement in Inverted Sentences

In inverted sentences, which often begin with *there* or *here*, the verb precedes the subject. However, the verb must still agree in number with its subject. Look at the following sentence from "The First Year of My Life":

There *were* those black-dressed people, females of the species to which I appeared to belong. . . .

The verb *were* agrees with the plural subject *people*, not with *There*.

A. PRACTICE: *Underline the subject or subjects of each sentence, and circle the verb that agrees with your choice.*

1. Here *(is, are)* a letter and an invitation delivered by the postman.

2. There *(was, were)* a suggestion of depth and intelligence in the occupant's room.

3. In the end, there *(is, are)* no interesting thoughts in Isabella's brain.

4. There *(was, were)* many soldiers scarred and killed by poisonous gas during the war.

5. In this anthology *(is, are)* poems by Wilfred Owen and Alan Seegar.

6. Here *(is, are)* an interesting theory on infant development.

B. Writing Application: *Write a paragraph describing the first birthday party you can recall, either your own or someone else's. Use at least two inverted sentences. Make sure to use the correct subject-verb agreement in your inverted sentences.*

_____

_____

_____

_____

_____

_____

_____

_____

_____

_____

_____

"The Lady in the Looking Glass: A Reflection" by Virginia Woolf
"The First Year of My Life" by Muriel Spark
Support for Writing

Review "The Lady in the Looking Glass." List details about Isabella that tell about the "real" woman. Then, list details about the Isabella seen through the looking glass. Based on a comparison of the two sets of details, make a judgment about Woolf's ideas about knowing others, and write a response below.

Inference from "Mirror" View	Evidence

Inference about "Real" View	Evidence

Your response: _____

_____

_____

_____

On a separate page, use your response to help you write a topic sentence for your essay on a literary theme. Use information from the charts to explain and support your ideas.

"The Lady in the Looking Glass: A Reflection" by Virginia Woolf
"The First Year of My Life" by Muriel Spark
Support for Extend Your Learning

Research and Technology

Do research on Freud's technique of free association and Woolf's technique of stream-of-consciousness. Enter the information in the chart. Use the details in your **report on cultural trends.**

Freud's Techniques	Woolf's Techniques

Listening and Speaking

Use the Venn diagram to compare the tone and mood in Seeger's poems with those in Owen's poems. List ways they are different in the left and right parts of the circles. List ways they are similar where the circles overlap. Use the details for your discussion on how the poems compare to the tone and mood of Spark's story.

"Tone and Mood in Seeger's Poems"   **"Tone and Mood in Owen's Poems"**

Name _____ Date _____

"The Lady in the Looking Glass: A Reflection" by Virginia Woolf
"The First Year of My Life" by Muriel Spark
Enrichment: Science

Mirrors

In "The Lady in the Looking Glass," the narrator describes the reflections she sees in a looking glass, or mirror. Unlike contemporary glass objects, the first mirrors, used in ancient Greece and Rome and in Europe during the Middle Ages, were convex disks of polished silver, bronze, or tin. By the late 1300s, mirrors consisted of a flat piece of glass backed with a thin sheet of reflecting metal. During the Renaissance, this mirror-making technique was refined. However, mirrors were still very expensive, and only the wealthiest people used them as household objects. Not until the seventeenth century did mirrors come into wider use as decorations. In 1835, a chemical innovation allowed manufacturers to coat the back of a sheet of glass with metallic silver. Contemporary methods of mirror making are refinements on this same technique. When light hits the glass surface of a mirror, it is reflected. The smoother the mirror's surface, the better the reflection.

DIRECTIONS: *Write your answers to the following questions.*

1. What quality reflection might you have seen in a mirror made in ancient Greece? Explain.

   _____

   _____

2. What advances in mirror making have improved the quality of reflected images?

   _____

   _____

3. Is an image reflected in a mirror real or an illusion? Explain.

   _____

   _____

4. What are the literal and figurative functions of the mirror in "The Lady in the Looking Glass"?

   _____

   _____

5. Why is a mirror a fitting metaphor in Woolf's story?

   _____

   _____

   _____

   _____

   _____

"The Lady in the Looking Glass: A Reflection" by Virginia Woolf
"The First Year of My Life" by Muriel Spark
Selection Test A

Critical Reading *Identify the letter of the choice that best answers the question.*

____ 1. What question might you ask after reading that people should not hang looking glasses (mirrors) "any more than they should leave open . . . letters confessing some hideous crime" in "The Lady in the Looking Glass"?
A. How do looking glasses used in crimes?
B. What kinds of looking glasses are most dangerous?
C. Where does the narrator see a looking glass?
D. What is wrong with hanging looking glasses?

____ 2. Which is mostly missing from "The Lady in the Looking Glass" because it is a stream-of-consciousness narrative?
A. a narrator
B. a plot
C. a conflict
D. a description

____ 3. In "The Lady in the Looking Glass," what kinds of letters are delivered to Isabella?
A. bills
B. love letters
C. letters from faraway friends
D. invitations to parties

____ 4. What does the narrator learn by looking into the looking glass in "The Lady in the Looking Glass"?
A. where Isabella keeps her private letters
B. who Isabella's secret lover is
C. how old Isabella is and how empty her life is
D. why Isabella takes special care of her garden

____ 5. What is the main idea of "The Lady in the Looking Glass"?
A. People are not what they seem.
B. No one cares about older people.
C. Some people like living alone.
D. Looking glasses tell the truth.

____ 6. How does the reader know that "The First Year of My Life" uses an omniscient narrator?
   A. The baby was born on a Friday.
   B. The baby is cared for by women.
   C. The baby has an older brother.
   D. The baby is aware of world events.

____ 7. In "The First Year of My Life," what did people think was most unusual about the narrator?
   A. She cried constantly.
   B. She walked at an early age.
   C. She did not laugh.
   D. She did not speak.

____ 8. In "The First Year of My Life," what can you conclude from the adults' admiration of the narrator's brother as he marches with a toy rifle?
   A. They strongly disapprove of all war.
   B. They are frightened by it.
   C. They are numbed by the many deaths.
   D. They think it is heroic and exciting.

____ 9. What question would a reader ask about why the baby bangs a spoon on the table after hearing the number of dead and wounded in the war in "The First Year of My Life"?
   A. What were the exact numbers of people who died or were wounded?
   B. Does her banging the spoon connect to the author's opinion of war?
   C. Why is the baby still unable to properly use a spoon?
   D. How do adults put up with the baby's bad manners during wartime?

____ 10. What can you conclude about why the narrator smiles at the end of the story?
   A. She thinks the absurdity of the war is amusing.
   B. She wants to reward her family for the birthday cake.
   C. She thinks the glowing candle and cake are lovely.
   D. She has lost her ability to understand the world.

____ 11. What is the effect of combining a baby's autobiography with events of World War I?
   A. to say that war is insignificant compared to the lives of children
   B. to demonstrate that babies really do know everything
   C. to contrast the peace of a baby's life with the horrors of war
   D. to emphasize that babies are aware of events around them

Vocabulary and Grammar

____ 12. Which word best replaces *authenticity* in this sentence: "The *authenticity* of my driver's license has been checked"?
A. scolding
B. knowledge
C. ability
D. genuineness

____ 13. Which of the following is an inverted sentence in which the verb comes before the noun?
A. "The room that day was full of such shy creatures."
B. "In each of these cabinets were many little drawers."
C. "Suddenly these reflections were ended violently"
D. "One must refuse to be put off any longer."

Essay

14. During most of the "The Lady in the Looking Glass," the narrator describes Isabella as interesting with many secrets, exciting experiences, and aspects to her character. Then, at the end of the story, she suddenly says that Isabella was "perfectly empty." Which is a truer description of Isabella? State your opinion in an essay, and give evidence from the story to support it.

15. Choose either "The Lady in the Looking Glass" by Virginia Woolf or "The First Year of My Life" by Muriel Spark. In an essay, discuss how the author experimented with point of view. Did the author use stream-of-consciousness to tell her story? Did she use an omniscient narrator? Do you think the experiment was successful? Why or why not? Give evidence from the story to support your responses.

"The Lady in the Looking Glass: A Reflection" by Virginia Woolf
"The First Year of My Life" by Muriel Spark
Selection Test B

Critical Reading *Identify the letter of the choice that best completes the statement or answers the question.*

_____ 1. Virginia Woolf most likely wrote "The Lady in the Looking Glass" to
   A. re-create the sensation of a mental breakdown.
   B. examine the philosophical issue of reality.
   C. teach a lesson about upper-middle-class life.
   D. indulge her passion for vivid description.

_____ 2. What question about Woolf's narrator is invited by this passage?
   The house was empty, and one felt, since one was the only person in the drawing room, like one of those naturalists who, covered with grass and leaves, lie watching the shyest animals . . .
   A. Where is the narrator?
   B. Is the narrator a naturalist?
   C. Who is the narrator?
   D. What kind of animals is the narrator watching?

_____ 3. Woolf stylistically re-creates the thought process of the narrator by
   A. allowing ideas to accumulate into long paragraphs.
   B. jumping erratically from subject to subject.
   C. producing a rhythmic, dreamlike effect.
   D. using informal grammatical constructions.

_____ 4. What is Woolf's attitude toward factual information about Isabella?
   A. She finds the facts meaningless.
   B. She ridicules the facts as conventional.
   C. She is overwhelmed by the variety of facts.
   D. She deliberatly ignores the facts.

_____ 5. One of the most striking aspects of a stream-of-consciousness narrative is the relative absence of
   A. conflict.
   B. motivation.
   C. tone.
   D. plot.

_____ 6. What is the theme of "The Lady in the Looking Glass"?
   A. Familiarity breeds contempt.
   B. It is impossible to really know and understand another person.
   C. Money can't buy happiness.
   D. Imagination is as important as information the senses obtain.

_____ 7. Which quotation from "The First Year of My Life" reveals that the story has an omni-scient narrator?
   A. "Babies, in their waking hours, know everything that is going on everywhere in the world . . ."
   B. "There were those black-dressed people, females of the species to which I appeared to belong, saying they had lost their sons."
   C. "I woke and tuned into Bernard Shaw who was telling someone to shut up."
   D. "My mother's brother, dressed in his uniform, came coughing."

_____ 8. The predominant tone of "The First Year of My Life" is
   A. pessimistic.
   B. bemused.
   C. anxious.
   D. scornful.

_____ 9. What question is invited by the following passage from "The First Year of My Life"?
   Now the sentries used bodies for barricades and the fighting men were unhealthy from the start. I checked my toes and fingers, knowing I was going to need them.
   A. How does the narrator know these details about the war?
   B. What role does the narrator expect to play in world affairs?
   C. Why were the fighting men unhealthy?
   D. What does the narrator think of the war?

_____ 10. Why does Spark interweave the narration of her development with the events of World War I?
   A. to contrast a baby's healthy development with the war's destruction
   B. to distract from the atrocities of war
   C. to balance the story
   D. to condemn Britain's role in the war

_____ 11. In the "First Year of My Life," what is the significance of the narrator's smile at the end of the story?
   A. She finally develops a sense of humor.
   B. She finds men more amusing than women.
   C. She is overcome by the absurdity of war.
   D. She loses her ability to tune in to everything in the world.

Vocabulary and Grammar

_____ 12. By peering at Isabella's image in the looking glass, the narrator _____ the woman's true character.
   A. discerned
   B. omniscient
   C. authenticity
   D. suffused

____ 13. A baby who never smiles will probably become a (an) _____ child.
   A. suffused
   B. transient
   C. omniscient
   D. reticent

____ 14. Which sentence contains correct subject-verb agreement?
   A. From the hallway are sighs and whispers of passersby.
   B. There were the sound of shy animals stepping cautiously into the room.
   C. Here is the shadows of leaves cast by light.
   D. In the garden is traveler's joy and convolvulus.

____ 15. The narrator recalled that on her first birthday, there _____ a birthday cake with one candle.
   A. is
   B. was
   C. are
   D. were

Essay

16. What role do imagination and reality play in these stories by Woolf and Spark? In an essay, explain how each writer views imagination and reality and how the contrasting qualities are presented in their stories. Use examples from the stories to support your main ideas.

17. Woolf and Spark experiment with point of view. How successful are these experiments? In an essay, describe and analyze each writer's technique. Determine what effect each writer achieves and how point of view affects the story's meaning.

Vocabulary Warm-up Word Lists

Study these words from the selections. Then, complete the activities that follow.

Word List A

colleagues [KAHL eegz] *n.* fellow workers in a profession or organization
Jerry's <u>colleagues</u> all advised him not to ask for a raise.

commiseration [kuh miz uh RAY shuhn] *n.* expression of sympathy
After Bonnie's words of <u>commiseration</u>, Jane felt better.

distinguished [dis TING wisht] *adj.* dignified
In his tuxedo, Harry looked quite <u>distinguished</u>.

extraordinarily [eks truh AWR duh ner uh lee] *adv.* remarkably
Jesse is <u>extraordinarily</u> strong for a boy his age.

furnishings [FER nish ingz] *n.* furniture or appliances, as for a room
Sam's new <u>furnishings</u> were all very modern and sleek.

inevitably [in EV uh tuh blee] *adv.* unavoidably; certainly
If Tammy keeps spending so recklessly, she will <u>inevitably</u> go into debt.

moderately [MAHD uhr it lee] *adv.* not extremely or excessively
If you eat <u>moderately</u> and exercise regularly, you can control your weight.

noiselessly [NOYZ lis lee] *adv.* silently; quietly
The cat <u>noiselessly</u> stalked the mouse.

Word List B

appeased [uh PEEZD] *v.* satisfied; gave in to demands
The simple meal <u>appeased</u> the child's hunger.

assertion [uh SER shuhn] *n.* a firm statement; claim
Pam's <u>assertion</u> that she was first in line was rudely disregarded.

exclamations [eks kluh MAY shuhnz] *n.* sudden outcries; forceful words
Diane's <u>exclamations</u> of delight over her gifts sounded false and insincere.

frenzy [FREN zee] *n.* a wild fit
Brian finished the gardening in a <u>frenzy</u> of activity.

inspiration [in spuh RAY shuhn] *n.* a sudden good idea or impulse.
Donald's great <u>inspiration</u> was to decorate the tables with flower petals.

potential [puh TEN shuhl] *adj.* possible, but not yet actual
Darla regarded each new person she met as a <u>potential</u> friend.

shortage [SHAWR tij] *n.* a lack in the amount needed
The cash register has a <u>shortage</u> of pennies.

successive [suhk SES iv] *adj.* following in order
Our win tonight represents our fifth <u>successive</u> victory.

Name _____ Date _____

"The Rocking-Horse Winner" by D. H. Lawrence
"A Shocking Accident" by Graham Greene
Vocabulary Warm-up Exercises

Exercise A *Fill in each blank in the paragraph below using each word from Wordlist A only once.*

Jo was looking for new [1] _____ for her office. She tried to tiptoe through the furniture store as [2] _____ as possible, because she didn't want to attract the salesperson's attention. Her budget was tight and so she was interested only in [3] _____ priced pieces, but she knew that, without fail, the salesperson would [4] _____ try to steer her toward more expensive items. She wished she could find a desk that would impress her [5] _____ at work when they passed her office. She kept looking at elegant, [6] _____ pieces, which of course were all too costly for her. Then she spotted exactly what she wanted—an [7] _____ well-designed desk, both beautiful and practical, on sale, just within her price range. She couldn't believe her eyes. When the salesperson came over, however, she noticed the kind expression of [8] _____ on his face. "I'm sorry, miss," he said sympathetically. "That piece has already been sold."

Exercise B *Write a complete sentence to answer each question. For each item, use a word from Word List B to replace each underlined word without changing its meaning.*

1. What underlined declaration might you make if someone got credit for something you did?
   _____

2. Describe what a maple tree might look like in the fall and in each following season.
   _____

3. How would a dog react to an insufficiency of food in its bowl?
   _____

4. What is a possible problem that a family might face at an amusement park?
   _____

5. Name one idea you have for an interesting party theme.
   _____

6. What outcries might you hear if you brought a snake into the kitchen?
   _____

7. Describe a status symbol that led to a fit of buying among your friends.
   _____

8. What would happen if you satisfied every demand a child made?
   _____

"The Rocking-Horse Winner" by D. H. Lawrence
"A Shocking Accident" by Graham Greene
Reading Warm-up A

Read the following passage. Pay special attention to the underlined words. Then, read it again, and complete the activities. Use a separate sheet of paper for your written answers.

Mr. Appleby, better known as "Grandpa" to young William Appleby, was on a mission. He had already provided most of the underlined furnishings for William's bedroom, such as a "big boy" bed and a dresser. Now, he was looking for the perfect rocking horse. A well-groomed, distinguished gentleman of eighty, Mr. Appleby remembered fondly the beautifully carved rocking horse he had had as a child. He hoped to find something like it for William, an extraordinarily gifted young boy who deserved only the best.

As Mr. Appleby entered the finest children's store in town, he was approached by a young saleswoman. She had just broken away from a few of her colleagues who appeared to be having a meeting in the center of the floor. "How may I help you?" she asked.

"I'm looking for a very special rocking horse," Mr. Appleby said. "It's a gift for my grandson. That's why it has to be wonderful. I want a traditional wooden horse. None of those plastic things."

"Well, follow me, sir," she said. They walked into an area filled with rocking horses. Inevitably, each was plastic. All were battery-powered, and every one had a gimmick of some kind. Some were able to make noises that sounded moderately realistic, as if an actual horse's neigh had been badly recorded. Mr. Appleby sighed, and the salesperson smiled in commiseration. She sympathized with the difficulty of finding a traditional horse. Then, a gorgeous wooden horse caught Mr. Appleby's eye. It had no batteries. It did not snort or neigh. It rocked noiselessly and naturally when he pushed it. Best of all, it looked very much like the one Mr. Appleby had had as a child. "I'll take it," he said. Then he added, "Actually, I'd like two." The saleswoman smiled.

1. Circle some examples of underlined furnishings. Define *furnishings*.

2. Underline the phrase that is a sign that Mr. Appleby looks underlined distinguished. Then, use *distinguished* in a sentence.

3. Circle the phrase that tells what Mr. Appleby thinks his extraordinarily gifted grandson deserves. Name an animal that jumps *extraordinarily* high.

4. Underline the words that tell what the saleswoman's colleagues were doing.

5. Circle the words in these sentences that reinforce the meaning of the word inevitably. Name one thing that will *inevitably* happen today.

6. Underline the words that explain what moderately realistic means. Where do you buy *moderately* priced clothing?

7. Circle the words that suggest the reason for the woman's commiseration. Describe a time that *commiseration* with a friend comforted you.

8. Circle the words that contrast with noiselessly. Describe something that you do *noiselessly*.

"The Rocking-Horse Winer" by D. H. Lawrence
"A Shocking Accident" by Graham Greene
Reading Warm-up B

Read the following passage. Pay special attention to the underlined words. Then, read it again, and complete the activities. Use a separate sheet of paper for your written answers.

While some people would never consider taking a pig for a pet, others might find the idea a strange and wonderful <u>inspiration</u>. When we talk about pet pigs, we are referring to a special breed called Vietnamese pot-bellied pigs. Although the breed has been available in the United States only since 1985, there is no <u>shortage</u> of these animals today. When breeders realized the <u>potential</u> profit that could be made, they bred many <u>successive</u> generations of the animal. For a while, the popularity of this exotic pet led to almost a buying <u>frenzy</u>, although this craze has died down somewhat in recent years. Still, if you talk to a fan of pot-bellied pigs, you are likely to hear emotional <u>exclamations</u> about what wonderful pets they make.

Compared to its cousin, the farm hog, which can weigh more than 1,000 pounds, the pot-bellied pig is relatively quite small. It reaches an average weight of 120 to 150 pounds. Its body is very compact and solid, so that a 100-pound pig looks no larger than a medium-sized dog of 35 or 40 pounds—until you try to lift it! Like dogs, pigs are quite trainable. They can be house trained and leash trained, and they can even learn a few tricks. They are intelligent, curious, and playful, and so require frequent stimulation. If ignored or mistreated, they will demonstrate <u>assertion</u> to the point of aggression, and this behavior can become a problem to the pet owner. Like most creatures, pigs respond well to affection and praise, and they do not respond well to physical punishment. Pigs have huge appetites, and their relentless demands for food must be <u>appeased</u> if you want to have a happy pet.

1. Underline the words that tell the idea that some people consider an <u>inspiration</u>. Describe a time you had a sudden *inspiration*.

2. Circle the words that tell what there is no <u>shortage</u> of today. Then, tell what *shortage* means.

3. Describe an idea of yours that you think could lead to <u>potential</u> profit.

4. How many <u>successive</u> generations in your family are represented by people who are still living?

5. Underline a word that means about the same as <u>frenzy</u>. Use *frenzy* in a sentence.

6. Underline the words that tell what kinds of <u>exclamations</u> you might hear from a fan of pot-bellied pigs. What *exclamations* would you expect to hear if you gave a friend a thoughtful gift?

7. Circle the word that indicates a more forceful kind of <u>assertion</u>. If someone pushed his or her way in front of you on a line, what *assertion* would you be likely to make?

8. Circle the phrase that tells what must be <u>appeased</u> in order for the pig to be happy. What does *appeased* mean?

"The Rocking-Horse Winner" by D. H. Lawrence
"A Shocking Accident" by Graham Greene
Literary Analysis: Theme and Symbol

In most short stories, a **theme** conveys a main idea or message about life to the reader. Writers often use **symbols** to enhance their themes. A symbol is a person or object that represents an idea or a connection point for several ideas. Lawrence uses the rocking horse as a symbol with multiple meanings. Greene, in "A Shocking Accident," strengthens his theme by using the pig as a symbol for what is out of place.

DIRECTIONS: *Write your answers to the following questions.*

1. What is the literal meaning of the rocking horse in "The Rocking-Horse Winner"?

_____

_____

_____

2. What other meanings might the rocking horse have in Lawrence's story? In other words, what does the rocking horse symbolize?

_____

_____

_____

3. How does the symbol of the rocking horse help you define the theme of "The Rocking-Horse Winner"?

_____

_____

_____

4. How does the pig serve as a symbol in "A Shocking Accident"?

_____

_____

_____

"The Rocking-Horse Winner" by D. H. Lawrence
"A Shocking Accident" by Graham Greene
Reading Strategy: Identify With a Character

When you **identify with a character,** or put yourself in that character's place, you can better understand his or her thoughts, feelings, problems, or motivations. Identifying with a character can lead you to understand a writer's purpose and a literary work's overall theme. For example, identifying with Paul when he first discusses his winners with Uncle Oscar means putting yourself in the boy's situation. You imagine that Paul is proud of his luck, careful not to reveal too much, and concerned that an adult might disapprove of his actions. Empathizing with Paul makes it easier to understand his actions.

DIRECTIONS: *For each situation described, identify the character's thoughts, feelings, problems, or motivations. Then state how you would respond.*

"The Rocking-Horse Winner"

1. Paul proclaims to his mother that he is lucky, but she doesn't believe him.

   _____

   _____

   _____

2. After Paul's mother receives the five thousand pounds, Paul hears the house screaming for even more money.

   _____

   _____

   _____

"A Shocking Accident"

3. After his classmates learn the details of his father's death, Jerome is called Pig.

   _____

   _____

   _____

4. Jerome delays telling Sally the story of his father's death.

   _____

   _____

   _____

"**The Rocking-Horse Winner**" by D. H. Lawrence
"**A Shocking Accident**" by Graham Greene
Vocabulary Builder

Using the Prefix *ob-*

A. DIRECTIONS: *Replace the italicized word or words with the word* object, obscures, *or* obstacles.

1. During a solar eclipse, a celestial body *blocks* our view of the sun.
2. I *firmly am opposed* to your interpretation of the scientific findings.
3. We must remove any *items that block the way* before we can proceed.

Using the Word List

discreet	brazening	careered	obstinately	uncanny
remonstrated	apprehension	embarked	intrinsically	

B. DIRECTIONS: *For each numbered word, choose the word or phrase that is the most similar in meaning. Circle the letter of your choice.*

1. discreet
   A. showing good judgment
   B. behaving wildly
   C. showing favor
   D. acting mysteriously

2. brazening
   A. acting courageously
   B. thinking innovatively
   C. daring shamelessly
   D. accepting willingly

3. careered
   A. skidded
   B. dashed
   C. jumped
   D. glided

4. obstinately
   A. regretfully
   B. admittedly
   C. stubbornly
   D. happily

5. uncanny
   A. unique
   B. feverish
   C. unfamiliar
   D. eerie

6. remonstrated
   A. reverted
   B. exemplified
   C. protested
   D. approved

7. apprehension
   A. reluctance
   B. misgiving
   C. refusal
   D. avoidance

8. embarked
   A. made a start
   B. planned a party
   C. left the scene
   D. greeted a host

9. intrinsically
   A. thoroughly
   B. quickly
   C. superficially
   D. innately

"The Rocking-Horse Winner" by D. H. Lawrence
"A Shocking Accident" by Graham Greene

Grammar and Style: Subjunctive Mood

The **subjunctive mood** of a verb is used to state a wish or condition contrary to fact. It is usually expressed with the verb *were*. Notice the use of the subjunctive mood in the following sentence from "The Rocking-Horse Winner":

"I needn't worry, mother, if I *were* you."

The subjunctive is also used in *that* clauses of recommendation, command, or demand. Used with third-person singular subjects, the subjunctive form is the present form of the verb without *s*. For the verb *to be*, the present subjunctive form is *be* and the past is *were*.

Recommendation: It is suggested that Paul *go* to the seaside.

Demand: His mother insisted that the money *be* advanced all at once.

A. PRACTICE: *Circle the correct verb in parentheses for each of the following sentences.*

1. When he was on his rocking horse, Paul looked as if he (*was*, *were*) possessed.

2. Initially, Oscar recommended that Paul (*is*, *be*) cautious with his betting.

3. Paul wished that the house (*was*, *were*) satisfied.

4. The housemaster's shoulders shook as if he (*was*, *were*) laughing.

5. Jerome wishes that his father (*were*, *be*) remembered for his writing, not his bizarre death.

6. It is important to Jerome that Sally (*respond*, *responds*) appropriately to the story.

B. Writing Application: *Write a brief paragraph describing a dream, wish, or goal you have. Use the subjunctive mood at least twice in your description.*

_____

_____

_____

_____

_____

_____

_____

_____

_____

_____

Name _____ Date _____

"The Rocking-Horse Winner" by D. H. Lawrence
"A Shocking Accident" by Graham Greene
Support for Writing

Collect ideas for your product description by sketching your idea for a new toy in the box below. Then, jot notes about its function, size, sounds, color, and moving parts in the surrounding circles.

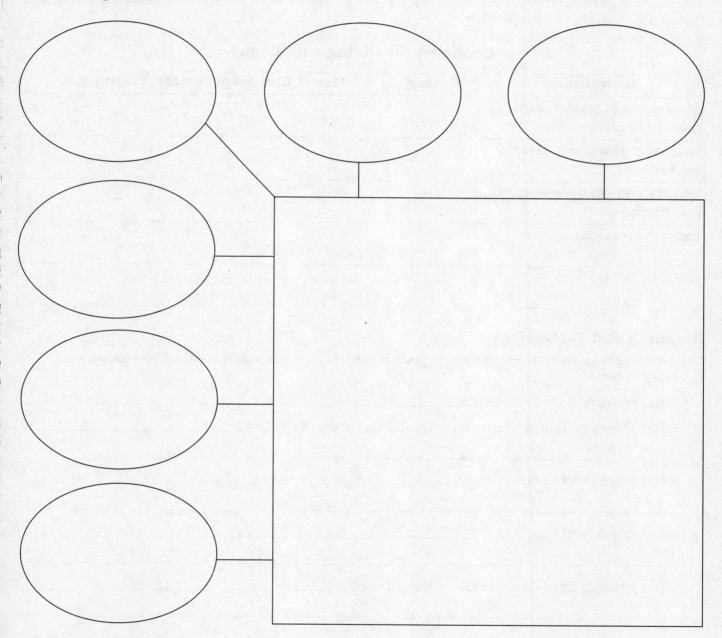

Use the information you have gathered in the graphic organizer as you write your product description on a separate page. Use vivid verbs and adverbs to describe the toy.

"The Rocking-Horse Winner" by D. H. Lawrence
"A Shocking Accident" by Graham Greene
Support for Extend Your Learning

Listening and Speaking

Use the following checklist to prepare and rehearse your **soliloquy** as the character Jerome. Assess your performance by jotting down a score of from 1 to 5. Work on ways to improve those techniques you do not rate highly.

Checklist for Giving a Soliloquy

Techniques	Rating	How I Can Improve My Technique
Slow down or speed up my pace of reading		
Use hand gestures and facial expressions		
Use staging—movement and positioning		
Express emotions		
Create drama		

Research and Technology

Use these questions to help you focus your research for your **multimedia travelogue** about Greene's travels.

What country have I chosen? _____

What places or topics in this country did Greene write about? _____

_____

What places will I show? _____

_____

What music will I use? _____

_____

What reading from Graham Greene will I use? _____

_____

"The Rocking-Horse Winner" by D. H. Lawrence
"A Shocking Accident" by Graham Greene
Enrichment: The Greek Notion of Fate

The theme that one cannot escape fate, as expressed in "The Rocking-Horse Winner," has haunted human beings since antiquity. *Fate* often means "ruin or disaster that cannot be controlled or avoided." The ancient Greeks believed three goddesses determined the course of human life: Clotho (Spinner), who spins life's thread; Lachesis (Dispenser of Lots), who determines life's length; and Atropos (Inflexible), who cuts it off.

DIRECTIONS: *Write your answers to the following.*

1. What idea of life do the three Greek Fates symbolize? Explain.

   _____

   _____

2. Which character in "The Rocking-Horse Winner" echoes the Greek notion of fate? Provide an example from the story to support your opinion.

   _____

   _____

   _____

3. In "The Rocking-Horse Winner," what is Paul's fate at birth?

   _____

   _____

4. How does Paul attempt to avoid his fate?

   _____

   _____

5. How would the conflict that Paul faces in "The Rocking-Horse Winner" be expressed in light of the Greek notion of fate?

   _____

   _____

6. Does Paul's plan to make his own luck fit within the Greek notion of fate? Explain.

   _____

   _____

   _____

   _____

   _____

   _____

"The Rocking-Horse Winner" by D. H. Lawrence
"A Shocking Accident" by Graham Greene
Selection Test A

Critical Reading *Identify the letter of the choice that best answers the question.*

____ 1. In "The Rocking-Horse Winner," what does Paul keep hearing the house whisper?
    A. "Your mother does not love you!"
    B. "Your luck will change!"
    C. "There must be more money!"
    D. "You must leave while you can!"

____ 2. If you were Paul in "The Rocking-Horse Winner," how would the house's whisperings make you feel?
    A. anxious
    B. joyful
    C. confused
    D. surprised

____ 3. Why does Paul bet on horse races in "The Rocking-Horse Winner"?
    A. because he cannot help it
    B. to get money to help his mother
    C. to pay for his schooling at Eton
    D. to pay his father's debts

____ 4. How does Paul pick winning horses in "The Rocking-Horse Winner"?
    A. He picks the name of the winning horse in the newspaper.
    B. He follows Bassett's choices for winning horses.
    C. He dreams the name of the winning horse.
    D. He discovers the name of the horse while on his rocking horse.

____ 5. What does horse-racing symbolize in "The Rocking-Horse Winner"?
    A. family
    B. luck
    C. money
    D. childhood

____ 6. What is one of the themes of "The Rocking-Horse Winner"?
    A. how money changes people
    B. the need for friends
    C. how gambling ruins people
    D. the need to supervise children

____ 7. Why does Paul avoid telling the secret of his rocking horse in "The Rocking-Horse Winner"?
   A. He fears someone will take the rocking horse.
   B. He knows that no one will believe him.
   C. He fears that the horse will lose its magic.
   D. He has promised Bassett that he would not tell anyone.

____ 8. What is the "shocking accident" referred to in "A Shocking Accident"?
   A. Jerome's family has suddenly lost all its money.
   B. Jerome's father was killed in a gun fight in Naples.
   C. Jerome's parents died in a car accident.
   D. Jerome's father died when a pig fell on him.

____ 9. How would you feel toward Jerome's father if you were Jerome in "A Shocking Accident"?
   A. angry
   B. uncaring
   C. adoring
   D. fearful

____ 10. How do most people react to the story of the death of Jerome's father in "A Shocking Accident"?
   A. They laugh.
   B. They weep.
   C. They understand.
   D. They are annoyed.

____ 11. If you were Jerome in "A Shocking Accident," why would you worry about how Sally will react when she hears how Jerome's father died?
   A. He thinks she will be ashamed of him.
   B. He knows she will think less of him when she hears.
   C. He assumes she will cry and feel sorry for him.
   D. He fears their relationship will end if she laughs.

____ 12. One of the themes of "A Shocking Accident" is that events are out of place. What symbol best supports this theme?
   A. Jerome's marriage
   B. the pig
   C. school
   D. the father's books

Vocabulary and Grammar

____ 13. Which word best replaces *obstinately* in this sentence: "The toddler *obstinately* refused to pick up her toys"?
  A. stubbornly
  B. fearfully
  C. happily
  D. pleasantly

____ 14. Which word *correctly* completes the subjunctive mood in this sentence: "Jerome worried that if people _____ to learn about his father, they would laugh"?
  A. was
  B. were
  C. are
  D. is

Essay

15. In the final line of "The Rocking-Horse Winner," Uncle Oscar tries to comfort his sister by saying that Paul is "best gone out of a life where he rides his rocking horse to find a winner." What does Uncle Oscar mean? Do you agree with him? Explain your answer, using examples from the story to support your explanation.

16. In "A Shocking Accident," Jerome is faced with a problem not of his making. In an essay, describe what happened and why it has become a problem for Jerome. Then, tell how you would feel about this shocking accident if you were Jerome and had to explain the situation to friends.

Name _____ Date _____

Selection Test B

Critical Reading *Identify the letter of the choice that best completes the statement or answers the question.*

____ 1. In "The Rocking-Horse Winner," how is Paul's attitude toward luck different from his mother's?
   A. He doesn't believe luck and money are related.
   B. He believes people can create their own luck.
   C. He blames other people for his bad luck.
   D. He relies on luck to make up for recklessness.

____ 2. In "The Rocking-Horse Winner," Paul starts betting on horse races because he
   A. succumbs to Bassett's urgings.
   B. listens to his rocking horse.
   C. hopes to relieve his mother's anxiety.
   D. inherits the family's weakness for gambling.

____ 3. The rocking horse in "The Rocking-Horse Winner" adds to the story's fairy-tale style because it
   A. is used as another character.
   B. ultimately causes Paul's death.
   C. brings Paul and his mother together.
   D. seems to have supernatural powers.

____ 4. In "The Rocking-Horse Winner," the character of Paul is portrayed as
   A. immoral beyond redemption.
   B. victimized by his parents' greed.
   C. spoiled and irresponsible.
   D. passive in the face of opportunity.

____ 5. In "The Rocking-Horse Winner," Paul doesn't reveal the secret of his rocking horse because he
   A. wants to preserve its special powers.
   B. is a deceitful child.
   C. fears ridicule.
   D. has been sworn to secrecy by Bassett.

____ 6. One of Lawrence's themes in "The Rocking-Horse Winner" is the
   A. ways that materialism can warp people psychologically.
   B. power of supernatural forces over people's lives.
   C. need children have for strict discipline.
   D. high cost of taking unnecessary risks.

_____ **7.** What is the "shocking accident" of Greene's story?
    A. A spy is shot by secret police.
    B. A pig falls on a man and kills him.
    C. An ostracized boy takes his revenge on his tormentors.
    D. An engaged couple dies in a car accident.

_____ **8.** In relation to "A Shocking Accident," what word best describes Jerome's attitude toward his father's memory?
    A. worshipful
    B. conflicted
    C. negative
    D. rejecting

_____ **9.** In "A Shocking Accident," why does it pain Jerome to hear his aunt tell strangers the story of his father's death?
    A. He is embarrassed by the story.
    B. He resents his aunt because his father favored her.
    C. He feels his aunt doesn't cherish his father's memory as he does.
    D. He wants to tell the story himself.

_____ **10.** Which symbol from "A Shocking Accident" best supports the theme that things are out of place?
    A. the school
    B. the album
    C. the pig
    D. Sally

_____ **11.** In reading "A Shocking Accident," a reader identifying with Jerome's dilemma about sharing his father's story with Sally would feel
    A. frustrated.
    B. ambivalent.
    C. amused.
    D. sad.

_____ **12.** Sally's question in "A Shocking Accident" about the pig is ironic because
    A. the same question that isolated Jerome from others forms a tighter bond between Jerome and Sally.
    B. no one knows for certain what became of the pig.
    C. she seems to care more about the pig than about Jerome's father.
    D. Jerome has pondered that question since his father's death.

Vocabulary and Grammar

_____ **13.** In "The Rocking-Horse Winner," Paul's ability to predict winning horses is _____.
    A. discreet
    B. brazening
    C. uncanny
    D. remonstrated

___ **14.** Despite his mother's objections, Paul _____ refused to stop riding the rocking horse.
   A. careered
   B. obstinately
   C. embarked
   D. intrinsically

___ **15.** "If you _____ me and I _____ you," said his mother, "I wonder what we *should* do!"
   A. was, was
   B. were, was
   C. was, were
   D. were, were

___ **16.** Jerome is not certain what he would do if Sally _____ to laugh at the story.
   A. is
   B. was
   C. were
   D. weren't

Essay

17. Both Paul in "The Rocking-Horse Winner" and Jerome in "A Shocking Accident" experience difficulties due to events beyond their control. What problems does each character face? What does he feel? As a reader, how do you identify with the character? Focusing on either Paul or Jerome, explore and answer these questions in an essay, incorporating appropriate details from the stories.

18. In "The Rocking-Horse Winner," symbolism enhances Lawrence's theme. What meaning or meanings does the symbol of the rocking horse have? What theme or themes does it reflect? In an essay, explain how Lawrence uses symbolism to convey theme. Support your ideas with evidence from the story.

Unit 6: A Time of Rapid Change
Benchmark Test 11

MULTIPLE CHOICE

Literary Analysis and Reading Skills

1. Which of the following is an example of a cultural conflict?
   A. a child wants to take on social responsibilities that he or she may be too young to handle
   B. an immigrant wants a child to follow old-country customs that the child wants to abandon
   C. a farm family battles to save its small farm from the company that is trying to buy it
   D. a college graduate struggles to come to a decision about which career path to follow

Read this speech. Then, answer the questions that follow.

(1) A hundred years ago today, Governor James Morris passed into law the Helping Hand Act to help the citizens of our state at a time of great need. (2) Flood had ravaged much of the region; lives had been devastated; homes and businesses had been destroyed. (3) The Helping Hand Act provided funds for food, water, temporary shelter, cleanup, and construction. (4) Today, our state is again facing great devastation. (5) People are losing higher-paying jobs in record numbers. (6) As governor of your state, I have therefore chosen to follow in the footsteps of James Morris, proposing a bill to deal with this crisis. (7) I call this bill the Second Helping. (8) I call on all good citizens of our state to give this bill their support, and I call on our state legislators to pass it.

2. What is the main point made in this speech?
   A. The state legislature is no longer the honorable body that it once was.
   B. The speaker cares for the citizens and hopes to be reelected.
   C. The state needs Second Helping today just as it needed the Helping Hand Act in the past.
   D. James Morris was a great governor of the past.

3. What is the occasion of this speech?
   A. the hundredth anniversary of passage of the Helping Hand Act
   B. the annual opening of the state legislature
   C. the need to persuade voters to reelect the governor
   D. a gathering of political supporters working on the governor's reelection

4. Which of these questions should a listener ask about how this speech might affect citizens?
   A. Why did the governor call the plan Second Helping?
   B. What is the role of the state legislature?
   C. When did James Morris serve as governor?
   D. How much of a tax increase does the governor's plan involve?

5. Which sentence uses parallel structure to make its ideas more powerful and memorable?
   A. sentence 1
   B. sentence 2
   C. sentence 4
   D. sentence 5

Name _____ Date _____

Read this short story. Then, answer the questions that follow.

When the British-Nigerian Petroleum Company sent a crew to Okike to hunt for oil, the people of Okike were thrilled about the boost it would give their economy. Then they saw that the crew planned to dig right across the path leading to their ancestral burying ground. An old villager came to John Drake, the head of the crew. "You must not dig there," he told Drake, "for that is the path on which our dead relatives leave this world and our new children come in.

"I will explain with a little story. This same path goes through the hospital grounds, and the villagers have always had the right of way. One year a new administrator came. He put up a fence to keep villagers from walking across the hospital grounds. There were three women in the hospital due to have babies. The babies did not come. No one could explain why they were late. Finally, many villagers tore down the fence and began walking the path again."

"And what happened next?" asked Drake.

"The babies were born soon afterwards," said the old man, "or so I am told—for I was one of them."

"All right," said Drake, respectfully. "We will bypass your path."

"Then you are welcome to begin," said the old man.

6. What is the central conflict of the story?
   A. traditional customs vs. modern commercial ways
   B. people who do not value wealth vs. people who do
   C. an older generation vs. a younger generation
   D. a known language vs. an unfamiliar language

7. Which of these plot devices does the story contain?
   A. stream of consciousness
   B. surprise ending
   C. multiple versions of the same events
   D. story within a story

8. Which statement best expresses the theme of the story?
   A. Human beings can take comfort from nature if they learn to appreciate its beauty.
   B. Birth and death are both key parts in the natural cycle of life.
   C. Modern life goes more smoothly when traditional beliefs and values are respected.
   D. The more things change, the more they stay the same.

Read this excerpt from a story. Then, answer the questions that follow.

Brenda had not seen her old home in some time but had heard that the new owner was having a lot of work done. Now she wheeled her chair down the road to see for herself. Oh, what a ridiculous gate stood at the foot of the drive! And the driveway had become a sweeping semicircle.

Her father had built this house, and now it was being turned into a pretentious mansion. And was that a pool house they were building? For a heated indoor monstrosity! Her thoughts were interrupted by the sight of a middle-aged man walking down the drive—the new owner, she supposed.

"Hello," Brenda said. "I was curious to see what you were building. My dad built this house. I live down the road now."

"You're welcome to take a look," the man said. "Gate's a bit much, isn't it? Contractor went overboard, I'm afraid. And we had the driveway redone to make room for the pool house."

"That will be nice," Brenda replied, a false smile pasted on her face.

"It will, indeed. For my wife's daily swims. She's in a wheelchair just like you . . . the doctor recommended light swimming." His smile was genuine. "You might come by and join her, if you can. I mean, you're more than welcome."

Brenda was shocked. How wrong about this man she had been!

9. Where in the selection does Brenda's stream of consciousness start?
   A. the sentence beginning, "Oh, what a ridiculous gate"
   B. the sentence beginning, "And the driveway"
   C. the sentence beginning, "Her father had built"
   D. the sentence beginning, "I was curious"

10. Which of these pictures do the selection details paint?
    A. a huge mansion with a pool house being constructed beside it
    B. a road across an empty landscape, with a single home on it
    C. an overly decorated gate at the foot of a semicircular driveway
    D. a middle-aged woman in a wheelchair who lives in a mansion

11. Which of these experiences can best help you relate to the character of Brenda?
    A. moving to a new home
    B. swimming in an indoor pool
    C. studying local architecture
    D. visiting a place you recall from childhood

12. What epiphany does Brenda have at the end of the selection?
    A. She realizes that she is more independent than she thought.
    B. She realizes that her old home has not changed very much at all.
    C. She realizes that it is time to stop thinking about the past.
    D. She realizes that she has completely misjudged the new owner.

Read this poem by British poet Edward Thomas. Then, answer the questions that follow.

Adlestrop

Yes, I remember Adlestrop—
The name, because one afternoon
Of heat the express-train drew up there
Unwontedly.° It was late June.

                                                     ° unwontedly unaccustomedly; not as usually scheduled

5 The steam hissed. Someone cleared his throat.
No one left and no one came
On the bare platform. What I saw
Was Adlestrop—only the name

And willows, willow-herb, and grass,
10 And meadowsweet, and haycocks dry,
No whit° less still and lonely fair   °**no whit** not a bit
Than the high cloudlets in the sky.

And for that minute a blackbird sang
Close by, and round him, mistier,
15 Farther and farther, all the birds   °**Oxfordshire** (OKS ferd sher)
Of Oxfordshire, and Gloucestershire.°   **Gloucestershire** (GLOS ter sher): English counties

13. Which statement best summarizes the poem?
   A. When his train stops unexpectedly in a peaceful, out-of-the-way town, the speaker's appreciation of the natural landscape is heightened.
   B. The speaker's train stops unexpectedly in Adlestrop, a suburb he remembers from childhood but which he has not visited in many years.
   C. When his train stops in a small town on a hot day in summer, the speaker sees many varieties of plant life.
   D. At a train station far from the fields of battle, the speaker hears a blackbird sing and sees high clouds in the sky.

14. What sort of diction does the poem use?
   A. simple and conversational
   B. technical and scientific
   C. formal and complicated
   D. casual and a bit crude

15. Which phrase best describes the tone of the poem?
   A. bitter and angry
   B. tired and bored
   C. sad and mournful
   D. peaceful and reflective

16. What does Adlestrop seem to symbolize, or represent?
   A. the dull routine of suburban life
   B. peace and greater awareness
   C. violence and warfare
   D. the intensity of summer heat

Vocabulary and Grammar

17. Which of the following is generally a *laudable* achievement?
   A. winning a prize
   B. tripping over a rock
   C. falling asleep
   D. losing a glove

18. Which of the following are *durable* goods?
    A. marshmallows
    B. tissue paper
    C. refrigerators
    D. oranges

19. Based on your understanding of the Latin root *-mort-*, what is a *mortal* illness?
    A. an illness that goes on for a long time
    B. an illness that puzzles doctors
    C. a childhood illness
    D. an illness that generally results in death

20. Based on your understanding of the Latin root *-vinc-*, what is an *invincible* army?
    A. an army that has just been defeated
    B. an army that cannot be defeated
    C. an army that needs better leadership
    D. an army that needs better supplies

21. Which of these adjectives best describes a person who is a *skeptic*?
    A. enthusiastic
    B. innocent
    C. doubting
    D. unwise

22. The Latin root *-vert-* or *-vers-* can mean "to turn." Which of these words probably means "turned against the speaker" or "opposite from what was previously stated"?
    A. obverse
    B. transverse
    C. divert
    D. vertical

23. Which sentence uses *who* or *whom* correctly?
    A. The character whom the novel explores in depth is an old woman.
    B. The woman, who we meet in the first chapter, tells a story within the story.
    C. She is the character about who we learn through stream of consciousness.
    D. After her epiphany, she is no longer the person whom she was before.

24. What is the best way to improve this sentence by using parallel structure?

    Speak loudly, with pride, and in a clear voice.

    A. Change "with pride" to "proudly."
    B. Change "in a clear voice" to "clearly."
    C. Change "with pride" to "proudly" and "in a distinct voice" to "clearly."
    D. Do not make any changes; the sentence is best left as it is.

25. Which of these words is a concrete noun?
    A. life
    B. fantasy
    C. jealousy
    D. stomach

26. Which sentence contains no errors in the usage of the word *like*?
    A. Cathy's Welsh accent sounds like music.
    B. Millie spoke like she lived in northern England.
    C. Jordan speaks like a Scotsman usually speaks.
    D. None of them speak as quickly like a Londoner.

27. What is the adverb clause in this sentence?

    After lunch, we will go to the library that is two blocks away.

    A. after lunch
    B. we will go
    C. to the library
    D. that is two blocks away

28. In which sentence do the subject and verb agree?
    A. Right now here is two hummingbirds in our garden.
    B. On the flowers near the pond sits several bumblebees.
    C. Here is a group of flowers that my mom has planted.
    D. Beside the statue is a rose bush and a lilac bush.

29. Which sentence correctly uses the subjunctive mood?
    A. If I was in charge, we would visit England next year.
    B. If my brother was choosing, he would pick New Orleans.
    C. My dad wishes that he was staying home.
    D. If my mother were the boss, the whole family would go camping.

ESSAY

30. Think about a problem that you would like to see solved. It might be something in your school or local community, or it might be a broader problem in the nation or world. Write a short problem-and-solution essay or the text of a persuasive speech in which you offer suggestions about how to solve the problem.

31. Many short lyric poems have one strong central image. Write a short lyric poem—rhymed or in free verse—in which the strong, central image is a product that people buy. Describe the image, and convey your feelings about it. You might use the product as a concrete symbol of an abstract idea.

32. Write a brief literary essay about the images, symbolism, or theme of a modern poem or story you have read. Trace a central image, symbol, or theme throughout the story, and give your insights about it. You might write about a poem or a story that appears in your textbook or one that you found elsewhere.

Unit 6: A Time of Rapid Change
Diagnostic Test 12

MULTIPLE CHOICE

Read the selection. Then, answer the questions that follow.

The bond between two friends is a literary theme that can be found in the earliest tales told by humans. One such tale, *The Epic of Gilgamesh,* is among the world's oldest written works of literature. It tells the tale of a cruel king, Gilgamesh, for whom the gods create a friend, Enkidu, in the hopes that he will help the king to become a just ruler. Enkidu challenges Gilgamesh to a fight, in which Gilgamesh emerges victorious. The two men become fast friends, and their friendship makes Gilgamesh a better king.

Later in the epic, Gilgamesh is wooed by the goddess of love, Ishtar, but he rejects her. Humiliated, Ishtar punishes Gilgamesh's kingdom by sending a bull, which brings famine with it. When Gilgamesh and Enkidu kill the bull, the gods agree that one of the friends must die, and Enkidu suffers a painful death.

Enkidu's death prompts Gilgamesh to seek eternal life. He meets a man who has been granted immortality. The man gives Gilgamesh a test: if Gilgamesh can stay awake for a week, he will be granted never-ending life. Gilgamesh agrees, but before long he feels enormous fatigue and falls asleep, failing the test. The man decides to give Gilgamesh another chance. He furnishes him with a miraculous plant that will restore his youth, but a snake steals the plant from him. As a result of these trials, Gilgamesh learns to appreciate life and returns to his kingdom where he becomes a great and wise king.

1. What is one reason why *The Epic of Gilgamesh* is an important literary work?
   A. It is a story about immortality.
   B. It is a story of the gods.
   C. It is a story of the love between friends.
   D. It is one of humanity's oldest recorded stories.

2. The gods send Gilgamesh a friend in the hopes that it will make him a better king. What does this imply about friendship?
   A. Friendship can transform people.
   B. Friendship is important.
   C. Friends make kings better.
   D. All kings need a friend to rule.

3. What happens when Gilgamesh and Enkidu first meet?
   A. They kill a bull.
   B. They fight the gods.
   C. They have a grueling fight.
   D. They become friends.

4. How does Ishtar punish Gilgamesh for rejecting her?
   A. She sends a man to make him immortal.
   B. She executes Enkidu.
   C. She sends a bull that brings famine.
   D. She makes him mortal.

5. How does Gilgamesh's response to Ishtar's punishment bring about Enkidu's death?
   A. When he and Enkidu attempt to kill the bull, the bull kills Enkidu.
   B. When he and Enkidu kill the bull, the gods punish them by killing Enkidu.
   C. When he and Enkidu attempt to kill the bull, Ishtar kills Enkidu.
   D. When Enkidu attempts to kill the bull, the gods decide to kill Enkidu.

6. How does Gilgamesh respond to Enkidu's death?
   A. He searches for immortality.
   B. He learns to appreciate life.
   C. He tries to find death.
   D. He tries to bring Enkidu back to life.

7. Which of the following must Gilgamesh accomplish in order to achieve immortality?
   A. He must find a miraculous plant.
   B. He must kill a bull.
   C. He must go without sleep for a week.
   D. He must eat a special plant.

8. What does Gilgamesh learn from his search for immortality?
   A. that immortality is impossible
   B. to appreciate mortality
   C. that immortality is not desirable after all
   D. to appreciate life

Read the selection. Then, answer the questions that follow.

Horses have been an important part of the Blackfeet Indians culture for hundreds of years and yet the horse is not native to North America. The Blackfeet first acquired horses, which they called Elk Dogs, from Spanish explorers, who brought their world-renowned Mustangs with them when they arrived in North America. Horse allowed the Blackfeet to move faster, hunt more efficiently, and gave them a strategic advantage in combat. The Blackfeet lived in America's Great Plains and hunted bison, elk, and deer. They were particularly reliant on the bison, which they used to make material for clothing, tipis, moccasins, and a variety of tools. As America expanded westward, bison were hunted nearly to extinction, the Blackfeet were confined to reservations, and their beloved horses were confiscated.

Today a small herd of Spanish Mustangs is once again living with the Blackfeet. In 1994, Robert Blackbull received a Mustang stallion as a gift and later bought six mares. There are now over 100 Spanish Mustangs on the Blackfeet reservation, and Blackbull has founded the Blackfeet Buffalo Horse Coalition. The Coalition focuses on using horses as a means of connecting Blackfeet youth to the history and traditions of their people. Young Blackfeet train to ride horses in much the same ways that their ancestors did and come to learn how vital horses were to their culture.

9. Who was responsible for bringing horses to the Plains?
   A. European Americans
   B. the Spanish
   C. the Mustangs
   D. the Blackfeet

10. How long did the Blackfeet have horses?
    A. from ancient times
    B. for centuries
    C. since the coming of European Americans
    D. since 1994

11. Which best describes why horses were important to the Blackfeet?
    A. The horse helped them hunt more efficiently.
    B. The horse allowed them to move westward and to escape the reservation.
    C. The horse became their most valued companion.
    D. The horse provided them with food and clothing.

12. How did the Blackfeet use the bison?
    A. as the object of hunting
    B. as companions
    C. to help them live on the Plains
    D. for food, clothing, and shelter

13. Why did the Blackfeet give up their horses?
    A. They no longer relied on hunting buffalo for food.
    B. They were forced on to reservations and forced to give up the horses.
    C. The Spanish Mustangs gradually disappeared from the Plains.
    D. Most of the horses had been captured or killed by the European Americans.

14. When did horses return to the Blackfeet reservation?
    A. in 1994, when Robert Blackbull was given a Spanish Mustang
    B. when Blackfeet captured Spanish Mustangs in the last century
    C. when the European Americans completed their settlement of the Plains
    D. when the Blackfeet brought a large group of horses to the reservation

15. What is the purpose of the Blackfeet Buffalo Horse Coalition?
    A. to help people understand the relationship between the buffalo and the horse
    B. to connect Blackfeet youth to their history and ancestral way of life
    C. to acquire and raise Spanish Mustang horses
    D. to attempt to bring back the bison and horse herds on the plains

Vocabulary Warm-up Word Lists

Study these words from the selections. Then, complete the activities that follow.

Word List A

barricade [BAR uh kayd] *n.* something that blocks passage; barrier
    The <u>barricade</u> prevented cars from continuing down the street.

blundering [BLUHN duh ring] *n.* making a stupid mistake
    Hal could just kick himself for <u>blundering</u> yet again and looking foolish.

bombardment [bahm BAHRD muhnt] *n.* the act of attacking persistently
    Their snow fort protected the children from the snowball <u>bombardment</u>.

fierce [FEERS] *adj.* frighteningly cruel, violent, savage, or intense
    The dog's <u>fierce</u> attack drove the intruder away.

rectangular [rek TANG yuh luhr] *adj.* having the shape of a rectangle
    Denise prefers <u>rectangular</u> frames to oval or circular ones.

sodden [SAH duhn] *adj.* soaked with moisture
    After the downpour, the patio and all the patio furniture were <u>sodden</u>.

tortuous [TAWR choo uhs] *adj.* full of twists, turns, and windings
    The bus trip up the <u>tortuous</u> mountain road was extremely frightening.

unaccustomed [un uh KUS tuhmd] *adj.* not used; not familiar
    The speaker announced that he was <u>unaccustomed</u> to public speaking.

Word List B

attentive [uh TEN tiv] *adj.* giving or showing thought or care
    The nurse was <u>attentive</u> to all the patient's needs.

awash [uh WAHSH] *adj.* covered or overflowing with water
    Because of the leaky pipe, the kitchen floor was <u>awash</u>.

backdrop [BAK drahp] *n.* background; setting, as of a historical event
    We admired the skyline against the <u>backdrop</u> of the setting sun.

boredom [BAWR duhm] *n.* the condition of being made weary by something dull
    Robert could not conceal his <u>boredom</u> at the tedious performance.

circuit [SER kit] *n.* a route or path that that turns back to where it began
    Jogging comfortably, Phil completed the <u>circuit</u> in just under three hours.

instantaneous [in stuhn TAY nee uhs] *adj.* happening in a moment
    The sergeant expected <u>instantaneous</u> obedience of his orders.

trance [TRANS] *n.* a condition between sleep and wakefulness
    In a <u>trance</u>, the hypnotized woman lifted her arm slowly.

variations [var ee AY shuhnz] *n.* changed or altered forms
    The chef tried several <u>variations</u> of the same recipe, using different spices.

Poetry of Dylan Thomas and Ted Hughes
Vocabulary Warm-up Exercises

Exercise A *Fill in each blank below with the appropriate word from Word List A.*

Perry had just moved to the country, and he was [1] _____ to having so
much open space. His yard was a huge [2] _____ area, twice as big as the
park he had used in the city. He had horses, too, which were kept in their area by the
[3] _____ of a white wooden fence. One day, he rode one of the horses
along a [4] _____ path in the nearby woods. When they got lost, Perry
was angry at himself for [5] _____ so stupidly. Imagine his surprise when
the horse found the way back by himself. It was a lucky thing, too, because shortly after
they got back, a [6] _____ winter storm began. Soon it began to hail, and
the [7] _____ of the hailstones continued for twenty minutes. Perry and
the horse waited it out in the stable. Perry wondered when the [8] _____
ground would dry out enough so he could go riding again.

Exercise B *Decide whether each statement is true or false. Circle* T *or* F, *and explain your
answer.*

1. If you complete a <u>circuit</u>, you get back to where you started.
   T / F _____

2. If you are <u>attentive</u> when someone is speaking, you will probably miss most of what
   the person says.
   T / F _____

3. The <u>backdrop</u> includes important details that are in the foreground.
   T / F _____

4. Medicine that gave <u>instantaneous</u> relief of pain would add to the suffering of
   patients.
   T / F _____

5. After a dry, sunny, hot day, the ground would probably be <u>awash</u>.
   T / F _____

6. You might say a sleepwalker was in a <u>trance</u>.
   T / F _____

7. One way to show <u>boredom</u> is to jump up and down and cheer.
   T / F _____

8. If you play <u>variations</u> of a song, you play the same thing over and over.
   T / F _____

Poetry of Dylan Thomas and Ted Hughes
Reading Warm-up A

Read the following passage. Pay special attention to the underlined words. Then, read it again, and complete the activities. Use a separate sheet of paper for your written answers.

Suppose you find yourself out on some path to which you are <u>unaccustomed</u>; because you are unfamiliar with the area, you are not sure where you are or how to get back to where you were. This <u>tortuous</u> path winds in and out and up and down, and you are very confused. Well, if you have a compass and some common sense, you can just calm down and try to enjoy your surroundings as you head in the right direction.

However, what if you notice that the sky is darkening with angry, <u>fierce</u> storm clouds? That's a whole different story, and it would be difficult to stay calm under such circumstances; you would know that the weather would soon be changing drastically, and you would be exposed to the <u>bombardment</u> of heavy raindrops and maybe even hail. You would try to remember everything you had ever heard about finding shelter from a storm: were you supposed to huddle near a tree, hoping to be protected by the branches from the rain, or had you heard that a tree was the worst place to be in a storm because of the threat of lightning? Just about then, you would start to regret your terrible error of <u>blundering</u> into this mess.

Suppose that, after a bit more hiking, you notice that the path straightens out as you come upon an open meadow, and then you see some kind of structure in the center of it. It looks like a gazebo surrounding a <u>rectangular</u> picnic table. "Perfect!" you think to yourself: the gazebo can act as a <u>barricade</u>, blocking the rain from hitting the picnic table. You can sit out the storm and, later, make your way back over the <u>sodden</u>, rain-soaked ground. Aren't you lucky that you remembered to pack a lunch?

1. Underline the word that means about the same as <u>unaccustomed</u>. Use *unaccustomed* in a sentence.

2. Circle the words that describe what a <u>tortuous</u> path does. Describe a ride or walk you once took on a *tortuous* road.

3. Underline the word that means about the same as <u>fierce</u>. Name one common occurrence in nature that you would describe as *fierce*.

4. Circle the words that tell what might contribute to a <u>bombardment</u>. What does *bombardment* mean?

5. Circle the words that tell what <u>blundering</u> is. Describe a time you or someone you know regretted *blundering*.

6. Underline the words that tell what had a <u>rectangular</u> shape. Name one thing in the classroom that is *rectangular*.

7. Underline the word that tells what a <u>barricade</u> does. In a zoo, what kind of *barricade* usually exists between people and animals?

8. Circle the word that means about the same as <u>sodden</u>. How can you prevent getting *sodden* shoes if you go walking in the rain?

Poetry of Dylan Thomas and Ted Hughes
Reading Warm-up B

Read the following passage. Pay special attention to the underlined words. Then, read it again, and complete the activities. Use a separate sheet of paper for your written answers.

Some horse owners think that horse care is simple: just give them the <u>backdrop</u> of a pasture, allow them to graze all day, and put them in the stable at night. Such horse owners must be in some kind of a daze or <u>trance</u>, for they could not be more mistaken—horses have many needs, some physical and some psychological, and it is the owner's responsibility to be <u>attentive</u> to those needs.

As a general rule, the horse owner should have one acre of land per horse for grazing purposes. Frequently, the field should be checked for rubbish and anything else that might be harmful to the horse. The field should have a sturdy fence in good repair so the horse cannot escape. There are many <u>variations</u> in fence types that are suitable for horse pastures: they can be made of wooden posts and rails, painted white, or they can be made of plain wire secured to wooden posts. If the field happens to become <u>awash</u>, due to rain or flooding, the horses need an alternative environment.

Horses can suffer from <u>boredom</u> just as humans can, so it is imperative that horses enjoy the companionship of humans and other horses. As for shelter other than the stable, horse must be protected from the elements of the sun, wind, and rain; a grove of trees can serve as an <u>instantaneous</u> shelter, but a better alternative is a three-sided shelter. The prevailing wind should hit the back of the structure.

Horses need to get exercise daily: horses that don't get a chance to run free in a pasture will need to be walked on some kind of <u>circuit</u> or track. If you want a horse, you have to be prepared for the work that is involved.

1. Underline the word that describes the kind of <u>backdrop</u> a horse might enjoy. What is a *backdrop*?

2. Circle the word that means about the same as <u>trance</u>. Describe how a person in a *trance* might act.

3. What is a synonym for <u>attentive</u>? Use *attentive* in a sentence.

4. Circle the phrases that explain two types of <u>variations</u> in fence types. Describe two *variations* of tops you might wear with jeans.

5. Underline the words that explain what might cause a field to become <u>awash</u>. What does *awash* mean?

6. Describe a time you suffered from <u>boredom</u>.

7. What does <u>instantaneous</u> mean? Use *instantaneous* in a sentence.

8. Circle the word that means about the same as <u>circuit</u>. Describe a *circuit* you can walk to get exercise.

"Do Not Go Gentle into That Good Night" and **"Fern Hill"** by Dylan Thomas
"The Horses" and **"The Rain Horse"** by Ted Hughes
Literary Analysis: Voice

What did you "hear" when you read these poems by Dylan Thomas and Ted Hughes? Did you hear Thomas raging against death? Did you hear Hughes relishing his memory? What is it, exactly, that causes you to "hear" anything in a poem? What produces a poem's voice?

Voice in literature is usually produced by variations in word choice, rhythm, and diction. Writers use these elements carefully to produce the "sound" they want. Many writers, like Dylan Thomas, have a characteristic voice, although most can vary their sound considerably.

Word choice, or vocabulary, affects the voice. A word like *hush* is an obvious example of a word that readers can "hear." In a similar way, Hughes's use of the word *frost* seems almost hushed, and adds to the image he is creating.

Rhythm also makes a difference. Hughes sets up his sentences in stanzas so that they cannot be read quickly, and in "Fern Hill," Thomas's lilting rhythm invites the poem to be read aloud to play with its voice.

Diction affects voice. Diction is the way words are put together, and includes language level, narrative form, and grammatical structure. Are sentences complex or simple? Is the language casual or formal? Choices about word order also make the rhythm, of course, but so do repetitions. When Thomas repeats *rage* in "Rage, rage against the dying of the light," you can almost hear the rolling Welsh *r*'s. This line is a good example of word choice, rhythm, and diction combining to make a distinctive voice.

DIRECTIONS: *Review "Fern Hill" and record lines or phrases in the following table that seem particularly indicative of the voice of the poem. Then indicate whether the effect is produced by word choice, rhythm, or diction. Then, in the third column, describe the voice of the passage and what effect it has on the poem as a whole.*

Line or Passage	How Voice Is Produced	Description of Voice

Name _____ Date _____

"Do Not Go Gentle into That Good Night" and **"Fern Hill"** by Dylan Thomas
"The Horses" and **"The Rain Horse"** by Ted Hughes
Reading Strategy: Judge the Writer's Message

Whenever you read a poem, a story, or an editorial, it is only natural to weigh the writer's ideas or events against your own experience. Does the writer's expression of an idea or an event match with your own experience, or have you had a different experience?

Readers should **judge the message** of what they read. Some ideas you come across simply won't make sense to you; other ideas will contradict what you may already believe or know to be true. Test a writer's message against your own experience and accept or reject ideas accordingly.

DIRECTIONS: *As you read each poem in this section, note its message in the appropriate area in the table. Then judge each message, deciding whether you agree or disagree, accept or reject the message.*

Poem	Message	Reader's Judgment and Explanation
"Do Not Go Gentle into That Good Night"		
"Fern Hill"		
"The Horses"		

"Do Not Go Gentle into That Good Night" and **"Fern Hill"** by Dylan Thomas
"The Horses" and **"The Rain Horse"** by Ted Hughes
Vocabulary Builder

Using the Root -vol-

A. DIRECTIONS: *The following words contain the root -vol-, meaning "to will" or "to wish." Complete each sentence by writing the appropriate word in the blank.*

volition   voluntary   voluntarism

1. The not-for-profit organization relied almost completely on _____ for its work among the community of homeless people.

2. Though her parents expressed their opinions, Sheila chose the field of social work of her own _____.

3. After seeing the news report, dozens of residents _____ turned out to show their support for preserving the historical building.

Using the Word List

grieved	transfiguring	exasperated
nondescript	malevolent	

B. DIRECTIONS: *Each numbered word is followed by four lettered words or phrases. Choose the word or phrase that is most similar in meaning to the numbered word, and circle the letter of your choice.*

1. exasperated
   A. out of breath
   B. without hope
   C. very irritated
   D. filled with longing

2. grieved
   A. sighed
   B. mourned
   C. hailed
   D. resented

3. nondescript
   A. lacking authority
   B. having no destination
   C. lacking form or shape
   D. without character

4. malevolent
   A. wishing harm
   B. hard or brittle
   C. against one's will
   D. clearly disinterested

5. transfiguring
   A. moving from place to place
   B. changing form
   C. performing experiments
   D. calculating values

Name _____ Date _____

Grammar and Style: Sentence Beginnings: Adverb Clauses

An adverb modifies a verb, an adjective, or another adverb. Similarly, an **adverb clause** is a subordinate clause that modifies a verb, an adjective, or an adverb, telling *how, when, where, why, to what extent,* or *under what condition.* In the sentence below, the italicized adverb clause modifies the verb *defend* and tells *under what condition.*

There were deep hollows in the river-bank, shoaled with pebbles, . . . perfect places to defend himself from *if the horse followed him out there.*

Adverb clauses are always introduced by subordinating conjunctions. Here are some common subordinating conjunctions.

after	as though	since	when
although	because	so that	whenever
as	before	than	where
as if	if	through	wherever
as long as	in order that	unless	while
as soon as	provided that	until	

To create variety—and, therefore, interest—in your writing, you can begin sentences with adverb clauses, as Ted Hughes does.

Since the horse seemed to have gone on down the wood, his way to the farm over the hill was clear.

A. PRACTICE: *Circle the number of each sentence that begins with an adverb clause. For each sentence that does begin with an adverb clause, underline the clause and circle the word it modifies.*

1. "At the woodside he paused, close against a tree."

2. "As he went, he broke a yard length of wrist-thick dead branch from one of the oaks."

3. "Through the bluish veil of bare twigs he saw the familiar shape out in the field below the wood."

4. "Whenever it seemed to be drawing off he listened anxiously until it closed in again."

B. Writing Application: *Write two sentences about "The Rain Horse." Begin each sentence with an adverb clause, and use three different subordinating conjunctions.*

1. _____

2. _____

"Do Not Go Gentle into That Good Night" and **"Fern Hill"** by Dylan Thomas
"The Horses" and **"The Rain Horse"** by Ted Hughes
Support for Writing

Use the following diagram to develop ideas for your parody of Thomas's or Hughes's voice. In the center circle, write your ridiculous subject. In each of the surrounding circles, write a detail about your subject that you can develop in your parody.

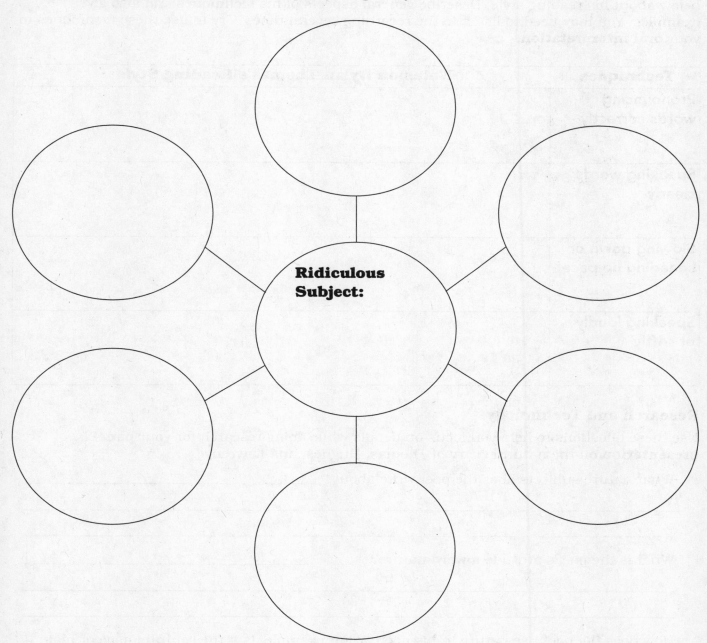

Ridiculous Subject:

On a separate page, use details that you have developed about your subject, as well as the poet's forms, rhythms, and words to help you write a parody. Use vivid language to exaggerate characteristics of the voice of the poet you have chosen.

"Do Not Go Gentle into That Good Night" and **"Fern Hill"** by Dylan Thomas
"The Horses" and **"The Rain Horse"** by Ted Hughes
Support for Extend Your Learning

Listening and Speaking

Listen to a recording of Dylan Thomas reading his poetry. As you listen, jot notes in the chart below about his reading style. Describe general aspects of his techniques and also give examples. You may need to listen to the recording several times. Try to use these techniques in your **oral interpretation**.

Techniques	Notes on Dylan Thomas's Reading Style
Pronouncing words correctly	
Speaking words clearly	
Slowing down or speeding up pace	
Speaking loudly or softly	

Research and Technology

Use these questions to help you focus on details while doing research for your **panel presentation** on the nature poetry of Thomas, Hughes, and Lawrence.

What nature subjects does the poet write about? _____

_____

_____

What is the poet's attitude toward nature? _____

_____

_____

How does the poet use nature in his poetry? For example, is it the central image or main idea, or is it a secondary theme? _____

_____

_____

"Do Not Go Gentle into That Good Night" and **"Fern Hill"** by Dylan Thomas
"The Horses" and **"The Rain Horse"** by Ted Hughes

Enrichment: Preservation of Wilderness Lands

Both Thomas and Hughes evoke rich, memorable images of the natural world through their works. They make it easy to imagine the "apple boughs," the "sun / Orange, red, red" erupting, and "raw, flapping wetness in the air." It is not difficult to appreciate the beauty and the power of nature, as these writers depict it.

In modern America, there are those who claim that the natural world is receding in the face of constant, even rampant, development. Other Americans believe that the development is natural and good and will lead to an improved quality of life for residents of city and country alike. They feel that the land's resources should be put to work for America's growing population.

In the United States, there are approximately 272 million acres of public land—land that is largely vacant and *not* privately owned. This land, primarily in the far Western states and Alaska, is administered by the Bureau of Land Management (BLM), part of the U.S. Department of the Interior. The BLM takes into consideration multiple uses and sustained yield in its management of the land. Their plans encompass the long-term needs of future generations in terms of the land's resources, which include timber, rangeland, minerals, wildlife, wilderness, and natural scenic beauty.

One example of the BLM's work is its overseeing of about 40,000 wild mustangs that live on public lands in nine Western states. Protected by the Wild Free-Roaming Horse and Burro Act of 1971, the mustang population now increases by fifteen to twenty percent each year. To prevent overgrazing, the BLM conducts periodic roundups, offering the surplus animals for adoption to private owners.

There are people who feel that this use of thousands of acres of public land is a waste. They argue that the land should be logged, pumped for oil, and mined, to the exclusion of the mustangs. The supporters of undeveloped public land hold that this land should remain untouched to preserve its natural beauty as well as the habitat it provides for mustangs and thousands of other species of animals and of plants.

DIRECTIONS: *Take a stand on whether public lands should be "used" for their timber, oil, and mineral resources, whether they should remain untouched and undeveloped, or whether you think it is possible to strike a balance between the two. Use the following space and the back of this page to formulate and support your argument.*

_____

_____

_____

_____

_____

_____

_____

_____

"Do Not Go Gentle into That Good Night" and **"Fern Hill"** by Dylan Thomas
"The Horses" and **"The Rain Horse"** by Ted Hughes

Selection Test A

Critical Reading *Identify the letter of the choice that best answers the question.*

____ 1. In "Do Not Go Gentle into That Good Night," what does "night" symbolize?
   A. nature
   B. death
   C. society
   D. faith

____ 2. Who is the dying person in "Do Not Go Gentle into That Good Night"?
   A. the speaker's friend
   B. God
   C. the speaker's father
   D. the speaker

____ 3. What is the main idea of "Do Not Go Gentle into That Good Night"?
   A. Society treats poets as outsiders.
   B. People's faith grows stronger as death nears.
   C. People should not regret how they act.
   D. Life is short and we should hold onto it.

____ 4. Which statement best illustrates a reader judging the message in "Fern Hill"?
   A. I really like this poem because it was easy to understand.
   B. I agree with Thomas that life is short.
   C. My favorite lines are the ones that rhyme.
   D. The poem has many good nature images.

____ 5. What tone is suggested by the line: "Now as I was young and easy under the apple boughs" from "Fern Hill"?
   A. an angry tone
   B. a bitter tone
   C. a joyful tone
   D. a proud tone

____ 6. Which statement identifies an element of voice, such as word choice, in "Fern Hill"?
   A. Thomas chooses words that express the freedom of childhood.
   B. The theme of the poem is the happiness of childhood.
   C. Thomas recalls childhood on his grandfather's farm in Wales.
   D. Thomas reminds the reader that childhood is brief.

_____ 7. In "The Horses," how is "Not a leaf, not a bird— / A world cast in frost" an example of the poet's voice?
   A. The speaker is examining the world of nature.
   B. Readers have taken similar walks.
   C. These lines describe how quiet it was.
   D. Hughes writes in brief, tight images.

_____ 8. Which statement best paraphrases "Then the sun / Orange, red, red erupted" from "The Horses"?
   A. The sun exploded into many parts.
   B. It grew lighter and suddenly the sun rose.
   C. A volcano exploded.
   D. The sunrise made strange colors.

_____ 9. What is "The Rain Horse" about?
   A. A man walking on a rainy day sees a horse that seems to want to attack him.
   B. A man recalls a walk when he saw a horse standing in the rain.
   C. The narrator chases his horse across a farmer's land but fails to catch it.
   D. A memory of a horse reminds the narrator of the beauty of nature.

_____ 10. Read the following: "His scalp went icy and he shivered. What was he to do?" from "The Rain Horse." Based on these sentences, what seems to be the narrator's attitude?
   A. He is relieved and refreshed.
   B. He feels confident and in control.
   C. He is relaxed and calm.
   D. He is anxious and unsettled.

_____ 11. How does the rain contribute to the effect of "The Rain Horse"?
   A. It blurs the line between reality and imagination.
   B. It is a normal part of English weather.
   C. The rain makes the narrator cold.
   D. The rain shows the horse's fear.

Vocabulary and Grammar

_____ 12. Which word best replaces *grieved* in this sentence: "She *grieved* due to the loss of her dear friend"?
   A. laughed
   B. forgot
   C. mourned
   D. imagined

_____ **13.** Which sentence begins with an adverb clause that shows *when, why,* or *under what conditions?*
   A. As the young man climbed the hill, the rain came.
   B. He waited, trying to make himself warmer.
   C. He hugged his knees to squeeze out the cold.
   D. He took control of himself and turned back.

Essay

14. In "Fern Hill," the speaker says that as a child, he did not care that time would eventually catch up with him and that the joyous and free way of childhood would one day suddenly disappear. In an essay, explain whether you agree with this message, based on your own experience and your reading of the poem.

15. In "The Rain Horse," the narrator returns to the place where he grew up. He takes a walk to visit a place he once knew. One of the themes of the essay is how the narrator feels distant from both his childhood home and from nature. In an essay, explain how details from the story support this theme.

"Do Not Go Gentle into That Good Night" and **"Fern Hill"** by Dylan Thomas
"The Horses" and **"The Rain Horse"** by Ted Hughes

Selection Test B

Critical Reading *Identify the letter of the choice that best completes the statement or answers the question.*

_____ 1. Whom does the speaker in "Do Not Go Gentle into That Good Night" address?
    A. the sun
    B. good men and wild men
    C. his father
    D. death

_____ 2. In "Do Not Go Gentle into That Good Night," the wise men " [d]o not go gentle into that good night" because
    A. they doubt their own wisdom.
    B. they envy those who were less wise.
    C. they are afraid of death.
    D. their wisdom has not inspired others.

_____ 3. Choose the statement that illustrates a reader judging the message of "Do Not Go Gentle into That Good Night."
    A. I don't like this poem.
    B. The line "Rage, rage against the dying of the light" is my favorite.
    C. Thomas uses a three-line stanza with alternating end rhyme.
    D. I think people should be more accepting of death than Thomas is.

_____ 4. The central idea of "Do Not Go Gentle into That Good Night" is that
    A. people die in the same spirit in which they lived.
    B. death always comes too soon and should be resisted.
    C. having regret at the end of one's life is pitiful.
    D. people of all ranks and stations are equal in death.

_____ 5. Which image in "Fern Hill" evokes the idea of natural simplicity and freshness?
    A. ". . . happy as the grass was green . . ."
    B. ". . . the pebbles of the holy streams."
    C. ". . . fire green as grass."
    D. ". . . a wanderer white / With the dew . . ."

_____ 6. The line "Though I sang in my chains like the sea" closes "Fern Hill" with a feeling of
    A. bitterness.
    B. frustration.
    C. relief.
    D. triumph.

____ 7. Which statement most accurately describes Thomas's voice in "Fern Hill"?
   A. Thomas uses multiple natural images to evoke the carefree feeling of childhood.
   B. Thomas expresses bitterness that children become "out of grace."
   C. Thomas expresses his belief that children can only thrive if brought up in a natural environment.
   D. Thomas implies that children are thoughtless and "heedless" of the advantages they have.

____ 8. In "The Horses," the speaker describes
   A. a vivid memory of an early-morning walk in the country.
   B. an experience with a herd of horses that he recently had.
   C. a frightening encounter with a herd of stampeding horses.
   D. a nighttime walk through a dark field.

____ 9. Readers who are judging the message of "The Horses" might consider
   A. experiences they have had with horses in a horse stable.
   B. their own memories of an experience in a solitary natural setting.
   C. a walk they have taken at sunset.
   D. their recollection of a steamy summer night.

____ 10. In these lines from "The Horses," how does the poet use diction to contribute to the image?
   > Huge in the dense gray—ten together—
   > Megalith-still . . .

   A. The short phrases stand separately, as if each is a stone-still horse.
   B. The words have a "heavy" sound that contributes to the sense of the word *huge*.
   C. The separation of the phrases slows the speaker down, giving the reader the feeling that he is counting the horses.
   D. The words *huge, gray,* and *megalith* convey the sense that the horses are statues.

____ 11. Choose the best restatement of the basic story line of Hughes's "The Rain Horse."
   A. An old man remembers a time during his boyhood when a farmer's horse threatened him.
   B. A man reconstructs a boyhood experience with a horse in an attempt to analyze the animal's behavior.
   C. A young man trespasses on a farmer's land in an attempt to catch his horse.
   D. A man encounters a horse that seems intent on trampling him.

____ 12. What role does the weather play in "The Rain Horse"?
   A. It adds to the man's discomfort and also tends to blur the reality of the story.
   B. It foreshadows that the man's walk will turn out unhappily.
   C. It is only natural, because the English climate is characteristically rainy.
   D. It adds to the conflict by making it harder for the man to get away from the horse.

Vocabulary and Grammar

____ 13. The man in "The Rain Horse" is *exasperated* by his situation. *Exasperated* means
   A. "full of anxiety about."
   B. "out of breath."
   C. "extremely annoyed."
   D. "distracted, bored."

____ 14. The trees in the woods are nondescript saplings, which means they are
   A. without significant identifying characteristics.
   B. very young and unformed.
   C. incapable of being described.
   D. of a variety the narrator cannot identify.

____ 15. Which sentence begins with an adverb clause?
   A. This hill was shaped like a wave, a gently rounded back lifting out of the valley.
   B. As he watched it, the horse ran up to that crest.
   C. All around him the boughs angled down, glistening, black as iron.
   D. Over to his right a thin, black horse was running across the ploughland towards the hill.

Essay

16. In "The Rain Horse," a young man returns to a familiar site from his boyhood. In an essay, explore the following questions: What are his first impressions upon arriving at the top of the hill? How does it feel to be back after twelve years? How has that relationship changed? How does his episode with the horse affect that relationship? Finally, explain whether you think the horse was real or imagined, a thing of the past or of the present.

17. In "Do Not Go Gentle into That Good Night" and "Fern Hill," Dylan Thomas expresses feelings about various stages of life. What are those feelings, as revealed in the two poems? How do Thomas's attitudes about these stages of life fit with your own? Do you agree or disagree, accept or reject his attitudes on the basis of your own experience? In an essay, explain why.

Study these words from the selections. Then, complete the activities that follow.

Word List A

blurred [BLERD] *adj.* made less clear or distinct in form or outline
Ana's vision seemed blurred, but then she noticed her glasses were dirty.

comfort [KUM fuhrt] *n.* a pleasant condition, free from pain or worry
Les was happily living a life of comfort, but then his troubles began.

lodged [LAHJD] *v.* placed or left somewhere
Kimi lodged her special treasures in a tiny space beneath her floorboards.

moaning [MOHN ing] *v.* making a low, sad sound, as if from pain or grief
After twisting her ankle, Sharon lay on the ground, moaning in pain.

persisted [puhr SIS tid] *v.* continued stubbornly in spite of difficulty
Roland found math hard, but he persisted until he understood it.

prolong [proh LONG] *v.* to make longer in time or space; continue
Having a good time, they decided to prolong their visit another hour.

trough [TRAWF] *n.* a long, narrow depression, as between ridges
Water collected in the trough formed by wheel ruts in the mud.

vaguely [VAYG lee] *adv.* not precisely, clearly, or distinctly
Chad vaguely remembered his mom telling him to be home early.

Word List B

absurd [uhb SERD] *n.* something that is ridiculously unreasonable
The little boy's silly behavior verged on the absurd.

damage [DAM ij] *n.* injury or harm
The storm did considerable damage to the farm.

dart [DAHRT] *v.* to move suddenly and swiftly
The yellow fish dart through the water as the children watch them.

explosion [ek SPLOH zhuhn] *n.* a sudden blowing up or bursting
The explosion of the dynamite could be heard from miles away.

pellets [PEL its] *n.* small, round balls, as rolled from paper, bread, or wax
We rolled pellets out of putty and stuffed them into the holes in the wall.

rigidly [RIJ id lee] *adv.* in a fixed and unmoving manner
The guards stood rigidly at attention for more than an hour.

stationary [STAY shuhn eh ree] *adj.* remaining in one place
Every day, Joan rode a stationary bike to burn calories.

tremor [TREM uhr] *n.* a quick, vibrating movement; a shaking
The first signal that we were having an earthquake was a slight tremor.

Poetry of Philip Larkin, Peter Redgrove, and Stevie Smith
Vocabulary Warm-up Exercises

Exercise A *Fill in each blank below with the appropriate word from Word List A.*

Running forward to catch the softball, Carol tripped in a small [1] _____ in the ground and twisted her ankle. As she lay [2] _____ on the ground, her friend Lucy tried to offer some [3] _____. Carol looked up at Lucy but could not see her clearly, as her vision was slightly [4] _____. Carol [5] _____ remembered questioning the wisdom of playing in the old, abandoned field. Now, as her pain [6] _____, she knew it had been a bad idea. Not only had she twisted her ankle, but she could tell that a small pebble was [7] _____ firmly in her knee. She did not want to [8] _____ her pain, so she asked Carol to call emergency services so that she could get help quickly.

Exercise B *Decide whether each statement is true or false. Circle T or F, and explain your answer.*

1. If you see someone <u>dart</u> out into the street, that person is moving slowly.
   T / F _____

2. You could make <u>pellets</u> out of snow.
   T / F _____

3. A <u>tremor</u> in the earth is a sign of an earthquake.
   T / F _____

4. It would be <u>absurd</u> to expect a thank-you note for a gift.
   T / F _____

5. You could ride down a mountain trail on a <u>stationary</u> bike.
   T / F _____

6. People who dance <u>rigidly</u> are very graceful and fluid in their movements.
   T / F _____

7. If you blow up a balloon too much, you might see an <u>explosion</u>.
   T / F _____

8. If you <u>damage</u> a painting, it goes up in value.
   T / F _____

Name _____ Date _____

Read the following passage. Pay special attention to the underlined words. Then, read it again, and complete the activities. Use a separate sheet of paper for your written answers.

Abby enjoyed bike riding, and she did it often to keep in shape. She rode a minimum of four times per week. It was an activity that she <u>persisted</u> in, refusing to give it up. She particularly enjoyed riding though the country near her home. Today was a particularly beautiful day, sunny and clear but not too hot. Looking forward to her ride, she set out eagerly.

As she rode along, Abby enjoyed the sights and sounds around her. An abundance of wildflowers grew in the <u>trough</u> of the ditch beside the road, and she saw birds flitting between the trees. Occasionally, she heard the distant <u>moaning</u> sound of large farm equipment operating in the fields. But otherwise, it was so quiet that she could hear the pebbles <u>lodged</u> in the treads of her wheels making a soft crunching noise on the roughly paved country road.

Enjoying her ride immensely, Abby was only <u>vaguely</u> aware of the passing miles. She suddenly realized that it was getting late, and she did not want to <u>prolong</u> her ride past dark. It was time to turn around. Unfortunately, she had taken several turns and was no longer sure where she was. She looked for a road sign to point her in the right direction, but the only one she could find was too <u>blurred</u> from age and weather for her to read. She realized that nothing around her looked familiar, and she began to get slightly worried. She took <u>comfort</u> in knowing that she had a cell phone in her pocket and could call for help if she needed to.

Abby knew her house was to the west, so she followed the direction of the setting sun. Soon enough, she began to recognize landmarks and knew she was going the right direction.

1. Underline the words that prove that Abby <u>persisted</u> in her favorite activity. What is one activity in which you have **persisted**?

2. Circle the words that tell where the <u>trough</u> was located. What is a **trough**?

3. Underline the words that tell what was making a <u>moaning</u> sound. Describe what **moaning** sounds like.

4. Circle the word that tells what was <u>lodged</u> in Abby's wheels. Use **lodged** in a sentence.

5. Underline the words that tell what Abby was <u>vaguely</u> aware of. What is a word or phrase that means about the same as **vaguely**?

6. Circle the words that tell what Abby did not want to <u>prolong</u>. What is an example of something that people usually want to **prolong**?

7. Underline the words that tell what caused the road sign to be <u>blurred</u>. Tell what might cause a photograph to be **blurred**.

8. Underline the words that tell what gave Abby <u>comfort</u>. What other things might give a lost person **comfort**?

Name _____ Date _____

Read the following passage. Pay special attention to the underlined words. Then, read it again, and complete the activities. Use a separate sheet of paper for your written answers.

Michael got up early and did his morning exercises, including forty minutes on the <u>stationary</u> bike. After a shower, Michael got dressed for another day as a coal miner, a job he did not particularly enjoy but one that he needed for now.

His mother had prepared a substantial breakfast for him, and she poured him a second glass of milk as they talked. Soon, she was giving him his good-bye kiss and watching him <u>dart</u> out the door, in a hurry to get to work on time. "Be careful, son," she called. "If you feel the slightest movement or <u>tremor</u> down there, get out right away!"

Michael thought his mother's fears were <u>absurd</u>; it was unreasonable, he thought, to assume that the mining company would take any chances. He felt perfectly safe, knowing that no <u>explosion</u> of any kind had ever taken place in a mine owned by Corti Brothers—at least none that were unplanned. The ones that were planned did no real <u>damage</u> or harm; instead, they opened up blocked areas so the miners could go deeper into the earth.

As he walked to work, Michael noticed a few small <u>pellets</u> of stone inside his right boot, so he had to stop and get rid of the small, round pebbles. He was worried this would make him late for work, but he managed to get there on time anyway. That was one thing the boss was <u>rigidly</u> strict about—he never changed his attitude about punctuality. If a worker got there two minutes late, he would lose fifteen minutes of pay. Michael always thought that policy was a little harsh, but there was nothing he could do about it. "One more year of this," Michael thought, "and I'll have enough money saved to go to college!"

1. Underline the words that tell for what Michael used his <u>stationary</u> bike. What does *stationary* mean?

2. Circle the words that explain why Michael might <u>dart</u> out the door. Use *dart* in a sentence

3. Underline the word that means about the same as <u>tremor</u>. What is one thing that might cause you to feel a *tremor* in the ground?

4. Circle the word that means about the same as <u>absurd</u>. Describe an *absurd* fear a child might have.

5. Underline the words that tell why Michael did not fear an <u>explosion</u>. What is an *explosion*?

6. Underline the word that means about the same as <u>damage</u>. Describe a time you accidentally did some *damage* to one of your possessions.

7. Circle the words that describe the <u>pellets</u> of stone inside Michael's boot. Use *pellets* in a sentence.

8. Underline the words that prove the boss was <u>rigidly</u> strict. What is a word that means the opposite of *rigidly*?

"An Arundel Tomb" and **"The Explosion"** by Philip Larkin
"On the Patio" by Peter Redgrove
"Not Waving but Drowning" by Stevie Smith
Literary Analysis: Free Verse and Meter

Whether a poet uses free verse or a conventional form of poetry, the lines of poetry likely have some kind of rhythm, or alternation of strong and weak—or stressed and unstressed—syllables. That rhythm may or may not create a regular pattern, or meter. Whether it does or not, though, the poet probably uses the rhythm to add to the meaning of the poem.

The meter of a poem is measured in feet. One foot is made up of one stressed syllable and any number of unstressed syllables. Following is a summary of the kinds of meter Larkin uses in "An Arundel Tomb" and "The Explosion."

Meter	Pattern of Syllables	Example
iambic tetrameter	four sets of iambs per line (˘ ˊ)	The earl and countess lie in stone
trochaic tetrameter	four sets of trochees per line (ˊ ˘)	Shadows pointed towards the pithead:

When poets vary the rhythm of a conventional meter, they add emphasis to a line or give special significance to the meaning of the line. Free-verse poets vary their rhythms frequently to add to or create meaning in their poems.

DIRECTIONS: *Examine the rhythm and meter in the poems in this section, as directed by the following questions.*

1. Following is the first line of "An Arundel Tomb." Notice how the stressed and unstressed syllables fall.

   Side by side, their faces blurred,

   How is this line different from the other lines in the poem? Why do you think Larkin made this line different?

   _____

   _____

2. Scan line 15 of "The Explosion." How many feet does it have? What effect does its rhythm have?

   Scarfed as in a heat-haze, dimmed.

   _____

   _____

Name _____ Date _____

"An Arundel Tomb" and **"The Explosion"** by Philip Larkin
"On the Patio" by Peter Redgrove
"Not Waving but Drowning" by Stevie Smith
Reading Strategy: Read in Sentences

The key to reading and understanding poetry is to read the punctuation rather than the line endings. The rhythm or rhyme of a poem may seem to require a reader to pause at the end of each line, but one must think beyond the physical line endings to the sense of the words. If you **read in sentences,** ignoring the line endings, you will find that sense.

In Philip Larkin's "An Arundel Tomb," each of the first three stanzas is one sentence. Though some lines end with a comma, a dash, or a colon, the unit of thought does not end until the end of the stanza.

A. DIRECTIONS: *Write each sentence in stanzas 4–7 of "An Arundel Tomb." Do not pay attention to line endings; write the sentences in the space provided as if they are in narrative form.*

Sentence 1: _____

_____

Sentence 2: _____

_____

Sentence 3: _____

_____

Sentence 4: _____

_____

Sentence 5: _____

_____

Sentence 6: _____

_____

Sentence 7: _____

_____

Sentence 8: _____

_____

B. DIRECTIONS: *Now review the entire poem. Remember that each of the first three stanzas is one sentence. Practice reading them in sentences. Then continue to stanzas 4–7, which you have written on this page. Mark places to pause and breathe that fit with the meaning of the sentences. Practice several times, and then read the poem aloud to an audience.*

"An Arundel Tomb" and **"The Explosion"** by Philip Larkin
"On the Patio" by Peter Redgrove
"Not Waving but Drowning" by Stevie Smith
Vocabulary Builder

Using the Root *-fid-*

A. DIRECTIONS: *The root -fid-, meaning "faith," is included in each of the numbered words. Match each numbered word with its definition. Write the letter of the definition next to the word it defines.*

___ 1. confidant
___ 2. confidential
___ 3. perfidious

A. one to whom secrets are entrusted
B. faithless
C. private, secret

Using the Word List

effigy	supine	fidelity	larking

B. DIRECTIONS: *Complete each sentence by writing the appropriate Word List word in the blank.*

1. Without knowing anything about the earl and countess, it is hard to tell whether their _____ was the sculptor's imagination or not.

2. Many tombs of royalty traditionally include a(n) _____ of the noble person, in commemoration of his or her rank and importance.

3. The children were only _____; they hadn't meant to tramp through old Mrs. Wilson's flower garden.

4. When performing CPR, the victim should be lying _____ unless other injuries prevent him or her from being so positioned.

C. DIRECTIONS: *Choose a lettered pair that best expresses a relationship similar to that expressed in the numbered pair. Circle the letter of your choice.*

1. EFFIGY : LIKENESS ::
   A. canvas : easel
   B. water : wet
   C. portrait : painting
   D. horse : animal

2. FIDELITY : TRUST ::
   A. greed : money
   B. hope : future
   C. anger : calm
   D. betrayal : disloyalty

3. LARKING : PLAYFUL ::
   A. working : easy
   B. aiming: target
   C. troubling : avoidance
   D. studying : scholarly

4. SUPINE : ERECT ::
   A. recline : stand
   B. careful : mistake
   C. favorable : false
   D. run : jog

Name _____ Date _____

"An Arundel Tomb" and **"The Explosion"** by Philip Larkin
"On the Patio" by Peter Redgrove
"Not Waving but Drowning" by Stevie Smith
Grammar and Style: Sequence of Tenses

The tense of a verb indicates the time of the action or state of being expressed by the verb. Each verb has six tenses. The following summary focuses on just four tenses.

Tense	The tense expresses . . .	Examples
Present	an action that is occurring now	I *write* a story.
Past	an action that occurred in the past and did not continue into the present	I *wrote* a story.
Present Perfect	an action that occurred at some indefinite time in the past, or that began in the past and continues into the present	I have *written* a story. (Requires *has* or *have* + past participle.)
Past Perfect	an action that was completed in the past before some other past occurrence	I *had written* a story. (Requires *had* + past participle.)

When you write, it is important to make sure that your verbs express actions in the order in which they occurred. Writers must pay attention to this **sequence of tenses** to make sure their writing is clear and accurate. Using the sequence of tenses carefully can also add expressiveness to your writing, as it does to Philip Larkin's in "An Arundel Tomb."

A. PRACTICE: *Identify the tense of the italicized verb in each of the following sentences.*

1. Time *has transfigured* them into untruth. _____

2. The earl and countess *lie* in stone. _____

3. Rigidly they *persisted*, linked, through lengths of time. _____

B. Writing Application: *Write sentences according to the instructions.*

1. Use a past perfect verb in a sentence about a book you've read. Show that one action happened before another. _____

2. Use a present tense verb in a sentence about your morning routine. _____

_____

3. Use a past tense verb in a sentence about something you did yesterday. _____

_____

Name _____ Date _____

"An Arundel Tomb" and **"The Explosion"** by Philip Larkin
"On the Patio" by Peter Redgrove
"Not Waving but Drowning" by Stevie Smith
Support for Writing

Complete the organizer below to collect information for your reflective essay. Write the everyday sight or event that will be the subject of your essay in the center circle. In the surrounding circles, jot down the ideas, feelings, and comparisons that this event evokes in you.

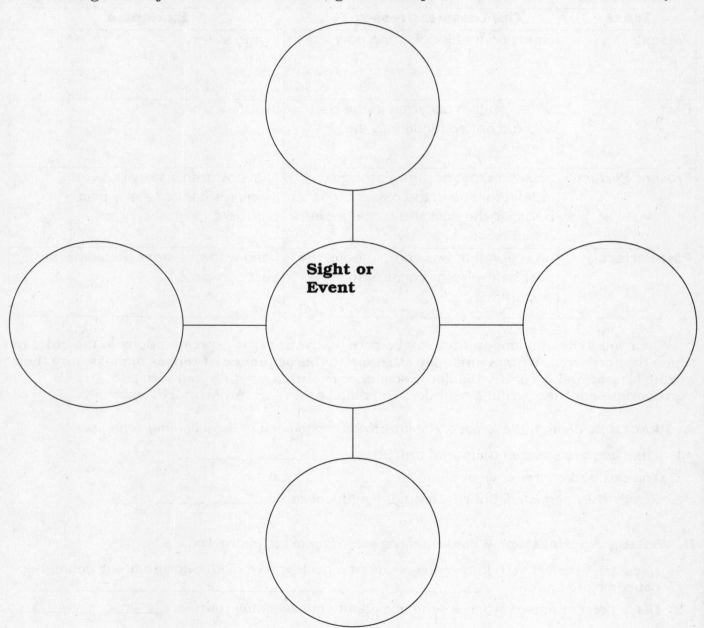

As you write your reflective essay on a separate page, draw on details you have recorded in the organizer. Use them to create deeper meaning about the event or sight you have experienced.

"An Arundel Tomb" and **"The Explosion"** by Philip Larkin
"On the Patio" by Peter Redgrove
"Not Waving but Drowning" by Stevie Smith

Support for Extend Your Learning

Research and Technology

Develop ideas for your **slide show** by completing the following chart. In the left column, write details about Arundel's tomb. In the second column, write details from the tomb statuary that compares and contrasts with the details on Arundel's tomb.

Details of Arundel's Tomb	Details About Medieval Tomb Statuary

Listening and Speaking

Reread "The Explosion," and think about the miners. Jot two ideas for rhetorical questions and two ideas for figurative language in the chart below. Use your ideas as you write your **eulogy.**

Rhetorical Questions	1.
	2.
Figurative Language	1.
	2.

"An Arundel Tomb" and **"The Explosion"** by Philip Larkin
"On the Patio" by Peter Redgrove
"Not Waving but Drowning" by Stevie Smith
Enrichment: Social Studies

Coal Mining in England

Many of us can imagine—based on history lessons or stories we've read—the early days of coal mining. Perhaps you envision workers, wearing helmets with candles or small gas lamps on them, descending dark tunnels to chip away at the rock face with metal shovels and pick axes. In fact, this picture developed relatively late in coal-mining history.

Imagine, if you can, *thirteenth-century* coal miners. At that early date, coal was already being shipped from Durham and Northumberland, two areas that are now counties in northern England. Coal was a regular trade commodity for the next several hundred years, becoming more and more widely used as a household fuel. In the 1700s, with the onset of the Industrial Revolution and the use of steam power, coal mining virtually exploded. Between 1815 and 1865, Britain's coal production increased five-fold due to the increased demand made by Britain's factories.

The coal industry has long been important in Wales. Prior to World War I, South Wales boasted 630 coal mines and 230,000 miners. Keep in mind that all of Wales is just a little larger than the state of Massachusetts. Today, however, due to changes in the industry and changes in demand, there are perhaps seven mines and 4,000 miners in South Wales.

DIRECTIONS: *Use the information on this page about the history of coal mining in England to draw conclusions about the impact of changes in the coal industry on the people of Britain.*

1. Suppose you belong to a family that has lived in Northumberland for generations. Your ancestors, grandfathers, uncles, and father have all been coal miners. What, do you suppose, is your family's attitude toward coal mining?

   _____

   _____

2. In the mid-1850's in Britain, industry and technology created a boom in the coal industry. How might this have affected people's attitudes toward coal mining?

   _____

   _____

3. To residents of South Wales in 1913, it seemed as if the whole world was one continuous coal mine. In the early 1930's, however, there was a significant decrease in demand for Welsh coal. What effect would this have had on the people of South Wales, who were so heavily involved in mining?

   _____

   _____

   _____

   _____

"An Arundel Tomb" and **"The Explosion"** by Philip Larkin
"On the Patio" by Peter Redgrove
"Not Waving but Drowning" by Stevie Smith

Selection Test A

Critical Reading *Identify the letter of the choice that best answers the question.*

____ 1. What is shown on the tomb described by the speaker in "An Arundel Tomb"?
   A. a knight on horseback
   B. a poem on faithfulness
   C. a crown and sword
   D. a husband and wife

____ 2. Read these lines from "An Arundel Tomb." How many times would you pause, including at the end?
   They would not think to lie so long. / Such faithfulness in effigy / Was just a detail friends would see:
   A. two times
   B. three times
   C. four times
   D. five times

____ 3. In "An Arundel Tomb," why is the line "The endless altered people came" described as iambic?
   A. It has a rhyme inside the sentence.
   B. Each foot has an unstressed and a stressed syllable.
   C. There is no regular rhythmic pattern to the line.
   D. People cannot understand what the poet is saying.

____ 4. What disaster occurs in "The Explosion"?
   A. The eggs in a lark's nest are broken.
   B. A miner falls and is seriously injured.
   C. Men die in an explosion in the mine.
   D. The mine starts to slide into the town.

____ 5. Why does the poem call the miners "fathers" and "brothers" in "The Explosion"?
   A. to tell that the miners were all men
   B. to show how careless the men were
   C. to complete the poem's regular meter
   D. to help readers identify with them

____ 6. Why is "Suddenly I dart out into the patio, / Snatch the bright glass up and drain it" from "On the Patio" described as free verse?
    A. It has lines that rhyme at the end.
    B. There are stressed and unstressed syllables.
    C. There is no end rhyme or regular meter.
    D. It uses the form of a ballad stanza.

____ 7. What does the glass of water become in "On the Patio"?
    A. a cloud
    B. lost love
    C. the speaker
    D. a sunny day

____ 8. Read these lines from "Not Waving but Drowning": "I was much too far out all my life / And not waving but drowning." How should they be read?
    A. as a rhyme
    B. as a song
    C. as two separate sentences
    D. as one sentence

____ 9. What is the speaker's tone in "Not Waving but Drowning"?
    A. happiness
    B. anger
    C. satisfaction
    D. sadness

Vocabulary and Grammar

____ 10. Which word best replaces *fidelity* in this sentence: "The husband and wife had a great sense of *fidelity* to one another"?
    A. competition
    B. fearfulness
    C. loneliness
    D. faithfulness

____ 11. Which sentence uses the present tense?
    A. I look at the statue each day.
    B. The snow fell yesterday
    C. Birds interrupted my thoughts.
    D. Time has stood still for us.

Essay

12. "On the Patio" builds dramatically to its conclusion. In an essay, tell what the poem is about. Explain how the main images develop an idea that is a surprise, as the speaker performs an unexpected action by putting the glass back.

13. In an essay, explain the message of the poem "Not Waving but Drowning." In your response, explain the meaning of these lines spoken by the dead man: "I was much too far out all my life / And not waving but drowning."

Name _____ Date _____

"An Arundel Tomb" and **"The Explosion"** by Philip Larkin
"On the Patio" by Peter Redgrove
"Not Waving but Drowning" by Stevie Smith
Selection Test B

Critical Reading *Identify the letter of the choice that best completes the statement or answers the question.*

_____ 1. In "An Arundel Tomb," the effigy shows a
  A. dog.
  B. knight and his armor.
  C. likeness of the sculptor.
  D. husband and a wife.

_____ 2. Which would be a strategy for reading and understanding "An Arundel Tomb"?
  A. visualizing falling snow
  B. knowing something about birdcalls
  C. visualizing "bone-riddled ground"
  D. reading in sentences

_____ 3. Choose the item in which the line of iambic tetrameter from "An Arundel Tomb" is correctly scanned.
  A. "Such plainness of the pre-baroque"
  B. "They would not think to lie so long".
  C. "The little dogs under their feet."
  D. "Of smoke in slow suspended skeins"

_____ 4. In "The Explosion," what is the immediate effect of the explosion?
  A. Normal, above-ground activities are momentarily interrupted.
  B. The wives rush to the entrance to the mine.
  C. The rabbits and larks all hide.
  D. The slagheap collapses.

_____ 5. Which is a theme of "The Explosion"?
  A. People's memories keep the dead alive.
  B. Death may occur suddenly and unexpectedly.
  C. Disasters are tragic and inevitable.
  D. Grieving is an important process.

_____ 6. Which line from "The Explosion" is in straight trochaic tetrameter?
  A. In the sun the slagheap slept.
  B. One showing the eggs unbroken.
  C. Down the lane came men in pit boots
  D. We shall see them face to face—

____ 7. In "The Explosion," the poet alters the rhythm of the lines that tell that the explosion occurs. What effect does this have?
  A. The lines sound more like an explosion.
  B. The lines get the reader's attention.
  C. The new rhythm is meant to sound like the speech of the now-dead miners.
  D. The altered rhythm conveys the sense that something "wrong" or unnatural has happened.

____ 8. In "On the Patio," what scene is the speaker watching?
  A. the gray clouds of a thunderstorm
  B. a wineglass filling up with rainwater
  C. lightning and thunder
  D. paint chipping off a rusty patio table

____ 9. The speaker in "On the Patio" empties the glass because he wants to
  A. fill it up with another cloud.
  B. clean up the mess.
  C. bring the table in out of the rain.
  D. see how much it will rain.

____ 10. In "Not Waving but Drowning," what is the gesture on which the poem focuses?
  A. a greeting
  B. a gesture of resignation
  C. a plea for help
  D. a farewell

____ 11. Which best describes the voice of the dead man in "Not Waving but Drowning"?
  A. cold
  B. frightened
  C. violent
  D. remorseful

____ 12. What sense does the word *cold* have when the dead man in "Not Waving but Drowning" says "it was too cold always"?
  A. The water was always too cold when he swam.
  B. The world was uninviting and unfriendly to him.
  C. The climate never suited him.
  D. It was too cold to have gone swimming in the first place.

Vocabulary and Grammar

____ 13. Their fidelity, or _____, is what will be remembered of the earl and countess.
  A. long lives
  B. eccentricity
  C. wealth
  D. faithfulness

____ 14. An effigy is a (an)
A. tomb.
B. image.
C. disguise.
D. copy.

____ 15. The sense of the verb tense used in the line "Time has transfigured them into / Untruth" is that the action
A. occurred in the past.
B. is occurring in the present.
C. occurred in the past and continues into the present.
D. occurred in the past before some other event.

____ 16. What tense should a writer use to express an action or state of being that happened in the past before some other event?
A. present
B. present perfect
C. past
D. past perfect

Essay

17. In "Not Waving but Drowning," the poet reveals the thoughts of the dead man. What are those thoughts and what is their message? What is the effect of the comments being made by the other people present? What is the effect of the poet's use of first person when expressing the dead man's thoughts? Write an essay responding to these questions.

18. In an essay discuss the central visual image of "An Arundel Tomb." How does the speaker reveal that image? What is the speaker's attitude toward the tomb? Does he admire it? Scorn it? Or something else? What legacy, according to the speaker, do the earl and countess pass on to us?

Vocabulary Warm-up Word Lists

Study these words from the selection. Then, complete the activities that follow.

Word List A

botanical [boh TAN uh kuhl] *adj.* having to do with plants or botany
　　Jerome's <u>botanical</u> interests are limited to ferns.

constellation [kahn stuh LAY shuhn] *n.* a group of stars that has been named
　　If you use your imagination, that <u>constellation</u> looks like a pot with a handle.

existed [eg ZIST id] *v.* lived; continued to be real
　　Dinosaurs <u>existed</u> long before humans came into being.

particularly [puhr TIK yuh luhr lee] *adv.* in a certain manner; especially
　　Of all the flowers in the garden, Clara <u>particularly</u> likes the irises.

poet [POH it] *n.* a person who writes compositions in verse and often in rhyme
　　Ralph Waldo Emerson was a philosopher, essayist, and <u>poet</u>.

poetry [POH uh tree] *n.* the art of writing compositions in verse
　　Haiku is a type of Japanese <u>poetry</u>.

rate [RAYT] *n.* amount or degree measured in proportion to something else
　　The automobile traveled at an excessive <u>rate</u> of speed.

tragedy [TRAJ uh dee] *n.* a sad or disastrous event
　　The tsunami in Indonesia was a terrible <u>tragedy</u> that caused great loss of life.

Word List B

calypso [kuh LIP soh] *n.* a type of West Indian music
　　Maryanne has loved <u>calypso</u> ever since she heard this music during her trip to Trinidad.

coconut [KOH kuh nut] *n.* the fruit of the coconut palm
　　One of the most important ingredients of this pie filling is <u>coconut</u>.

hospitable [HAHS pi tuh buhl] *adj.* showing welcome and generosity toward guests
　　The party guests all felt comfortable because of Juana's <u>hospitable</u> attitude.

humanity [hyoo MAN uh tee] *n.* the human race
　　A cure for cancer would benefit all <u>humanity</u>.

mango [MANG goh] *n.* a juicy tropical fruit with a slightly acid taste
　　This <u>mango</u> is ripe, juicy, and delicious.

negotiate [nuh GOH shee ayt] *v.* to bargain with others in hope of reaching an agreement
　　Pete tried to <u>negotiate</u> for a lower price, but Nora refused to budge.

punctually [PUNGK choo uh lee] *adv.* finished or arriving on time
　　Todd arrived <u>punctually</u> at the train station, but the train was late.

rite [RYT] *n.* a formal, solemn, or religious ceremony performed in a set way
　　A wedding is an emotional <u>rite</u> joining two lives together.

"B. Wordsworth" by V. S. Naipaul
Vocabulary Warm-up Exercises

Exercise A *Fill in each blank below using the appropriate word from Word List A.*

Esther had been working on her [1] _____ project all day, planting and transplanting in her garden, [2] _____ among the flower beds. She was grateful for nightfall because it meant she could rest. As Esther looked up at the night sky, she found her favorite [3] _____, Ursa Major. She began to think about how long those stars had [4] _____. She knew that they had been burning far before any human joy or [5] _____ had taken place on Earth, and that they would be burning long after she was gone. Esther was not a [6] _____, but she was fairly sure that thoughts about the immensity of the universe had been the subject of some great [7] _____. Even if great poems were created at the [8] _____ of a hundred a day, she thought, they would never explain the universe.

Exercise B *Decide whether each statement is true or false. Circle* T *or* F, *explain your answer.*

1. A visitor would be likely to hear <u>calypso</u> in Alaska.
   T / F _____

2. <u>Humanity</u> includes all the living things on Earth.
   T / F _____

3. A <u>hospitable</u> host at a party would probably make a guest feel very uncomfortable.
   T / F _____

4. If you hoped to get a bargain, you might <u>negotiate</u> with the seller.
   T / F _____

5. A child's graduation is an important <u>rite</u> that parents and grandparents often want to attend.
   T / F _____

6. You could use the juice from a <u>mango</u> to flavor some home-made sherbet.
   T / F _____

7. You could put a whole <u>coconut</u> on a toothpick and serve it as an appetizer.
   T / F _____

8. A person who arrives <u>punctually</u> at a bus station would probably miss the bus.
   T / F _____

"B. Wordsworth" by V. S. Naipaul
Reading Warm-up A

Read the following passage. Pay special attention to the underlined words. Then, read it again, and complete the activities. Use a separate sheet of paper for your written answers.

William Wordsworth was perhaps the greatest <u>poet</u> of the English Romantic period. He was born in 1770 in the Lake District in northwestern England, where he spent most of his life. Along with Samuel Taylor Coleridge, Wordsworth changed the direction of <u>poetry</u> completely, simplifying its language and style.

His poem "I Wandered Lonely as a Cloud," is a <u>particularly</u> good example. With fresh insight, he explores the emotional impact that "a host of golden daffodils" had on him when he suddenly came upon it. He compares them not just to a single <u>constellation</u> in the night sky, but to all the "stars that shine / And twinkle on the Milky Way." This is not his only poem that deals with a <u>botanical</u> subject like flowers. For example, in 1802, he wrote not one but two poems called "To the Daisy."

Wordsworth's life was marked by some <u>tragedy</u>. He became an orphan at age thirteen. When he was in his early forties, two of his five children died in the same year. Finally, his beloved sister Dorothy, who had been a great inspiration to him earlier, suffered a serious illness in 1829. This greatly affected her mind. It destroyed almost all of her memory. She became completely dependent on her brother and his wife, Mary. For the last twenty years of her life, Dorothy merely <u>existed</u> as she sat by the fire, occasionally reciting lines from her brother's poetry.

Wordsworth's best poems were written between 1797 and 1808. He continued to produce poetry until about 1823, though it was not as good as his earlier work. He wrote at an amazing <u>rate</u>, producing 70,000 lines of poetry. This is double the number of lines written by any other recognized poet.

1. Circle the name of the greatest <u>poet</u> of the English Romantic period. Explain what you like best about your favorite **poet**.

2. Underline the phrase that tells how Wordsworth and Coleridge changed the direction of <u>poetry</u>. What do you enjoy about **poetry**?

3. Circle the name of a <u>particularly</u> good example of Wordsworth's poetry. What does **particularly** mean?

4. Underline the word that tells what makes up a <u>constellation</u>. Name an example of a **constellation**.

5. Circle the word that is an example of a <u>botanical</u> item. Name three plants you might find in a local **botanical** garden.

6. Underline a nearby sentence that describes a <u>tragedy</u> in Wordsworth's life. Use **tragedy** in a sentence.

7. Circle the words that tell what Dorothy did as she merely <u>existed</u>. Name an animal that **existed** in the past but is now extinct.

8. Underline the phrase that proves Wordsworth wrote at an amazing <u>rate</u>. At a **rate** of four miles an hour, how far would you walk in two hours?

"B. Wordsworth" by V. S. Naipaul
Reading Warm-up B

Read the following passage. Pay special attention to the underlined words. Then, read it again, and complete the activities. Use a separate sheet of paper for your written answers.

Trinidad is one of the most exciting tropical tourist destinations you could ever hope to visit. The <u>hospitable</u> inhabitants of this lovely Caribbean island have ancestors from Africa, India, Europe, China, and the Middle East, which explains the rich, multi-ethnic feel of the country. The people will extend a friendly welcome to the traveler looking to relax in beautiful natural surroundings. Sun, sea, sand, parties, and music are what await those who come here, no matter what the season. For the traveler who arrives in time for Carnival, that yearly springtime <u>rite</u> of celebration and fun, Trinidad can be the vacation of a lifetime.

Carnival is the most famous cultural phenomenon of Trinidad, and for good reason. During Carnival, men and women dress in vibrant and colorful costumes to enjoy this unusually outrageous street event. Participants perform dances and sing songs—including <u>calypso</u>—as thousands of people fill the streets and enjoy the food, drink, and music that Trinidad has to offer. There's nothing like Carnival to show a cross-section of <u>humanity</u>, for people from all over the world participate in this wild party.

You don't have to go during Carnival to sample Trinidad culture; you can enjoy Trinidad all year long. The first thing you have to do is purchase a plane ticket. You might even be able to <u>negotiate</u> a bargain price. Then arrive <u>punctually</u> at the airport on the designated day—don't be late. Soon you will find yourself in a tropical paradise, where you can sit on the beach and order a shake made with a <u>mango</u>, a banana, and some pineapple—or any other tropical fruit that you enjoy. Just don't sit under a palm tree—you never know when a <u>coconut</u> might fall down and hit you on the head!

1. Underline the word in a nearby sentence that means about the same as hospitable. What is an example of a *hospitable* gesture that makes guests feel comfortable?

2. Circle the words that tell what kind of <u>rite</u> Carnival is. What is one *rite* in which high school seniors usually participate?

3. Circle the word that indicates what <u>calypso</u> is. Use *calypso* in a sentence.

4. Underline the word that means about the same as <u>humanity</u>. Name a historical discovery that benefited all of *humanity*.

5. Circle the word that hints at the meaning of <u>negotiate</u>. Describe how you might *negotiate* prices at a garage sale.

6. Underline the word that suggests the opposite of <u>punctually</u>. To arrive *punctually* at school, what time do you leave home?

7. Underline the phrase that tells what a <u>mango</u> is. Use *mango* in a sentence.

8. Circle the words that tell where a <u>coconut</u> grows. What is an example of a food that has *coconut* as an ingredient?

Name _____   Date _____

"**B. Wordsworth**" by V. S. Naipaul

Literary Analysis: First-Person Narrator

Point of view determines what the author can or cannot tell readers about a character's thoughts and actions. For instance, when we read a story written in **first-person narration,** we see, hear, and learn everything through the narrator. As a result, we can only guess why B. Wordsworth takes a liking to the narrator, what his motive might be, and whether or not he is what and who he says he is. We know only what the narrator tells us, and he can share information only from his own senses: what he sees, hears, thinks, imagines, assumes.

The following sentences are written from a variety of points of view. Identify with the word "yes" those sentences that could have been included in "B. Wordsworth" because they are written in the first person. Write "no" next to those sentences that are *not* in first person. Beneath each sentence marked "no," rewrite the sentence in first-person narration, as if it were part of the story.

_____ **1.** I was glad to see B. Wordsworth again and happy to be invited to eat his mangoes.

_____

_____

_____ **2.** B. Wordsworth was glad to see the boy.

_____

_____

_____ **3.** His mother was angry with the boy for coming home late from school and wondered where he'd been.

_____

_____

_____ **4.** B. Wordsworth told me, "I think you have the poet's eye."

_____

_____

_____ **5.** B. Wordsworth told him a story about a girl poet and a boy poet.

_____

_____

_____ **6.** B. Wordsworth and the boy took long walks through parks and along the waterfront.

_____

_____

Name _____ Date _____

"B. Wordsworth" by V. S. Naipaul
Reading Strategy: Respond to Characters

You can become a more active reader by envisioning the world a writer creates. One way to do this is to **respond to character** as you read. Each character reveals himself or herself through words, actions, personal qualities, and responses to other characters. For example, when B. Wordsworth asks the narrator if he may watch the bees, you are alerted to the character's unusual behavior. Then, when B. Wordsworth says, "I can watch a small flower like the morning glory and cry," you experience a glimpse of the man's sensitivity to the world around him.

DIRECTIONS: *As you read "B. Wordsworth," record in the following chart your responses to the behavior, words, and qualities expressed by B. Wordsworth and the narrator as they encounter specific events.*

Character: B. Wordsworth

Behavior/Words/Qualities	My Responses
Event:	
Event:	
Event:	

Character: the narrator

Behavior/Words/Qualities	My Responses
Event:	
Event:	
Event:	

Name _____ Date _____

Vocabulary Builder

Using Related Forms of *patron*

The Word Bank word *patronize* is a form of the word *patron,* which means "customer, supporter, or benefactor."

A. DIRECTIONS: *Write the form of the word* patron *that best completes each of the following sentences. Use context clues and your knowledge of the word* patron *to choose the correct word.*

| patronize | patronizing | patronage | patroness |

1. The wealthy _____ entered the gallery dressed in jewels and a lavish gown.
2. Unfortunately, the shopkeeper's _____ manner turned away many customers.
3. The wisest shopkeepers appreciate the _____ of each and every customer.
4. We decided to _____ the new Italian restaurant in our neighborhood.

Using the Word List

| rogue | patronize | distill | keenly |

B. DIRECTIONS: *Match each word in the left column with its definition in the right column. Write the letter of the definition on the line next to the word it defines.*

___ 1. keenly   A. to be a customer of a store

___ 2. rogue   B. to obtain the essential part

___ 3. patronize   C. sharply or intensely

___ 4. distill   D. scoundrel

C. DIRECTIONS: *Complete each of the sentences with the most appropriate word from the Word List.*

1. The poet sought to _____ life in a single line of poetry.
2. "What a _____ am I!" exclaimed Don Juan.
3. Writers seek to express thoughts and feelings _____.
4. Great minds _____ the resources of great literature.

Name _____ Date _____

"B. Wordsworth" by V. S. Naipaul

Grammar and Style: Pronoun Case in Compound Constructions

Pronoun case refers to the different forms a pronoun takes to indicate its function in a sentence. The subjective case is used when the pronoun performs the action—acts as the subject of the sentence—or when it renames the subject. The objective case is used when the pronoun receives the action of the verb—as a direct or an indirect object—or is the object of a preposition.

Subjective case pronouns: *I, we, you, he, she, it, they*

Objective case pronouns: *me, us, you, him, he, it, them*

The following sentences show the use of subjective and objective pronoun cases:

Subjective case: The narrator eats a fresh mango.

He is delighted with the flavor.

Objective case: B. Wordsworth tells the narrator a secret.

The poet asks *him* to keep a secret.

When **personal pronouns** are used in **compound structures**, that is, when they are linked by conjunctions such as *and* or *or,* they use the case that would be correct if the pronoun were used alone.

Subjective case: *He and B. Wordsworth* become friends.

B. *Wordsworth and I* talked about poetry.

Objective case: Orion shined brightly in the sky for the *poet and him.*

The yard on Miguel Street is a secret between *B. Wordsworth and me.*

A. PRACTICE: *Circle the correct pronouns for each sentence.*

1. The poet and (*I, me*) live on Miguel Street.

2. The narrator's mother and (*he, him*) do not have a close relationship.

3. They became friends, B. Wordsworth and (*he, him*).

B. Writing Application: *Each of the following sentences contains a compound pronoun construction. Rewrite each of these sentences, replacing the italicized word or words with a pronoun in the correct case.*

1. Mr. Wordsworth and *the narrator* take long walks together.

_____

2. *Mr. Wordsworth and the narrator* live on the same street.

_____

3. The relationship between the narrator and *his mother* is not loving.

_____

Name _____ Date _____

"**B. Wordsworth**" by V. S. Naipaul
Support for Writing

Use the diagram to collect details for your account of a remarkable person. Write the person's name in the center circle. In the surrounding boxes, write words and phrases to describe the person's remarkable qualities. Also, imagine the person in the scene you will describe. Jot notes about the person's reactions, words, and actions.

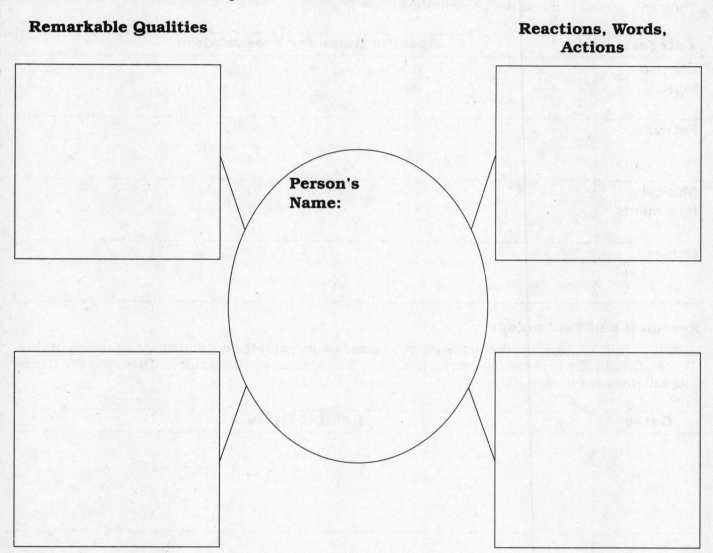

Remarkable Qualities

Reactions, Words, Actions

Person's Name:

As you write your first-person account of a remarkable person on a separate page, draw on ideas from your diagram. Use the details to help your readers see and understand the character and the situation.

"B. Wordsworth" by V. S. Naipaul
Support for Extend Your Learning

Listening and Speaking

Use the chart below to plan your contributions to the **multimedia tour.** List specific recordings, slides, photographs, and other items for the tour. Work with your group to select those the group will actually use in the presentation.

Categories	Specific Items for Presentation
Calypso Music	
Festivals	
Musical Intruments	
Others	

Research and Technology

Use this chart to organize the items for your **classroom exhibit** on the British influence in the West Indies. In the first column, write the dates for each part of the exhibit. Then, list the items you will display for each date.

Dates	Exhibit Items

Name _____ Date _____

"B. Wordsworth" by V. S. Naipaul

Enrichment: Astronomer

In V. S. Naipaul's short story, B. Wordsworth introduces the narrator to the names of the stars, including the constellation of Orion, the hunter. In that quiet moment between the two main characters, B. Wordsworth connects the small world of the young, frightened narrator to the larger, unknown universe.

If you were an astronomer, it would be your job to expand our knowledge about the universe. Not only do astronomers study the stars and other galaxies, they try to determine how our solar system evolved. To do this, they use laws of mathematics and physics.

Instead of spending the majority of their time looking through telescopes, astronomers today employ photographic and electronic equipment attached to telescopes to collect distant light and turn it into digital images on a computer. Observations are made and recorded by this sophisticated equipment from telescopes and observatories on earth and in space. Hot-air balloons, rockets, and satellites are all used to put observational equipment where it will be most effective. The astronomer decides what to observe and what methods of observation to use. He or she then analyzes the results of these observations, explains their significance or relevance to an existing theory, often publishing the findings in a scientific journal.

Because astronomy is a very competitive field, more opportunities exist for those who have a master's or doctor's degree in astronomy or in a related field, such as mathematics or physics. Most opportunities are in the government or education sectors.

DIRECTIONS: *Answer each of the following questions.*

1. What high school courses would best help you prepare for a career in astronomy?

   _____

   _____

   _____

2. How have an astronomer's tools of observation changed over the years?

   _____

   _____

   _____

3. Why are critical thinking and writing skills probably important for an astronomer?

   _____

   _____

   _____

4. In what way does the field of astronomy connect our smaller world with the larger universe?

   _____

   _____

   _____

"B. Wordsworth" by V. S. Naipaul
Selection Test A

Critical Reading *Identify the letter of the choice that best answers the question.*

____ 1. Who is the narrator of "B. Wordsworth"?
A. an outside narrator
B. V. S. Naipaul
C. a young boy
D. B. Wordsworth

____ 2. How do you know "B. Wordsworth" is told by a first-person narrator?
A. The narrator refers to himself as "I."
B. The narrator tells about other people in the story.
C. There is only one narrator for the entire story.
D. The narrator tells about B. Wordsworth.

____ 3. How does the narrator meet B. Wordsworth in "B. Wordsworth"?
A. He meets B. Wordsworth while he is singing Calypso music.
B. B. Wordsworth comes to his house and asks to watch the bees.
C. He meets B. Wordsworth when he is selling mangoes.
D. He meets B. Wordsworth when he is on a street corner.

____ 4. In "B. Wordsworth," what does B. Wordsworth claim to be?
A. a beekeeper
B. a gardener
C. a poet
D. a teacher

____ 5. What does B. Wordsworth mean when he tells the boy he is a poet in "B. Wordsworth"?
A. The boy speaks in rhymes.
B. The boy likes to read poetry.
C. The boy understands science.
D. The boy has many feelings.

____ 6. Which word best describes B. Wordsworth's manner of speaking in "B. Wordsworth"?
A. perfectly
B. softly
C. hurriedly
D. poorly

____ 7. In "B. Wordsworth," which words best describe the relationship between B. Wordsworth and the boy?
A. father and son
B. servant and master
C. gardener and helper
D. teacher and pupil

_____ 8. What might be a reader's most likely response to B. Wordsworth after reading "B. Wordsworth"?
A. B. Wordsworth is a beggar with no purpose in the world.
B. B. Wordsworth is a failure who mourns the lost love of his youth.
C. B. Wordsworth is a sensitive man who sees the wonder of the world.
D. B. Wordsworth is a capable man who cannot appreciate his own worth.

_____ 9. Why does B. Wordsworth tell the boy to leave and never come back in "B. Wordsworth"?
A. He is dying and does not want the boy to watch him.
B. He is tired of having the boy around all the time.
C. He realizes that he has taught the boy all he can.
D. He knows the boy's mother does not like him.

_____ 10. In "B. Wordsworth," the boy's mother scolds him after he has returned from eating mangoes at B. Wordsworth's. How might readers most likely respond to her anger?
A. The boy should learn never to tell his mother what he has been doing.
B. The boy didn't do anything wrong and does not deserve to be whipped.
C. The boy isn't very smart to tell his mother where he has been.
D. The boy deserves to be whipped for running around with a beggar.

_____ 11. What is the significance of B. Wordsworth's name in "B. Wordsworth"?
A. He chose the name because it was the only English name he knew.
B. It is a name of affection given him by his grandfather.
C. His old English master gave him the name to make fun of him.
D. He claims he is the black brother of the poet William Wordsworth.

_____ 12. In "B. Wordsworth," why does B. Wordsworth leave his garden untrimmed?
A. He is a poor gardener who does not know how to care for it.
B. He does not care about gardening or plants.
C. He decided not to touch it after the girl whom he loved died.
D. He is too tired after working all day to care for his garden.

Vocabulary and Grammar

_____ 13. Which word best replaces *keenly* in this sentence: "I *keenly* felt the sting of his words"?
A. sharply
B. joyfully
C. wisely
D. surprisingly

_____ 14. Which sentence uses the pronoun in the nominative case, as the subject of the sentence?
A. B. Wordsworth and I walked down to the park.
B. Others did not give B. Wordsworth and him a glance.
C. B. Wordsworth told him the line of poetry for that month.
D. The two people talked of poetry and many other things.

Essay

15. A first-person narrative is told from the point of view of a character who participates in the action of a story. A third-person narrative is told from the point of view of a character who does not participate. In an essay, explain how "B. Wordsworth" would be different if told by a third-person narrator. How might it change your response to the characters?

16. Near the end of "B. Wordsworth," B. Wordsworth sends the boy away and tells him not to come back. Then, the boy says, "I left the house, and ran home crying, like a poet, for everything I saw." In an essay, explain what the boy means. What does he mean in saying he cries like a poet? Give evidence from the story to support your response.

"B. Wordsworth" by V. S. Naipaul
Selection Test B

Critical Reading *Identify the letter of the choice that best completes the statement or answers the question.*

_____ 1. The narrator of this story is
   A. an unnamed boy.
   B. B. Wordsworth.
   C. V. S. Naipaul.
   D. the mother of a young boy.

_____ 2. The passage of the story that describes the beggars shows that the narrator's family is
   A. charitable and naive.
   B. stingy and suspicious.
   C. poor but kindly.
   D. artistic and wealthy.

_____ 3. How does the narrator meet B. Wordsworth?
   A. The boy sees Wordsworth perform with calypso singers.
   B. They live on the same block.
   C. Wordsworth is a well-known neighborhood poet.
   D. Wordsworth begs at the boy's home.

_____ 4. Which word best characterizes B. Wordsworth's request to watch bees in the narrator's yard?
   A. typical
   B. friendly
   C. unusual
   D. threatening

_____ 5. B. Wordsworth refers to the boy as a poet, meaning that he
   A. speaks in rhyme.
   B. is a sensitive person.
   C. is a writer.
   D. speaks in elegant language.

_____ 6. What makes this selection a first-person narrative?
   A. It relates an experience from the viewpoint of someone directly involved.
   B. It tells a story from beginning to end.
   C. It relates the experiences of the first person mentioned.
   D. It provides insight into the author's personal views.

____ 7. Which sentence might be spoken by the first-person narrator?
    I. My mother was angry with me for asking for four cents.
    II. B. Wordsworth was secretly glad to see the young boy.
    III. B. Wordsworth told a story about a girl poet and a boy poet.
    IV. I enjoyed eating the juicy mangoes.
    A. I and IV
    B. I, II, and III
    C. I, III, and IV
    D. all of the above

____ 8. Which best describes the relationship between B. Wordsworth and the narrator?
    A. teacher and student
    B. father and son
    C. merchant and customer
    D. patron and artist

____ 9. Which statement summarizes the likeliest reader's response to B. Wordsworth?
    A. He is a smooth-talking bum.
    B. He is a warm man with a talent for wonder, with something pitiable about him.
    C. He is an inspiring model.
    D. He is a vivid warning of the folly of poetry.

____ 10. The girl whom poet B. Wordsworth describes was most likely
    A. his mother.
    B. the narrator's mother.
    C. his wife.
    D. the woman who came begging at noon.

____ 11. Why does B. Wordsworth ask the boy to go away and never return?
    A. He knows his home is going to be torn down.
    B. He is afraid the boy will learn that he has lied to him.
    C. He has been angered by the boy.
    D. He doesn't want the boy to watch him die.

____ 12. By using a first-person narrator, Naipaul emphasizes
    A. B. Wordsworth's unusual behavior.
    B. the young boy's limited knowledge of poetry.
    C. the narrator's growing relationship with B. Wordsworth.
    D. the narrator's all-knowing character.

Vocabulary and Grammar

____ 13. What does the word *distill* mean?
    A. to be very quiet
    B. to obtain the essential part
    C. to comprehend
    D. to distinguish between parts

____ 14. Which of the following would you feel *keenly*?
   A. bumping into someone
   B. a shoulder massage
   C. a sharp pang of hunger
   D. stepping on a cat's tail

____ 15. Which sentence from "B. Wordsworth" contains pronouns in a compound construction?
   A. "One day a man called and said he was hungry."
   B. "He spoke very slowly and very correctly, as though every word was costing him money."
   C. "He said, 'That's what I do, I just watch.'"
   D. "He said, 'This is just between you and me, remember.'"

____ 16. Which sentence contains an incorrect pronoun case in a compound construction?
   A. Between you and I, that was the juiciest mango I've ever eaten.
   B. The narrator and he took long walks.
   C. They became friends, the poet and he.
   D. Mr. Wordsworth's yard and mango were a secret between him and me.

Essay

17. The young narrator rarely describes his feelings about B. Wordsworth directly. Yet the narrator clearly responds to Wordsworth. In an essay, describe the narrator's response to Wordsworth. Support your response with details from the story.

18. Naipaul's story is written from first-person point of view. The narrator, a young boy who lives in Trinidad, provides information about characters and events from his point of view. In an essay, explain how this story might be different if it were related from an omniscient, or all-knowing, point of view. Furthermore, explain why you do or do not think first-person narration is an effective point of view for relating the story. Support your assertion with several details from the story.

Vocabulary Warm-up Word Lists

Study these words from the selection. Then, complete the activities that follow.

Word List A

associated [uh SOH shee ay tid] *v.* connected in one's mind
Eddie always <u>associated</u> the smell of cut grass with his childhood.

bargaining [BAHR guh ning] *n.* the making of an agreement
When their <u>bargaining</u> was over, Sylvia was happy with the deal.

careered [kuh REERD] *v.* moved along at great speed
Steve <u>careered</u> dangerously down the hill on his new ten-speed bike.

compartments [kuhm PAHRT mints] *n.* sections of an enclosed area
David's sock drawer is divided into two <u>compartments</u>.

coordinated [koh AWR dn ay tid] *adj.* working together
With <u>coordinated</u> efforts, Alice and Sam cleaned the house quickly.

incredulous [in KREJ uh luhs] *adj.* feeling or having doubt or disbelief
With an <u>incredulous</u> look, Claire let us know she did not believe our story.

oneself [wun SELF] *pron.* one's own self
Taking care of <u>oneself</u> is the best way to stay healthy.

sinews [SIN yooz] *n.* tendons
Brad's injuries to his <u>sinews</u> took months to heal.

Word List B

chalet [sha LAY] *n.* a Swiss cottage with very wide eaves
The <u>chalet</u> looked so picturesque in the snow-covered mountains.

dwindling [DWIN dling] *adj.* gradually decreasing
Our <u>dwindling</u> supplies were a signal that we needed help quickly.

imprint [IM print] *n.* a mark made by printing, stamping, or pressing
Each child made an <u>imprint</u> that looked like an angel in the snow.

interrogating [in TER uh gayt ing] *v.* questioning in a formal setting
The police officer began <u>interrogating</u> the suspect.

preparedness [pree PAIR id nis] *n.* the state of being ready
Our storm <u>preparedness</u> included stocking the cellar with water.

readiness [RED ee nis] *n.* the state of being equipped or prepared
After installing the storm windows, Sam was in <u>readiness</u> for winter.

recur [ri KER] *v.* to occur again after an interval
Thoughts about Jane continued to <u>recur</u> in Albert's mind.

rhythmical [RITH mi kuhl] *adj.* marked by a repeated pattern
The song had a <u>rhythmical</u> beat that urged us to get up and dance.

"The Train from Rhodesia" by Nadine Gordimer
Vocabulary Warm-up Exercises

Exercise A *Fill in the blanks, using each word from Word List A only once.*

As Manuel [1] _____ down the street on his bike, he remembered his

mother's words, "One must always take care of [2] _____, so be careful!"

He tried to avoid falling after riding over a pothole in the street, but despite all his

[3] _____ efforts, he fell hard. His leg was injured so badly that he

suspected his [4] _____ were torn. He looked into the various

[5] _____ in his first-aid kit, but could find nothing for pain. Later, a

doctor told him that some amount of pain would be [6] _____ with his

recovery. [7] _____, Manuel said, "What do you mean? Can't modern

medicine control that? I would be willing to do any kind of [8] _____ that

was necessary!" The doctor just shook her head and told Manuel to stop whining.

Exercise B *Decide whether each statement is true or false. Circle T or F, and explain your answer.*

1. An <u>imprint</u> of a hand in wet cement will be invisible when the cement dries.
   T / F _____

2. <u>Readiness</u> for kindergarten includes some familiarity with the alphabet.
   T / F _____

3. Dreams that <u>recur</u> are dreams that you have only once.
   T / F _____

4. Earthquake <u>preparedness</u> includes having an adequate supply of water.
   T / F _____

5. <u>Dwindling</u> supplies are supplies that keep growing in volume.
   T / F _____

6. A <u>chalet</u> is a tent that is easy to set up.
   T / F _____

7. The reason a person might be <u>interrogating</u> another is to get answers.
   T / F _____

8. It is hard to dance to a <u>rhythmical</u> piece of music.
   T / F _____

Name _____ Date _____

"**The Train from Rhodesia**" by Nadine Gordimer
Reading Warm-up A

Read the following passage. Pay special attention to the underlined words. Then, read it again, and complete the activities. Use a separate sheet of paper for your written answers.

If you have never taken a long train ride, then you owe it to yourself to do so. After all, one should never deny <u>oneself</u> the chance for an interesting educational experience. Many people who travel only by automobile may not believe that train travel can be comfortable. To this <u>incredulous</u> traveler, I would say that train travel is easy and enjoyable.

Some people, after a long car ride, feel pain or discomfort in their muscles, bones, and even <u>sinews</u>. This is because they might have been too crowded or cramped during the ride. This would never happen in a train. You can get up and stroll down the wide aisles on your way to the dining car, the observation car, or the cars that have private <u>compartments</u> for sleeping. All the aches and pains that are <u>associated</u> with a long car ride can be avoided by taking the train.

In the dining car, tables are set for four. If you are traveling alone, you can meet three new people at every meal. It is interesting to watch the <u>coordinated</u> efforts of the servers who work together to get three different seatings of passengers fed within a few short hours. You will not be doing any <u>bargaining</u> to negotiate prices of the meals. However, you might be able to persuade a server to give you an extra-large serving of your favorite dessert.

I have heard only one negative story about train travel. Once, my friend Agnes was in a train that <u>careered</u> down the track and moved at great speed. She was walking to the dining car, and lost her balance. The only thing that was really hurt was her pride, but she said that will not stop her from riding the train again.

1. Underline the word that means about the same as <u>oneself</u>. Then, use *oneself* in a sentence.

2. Underline the words in a nearby sentence that tell how an <u>incredulous</u> traveler feels about train travel. Then, tell what *incredulous* means.

3. Underline the words that give a clue to the meaning of <u>sinews</u>. Define *sinews*.

4. Circle the word that tells what the <u>compartments</u> are used for. How might *compartments* be useful in a kitchen drawer?

5. Underline the words that tell what are <u>associated</u> with a long car ride. What foods are *associated* with Thanksgiving?

6. Circle the words that hint at the meaning of <u>coordinated</u>. Describe one game in which *coordinated* effort is necessary in order to win.

7. Circle the a clue to the meaning of <u>bargaining</u>. Describe a time you used *bargaining* as a tool to get something you wanted.

8. Underline the words that hint at the meaning of <u>careered</u>. Describe a time you saw something that *careered*.

Name _____ Date _____

"**The Train from Rhodesia**" by Nadine Gordimer
Reading Warm-up B

Read the following passage. Pay special attention to the underlined words. Then, read it again, and complete the activities. Use a separate sheet of paper for your written answers.

Wood carving is an interesting and creative hobby. As a beginner, you should have the following tools in <u>readiness</u>: wood and a carving tool. Start out with soft woods rather than hard woods because they are much easier to carve. Your <u>preparedness</u> should also include a pattern, graphite paper, and protection for your fingers. Popular subjects that repeatedly <u>recur</u> include animals, people, and buildings. You might even become skilled enough to carve a model of a Swiss <u>chalet</u>, complete with decorative details and wide eaves.

Patterns are very useful and should have extremely simple lines. Make an <u>imprint</u> of the pattern on the wood by tracing it on graphite paper—do not use carbon paper because it is too difficult to erase the lines later without smudging them. When deciding where to make your first cut, you need to be aware of the grain of the wood, which runs vertically up the tree. If you were <u>interrogating</u> an expert about which way the grain should go, here is what your answer would be: For an animal shape, the grain should run up and down on fragile areas, such as legs. If you are carving a picture, the grain should run vertically.

Before you use sharp metal carving tools and wood, you might want to practice with a bar of soap and a plastic knife. You can sharpen the plastic knife by using sandpaper or a sander. Use short, <u>rhythmical</u> cutting strokes to remove the excess soap in a repeated pattern. Then, continue to carve your <u>dwindling</u> piece of soap by cutting and rubbing it by hand. After you have completed several soap sculptures, you are ready to start using wood and a carving knife. You should use thumb and finger guards, or a special kind of tape, to protect your hands.

1. Underline the words that tell what you should have in <u>readiness</u>. Use *readiness* in a sentence.

2. Circle the words that tell what your <u>preparedness</u> should include. Then, describe some first-aid *preparedness* that you should bring along on a hike.

3. Circle the word that provides a clue to the meaning of <u>recur</u>. Then, describe two events that *recur* in your daily schedule.

4. Underline the words that describe a <u>chalet</u>. Then, use *chalet* in a sentence.

5. Underline the words that tell how to make an <u>imprint</u> of the pattern. What does *imprint* mean?

6. Underline the words that tell what you might be <u>interrogating</u> an expert about. What is one question you might ask if you were *interrogating* an instructor in an art class?

7. Underline the words that hint at the meaning of <u>rhythmical</u>. What is one sport where you would use *rhythmical* movements?

8. Underline the words that describe why the soap is <u>dwindling</u>. What is a synonym for *dwindling*?

"The Train from Rhodesia" by Nadine Gordimer
Literary Analysis: Conflict and Theme

A **conflict** in a literary work is a struggle between two characters, or between a character and some outside force, such as society or nature. A **theme** is a literary work's central idea. To bring alive a theme for readers, writers often dramatize it by showing a character struggling with a conflict. The writer's theme is developed through the way in which a character resolves, or fails to resolve, the conflict. In simple stories with simple themes, the resolution may be straightforward. In more complex stories, the conflict may remain unresolved.

In Gordimer's story, there are many conflicts. The main character, a young woman, is not able to resolve the major conflict, but she finally does, through her own inner struggle and that with her husband, reach an understanding of what the true conflict is.

DIRECTIONS: *For each of the following passages from "The Train from Rhodesia," explain how conflict helps dramatize the theme.*

1. . . . she thought of the lion and smiled. That bit of fur round the neck. But the wooden buck, the hippos, the elephants, the baskets that already bulked out of their brown paper under the seat and on the luggage rack! How will they look at home? Where will you put them? What will they mean away from the places you found them? Away from the unreality of the last few weeks? The man outside. But he is not part of the unreality; he is for good now. Odd . . . somewhere there was an idea that he, that living with him, was part of the holiday, the strange places.

   _____

   _____

   _____

   _____

2. She was holding it [the lion] away from her, the head with the open jaws, the pointed teeth, the black tongue, the wonderful ruff of fur facing her. She was looking at it with an expression of not seeing, of seeing something different.

   _____

   _____

   _____

   _____

3. If you wanted the thing, she said, her voice rising and breaking with the shrill impotence of anger, why didn't you buy it in the first place? If you wanted it, why didn't you pay for it? Why didn't you take it decently, when he offered it? Why did you have to wait for him to run after the train with it, and give him one-and-six? One-and-six!

   _____

   _____

   _____

   _____

Name _____ Date _____

"The Train from Rhodesia" by Nadine Gordimer
Reading Strategy: Read Between the Lines

Writers do not always explain the meaning or significance of an event in a story. Just as a character needs to reflect and consider the significance of events that occur, the reader needs to **read between the lines** of the story to discover clues to meaning. Consider the following passage from the story:

> All up and down the length of the train in the dust the artists sprang, walking bent, like performing animals, the better to exhibit the fantasy held toward the faces on the train. Buck, startled and stiff, staring with round black and white eyes. More lions, standing erect, grappling with strange, thin, elongated warriors who clutched spears and showed no fear in their slits of eyes.

What is significant in the passage's contrasting description of the artists "walking bent" and the fearless "elongated warriors"?

DIRECTIONS: *As you read "The Train from Rhodesia," record in the first column events that you or a character do not fully understand. After you read between the lines, explain in the second column the full meaning or significance of the event.*

Event	Meaning of Event

"The Train from Rhodesia" by Nadine Gordimer
Vocabulary Builder

Using the Prefix *a-*

One of the meanings of the prefix *a-* is "without or not." When using this meaning of the prefix *a-*, the meaning of the base word is negated. For example, the Word Bank word *atrophy* means "without nourishment."

A. DIRECTIONS: *Complete each of the following sentences. Form the missing word by using the italicized context clue and your knowledge of the prefix a-.*

1. The _____ character in the story displayed a *lack of moral judgment*.
2. *Without a tonal center or key*, the _____ composition sounded like a chorus of squabbling birds.
3. Our _____ meal of popcorn was *not typical* of our dinner eating habits.

Using the Word List

impressionistic	elongated	segmented
splaying	atrophy	

B. DIRECTIONS: *Match each word in the left column with its definition in the right column. Write the letter of the definition on the line next to the word it defines.*

___ 1. atrophy   **A.** conveying a quick, overall picture

___ 2. impressionistic   **B.** separated into parts

___ 3. elongated   **C.** waste away

___ 4. segmented   **D.** spreading

___ 5. splaying   **E.** lengthened; stretched

C. DIRECTIONS: *Rewrite each sentence using an appropriate word from the Word List.*

1. Her memories of the incident were sketchy.

_____

2. After long hours on the train, he felt his muscles begin to lose strength.

_____

3. The suitcase fell, spreading its contents across the corridor.

_____

4. The journey was more restful because it was broken into manageable parts.

_____

5. Her face sagged, stretched by fatigue.

_____

"**The Train from Rhodesia**" by Nadine Gordimer
Grammar and Style: Nominative Absolutes

A **nominative absolute** is a group of words containing a noun or pronoun modified by a participle or participial phrase. In the following sentence from "The Train from Rhodesia," the nominative absolute is italicized.

The stationmaster was leaning against the end of the train, *green flag rolled in readiness.*

As you can see in the preceding example, a nominative absolute modifies the rest of the sentence in which it appears, instead of modifying a particular word. A nominative absolute is always set off by a comma. The details included in the phrase can heighten suspense and bring a scene to life.

A. PRACTICE: *Underline the nominative absolute in each of the following sentences from Gordimer's story.*

1. "A man passed beneath the arch of reaching arms meeting gray-black and white in the exchange of money for the staring wooden eyes, the stiff wooden legs sticking up in the air."

2. "Joints not yet coordinated, the segmented body of the train heaved and bumped back against itself."

3. "She was holding it away from her, . . . the wonderful ruff of fur facing her."

4. "He stood astonished, his hands hanging at his sides."

5. "She sat down again in the corner and, her face slumped in her hand, stared out of the window."

B. Writing Application: *Revise each of the following sentences by adding a nominative absolute.*

1. The train pulled into the station.

_____

_____

_____

2. The young woman stood on the platform.

_____

_____

_____

3. The stationmaster rang the bell.

_____

_____

_____

"The Train from Rhodesia" by Nadine Gordimer
Support for Writing

Use the chart below to develop ideas for your analysis of storytelling technique in "The Train from Rhodesia." First, review the story, and find examples of imagery and dialogue. Record them in the chart, and jot notes on how they relate to the theme.

	Examples	**How It Relates to Theme**
Imagery		
Dialogue		

On a separate page, draft your analysis of storytelling technique, using details from the chart. Organize your ideas logically. Discuss how Gordimer's technique works.

"The Train from Rhodesia" by Nadine Gordimer
Support for Extend Your Learning

Listening and Speaking

Use the chart below to organize your arguments for the **debate.** On the left side of the chart, write arguments to support the proposition. On the right side, write arguments against the proposition. Use both inductive arguments (that apply specific examples to general ideas) and deductive arguments (that apply general ideas to specific examples).

Proposition: One should always pay a fair price for a thing.	
Arguments for the Proposition	**Arguments Against the Proposition**

Research and Technology

Use the following chart to organize and plan the graphics for your **historical report** on South Africa. Record important details for your historical report in the left column. Then, list graphics that can help explain these details in the right column.

Historical Details	**Graphics**

"**The Train from Rhodesia**" by Nadine Gordimer
Enrichment: Social Studies

Cultural Attitudes

When we read a story about a time or place unlike our own, we often gain an understanding of another people's culture, attitudes, and customs. Much of the work of Nadine Gordimer, for example, is set in her native South Africa; when we read her fiction, we obtain a glimpse of a different way of life.

Below are three passages from Gordimer's story "The Train from Rhodesia." Read each passage, and then write the letter of the statement that expresses the attitude or cultural fact conveyed by the passage on the line.

1. _____ "A stir of preparedness ripples through the squatting native vendors waiting in the dust; the face of a carved wooden animal, eternally surprised, stuck out of a sack. The stationmaster's barefoot children wandered over. From the gray mud huts with the untidy heads that stood within a decorated mud wall, chickens, and dogs with their skin stretched like parchment over their bones, followed the piccains down to the track."

   A. The arrival of the train is routine, and people and dogs move out of the way.

   b. The arrival of the train is a surprise; people are afraid of this strange occurrence.

   C. The arrival of the train is a big event, and people respond to it with ritual-like actions.

2. _____ "All up and down the length of the train in the dust the artists sprang, walking bent, like performing animals, the better to exhibit the fantasy held toward the faces on the train."

   A. The natives think they must behave in this manner to sell their wares.

   B. The natives are entertainers who enjoy this attention.

   C. The artists know they will be treated with the respect and dignity they deserve.

3. _____ "A few men who had got down to stretch their legs sprang on to the train, clinging to the observation platforms, or perhaps merely standing on the iron step, holding the rail; but on the train, safe from the one dusty platform, the one tin house, the empty sand."

   A. Trains pass through rarely; the men want to make sure they see much of the town.

   B. The men feel threatened by the cries of the artists; they are glad to be away.

   C. Participating briefly in the ritual is one thing, but the men want no real exposure to the village.

"The Train from Rhodesia" by Nadine Gordimer
Selection Test A

Critical Reading *Identify the letter of the choice that best answers the question.*

____ 1. What can you conclude by reading between the lines in "The Train from Rhodesia" that state that "A stir or preparedness rippled through" the adults and children who left what they were doing to wait at the station?
A. The arrival of the train was an important event in people's lives.
B. People were disappointed by the train because travelers never stayed.
C. The people disliked the train's arrival because it meant they had to work.
D. The people generally ignored the arrival of the train.

____ 2. What is the carving that interests the young woman in "The Train from Rhodesia"?
A. a lion
B. an elephant
C. a train
D. an eagle

____ 3. In "The Train from Rhodesia," the old man holds up his carving for the young woman, "smiling, not from the heart, but at the customer." What can you tell about the old man by reading between the lines?
A. He is proud of his work.
B. He acts friendly only so he can make the sale.
C. He distrusts the young woman.
D. He likes the woman and wants to please her.

____ 4. Why does the young woman not buy the carving in "The Train from Rhodesia"?
A. She thinks it is poorly made.
B. She thinks it is too expensive.
C. She does not have the money.
D. The old man is rude to her.

____ 5. Who are the young man and woman in "The Train from Rhodesia"?
A. journalists
B. teachers
C. tourists
D. art collectors

____ 6. What is the main conflict in "The Train from Rhodesia"?
A. overcoming differences in religion
B. traveling in another country
C. settling on a fair price
D. remaining true to one's principles

_____ 7. How much does the young man finally pay for the carving in "The Train from Rhodesia"?
   A. what the old man asked
   B. more than the first asking price
   C. a little less than the first asking price
   D. less than half the first asking price

_____ 8. Why does the old man sell the carving at a low cost in "The Train from Rhodesia"?
   A. He wants to please the young woman.
   B. He needs the money.
   C. He knows the man is buying it for his wife.
   D. He is tired of bargaining.

_____ 9. After she has decided not to buy the carving in "The Train from Rhodesia," the young woman is struck by "the unreality of the last few weeks." To what is she referring?
   A. She is not feeling well or thinking clearly.
   B. The trip with her husband has been wonderful.
   C. The figures she has collected do not look like real animals.
   D. The poverty and culture of Africa seems unreal.

_____ 10. What is the theme of "The Train from Rhodesia"?
   A. Train trips bring travelers in touch with the real Africa.
   B. Only artists know the value of their work.
   C. Long trips test the patience of every married couple.
   D. A bargain that hurts someone else is no bargain.

_____ 11. What can you infer from the line that says the train "had cast the station like a skin" in "The Train from Rhodesia"?
   A. The train is once again behind schedule.
   B. Trains are common in Africa.
   C. The train is puffing clouds of smoke.
   D. The train stops at places that are easily forgotten.

Vocabulary and Grammar

_____ 12. Which word best replaces *segmented* in this sentence: "The *splaying* duck's foot stood in the mud"?
   A. sticky
   B. spread-out
   C. wet
   D. funny

_____ 13. Which sentence contains a nominative absolute that has a noun or pronoun that is modified by a participial phrase?
   A. The wife sat behind the mesh of her veranda.
   B. From a piece of string hung a tiny woven basket.
   C. Passengers drew themselves in at the corridor windows.
   D. He stood astonished, his hands hanging at his sides.

Essay

14. In an essay, explain why the young wife is angry with her husband in "The Train from Rhodesia." Think about why she refused to buy the carving because it was too expensive, and yet become angry with her husband when he got it at a bargain. What does her attitude show about the economic differences between the passengers and the local people?

15. After the bargain is struck in "The Train from Rhodesia," the narrator writes: "The old native stood, breath blowing out the skin between his ribs, feet tense, balanced in the sand, smiling and shaking his head. In his opened palm . . . was the retrieved shilling and sixpence." What can you conclude about the old man's feelings? Does he think he was taken advantage of? Explain your answer in an essay.

"The Train from Rhodesia" by Nadine Gordimer
Selection Test B

Critical Reading *Identify the letter of the choice that best completes the statement or answers the question.*

____ 1. "The Train from Rhodesia" explores which central idea?
   A. the economic dependence of blacks on the white minority in South Africa
   B. the marketplace economy in South Africa
   C. the varied geography of South Africa
   D. the psychological effects of moving between different cultures in South Africa

____ 2. Which sentence best summarizes the story's theme?
   A. Do unto others as you would have them do unto you.
   B. A bargain gained at the expense of another is no bargain.
   C. Dignity is the value you place on yourself, not the value others place on you.
   D. Neither a buyer nor a seller should go back on his or her word.

____ 3. Who are the young man and woman in the story?
   A. professional art collectors
   B. Rhodesians going home
   C. journalists
   D. tourists

____ 4. Which is a central conflict in the story?
   A. The prices paid for the crafts will never be equal to their worth.
   B. It is difficult to relate equally to people in an unequal social or economic setting.
   C. The crafts have meaning only in their original cultural context.
   D. No matter how much money the natives get, it will not improve their lives.

____ 5. Which event described in the story might be interpreted as a sign of inequality by an outside observer?
   A. The natives carve wooden animal figures to sell.
   B. The stationmaster's children fetch loaves of bread from the train.
   C. The native children ask tourists for pennies.
   D. The train passengers buy souvenirs during their travels.

____ 6. By reading between the lines, in which passage can you discover the underlying conflict between blacks and whites in the story?
   A. "The train came out of the red horizon and bore down toward them over the single straight track."
   B. "A stir of preparedness rippled through the squatting native vendors waiting in the dust; the face of a carved wooden animal, eternally surprised, stuck out of a sack."
   C. "A man passed beneath the arch of reaching arms meeting gray-black and white in the exchange of money for the staring wooden eyes, the stiff wooden legs sticking up in the air; . . ."
   D. "Passengers drew themselves in at the corridor windows and turned into compartments to fetch money, to call someone to look."

_____ 7. In this passage from the story, what can be understood about the artists by reading between the lines?

> All up and down the length of the train in the dust the artists sprang, walking bent, like performing animals, the better to exhibit the fantasy held toward the faces on the train. Buck, startled and stiff, staring with round black and white eyes. More lions, standing erect, grappling with strange, thin, elongated warriors who clutched spears and showed no fear in their slits of eyes.

A. They are proud of their warrior heritage and display this pride through their crafts.
B. Because of their economic dependence upon whites, they are no longer proud warriors, but vendors of their culture.
C. They need a creative outlet.
D. They enjoy performing for the white tourists.

_____ 8. In which way is the young woman in the story different from her husband?
A. She more actively treats the South African natives as equals.
B. She is less interested in buying crafts from South African natives.
C. She feels more at home amid the culture of South Africa.
D. She is more sensitive to the dignity of the South African natives.

_____ 9. Why does the old man finally offer to sell the carved lion for "one-and-six"?
A. He feels the lion isn't worth more.
B. He needs the money to survive.
C. He knows the man wanted to surprise his wife.
D. He does not want the lion to go to anyone else.

_____ 10. What do you discover about the young man's cultural attitudes by reading between the lines of this passage?

> Here, one-and-six baas!—As one automatically opens a hand to catch a thrown ball, a man fumbled wildly down his pocket, brought up the shilling and sixpence and threw them out; the old native, gasping, his skinny toes splaying the sand, flung the lion.

A. He sees himself as a father figure to the native South Africans.
B. He reveals his feelings of superiority through his disrespectful treatment of the old man.
C. He is caught up in a social system that encourages whites to see blacks as unworthy of respect.
D. He believes whites and blacks should receive equal treatment.

_____ 11. At the end of the story, the man and the woman are in conflict with each other because
A. the incident has brought to light their different values.
B. she no longer cares about the carving.
C. he resents that his wife has changed her mind.
D. she is more responsive to the old man than to her husband.

Vocabulary and Grammar

_____ 12. The word *elongated* means
A. relieved.
B. lengthened.
C. yearned.
D. enlightened.

____ 13. The word *atrophy* contains the prefix *a-*, which means
   A. on top.
   B. waste away.
   C. negate.
   D. without or not.

____ 14. Which sentence from "The Train from Rhodesia" contains an absolute phrase?
   A. "The stationmaster was leaning against the end of the train, green flag rolled in readiness."
   B. "The stationmaster went slowly in under the chalet."
   C. "The young man swung in from the corridor, breathless."
   D. "She was pushing it at him, trying to force him to take it."

____ 15. Which part of this sentence is an absolute phrase?
   Joints not yet coordinated, the segmented body of the train heaved and bumped back against itself.

   A. Joints not yet coordinated
   B. the segmented body of the train
   C. heaved and bumped back against itself
   D. The sentence does not contain an absolute phrase.

Essay

16. In an essay explain the significance of the train's arrival for the local townspeople. How do people respond to the arrival of the train? Why? Use details from the story to support your explanation.

17. Select a passage from "The Train from Rhodesia" that you think most vividly highlights the inner conflict felt by the young woman as well as the larger conflict central to the story. In an essay, explain the significance of the passage you've chosen.

Study these words from the selections. Then, complete the activities that follow.

Word List A

ashen [ASH uhn] *adj.* of, like, or pale as ashes; gray
Andrea's <u>ashen</u> appearance made us think she was ill.

fronds [FRAHNDZ] *n.* large, leaflike parts, as of a palm tree or fern
The palm <u>fronds</u> were all over the ground after the storm.

horizon [huh RY zuhn] *n.* the line where the earth and sky seem to meet
The shipwrecked sailor scanned the <u>horizon</u> for signs of a rescue ship.

quips [KWIPS] *n.* clever or witty, and sometimes sarcastic, remarks
Dave was a good talk show host because his <u>quips</u> were entertaining.

scurry [SKER ee] *n.* the act of running quickly or hastily
With a sudden <u>scurry</u>, the mice were gone.

thatched [THACHT] *adj.* covered with reeds, straw, or similar material
The lovely, rose-covered cottage had a <u>thatched</u> roof.

triangular [try ANG yuh luhr] *adj.* shaped like a three-sided figure
They threw the ball in a <u>triangular</u> pattern from Mel to Jack to Bobbie.

withered [WI<u>TH</u> uhrd] *v.* became limp, dry, or lifeless
Months without rain <u>withered</u> the crops.

Word List B

extinction [ek STINGK shuhn] *n.* the condition of no longer existing
The whooping crane is no longer in immediate danger of <u>extinction</u>.

muttering [MUT uhr ing] *v.* mumbling; speaking indistinctly
Marcus was <u>muttering</u> something about not wanting to go to this movie.

perpetuate [puhr PET choo ayt] *v.* to cause to last for a very long time
Wanda wished to <u>perpetuate</u> her brother's memory with her song.

prophetic [pruh FET ik] *adj.* having to do with a prediction or foretelling
The doctor's words about Sam's condition turned out to be <u>prophetic</u>.

radiated [RAY dee ay tid] *v.* spread out from a center, as wheel spokes
Concentric circles <u>radiated</u> out from the spot where the stone sank.

reverberation [ruh ver buh RAY shuhn] *n.* a vibration or echolike effect
The bell's <u>reverberation</u> could be heard for ten seconds.

seethe [SEE<u>TH</u>] *v.* to be excited or upset
Mr. Quinn will <u>seethe</u> with anger when he finds out about the window.

splendor [SPLEN duhr] *n.* brilliance or magnificence
The <u>splendor</u> of the bride's gown was dazzling.

Poetry of Derek Walcott
Vocabulary Warm-up Exercises

Exercise A *Fill in each blank below using the appropriate word from Word List A.*

Belle stood on the beach and looked out at the [1] _____, a hazy line in the distance. Would anyone ever find her on this remote island? From inside the [2] _____ hut she had constructed, her pet monkey peeked out. All along the beach, palm [3] _____ littered the sand. They had been [4] _____ by the heat of the sun. Belle searched a [5] _____ area, from her hut to the sea and back to the rainforest behind her. She saw nothing unusual, until she noticed the [6] _____ of twenty or so monkeys from one tree to another. "What are they up to?" she wondered. Being alone on this beach, Belle hadn't heard any good [7] _____ from a human being for about a year—she missed her best friend's clever jokes. All the conversation she ever heard was the chattering of the monkeys. She looked into the sliver of a mirror she had managed to save. Her face had lost its [8] _____ appearance as she had tanned under the tropical sun.

Exercise B *Create two different sentences for each word on Word List B. You may use different forms of the vocabulary word for your second sentence.*

Example: After our argument, she was <u>muttering</u> something but I could only guess what.
If you wish to be heard, do not <u>mutter</u>.

1. splendor: _____
   _____

2. perpetuate: _____
   _____

3. reverberation: _____
   _____

4. extinction: _____
   _____

5. prophetic: _____
   _____

6. seethe: _____
   _____

7. radiated: _____
   _____

Name _____   Date _____

Read the following passage. Pay special attention to the underlined words. Then, read it again, and complete the activities. Use a separate sheet of paper for your written answers.

Darryl and his sister Charlene were getting tired of hearing the quips, witty remarks, and jokes exchanged by their parents as they relaxed in the restaurant of the fancy hotel. "Please, can we go to the beach instead?" they whined.

Their parents gave them permission, and with a quick scurry, the kids were off. They ran past the plants in the lobby that had withered slightly in the heat, thinking that somebody should give those plants a misting so they wouldn't look so dry and lifeless.

They went up to the room to change into their bathing suits and then ran down to the beach. They ordered lemonades at a little thatched hut that served as a snack bar. Fronds of palm trees decorated the roof of the hut, with some hanging over to provide a little shade. The kids drank their lemonades on the beach and thought about going in for a little dip. Before they managed to get up off their beach towels, they noticed some sort of commotion down at the shore. "What could be the problem?" they wondered.

As they looked out to the water, they noticed a triangular shape swimming back and forth just beyond the waves. Then it turned around and headed west, toward the horizon. Could it have been the fin of a shark? Their question was answered when a man with an ashen face approached them. They learned later that his pale gray appearance was caused by fear. He had been in the water when he saw the shark approach. Luckily, he had been able to get out. No one had been hurt, but it looked as if the water would be off limits for a while.

1. Underline the words that mean about the same as quips. Use *quips* in a sentence.

2. Circle the word in a nearby sentence that tells how children move when they scurry. What does *scurry* mean?

3. Underline the words that tell what a plant that withered might look like. What can be done to help a plant that has *withered*?

4. Circle the words in a nearby sentence that tell what a hut might be thatched with. In what type of environment would you be very unlikely to find a *thatched* hut?

5. Circle the words that tell where the fronds came from. Use *fronds* in a sentence.

6. Underline the words in a nearby sentence that tell what the triangular shape might have been. What is an example of something that is *triangular*?

7. Circle the word that tells in what direction the horizon is, if you are watching the sunset. What is the *horizon*?

8. Underline the words in a nearby sentence that mean about the same as ashen. What kind of experience might give you an *ashen* face?

Poetry of Derek Walcott
Reading Warm-up B

Read the following passage. Pay special attention to the underlined words. Then, read it again, and complete the activities. Use a separate sheet of paper for your written answers.

A great lover of art, Samantha had long admired the work of J. M. W. Turner, but she had not had the opportunity to see many of his paintings in their original <u>splendor</u> and magnificence. The Tate Gallery in London had taken care of Turner's thousands of paintings since 1851 when he died, but in 1987, the Clore Gallery had been opened next door to the Tate to house Turner's work.

"I know you will just <u>seethe</u> with excitement the moment you get there," Samantha's friend Jessie had said, and Jessie's comment had certainly been <u>prophetic</u> since it came true. Here Samantha was, bubbling over with the excitement of the experience she was about to enjoy. Her face <u>radiated</u> pure joy as she said, "One, please," to the clerk at the counter. Moments later, she entered the gallery, eager to view the paintings she had only seen in books before.

She ignored the <u>reverberation</u> of footsteps echoing in the gallery and the low sound of people <u>muttering</u> to each other about the display, focusing entirely on her enjoyment of the art. One painting after another proved to her that Turner was indeed the most daring of painters in his time. His experiments with light and color had changed the course of painting forever.

To Samantha's mind, Turner's work was the absolute best art ever created. Her friend Jessie always tried to tell her that any art lover was entitled to an opinion that might contradict Samantha's, but Samantha would not listen. She considered it her own personal mission to <u>perpetuate</u> a universal appreciation for her favorite painter. If she had her way, Turner's reputation would never go into <u>extinction</u>—it would be a terrible shame to allow such a great artist's legacy to end.

1. Underline the word that means about the same as <u>splendor</u>. Use *splendor* in a sentence.

2. Circle the words in a nearby sentence that tell what <u>seethe</u> means. Use *seethe* in a sentence.

3. Underline the words that tell what <u>prophetic</u> means. What statement did someone once say to you or someone you know that turned out to be *prophetic*?

4. Circle the word that tells what <u>radiated</u> from Samantha's face. Use *radiated* in a sentence.

5. Underline the word that means about the same as <u>reverberation</u>. Tell about a *reverberation* of sound that you once heard.

6. Circle the words that tell what people were <u>muttering</u> about. Describe what *muttering* sounds like.

7. Underline the words that tell what Samantha wanted to <u>perpetuate</u>. What is one idea you would like to *perpetuate*?

8. Circle the word that gives a clue to the meaning of <u>extinction</u>. What does *extinction* mean?

from **Midsummer, XXIII** and *from* **Omeros** *from* **Chapter XXVIII** by Derek Walcott

Literary Analysis: Theme and Context

The **theme** is the main idea or basic meaning that a writer communicates in a literary work. Theme expresses a clear point of view about some aspect of life and human experience. The theme is understood through exploring the **context**—the local conditions from which it comes. Very often poets and other writers choose to reveal their themes indirectly—thorough characters' behavior, figurative language, details of setting or atmosphere, dialogue, and other elements—rather than to state their message directly.

DIRECTIONS: *Answer each of the following questions.*

1. One of Walcott's themes in both *Midsummer* and *Omeros* concerns the brutality and injustice that result from racial prejudice. Put the theme in context by listing the images and phrases from these poems in which Walcott touches on this idea.

from *Midsummer,* XXIII: _____

_____

_____

_____

_____

_____

from *Omeros,* from Chapter XXVIII: _____

_____

_____

_____

_____

_____

Name _____ Date _____

from Midsummer, XXIII and **from Omeros from Chapter XXVIII** by Derek Walcott
Reading Strategy: Apply Background Information

Sometimes it is helpful to **apply background information** to extend your understanding of a literary work. The fact that Derek Walcott was in England, for example, probably explains Brixton rather than Miami or Los Angeles, as a setting for a poem. First, focus closely on the words the writer has chosen to use in the work. After considering what exists on the page, you might seek more information from the larger context of the artist's life.

It is not always safe to assume that a writer's work gives the exact story of his or her life, or that events in a writer's life adequately explain his or her work. Having knowledge of a writer's life may help explain references and attitudes, though, such as Walcott's disappointment in English theater. Applying background information can enlarge your understanding and expand your comprehension of the artist's world and yours.

DIRECTIONS: *Use the background information from the biographical material and footnotes in your text to consider the following passages. For each, write what background information may apply, and how you think it affects the particular passage or how it may have influenced the ideas represented.*

Passage	Background Information	Effect or Influence on the Passage
1. "I was there to add some color to the British theater." *Midsummer*		
2. "Now he heard the griot muttering his prophetic song/ of sorrow that would be the past." *Omeros*		

from **Midsummer, XXIII** and *from* **Omeros** *from* **Chapter XXVIII** by Derek Walcott
Vocabulary Builder

Using the Root *-duc-*

The Word Bank word *inducted* contains the Latin root *-duc-*, which means "to lead." Many other words, such as *education* or *ductwork,* that connote "leading" or "bringing something toward" also share this origin.

A. DIRECTIONS: *Match each word with the -duc- word root in the left column with its meaning in the right column. Write the letter of the definition on the line next to the word it defines.*

___ 1. ductile

___ 2. ducat

___ 3. deduce

___ 4. abduct

___ 5. reduction

A. to lead or take away

B. to trace a course of thought

C. a cutting back in number or amount

D. easily drawn or shaped, as metal

E. a coin bearing the image of a duke

Using the Word List

antic	rancor	eclipse	inducted

B. DIRECTIONS: *Each item consists of a related pair of words in CAPITAL LETTERS, followed by four lettered pairs of words. Choose the pair that best expresses a relationship similar to that expressed in the pair in capital letters. Circle the letter of your choice.*

1. ANTIC : DIGNIFIED ::
   A. comic : funny
   B. rushed : sedate
   C. crazy : oddity
   D. frantic : nervous

2. RANCOR : ANIMOSITY ::
   A. malice : generosity
   B. spite : jealousy
   C. kindness : courtesy
   D. revenge : charity

3. INDUCTED : MEMBER ::
   A. honored : hero
   B. called : answer
   C. gave : donor
   D. rejected : quality

4. ECLIPSE : LIGHT ::
   A. darken : darkness
   B. dim : bright
   C. orbit : planet
   D. shade : sun

from **Midsummer, XXIII** and *from* **Omeros** *from* **Chapter XXVIII** by Derek Walcott
Grammar and Style: Commonly Confused Words: *Affect* and *Effect*

Two words commonly confused are ***affect*** and ***effect***. The words sound similar, and although *affect* is a verb, *effect* may be a noun or a verb, adding to the confusion.

Affect is nearly always a verb. The usual meaning of *affect* is "to influence." For example, "Caribbean backgrounds strongly *affect* the poetry of Walcott." You could substitute *influence* without changing the meaning.

Effect is usually a noun meaning "result." For example, "The *effect* of Walcott's poem is a new perspective of England." You can substitute *result* without changing the meaning.

When *effect* is a verb, it means "to bring about," or "achieve." The sense of *effect* when used as a verb is one of completion, as in "Walcott hopes to effect political change in England."

A. PRACTICE: *Indicate whether each sentence uses* affect *or* effect *correctly. Write* C *in the blank if the sentence is correct or* I *in the blank if the sentence is incorrect.*

____ 1. One *effect* of England's economic problems of the 1980's was increased competition for scarce jobs.

____ 2. This competition could not fail to *effect* an already tense racial climate.

____ 3. In order to *affect* reform, the country needed to improve its entire economy.

____ 4. The tension had its *effect* on every aspect of a long-overlooked issue.

B. Writing Application: *Write sentences using* affect *or* effect *according to the instructions given for each item.*

1. Write a sentence about the result of reading the selection from *Omeros* and your imagination of the slave trade.

   _____

   _____

   _____

2. Write a sentence about what change Walcott had hoped to bring about in British theater.

   _____

   _____

   _____

from Midsummer, XXIII and **from Omeros from Chapter XXVIII** by Derek Walcott

Support for Writing

Use the graphic organizer below to collect and organize ideas for your multimedia presentation of either Walcott poem. First, write the poem you have chosen. List the theme and main images in the boxes on the left. Then, list ideas for photographs, artwork, music, video clips, and sound effects that may illustrate the poem.

Poem: _____   **Audiovisual Aids**

Theme:

Image:

Image:

Image:

Draw on details from your graphic organizer as you draft your script on a separate page. Show the line-by-line relationship between the text and the aids you will use.

from **Midsummer, XXIII** and *from* **Omeros** *from* **Chapter XXVIII** by Derek Walcott
Support for Extend Your Learning

Listening and Speaking

Identify lines in *Midsummer* that are highly emotional. Jot parts of lines in the left column below. In the right column, write vivid words that describe the emotions. Think how you can express these feelings in your **recitation** by changing your volume, pace, or emphasis.

Emotional Lines	Description of the Emotions

Research and Technology

Write notes in the following chart as you do research for your **Caribbean culture festival**. Record ideas for items you may choose to exhibit, such as recordings of specific Caribbean music or a specialty food that might be prepared.

	Items in Exhibit
Language	
Food	
Music	

***from* Midsummer, XXIII** and ***from* Omeros *from* Chapter XXVIII** by Derek Walcott
Enrichment: Social Studies

British Royalty

Answer the following true-and-false quiz about British royalty:

1. _____ The Queen of England rules the British Empire.
2. _____ The monarchy operates independently of taxpayers.
3. _____ The Queen's husband is the King.
4. _____ Succession to the English throne has been unbroken since the Middle Ages.

The answer to all of the statements is false. The United Kingdom is a constitutional monarchy governed by Parliament. The queen has almost no real power, and taxpayers support the royal family. Prince Phillip, Queen Elizabeth's husband, Duke of Edinburgh and queen's consort, could never become king. The House of Windsor, formerly called Hanover, has reigned in England only since 1714.

Though the monarchy may not be all we think it is, it nevertheless has a hold on the imagination of America and the rest of the world. American history is tied heavily to Great Britain, and much of our population is descended from its emigrants. The close British-American alliance in World War II is still remembered by living Americans, and in the media we have watched England's royal family grow, age, err, and sometimes die.

The isolation of British royalty is both an advantage and a disadvantage. Without real power, the queen has no real responsibility for problems. She becomes a symbol for tradition, ritual, and stability, largely of an empire that is not as large or powerful as it once was. A fairy-tale sense of kings and queens inhabits our imaginations, though, and we watch the splendid ceremony with pleasure and wonder.

DIRECTIONS: *Answer the following questions.*

1. Why do you think the world pays attention to British royalty?

   _____

   _____

2. Give reasons why some Britons might feel isolated from the monarch, and reasons why some still feel highly loyal.

   _____

   _____

   _____

from Midsummer, *XXII* and *from* Omeros *Chapter XXVIII*, by Derek Walcott
Selection Test A

Critical Reading *Identify the letter of the choice that best answers the question.*

____ 1. What is the historical context of the excerpt from *Midsummer,* in which there are references to chains and whips?
   A. slavery in the West Indies
   B. a riot in London
   C. apartheid in South Africa
   D. New York City

____ 2. What background information would help you understand references to Boer cattle and apartheid in *Midsummer*?
   A. history of Great Britain
   B. background on the use of whips
   C. background on Boer cattle
   D. history of apartheid in South Africa

____ 3. To whom is Walcott alluding to in *Midsummer* when he refers the character called the Moor?
   A. a black character in Shakespeare's play *Othello*
   B. a griot, who is telling the story
   C. the poem's speaker, who is a West Indian
   D. the police chief who is handling a riot

____ 4. Why does the speaker in *Midsummer* say he was in London to "add color to the British theater"?
   A. The other actors were white.
   B. The other actors could not paint.
   C. The other actors were not poets.
   D. The other actors were rioters.

____ 5. What is the speaker's tone in *Midsummer* when he says, "But the blacks can't do Shakespeare"?
   A. He is humorous and joking.
   B. He is apologetic and sad.
   C. He is bitter and sarcastic.
   D. He is honest and realistic.

____ 6. What story does the griot, or oral historian, tell in the excerpt from *Omeros*?
   A. the story of how West Indians came to England in search of opportunity
   B. the story of the lives Africans once had before they were slaves
   C. the story of how Guinea gained its independence
   D. the story of enslaved Africans who were brought to the West Indies

____ 7. Why does the griot in *Omeros* say "remember us to the black waiter bringing the bill"?
   A. A people who once had a strong identity have been reduced to waiting tables.
   B. The griot once worked as a waiter and wants to be remembered to his friends.
   C. People who were once enslaved are now successful in their new land.
   D. The former slaves have been rewarded for their hard work with freedom.

____ 8. Which word best describes the tone of the excerpt from *Omeros*?
   A. satisfaction
   B. relief
   C. pleasure
   D. sorrow

____ 9. In *Omeros*, the speaker says the great "splendor" is the slaves' survival. Why?
   A. because they were given land
   B. because they found new freedom
   C. because they lived through hardship
   D. because they received a great welcome

____ 10. What does the speaker mean by these lines at the end of *Omeros*: "Now each man was a nation / in himself, without mother, father, brother"?
   A. Every African was proud of his or her country.
   B. The enslaved Africans were entirely alone, without a family or country.
   C. The African groups never joined together.
   D. Everyone is alone in life and has only himself or herself to rely on.

Vocabulary and Grammar

____ 11. Which word best replaces *rancor* in this sentence: "The griot must have felt *rancor*, although he acted friendly"?
   A. laughter
   B. bitterness
   C. changed
   D. dimmed

____ 12. Which sentence uses the word *effect* correctly to mean "result"?
   A. The griot's stories of slavery strongly *effect* his listeners.
   B. One *effect* of the slave trade was to destroy a culture.
   C. The lives of slaves still *effect* the stories of West Indians.
   D. How did conditions on the slave ships *effect* the Africans?

Essay

13. Derek Walcott's grandmothers were descendants of African slaves. His grandfathers were white. Both as a person and as an artist, Walcott has been caught between two cultures. Based on *Midsummer, XXIII*, what can you conclude about his feelings toward his place between these cultures? Use examples from the poem to help you respond.

14. In the first line of the excerpt form *Omeros*, the speaker mentions the griot's "prophetic song of sorrow" as he traces the history of Africans from their original free state, to enslavement, to their lives in the modern world. A prophecy is a prediction of what will happen. In an essay, explain how the griot's story is a prophecy.

Midsummer, *XXII* and *from* Omeros *Chapter XXVIII*, by Derek Walcott
Selection Test B

Critical Reading *Identify the letter of the choice that best completes the statement or answers the question.*

____ 1. The excerpt from *Midsummer,* XXIII, primarily concerns
   A. the passing of seasons in an English town.
   B. a view of England from a nonwhite perspective.
   C. race riots in England.
   D. the failure of Shakespeare's drama in modern times.

____ 2. Which would help a reader best appreciate Walcott's *Midsummer,* XXIII?
   A. visiting the site of the Brixton riots
   B. watching African actors in Shakespearean productions
   C. visualizing the life cycle of the leaves in the poem
   D. understanding literary allusions and cultural references

____ 3. In *Midsummer,* XXIII, Walcott refers to "Caedmon's raceless dew" and "Turner's ships" in order to
   A. show how far the British Empire has fallen.
   B. suggest that past artistic glories are put to shame by the brutality of this age.
   C. hint that these works of British art were never really of value.
   D. imply that the demonstrators have totally missed the point.

____ 4. The selection from *Omeros,* Chapter XXVIII, takes as its topic the
   A. destruction of African culture by modern life.
   B. preservation of tradition orally by the griot.
   C. speaker's struggle for his own identity.
   D. dislocation and grief brought by the slave trade.

____ 5. To what do these lines from *Omeros,* Chapter XXVIII, refer?
   So there went the Ashanti one way, the Mandingo another, the Ibo another, the Guinea . . .
   A. African tribes' unwillingness to adopt one another's customs
   B. loss of tribal identity in the New World
   C. warring tribal factions in Africa today
   D. dispersal of plant seeds from different parts of Africa

____ 6. When the speaker of *Omeros,* Chapter XXVIII, says "remember us to the black waiter bringing the bill," he suggests
   A. the destiny of people who have no past.
   B. that the griot must support himself with what he can get.
   C. the displacement of people who once had a rich identity.
   D. that financial gain will compensate for the wrong of slavery.

    7. What context is described by the speaker in *Midsummer* when he refers to "the stampeding hiss and scurry of green lemmings"?
      A. The rioters are acting dramatically.
      B. The rioters have gained the sympathy of many.
      C. The rioters act like frantic animals.
      D. The rioters are misunderstood.

    8. Which background information would help readers understand the griot's story about enslavement in *Omeros*?
      A. a map of west central Africa
      B. a review of the history of the triangle trade
      C. details about African traditions in the West Indies
      D. details about experiences on the slave ships

    9. Which statement best summarizes the theme of Walcott's two poems?
      A. Struggling people try to find a voice in the modern world.
      B. Gifted artists struggle for recognition.
      C. The beauty of nature lasts even during human struggle.
      D. The wisdom and experience of elders should be heard.

Vocabulary and Grammar

    10. Someone or something in *eclipse* is
      A. frightening.
      B. oval.
      C. fading.
      D. joyous.

    11. An *antic* behavior is
      A. quirky.
      B. secret.
      C. dangerous.
      D. old-fashioned.

    12. Which sentence employs a *correct* use of the word *affect*?
      A. The affect of the procedure is an enhanced life span.
      B. If one is to affect a reversal of events, one may have to reverse one's habits.
      C. A person can massively affect the lives of others without intention.
      D. Some literature, no matter how popular, has little lasting affect.

    13. Which sentence employs a *correct* use of the word *effect*?
      A. Using your car's safety equipment will effect your chances of survival in an accident.
      B. The careful researcher will do nothing to effect the integrity of his or her data.
      C. If you would effect the outcome of elections, you could begin by voting.
      D. The effect of long-term high doses of vitamins is not yet clear.

Essay

14. Outside information about the lives of poets and the subjects they write about helps in understanding poems. What information is particularly useful in grasping Walcott's poems? Write an essay in which you show how essential background information helps you understand the selections by Walcott. Use examples from *Midsummer*, Chapter XXIII and *Omeros*, Chapter XXVIII to support your ideas.

15. Walcott is intimately familiar with English language and culture. He also has an "outsider's" point of view on this tradition. Write an essay in which you explain how Walcott uses this double perspective in his poems. Use examples from *Midsummer*, Chapter XXIII and/or *Omeros*, Chapter XXVIII to support your points.

Name _____   Date _____

From the Author's Desk
Anita Desai Introduces "A Devoted Son"

DIRECTIONS: *Use the space provided to answer the questions.*

1. According to Anita Desai, why does writing a short story resemble writing a poem?

   _____

   _____

2. What examples does Desai give of "moments" that serve as inspiration or "seeds" for short stories?

   _____

   _____

   _____

   _____

3. Briefly explain Desai's process of writing a short story. How is this process like "planting seeds"?

   _____

   _____

   _____

   _____

4. According to Desai, what was the "seed" for her story "A Devoted Son"?

   _____

   _____

   _____

   _____

5. Desai claims that art can render complex and mysterious things "utterly pure, clear, and transparent." Do you agree with her claim? Briefly explain your answer, using at least one example from literature, painting, or music to support your opinion.

   _____

   _____

   _____

   _____

   _____

   _____

   _____

   _____

Anita Desai
Listening and Viewing

Segment 1: Meet Anita Desai
- What other languages does Anita Desai speak, and how does she incorporate them into her writing?
- Why do you think knowledge of other languages is important in character development?

_____

_____

_____

Segment 2: The Short Story
- What experience inspired Desai to write "A Devoted Son"?
- What truth about life does the story reveal?
- What experience would you write about that would express a truth about life?

_____

_____

_____

_____

Segment 3: The Writing Process
- According to Anita Desai, why are writing and playing music similar activities?
- Why do you think it is important to practice writing consistently?

_____

_____

_____

Segment 4: The Rewards of Writing
- Why does Anita Desai consider reading her "lifeline"?
- How can entering books add "another dimension" to your life?

_____

_____

_____

_____

Vocabulary Warm-up Word Lists

Study these words from the selection. Then, complete the activities that follow.

Word List A

amongst [uh MUNGST] *prep.* in the midst of; among
   Lily saw one weed <u>amongst</u> the lovely irises.

colleagues [KAHL eegz] *n.* fellow workers in a profession
   At lunchtime, Daisy and her <u>colleagues</u> ate together and talked about work.

distraught [dis TRAWT] *adj.* extremely upset; crazed
   Barbara was <u>distraught</u> when she brought her injured dog to the vet.

humiliating [hyoo MIL ee ayt ing] *adj.* extremely embarrassing; humbling
   It was <u>humiliating</u> for the team to lose by thirty points.

miraculously [muh RAK yoo luhs lee] *adv.* amazingly; wondrously
   The cat seemed extremely sick, but, <u>miraculously</u>, she recovered fully.

panicky [PAN ik ee] *adj.* showing sudden, overwhelming fear
   When Al yelled "Fire!" the <u>panicky</u> audience ran out of the theater.

thereafter [<u>th</u>ehr AF ter] *adv.* after that time
   Dee decided to save money; <u>thereafter</u>, she added to her account each week.

verandah [vuh RAN duh] *n.* a long, open, outdoor porch, usually with a roof
   Wanda sat on the <u>verandah</u>, sipping lemonade and admiring the sunset.

Word List B

adamantly [AD uh muhnt lee] *adv.* in an unyielding, stubborn way
   Roy <u>adamantly</u> refused to play ball with Jake.

deprived [dee PRYVD] *adj.* kept from getting, having, or enjoying
   <u>Deprived</u> of nutritious food, Don soon became ill.

efficiency [ee FISH uhn see] *n.* effectiveness achieved without waste
   With great <u>efficiency</u>, Marla washed the car in fifteen minutes.

exaggeration [eg zaj uh RAY shuhn] *n.* overstatement of what is real
   Paul was prone to <u>exaggeration</u> when talking about fish he caught.

multitude [MUHL tuh tood] *n.* a great number of persons or things
   Pat was surprised at the <u>multitude</u> that bought tickets for her speech.

prestigious [pres TEE juhs] *adj.* having or giving fame or respect
   The author of this book earned several <u>prestigious</u> awards for it.

sparse [SPAHRS] *adj.* meager; scattered thinly
   The rations given to the troops were <u>sparse</u> and stale.

surgeon [SER juhn] *n.* a doctor whose practice is limited to surgery
   The <u>surgeon</u> who took out Alan's tonsils was very skilled.

Name _____ Date _____

Exercise A *Fill in each blank below with the appropriate word from Word List A.*

Chad was feeling a bit depressed after his [1] _____ and embarrassing
performance at his new part-time job. He had gotten the job only two weeks before, and
he was told that he would be serving the tables that were out on the
[2] _____. He had been given a brief amount of training;
[3] _____, he had been on his own. All went well until this afternoon
when he carried a heavy tray [4] _____ the tables, chairs, and diners.
With a frightened, almost [5] _____ feeling, he realized the tray was
unbalanced. Within moments, his mood changed from slightly nervous to
[6] _____, or very upset. [7] _____, however, none of the
drinks spilled on any of the guests, and Chad still had his job. His
[8] _____ told him that they had all had similar experiences, which was
some comfort to Chad.

Exercise B *Find a **synonym** or **phrase** that means about the same as each word in the following vocabulary list. Then, use each vocabulary word in a sentence that makes the meaning of the
word clear.*

Example: Vocabulary word: *amongst* Phrase with similar meaning: *in the midst of*
　　　　　Sentence: Anna felt like a princess <u>in the midst of</u> peasants.

1. distraught Synonym: _____
　_____

2. colleagues Synonym: _____
　_____

3. miraculously Synonym: _____
　_____

4. thereafter Synonym: _____
　_____

5. verandah Synonym: _____
　_____

6. panicky Synonym: _____
　_____

7. humiliating Synonym: _____
　_____

"A Devoted Son" by Anita Desai
Reading Warm-up A

Read the following passage. Pay special attention to the underlined words. Then, read it again, and complete the activities. Use a separate sheet of paper for your written answers.

Ravi resided with her family in a comfortable home on the outskirts of Calcutta, India. The oldest of three children and the only girl, Ravi had always been interested in medicine; one of her quirks as a child was to patch up her dolls with bandages whenever they got a scratch. Now, as Ravi turned eighteen, her life was about to change drastically, and Ravi's family was <u>distraught</u>, in turmoil, and extremely upset.

It was time for Ravi to leave home. After much planning and preparation, Ravi was ready to begin studying medicine in the United States. She was enrolled in a university in Los Angeles, more than thirteen thousand miles away from home; her passport was in order, and she was packed. As she enjoyed her last evening <u>amongst</u> her beloved family, Ravi felt torn: on the one hand, she wanted to go, but on the other, she knew she'd miss her family, their pleasant evenings on the <u>verandah</u> in front of their home, and the familiarity of their customs.

Ravi had always been an excellent student, never having had a <u>humiliating</u> failure when it came to her studies. She had never had the <u>panicky</u>, frightened feeling that some of her friends had when they weren't prepared for a test. No, Ravi had made a resolution long ago to do her best at all times; <u>thereafter</u>, she had lived up to that promise to herself. Now, <u>miraculously</u> for someone whose family was not really wealthy, she was on her way to college, which would be followed by medical school. Ravi knew that she could look forward to a life among well-educated <u>colleagues</u>, the kind of coworkers who were dedicated to the idea of helping the sick get well. If only it weren't so difficult to leave home!

1. Underline two phrases that mean about the same as <u>distraught</u>. Tell about a situation that might make a person feel *distraught*.

2. Underline the words that describe the people <u>amongst</u> whom Ravi spent the evening. What is a more common word for *amongst*?

3. Circle the words that tell where the <u>verandah</u> is located. Use *verandah* in a sentence.

4. Circle the word that is described as <u>humiliating</u>. What does *humiliating* mean?

5. Circle the word that means about the same as <u>panicky</u>. What might cause you to have a *panicky* feeling?

6. Ravi made a resolution. Underline the words that tell what she did <u>thereafter</u>. Use *thereafter* in a sentence.

7. Circle the words that tell what was <u>miraculously</u> happening for Ravi. What is one thing that you wish would *miraculously* happen in your life?

8. Circle the word that means about the same as <u>colleagues</u>. What kind of *colleagues* would you like to work with in the future?

"A Devoted Son" by Anita Desai
Reading Warm-up B

Read the following passage. Pay special attention to the underlined words. Then, read it again, and complete the activities. Use a separate sheet of paper for your written answers.

A person who wants to become a doctor must be <u>adamantly</u> dedicated to the idea because the necessary education is a long and difficult process. Even if done with <u>efficiency</u>, with no wasted time, it will take at least eleven years beyond high school. It is not an <u>exaggeration</u> to say that a doctor's education can begin as early as high school, with such courses as chemistry, physics, and biology. After high school, the future physician must complete four years at a college or university.

Graduating with a four-year degree is just the first in a <u>multitude</u> of educational steps. The next step is four years at medical school, culminating in the earning of the <u>prestigious</u> doctor of medicine degree (M.D.). The step after that is a residency program: three to seven years or more of additional study and practice. The length of time required depends on the specialty in which the student is interested. Family practice, internal medicine, and pediatrics, among others, require three more years of training. For a general <u>surgeon</u> who will be performing operations, the requirement is five more years. For highly specialized forms of medicine, such as laparoscopic surgery or psychiatry, one to three more years beyond that are required. It is clear that a future doctor has <u>sparse</u> amounts of free time—maybe even none!

After all this study, one would think the graduate would be able to practice medicine. However, at this point, he or she would still be <u>deprived</u> of that opportunity. The right to practice medicine is denied until the future physician obtains a state license after a series of exams. Most physicians also become board certified, which means still more tests. Even then, a doctor's education does not cease. Doctors must continually keep up-to-date on new medical developments.

1. Underline the words that tell why a future doctor must be <u>adamantly</u> dedicated. What is another word that means about the same as *adamantly*?

2. Circle the words that explain what <u>efficiency</u> means. What is one task that you like to do with great *efficiency*?

3. Underline the words that tell what it is not an <u>exaggeration</u> to say. Use *exaggeration* in a sentence.

4. Underline the words in nearby sentences that prove the education of a doctor requires a <u>multitude</u> of steps. What does *multitude* mean?

5. Circle the item that is described as <u>prestigious</u>. What *prestigious* award do you think you might like to receive someday?

6. Underline the words that tell what a <u>surgeon</u> does. What kind of condition might require the services of a *surgeon*?

7. Circle the word that means even less than <u>sparse</u>. Use *sparse* in a sentence.

8. Circle the word in a nearby sentence that means about the same as <u>deprived</u>. What does *deprived* mean?

Name _____ Date _____

"A Devoted Son" by Anita Desai
Literary Analysis: Static and Dynamic Characters

Anita Desai's "A Devoted Son" presents an unusual example of **static** and **dynamic** characters. A static character is one who does not change during the course of a work, and a dynamic character is one who undergoes change as a result of what happens in the work. Readers might expect that the young man would be the one to change, but Desai reverses our expectations.

To understand static and dynamic characters, we need to consider what we mean by change. Varma never leaves the village. Yet he is not the same person at the end of the story as he was when Rakesh first showed him his test results. His feelings about the world and his son have altered dramatically. By contrast, Rakesh has many experiences, for he begins the story as a student, studies in America, returns, marries, raises a family, and founds a successful clinic. Yet Desai presents him as the same dutiful son at the end of the story as at the beginning, apparently unaffected internally by the things he has done.

How does Desai show the changes in Varma and the lack of change in Rakesh? Because the change occurs emotionally, we can look at descriptions of characters' feelings or responses to situations to follow each character's progress.

DIRECTIONS: *Answer the following questions by analyzing indications of change in Rakesh and Varma in "A Devoted Son."*

1. Describe Varma's emotional state at the beginning, middle, and at the end of the story.

_____

_____

_____

2. Identify three paragraphs from the beginning, the middle, and the end of the story that indicate this change. Write phrases or sentences from the paragraphs that evidence change.

_____

_____

_____

3. Describe Rakesh at the beginning and at the end of the story.

_____

_____

_____

4. Identify three paragraphs from the beginning, the middle, and the end of the story that support your description of Rakesh. Write phrases or sentences from the paragraphs that support your interpretation.

_____

_____

_____

320

"A Devoted Son" by Anita Desai
Reading Strategy: Evaluate Characters' Decisions

In good writing, characters and the situations they face often seem real. One test of a good story is whether you wonder about the characters outside the context of the story. Is Rakesh's father still alive? What is Rakesh like now? Has he learned what his father really needs?

As you read, you compare the things that characters do to what you think they ought to do, and develop attitudes about them. In much fiction, just as in life, actions have consequences, some of them not foreseen by the characters (or the reader). When Rakesh first did well on his exams, could his father have anticipated how success might affect his relationship with his son? Could you? As you read, try to **evaluate characters' decisions** in terms of the world of the story. What is being decided? What are the choices and consequences? How is each decision made? What are the values on which the decision is based?

DIRECTIONS: *Use the following chart to help you consider decisions the characters make in the story. The first column lists a decision that has been made. In the second column, write what you think the reason for that decision is, and how the decision is made. In the third column, write the consequences of the decision. What does it lead to in terms of events, and what effect does it have on this or other characters? In the fourth column, note your assessment or thoughts about the decision and the character.*

Decision	Motivation	Consequences	Evaluation
1. Rakesh pursues a career in medicine			
2. Rakesh seeks advanced education in America.			
3. Rakesh returns to India and sets up a clinic.			
4. Varma becomes increasingly irritable.			
5. Varma decides he wants to die.			

Name _____   Date _____

Vocabulary Builder

Using the Root *-fil-*

The Latin word *filius* means "son," and *filia* means "daughter." The Word Bank word *filial* comes from these roots, literally meaning "of or befitting a son or daughter." Words formed from the root *-fil-* imply obligation and association.

A. DIRECTIONS: *Match each word derived from the -fil- word root in the left column with its definition in the right column. Write the letter of the definition on the line by the word it defines.*

___ 1. affiliate (verb)   A. relationship between parent and child

___ 2. filiation   B. voluntary connection

___ 3. affiliate (noun)   C. to join or associate

___ 4. affiliation   D. a member or colleague

Using the Word List

exemplary	filial	encomiums	complaisant	fathom

B. DIRECTIONS: *Each item consists of a word from the Word List followed by four lettered words or phrases. Choose the word or phrase most nearly similar in meaning to the Word List word. Circle the letter of your choice.*

1. exemplary
   A. model
   B. necessary
   C. released
   D. principal

2. filial
   A. equine
   B. teeming
   C. belated
   D. respectful

3. encomiums
   A. campgrounds
   B. tributes
   C. environments
   D. savings

4. complaisant
   A. protesting
   B. supplement
   C. agreeable
   D. courtesy

5. fathom
   A. assist
   B. comprehend
   C. deny
   D. create

Name _____ Date _____

"A Devoted Son" by Anita Desai
Grammar and Style: Sentence Variety

Just as effective speakers change voice inflection to hold audiences, effective writers vary sentences to keep language moving.

Sentences vary by length. Some paragraphs begin with a short crisp sentence to make a point, followed by longer ones to provide details. Others may begin with long sentences to set the scene, and drive home a point with a single, blunt insight.

Sentences vary by type. Beginning a paragraph with a question or exclamation grabs readers' attention. Sentences are declarative, interrogative, imperative, or exclamatory.

Sentences vary by structure. Simple sentences, compound sentences (two or more independent clauses, but no subordinate clauses), or complex sentences (at least one independent and one subordinate clause) mix to vary the cadence of a paragraph.

Sentences vary in placement of elements. Within these types of variation exist options for more variety. Clauses, phrases, subjects, and predicates may shift for sentence diversity.

A. PRACTICE: *Identify the length, type, and structure of each sentence in the following passage. Then describe how all of the sentences work together to dramatize events in the paragraph.*

The old man who had been lying stretched out on his bed, weak and feeble after a day's illness, gave a start at the very sound, the tone of these words. He opened his eyes—rather, they fell open with shock—and he stared at his son with a disbelief that darkened quickly to reproach. A son who actually refused his father the food he craved? No, it was unheard of, it was incredible. But Rakesh had turned his back to him and was cleaning up the litter of bottles and packets on the medicine shelf and did not notice while Veena slipped silently out of the room with a little smirk that only the old man saw, and hated.

1. Sentence 1: _____

2. Sentence 2: _____

3. Sentence 3: _____

4. Sentence 4: _____

5. Sentence 5: _____

6. Paragraph Description: _____

_____

B. Writing Application: *Experiment with sentence variety by rewriting the third-to-last paragraph of "A Devoted Son." Reorder or recast sentences in the paragraph that begins "Varma's mouth. . . ."*

_____

_____

_____

_____

_____

Name _____ Date _____

"A Devoted Son" by Anita Desai
Support for Writing

As you brainstorm, record ideas for your proposal for a program for the elderly in the organizer below.

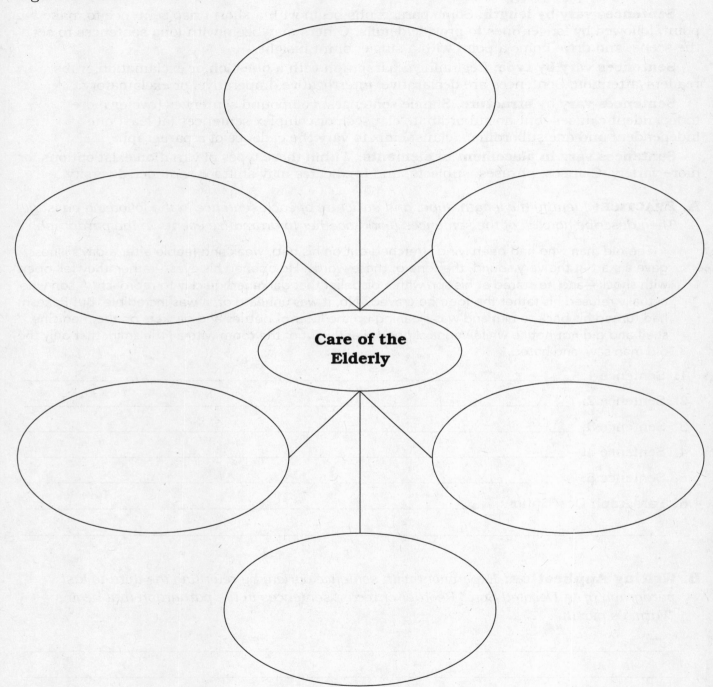

Use details from the diagram to draft your proposal for a program for the elderly on a separate page. State your objectives clearly, and use positive verbs.

"A Devoted Son" by Anita Desai
Support for Extend Your Learning

Listening and Speaking

Imagine yourself in the role of the character you will play. Think about your situation, your feelings, and what the other character is thinking. Then, respond to these questions as you prepare your **role play.** Practice by improvising before you perform.

What is the situation? _____

_____

How do I feel about what is happening? _____

_____

What do I want to happen? _____

_____

How can I make myself understood? _____

_____

Research and Technology

Do research on the Internet and in the library for your **social services report.** Write details about care for the elderly in the United States and India in the chart below.

The Elderly in the United States	The Elderly in India

"A Devoted Son" by Anita Desai
Enrichment: Physical Education

Cricket

The English game of cricket is played primarily in countries that are or were members of the British Empire, such as Australia, Canada, India, New Zealand, Pakistan, South Africa, and the West Indies. Cricket is sometimes seen as an upper-class remainder of the British colonial era.

The rules of cricket are complex, but the basic goal is to score runs by having a player strike a ball that is thrown (or *bowled*). The player must then run between two wickets sixty-six feet apart. A wicket is made up of three twenty-eight-inch stakes with two pieces of wood, called *bails,* lying across them. A player from the batting team stands at each wicket, and when the ball is struck, each may attempt to exchange places. If they can do so before either is put out, a run is scored. Batsmen may be put out in ten different ways, but the most common are for the opposing team to catch the ball in the air or use the ball to knock the bails off the wicket before a batsman reaches it. The same two batsmen continue until each is put out. When ten batsmen are out, the other team bats. Two innings usually constitute a match. High-level matches, called "Tests," may take three to five days to complete.

Cricket is played by eleven-player teams on a field about five hundred feet square. Balls may be hit to or fielded from anywhere. Four runs are scored if the ball leaves the field on the ground, six if in the air. The ball is made of hard leather and is about the size of a baseball. It can be spun, thrown or bounced to bowl. A cricket bat is flat, weighs about two-and-a-half pounds and is about thirty-eight inches long.

DIRECTIONS: *Answer the following questions.*

1. What similarities to baseball are apparent in cricket?

   _____

   _____

2. America is a former British colony and shares much culture with England. Why do you suppose cricket never became popular in the United States?

   _____

   _____

3. What is symbolized in "A Devoted Son" by Varma's grandsons playing cricket on the lawn?

   _____

   _____

   _____

   _____

   _____

   _____

"A Devoted Son" by Anita Desai
Selection Test A

Critical Reading *Identify the letter of the choice that best answers the question.*

_____ 1. What news does Rakesh get from reading the morning papers at the beginning of "A Devoted Son"?
A. He is getting married.
B. He has been admitted to college.
C. He is going to America.
D. He earned high marks on an examination.

_____ 2. As "A Devoted Son" begins, what makes Varma most proud of his son?
A. his respect for his father
B. his loyalty to his community
C. his professional achievements
D. his scholarship

_____ 3. Early in "A Devoted Son," what decision does the family make for Rakesh?
A. to keep him in India
B. to sacrifice so he can have a good education
C. to teach him to act independently like a modern Indian
D. to help him purchase the clinic

_____ 4. In "A Devoted Son," Rakesh agrees to marry a woman whom his mother has chosen. Which of the following statements gives the best evaluation of Rakesh's decision?
A. It is short-sighted because this wife will not help him achieve high social standing.
B. It is wise because he values his family's support and wants to stay in India as a doctor.
C. It is foolish because he should marry an American who would help him in his career.
D. It is wise because he knows an American wife would not treat his father respectfully.

_____ 5. In "A Devoted Son," where do Rakesh and his wife live?
A. in the United States
B. in a house near their clinic
C. in a new house outside the village
D. with Rakesh's father and mother

_____ 6. In "A Devoted Son," what happens to Varma after his wife dies?
A. He travels widely.
B. He helps his son in his clinic.
C. He becomes sick and frail.
D. He remarries.

____ 7. Which of the following shows that Rakesh is a static character who does not change in "A Devoted Son"?
A. He returns to his village to practice medicine.
B. He becomes wealthy and successful.
C. His devotion to his father never changes.
D. He uses all his medical skill to help his father.

____ 8. In "A Devoted Son," what does Varma begin to think of Rakesh's wife after he becomes ill?
A. that she makes fun of him
B. that she is a poor mother
C. that she spends money carelessly
D. that she is a kind nurse

____ 9. Which of these is a dynamic character who changes during "A Devoted Son"?
A. Rakesh, the son
B. Varma, the father
C. Veena, the daughter-in-law
D. Bhatia, the neighbor

____ 10. Why does Varma finally refuse to take the medicine given him by Rakesh in "A Devoted Son"?
A. He does not trust Western medicines.
B. He is just trying to annoy Rakesh.
C. He is getting ready to die.
D. He thinks Rakesh is mistreating him.

____ 11. What is the central conflict in "A Devoted Son"?
A. the conflict between Rakesh and his father about how Varma should be cared for
B. the conflict between Rakesh and his mother over whom he should marry
C. the conflict within Rakesh over whether to stay in his village or move to America
D. the conflict within Rakesh over whether to stay at the hospital or open a clinic

Vocabulary and Grammar

____ 12. Which word best replaces *fathom* in this sentence: "The father could not *fathom* why his son was trying to starve him"?
A. change
B. heal
C. deny
D. understand

____ 13. Which word best replaces *complaisant* in this sentence: "His wife was so quiet and *complaisant* that no one complained about her"?
A. disagreeable
B. angry
C. pleasant
D. talkative

____ **14.** What is one purpose for using sentence variety, or sentences of different lengths?
  A. to express angry emotions
  B. to call attention to dialogue
  C. to make writing interesting and lively
  D. to present facts and details

Essay

15. When his father becomes sick in "A Devoted Son," Rakesh becomes his doctor. He gives him many pills and controls what he eats. His decision does not always meet with his father's approval. In an essay, tell whether you think Rakesh makes the right decisions for his father's care. Support your opinion with details from the story.

16. In "A Devoted Son," Rakesh is a brilliant student who grows into a successful doctor, the richest in the village. Throughout his life, he shows respect for his father and does what he can to care for him. Nevertheless, people's opinions of him change from the beginning to the end of the story. Write an essay in which you describe how these opinions change. Use examples from the story to support your response.

"A Devoted Son" by Anita Desai
Selection Test B

Critical Reading *Identify the letter of the choice that best completes the statement or answers the question.*

_____ 1. What does Varma's family celebrate at the beginning of "A Devoted Son"?
   A. Rakesh's admission to college
   B. Rakesh's unexpected return from America
   C. Rakesh's wedding
   D. Rakesh's high marks in an examination

_____ 2. At the beginning of the story, Varma takes most pride in Rakesh's
   A. humility to all around him.
   B. extraordinary accomplishment.
   C. respect for his father.
   D. scholarship to America.

_____ 3. Which choice gives a reasonable evaluation of the family decision to sacrifice for Rakesh's education, considering only the beginning of the story?
   A. reasonable, because they hope to improve the family's prestige and fortunes by it
   B. foolish, because they are too poor to afford it
   C. selfish, because they are only thinking of the money Rakesh will bring them
   D. devoted, because they think only of their son

_____ 4. Rakesh shows that he is a static character by
   A. showing unwavering "devotion" to his father.
   B. changing dramatically once he returns from medical school.
   C. restricting his father's diet, despite his father's complaints.
   D. always getting his own way after his mother dies.

_____ 5. What was most surprising about Rakesh's marriage?
   A. His wife was pretty, plump, and uneducated.
   B. Rakesh followed traditional custom to acquire his bride.
   C. The wedding took place at home in India, not in America.
   D. His wife was good-natured, but lazy.

_____ 6. Rakesh and his wife lived
   A. near the hospital where he worked.
   B. just outside the increasingly shabby colony.
   C. a short drive from the clinic Rakesh founded.
   D. in his father and mother's house.

_____ 7. Rakesh's mother is a
   A. central character.
   B. static character.
   C. rounded character.
   D. dynamic character.

_____ 8. After his wife's death and his own retirement, Varma
  A. grew even closer to his son.
  B. was gratified by his son's attention.
  C. became irritable and fell ill often.
  D. longed for former times.

_____ 9. Which statement is a reasonable evaluation of Rakesh's decision to restrict his father's diet?
  A. Rakesh shows courage by doing what is right despite his father's complaints.
  B. Rakesh shows insensitivity in placing medical concerns before his father's happiness.
  C. Rakesh is being spiteful, avenging himself for the way his father tried to run his life when he was young.
  D. Rakesh is being stubborn and just wants to be right all the time.

_____ 10. The one dynamic character in "A Devoted Son" is
  A. Varma.
  B. Veena.
  C. Rakesh.
  D. Bhatia.

_____ 11. Which choice gives a reasonable evaluation of the family decision to sacrifice for Rakesh's education, considering the ending of the story?
  A. The family should have known better than to allow Western ideas to corrupt their son.
  B. The family should not have arrogantly assumed they could better themselves without cost.
  C. The family should have prepared to adjust their traditional thinking to match whatever new attitudes Rakesh adopted.
  D. The family could not have known in advance the true nature of what it was they wished for and eventually received.

_____ 12. What was the one remaining pleasure left to the elderly Varma?
  A. meals brought twice a day on a stainless steel tray
  B. *kheer,* a rice pudding served for dessert
  C. having the news read out to him
  D. visits from elderly neighbors

Vocabulary and Grammar

_____ 13. One who is *complaisant* is
  A. protesting.
  B. irritable.
  C. obliging.
  D. silent.

_____ 14. He could not *fathom* modern technology; he simply could not
  A. admire it.
  B. oppose it.
  C. understand it.
  D. afford it.

_____ 15. Writers vary sentences in order to
      A. embed dialogue in critical places.
      B. keep their writing interesting and lively.
      C. withhold plot information until the end.
      D. display their command of language.

_____ 16. Which is not a typical technique to provide sentence variety?
      A. varying the length of sentences
      B. varying the structure of sentences
      C. varying the type of sentences
      D. varying the coherence of sentences

Essay

17. In much modern fiction, characters do not see their fondest wishes come true. Yet everything that Varma hopes will happen for Rakesh does so, and Rakesh is "ever a devoted son." How does it all go wrong for Varma? Write an essay in which you trace the changes Varma goes through as Rakesh rises, and explain how Varma's dreams, in coming true, are ruined. Use examples from the story to illustrate your points.

18. The title "A Devoted Son" is ironic, for though Rakesh may be respectful, his father believes Rakesh treats him poorly. What larger point might Desai be making about the relations between India, and the West? How might Varma's story reflect India's ambivalent (two-sided) attitude towards Western culture?

Vocabulary Warm-up Word Lists

Study these words from the selection. Then, complete the activities that follow.

Word List A

analogy [uh NAL uh jee] *n.* a likeness that exists between two things
   Barbara pointed out the <u>analogy</u> between our arms and fishes' fins.

conservative [kuhn SER vuh tiv] *adj.* moderate; cautious
   Tim's budget is a <u>conservative</u> estimate of what he actually spends.

psychological [sy kuh LAHJ uh kuhl] *adj.* having to do with the mind; mental
   Despite its physical demands, tennis is said to be largely a <u>psychological</u> game.

separation [sep uh RAY shuhn] *n.* the condition of being disconnected or apart
   After a two-year <u>separation</u>, the two friends picked up where they'd left off.

ultimate [UL tuh mit] *adj.* greatest or highest possible; maximum
   Paula mistakenly thought that the <u>ultimate</u> honor was to be prom queen.

vertically [VER tuh kuhl ee] *adv.* in a straight up and down manner
   Richard threw the ball <u>vertically</u>, straight up into the air.

virtual [VER choo uhl] *adj.* existing in effect, though not in fact or form
   Our team's victory is a <u>virtual</u> certainty.

voyaging [VOY uh jing] *n.* a journey, especially by sea
   Our long years of <u>voyaging</u> began when we bought the sailboat.

Word List B

comprehension [kahm pruh HEN shuhn] *n.* the act of understanding
   Science fiction tests the limits of human <u>comprehension</u>.

decade [DEK ayd] *n.* a period of ten years
   Perry's favorite historical <u>decade</u> is the 1920s.

dispatches [DIS pach uhs] *n.* messages, especially from official sources
   The captain read the daily <u>dispatches</u> from headquarters before acting.

energetic [en uhr JET ik] *adj.* full of energy; forceful; vigorous
   Carla enjoyed playing with her <u>energetic</u> puppy.

profound [proh FOUND] *adj.* deep; complete
   The <u>profound</u> differences in our attitudes keep us from being friends.

restraints [ri STRAYNTS] *n.* things that hold other things back
   The <u>restraints</u> in the car seat kept the child in place.

substantial [sub STAN shuhl] *adj.* large, as in amount or extent
   Dave eats a <u>substantial</u> breakfast every morning.

velocity [vuh LAHS uh tee] *n.* speed or swiftness
   That car can travel at a <u>velocity</u> of 150 miles per hour.

"We'll Never Conquer Space" by Arthur C. Clarke
Vocabulary Warm-up Exercises

Exercise A *Fill in each blank below using the appropriate word from Word List A.*

Brad's favorite video game gave the feeling of [1] _____ reality—it seemed so real, but it was not. The game required that he move his characters [2] _____, horizontally, and at various angles against a watery background. The [3] _____ goal of all their [4] _____ was to reach a peaceful place where they could rest. In his mind, Brad made the [5] _____ to coming home after a long and difficult journey, finally able to end a long [6] _____ from the family. Brad was a [7] _____ player, not taking too many chances. He believed that this gave him a [8] _____ advantage over his opponent, his friend Darla, whose personality made her more likely to take chances that would cause her to lose the game.

Exercise B *Write a complete sentence to answer each question. For each item, use a word from Word List B to replace each underlined word or phrase without changing its meaning.*

1. In which <u>ten-year period</u> of the twenty-first century will you turn fifty?
   _____

2. What is the maximum <u>speed</u> allowed when driving in a residential area?
   _____

3. What is one <u>deep</u> thought that guides your life?
   _____

4. What is one school subject that challenges your skills of <u>understanding</u>?
   _____

5. How would you entertain a kitten who was <u>full of energy</u>?
   _____

6. What is one purchase that would require a <u>large</u> amount of money?
   _____

7. If you were getting ready to graduate, what kinds of <u>messages</u> from your school would you be expecting?
   _____

8. What <u>restrictions</u> might limit the freedom of prisoners?
   _____

Name _____ Date _____

"We'll Never Conquer Space" by Arthur C. Clarke
Reading Warm-up A

Read the following passage. Pay special attention to the underlined words. Then, read it again, and complete the activities. Use a separate sheet of paper for your written answers.

Some call space "the last frontier," an <u>analogy</u> that reminds us that frontiers on our own planet have, for the most part, been conquered. Not too long ago, however, most of our planet was unexplored. It's fun to imagine what it was like in, say, the time of Christopher Columbus, when the <u>ultimate</u> frontier seemed to be the wide, wild ocean, which no one had ever crossed.

The concept of a round world was not completely new in the late 1400s. What was unknown, of course, was that two huge continents separated the waters that were thought to be just one big ocean. The more cautious and <u>conservative</u> thinkers of the day, however, did not agree with this idea of a round world. That is why it was difficult for Columbus to get funding for his expedition. Persuading King Ferdinand and Queen Isabella of Spain to sponsor him must have been a great <u>psychological</u> victory for him, improving his mental state and boosting his confidence.

Ready for <u>voyaging</u>, Columbus set out on his historic ocean trip with a crew of about ninety men and three ships: the *Santa Maria,* the *Pinta,* and the *Niña.* If we could stand on the deck of one of those ships today and look up at the largest masts placed <u>vertically</u> on the decks, we would no doubt be astonished at how small they were. Compared to today's ships, Columbus's three ships were almost like toys.

Columbus's first voyage began on August 3, 1492. He arrived back in his home port on March 15, 1493. His <u>separation</u> from home lasted a little over six months, but it is a <u>virtual</u> certainty that those six months changed the world.

1. Underline two items that are compared in an **analogy**. Write an **analogy** comparing time to something else.

2. Underline the words that describe the <u>ultimate</u> frontier during the time of Columbus. Use **ultimate** in a sentence.

3. Circle the word that means about the same as <u>conservative</u>. What does **conservative** mean?

4. Circle the word that hints at the meaning of <u>psychological</u>. What might be a great **psychological** victory for a typical teenager?

5. Underline the words that mean about the same as <u>voyaging</u>. If you had time and money for **voyaging**, where would you like to go?

6. Circle the word that tells where you would have to look to see something that was placed <u>vertically</u>. Use **vertically** in a sentence.

7. Circle the words that tell what kind of <u>separation</u> Columbus had to endure. What is another word that is similar to **separation**?

8. Underline the words that tell what was a <u>virtual</u> certainty. What is one thing in your life that is a **virtual** certainty?

"We'll Never Conquer Space" by Arthur C. Clarke
Reading Warm-up B

Read the following passage. Pay special attention to the underlined words. Then, read it again, and complete the activities. Use a separate sheet of paper for your written answers.

The eventful <u>decade</u> of the 1950s saw the end of the Korean War and the beginning of the Cold War between the United States and the Soviet Union. It also saw the start of the space race, begun in 1957, when the Soviet Union successfully launched Sputnik I, the world's first artificial satellite. This launching triggered <u>profound</u> changes in the relationship between the two powerful countries. Before the launch of Sputnik I, the United States was assumed to be technologically superior; after the launch, the Soviet Union enjoyed <u>substantial</u> and significant amounts of prestige and respect as the most technologically advanced player.

The first satellite was about as big as a basketball and weighed about 183 pounds. It circled 500 miles above the earth at a <u>velocity</u> of about 18,000 miles per hour. At this speed, it completed one orbit in about 98 minutes. It transmitted radio signals, and even amateur ham radio operators could pick up these <u>dispatches</u>.

Americans were not only awed by the Soviet achievement but also frightened by it. The size of Sputnik I suggested that the Soviets had developed advanced rockets, possibly capable of delivering nuclear warheads. It became imperative for the United States to not only catch up but pass the Soviets as soon as possible. The space race was on, and all <u>restraints</u> were off. Nothing could hold back the march of technology.

Today, such launches are routine, but back then, it altered our <u>comprehension</u> of what the Soviets could do. This new understanding started the vigorous and <u>energetic</u> U.S. effort to put a man on the moon. By the time Neil Armstrong walked on the moon in 1969, the race was won.

1. Underline the words that name a <u>decade</u>. In what *decade* were you born?

2. Circle the nearby sentence that describes the <u>profound</u> changes. Use *profound* in a sentence.

3. Circle the word that means about the same as <u>substantial</u>. What kind of storm might cause *substantial* wind damage?

4. Underline the word in a nearby sentence that means the same as <u>velocity</u>. At what *velocity* do you think a jet can fly?

5. Circle the phrase that describes certain types of <u>dispatches</u>. What kinds of *dispatches* might make a traveler want to return home quickly?

6. Underline the words in a nearby sentence that tell what <u>restraints</u> normally do. Name two kinds of *restraints* that keep people safe.

7. Underline the words that tell what <u>comprehension</u> means. Use *comprehension* in a sentence.

8. Circle the word that means about the same as <u>energetic</u>. In what types of school activities do most people put forth an *energetic* effort?

Name _____ Date _____

from "We'll Never Conquer Space" by Arthur C. Clarke
Literary Analysis: Prophetic Essay

It is not hard for readers to guess what Clarke's viewpoint is as they begin to read *We'll Never Conquer Space.* Clarke's title makes it no secret. As in any essay, though, Clarke needs to back up his viewpoint with facts and evidence. Also, because Clarke's is a **prophetic essay,** readers may also expect predictions and speculations.

A modern prophetic essay is, in some ways, no different from ancient prophecies. The person who writes or speaks the prophecy wants to convince his or her audience of the accuracy and truth of the prophecy. Modern writers do this by using persuasive literary techniques such as presenting facts or evidence, making logical and/or emotional appeals, creating images, and using quotable language. Here are some examples from Clarke's essay.

Fact:	Radio and light waves travel at the same speed of 186,000 miles a second.
Logical appeal:	Our age is in many ways unique, full of events and phenomena which never occurred before and can never happen again.
Image:	The remotest of the planets will be perhaps no more than a week's travel from the earth.
Quotable language:	Man will never conquer space.

Keep in mind that these are persuasive techniques. Your job as a reader is to determine whether they *really* support Clarke's argument or not.

DIRECTIONS: *State the main point, or thesis, of Clarke's essay in your own words. Then identify four major points that Clarke uses to support his thesis. For each point, identify whether it is a fact, logical/emotional appeal, an image, a speculation, or whether it is stated in quotable language. Some points may be a combination of techniques.*

Clarke's thesis: _____

Support 1: _____

_____

Support 2: _____

_____

Support 3: _____

_____

Support 4: _____

_____

from **"We'll Never Conquer Space"** by Arthur C. Clarke
Reading Strategy: Challenge the Text

Do you believe, and accept, everything you read? Books, magazine articles, newspapers, office memoranda, and corporate newsletters all convey information. Is the newspaper's reporting unbiased? Does the memo address the heart of the issue, or just someone's side of it? Is the company revealing what employees have a right to know?

When you read an essay, even one by a famous, well-respected writer, you should **challenge the text,** just as you should challenge materials you read at school and home. Clarke's essay, in particular, addresses a controversial subject and should raise questions as you read. Some of Clarke's statements are straight facts. Others are opinions, assumptions, or speculations about what might—or might not—come to be. Test his ideas by raising those questions.

DIRECTIONS: *Following are some statements from Clarke's essay that are worthy of being challenged. For each statement, write a question with which to challenge the statement. (You need not know the answer to the question.) An example has been done for you.*

Because we have annihilated distance on this planet, we imagine that we can do it once again.

Have we really "annihilated distance" on earth? Do people assume we can do it again, as Clarke claims?

1. ". . . when the satellite communication network is established, we will be able to see friends on the far side of the earth as easily as we talk to them on the other side of the town."

   _____

   _____

   _____

2. "We have abolished space here on the little earth; we can never abolish the space that yawns between the stars."

   _____

   _____

   _____

3. "This achievement [using nuclear energy for spaceflight], which will be witnessed within a century, might appear to make even the solar system a comfortable, homely place . . ."

   _____

   _____

   _____

Name _____ Date _____

Vocabulary Builder

Using the Suffixes *-ible* and *-able*

A. DIRECTIONS: *Many words in the English language contain the suffixes -ible or -able, meaning "able to," "having qualities of," or "worthy of." Match the following words with their definitions. Write the letter of the definition next to the word it defines.*

___ 1. applicable

___ 2. commendable

___ 3. negligible

___ 4. negotiable

A. capable of being traversed or dealt with

B. able to be disregarded

C. capable of being brought into action

D. worthy of praise

Using the Word List

ludicrous	irrevocable	instantaneous
enigma	inevitable	zenith

B. DIRECTIONS: *Each item consists of a Word List word followed by four lettered words or phrases. Choose the lettered word or phrase that is most nearly* opposite *in meaning to the Word List word, and circle the letter of your choice.*

1. enigma
   A. query
   B. widely known
   C. negative image
   D. solution

2. inevitable
   A. sure
   B. unlikely
   C. satisfied
   D. unsafe

3. instantaneous
   A. delayed
   B. lacking attention
   C. rough-skinned
   D. precise

4. irrevocable
   A. without words
   B. changeable
   C. finely tuned
   D. permanent

5. ludicrous
   A. boring
   B. serious
   C. miserable
   D. not playful

6. zenith
   A. lowest point
   B. farthest point
   C. nearest point
   D. distant point

Name _____ Date _____

from "We'll Never Conquer Space" by Arthur C. Clarke
Grammar and Style: Linking Verbs and Subject Complements

A **linking verb** connects its subject with a word that identifies or describes that subject.

Arthur C. Clarke *is* a writer. (The word *writer* identifies the subject, *Clarke*.)

Following are the most commonly used linking verbs.

all of the forms of *be* (*am, is, are, was, were, will be, has been, could have been,* and so on)	*appear* *become* *feel* *grow* *look* *remain*	*seem* *smell* *sound* *stay* *taste* *turn*

The word or words that identify or describe the subject, such as *writer* in the previous example, are called the **subject complement.** There are two kinds of subject complements, the predicate nominative and the predicate adjective. A predicate nominative refers to the person or thing that is the subject of the verb. The previous example has a predicate nominative. Here is another example.

Arthur C. Clarke *was* once a radar *instructor*.

A predicate adjective is an adjective that follows a linking verb and modifies, or describes, the subject of the verb.

Clarke's essay *is interesting.* (The adjective *interesting* modifies the subject, *essay*.)

A. PRACTICE: *In each sentence, circle the linking verb and underline the subject complement. Indicate whether the subject complement is a predicate nominative or a predicate adjective by writing* PN *or* PA *above the complement.*

1. "The facts are far otherwise."

2. "In all earlier ages than ours, the world was wide indeed."

3. "Once again we are face to face with immensity."

4. "The velocity of light is the ultimate speed limit."

5. "Again they are wrong."

B. Writing Application: *Use two different forms of the verb* be *and two other linking verbs to write sentences about Arthur Clarke or his essay. Underline the subject complement in each sentence.*

1. _____

2. _____

3. _____

Name _____ Date _____

from "We'll Never Conquer Space" by Arthur C. Clarke
Support for Writing

Use the chart below to gather details for your analysis of an argument. Review the essay, and identify Clarke's assumptions. Write them in the left column. Then, analyze each assumption. In the right column, list evidence and reasons that support or contradict each assumption.

Clarke's Assumptions	Support or Evidence For or Against

Use information from the chart as you draft your analysis on a separate page. As you write, include an evaluation of whether Clarke's assumptions make sense.

Name _____ Date _____

Support for Extend Your Learning

Listening and Speaking

Prepare for the **panel discussion** by jotting down the implications of Clarke's essay. Write implications about the future of space travel in the left column. Write implications about humanity's place in the cosmos, or universe, in the second column.

Future of Space Travel	**Humanity's Place in the Cosmos (Universe)**

Research and Technology

Review the excerpt from "We'll Never Conquer Space." Jot down Clarke's major ideas in the diagram below. Then, think of a way to illustrate each idea for a **museum exhibit.**

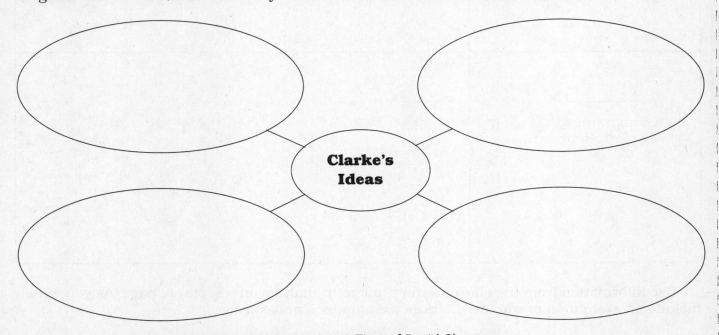

from **"We'll Never Conquer Space"** by Arthur C. Clarke
Enrichment: Science

The Theory of Relativity

Arthur C. Clarke's claim that we'll never conquer space depends on two things. The first is the mathematics of distance, to which he devotes much attention. The second is the constraint on how fast things, including messages, can move across space. This maximum speed of 186,000 miles per second—the speed of light—is a constant, as Clarke mentions, of the Theory of Relativity.

If you stand at the corner and watch a car pass, the car appears to be moving. If you are in the car, however, the lamppost on the corner appears to be moving. We assume our perception from the car is wrong, because we assume that the lamppost is a body at rest. Einstein asserted that it makes no difference which we say is moving, car or lamppost, for the motion or lack of motion is relative. There is in fact no absolute motion, only relative motion. Motion, Einstein said, can only be calculated by relative rates between perceived objects, as measured against the speed of light.

As implications of his theory, Einstein developed three ideas. Objects moving at very high speeds (approaching the speed of light) would theoretically change size. Mass would increase, length in the direction of motion would contract, and time would slow down. Second, nothing could move faster than the speed of light, because at this speed mass would increase to an infinite amount and length would decrease to zero. Third, mass is really a form of energy, and a small amount of mass equals a vast amount of energy. Thus the famous formula, $E=mc^2$, where E equals energy, *m* equals mass and *c*, the constant, is the speed of light.

Part of the theory of relativity has been proven experimentally. Subatomic particles accelerated to nearly the speed of light for brief instants do not decay at the same rate as others. For those particles, time is slower (though not for the observer).

Later scientists have expressed time as a fourth dimension, and mass is conceived as curved space. Here arises the popular conception—and some possibility—of traversing vast distances in an instant, by moving through strange "curves" in space created by black holes.

DIRECTIONS: *Answer the following questions.*

1. Because time differs for travelers and those staying home, what are the implications for deep space travel?

   _____

   _____

2. If communications cannot travel faster than the speed of light, what limits are imposed on space exploration?

   _____

   _____

from "We'll Never Conquer Space" by Arthur C. Clarke
Selection Test A

Critical Reading *Identify the letter of the choice that best answers the question.*

____ 1. Why does Clarke say in "We'll Never Conquer Space" that humans have an incorrect view of our ability to conquer space?
A. because space can be mapped and crossed by humans
B. because humans have accomplished many other advances
C. because space travel will one day be a reality
D. because light is part of the structure of space and time

____ 2. What prediction about the future does Clarke make in "We'll Never Conquer Space"?
A. Technological breakthroughs will allow humans to conquer space.
B. Humans will lose interest in space travel when it takes more than a few years.
C. If humans travel in space, they will be isolated from people on Earth.
D. Limits in technology will make travel to even the closest stars impossible.

____ 3. How might a reader challenge this statement from "We'll Never Conquer Space": "It will never be possible to converse with anyone on another planet"?
A. A reader would know that Clarke can support his statement.
B. A reader would assume that Clarke is exaggerating.
C. A reader would agree, wishing this were not the case.
D. A reader would want to see proof of Clarke's statement.

____ 4. In which quotation is Clarke making an analogy, or a comparison, in "We'll Never Conquer Space"?
A. "Man will never conquer space."
B. "Every technical device is always developed to its limit"
C. "Saturn or Jupiter [will play] the same role . . . [as] Africa or Asia today."
D. "Space can be mapped and crossed and occupied"

____ 5. Which analogy does Clarke make in "We'll Never Conquer Space" to emphasize his prediction?
A. It will not be possible to talk with people on other planets.
B. Voyages that last many years will be taken.
C. It is hard to imagine the number of planets that exist.
D. What we think of as news would actually be history.

____ 6. Why does Clarke argue in "We'll Never Conquer Space" that colonies established around other stars would be independent of Earth?
A. They would be too distant in time and space for Earth to control them.
B. Aliens on other planets would quickly take over these colonies.
C. People who travel in space would be independent by nature and rebel.
D. Communications would not reach that far, so they would not receive orders.

_____ 7. What does Clarke mean when he says "the price of Space is Time" in "We'll Never Conquer Space"?
 A. The technology for travel through space will be costly.
 B. It will take much time to travel vast distances through space.
 C. Spaceships, and the fuel to send them into space, are expensive.
 D. People will have to be paid a great amount to travel into space.

_____ 8. Which statement shows the complexity of the universe as described by Clarke in "We'll Never Conquer Space"?
 A. He says that the world will no longer shrink.
 B. He says that the space between stars will always exist.
 C. He says that radio and light waves travel at the same speed.
 D. He says that the number of other suns in our galaxy is about 10^{11}.

_____ 9. How might a reader challenge this statement from "We'll Never Conquer Space"?
 Every technical device is always developed to its limit . . . and the ultimate speed for spaceships is the velocity of light. They will never reach that goal . . .
 A. What evidence do you have that spaceships cannot go beyond the speed of light?
 B. Are scientists now working on ways to build spaceships that are as fast as light?
 C. What technical devices do we have right now that can go beyond the speed of light?
 D. How long will it take to develop fast spaceships, and will they take us to the stars?

_____ 10. At the end of "We'll Never Conquer Space," why does Clarke say that no person will ever return home from "beyond Vega"?
 A. No one will live long enough to return from so far away.
 B. People will be fascinated with the excitement of travel.
 C. Spacecraft will never be reliable enough to travel so far.
 D. By the time people reach Vega, they will have forgotten Earth.

Vocabulary and Grammar

_____ 11. Which word best replaces *inevitable* in this sentence: "It is *inevitable* that humans will one day travel in space"?
 A. silly
 B. frightening
 C. instant
 D. unavoidable

_____ 12. What is the linking verb that connects the subject to the other words in this sentence: "Most people are familiar with how scientists use notation to describe large numbers"?
 A. are
 B. familiar
 C. describe
 D. use

Essay

13. Clarke titles his essay "We'll Never Conquer Space." He seems absolutely certain that people will never conquer space. In an essay, tell whether he has convinced you that he is right. Give facts and reasons from the essay and from your own knowledge to support your position.

14. One of the sections of "We'll Never Conquer Space" is titled "Time Barrier." In an essay, explain how the "Time Barrier" will, according to Clarke, limit the ability of humans to conquer the universe. In your essay, answer these questions: What is this barrier? In what ways will it limit humans? Use details from the essay to support your response.

from "We'll Never Conquer Space" by Arthur C. Clarke
Selection Test B

Critical Reading *Identify the letter of the choice that best completes the statement or answers the question.*

_____ 1. What does Clarke predict in his prophetic essay?
   A. Our technology will not allow us to explore space any farther.
   B. Inability to communicate will hinder space travel.
   C. Humans' inability to comprehend space will prohibit us from going beyond the confines of our solar system.
   D. Travel across interstellar space, unlike modern travel on Earth, will always isolate travelers from those left at home.

_____ 2. Which is an example of a memorable phrase Clarke uses to convince readers of his viewpoint?
   A. "The ants have covered the world but have they conquered it . . .?"
   B. "Such a statement may sound ludicrous, now that our rockets are already 100 million miles beyond the moon. . . ."
   C. ". . . radio and light waves travel at the same limited speed of 186,000 miles a second."
   D. "Imagine a vast ocean, sprinkled with islands—some desert, others perhaps inhabited."

_____ 3. What is Clarke's main prophecy?
   A. We don't have the technology to conquer space.
   B. The vastness of space prevents us from conquering it.
   C. Humans are intimidated by the vastness of space.
   D. Our concept of the vastness of space is limited.

_____ 4. Why does Clarke mention the time lag caused by communicating on a planetary or stellar basis?
   A. to show how inadequate our technology is
   B. to emphasize the vastness of space
   C. to make a point about the speed of radio and light waves
   D. to convey how isolated space travelers would be from Earth

_____ 5. What would prevent instantaneous communication with a person on another planet?
   A. inferior communications technology
   B. the time transmissions take to cross such distances
   C. radio wave interference
   D. difference in time between one planet and the other

_____ 6. In addition to making his own prediction in his prophetic essay, Clarke is also
   A. displaying his technical knowledge.
   B. recounting the history of space exploration.
   C. painting a picture of humanity's place in the universe.
   D. casting doubt on the existing laws of physics.

____ 7. When Clarke compares space to a "vast ocean sprinkled with islands," he makes the point that
   A. there are too many planets to be explored.
   B. the distances between stars are so great that exploration would be impossible.
   C. current space technology is as primitive as a dugout canoe.
   D. the distance between stars would forever separate space travelers from Earth, just as island residents were from their original culture.

____ 8. Which does Clarke assume as an unchangeable fact?
   A. Nothing can move faster than the speed of light.
   B. Telephone technology is at its peak.
   C. Spaceflight technology may improve some, but not much.
   D. Humans will never comprehend a number like 10^9.

____ 9. Clarke asks us to picture an object five feet away, with nothing around it for 1,000 miles. He uses this image to illustrate the
   A. difference between travel on earth and travel in space.
   B. distance to our moon versus the distance to the sun.
   C. difference between our nearest star and the next galaxy.
   D. distance to the nearest planet as opposed to the distance to the nearest star.

____ 10. Given his use of the word *might*, what is Clarke doing in this statement?

   This achievement [harnessing nuclear energy for spaceflight], which will be witnessed within a century, might appear to make even the solar system a comfortable, homely place, with such giant planets as Saturn and Jupiter playing much the same role in our thoughts as do Africa or Asia today.

   A. He is partially agreeing to the opposing viewpoint for persuasive effect.
   B. He is stating when nuclear-powered spaceflight will be achieved.
   C. He is creating a picture of how we would view our solar system.
   D. He is guessing about the consequences of nuclear-powered spaceflight.

____ 11. How should a critical reader respond when seeing the word *never* in an essay?
   A. Accept this as a fact.
   B. Assume that the writer is using the term loosely.
   C. Be suspicious of an overgeneralization.
   D. Assume that the writer researched the issue and is correct.

____ 12. How would a reader best challenge this statement?

   These suns are on the average five light-years apart; in other words, we can never get from one to the next in less than five years.

   A. Are our measurements of the distances between the suns accurate?
   B. This assumes that faster-than-light travel is not possible. Is this a valid assumption?
   C. This assumes we can even get to the first sun. How far away is it?
   D. Are the suns habitable?

____ **13.** Why does Clarke say humans will never venture back from Vega of the Lyre, "the brightest star of the northern skies"?

    A. It is so pleasant that people would not want to leave.

    B. Given the average human life span, it is unlikely someone could make a round trip.

    C. We will never have the technology to go there.

    D. It is uninviting and uninhabitable.

Vocabulary and Grammar

____ **14.** Clarke identifies 61 Cygni as an *enigma,* meaning that it

    A. is unlike any other star.

    B. was only recently discovered.

    C. is unapproachable because it is so far away.

    D. poses a perplexing riddle.

____ **15.** Identify the sentence that contains a linking verb.

    A. "Self-contained cosmic arks . . . may be another solution . . ."

    B. "Imagine a vast ocean, sprinkled with islands."

    C. "But the messages will take minutes . . . on their journey . . ."

    D. "Returning messengers could report what had happened on the nearest colony—five years ago."

Essay

16. What, exactly, does Clarke predict in his essay? Why does he believe as he does? What arguments does he put forth in support of his prediction? As you summarize Clarke's argument in an essay, cite any particularly notable evidence or examples Clark uses to support his prediction.

17. Do you accept the ideas Clarke puts forth in "We'll Never Conquer Space"? What rings true? What doesn't? In an essay, challenge his assertions, stating what you agree and disagree with, and why. As you challenge the text, make note of assumptions Clarke makes and whether they are valid.

Writing About Literature—Unit 6
Evaluate Literary Trends

Prewriting: Finding a Focus

Complete the chart below to help you organize your thoughts and evaluate the poems you have read.

Poem	Accessibility (1=very accessible; 5=very obscure)	Author's Purpose	Reader's Needs

Drafting: Organizing an Outline

Complete the outline below to help you organize your essay.

    I. Introduction
       A. Interesting Opening
       B. Thesis Statement
   II. Body Paragraph 1—Topic Sentence
       A. Supporting Evidence
       B. Supporting Evidence
  III. Body Paragraph 2—Topic Sentence
       A. Supporting Evidence
       B. Supporting Evidence
  IV. Body Paragraph 3—Topic Sentence
       A. Supporting Evidence
       B. Supporting Evidence
   V. Conclusion
       A. Restatement of Thesis
       B. Memorable Closing

Writing About Literature—Unit 6
Evaluate Literary Trends: Integrating Grammar Skills

Avoiding Ambiguity

Poetry may or may not benefit from ambiguity, but the writing in an essay needs to be clear and easy to follow. As you revise, look for statements that are vague or could be interpreted in more than one way. Rewrite them to make your meaning clear.

Unclear: Modern poetry is complicated because of life.

Clear: Modern poetry's complexity reflects the confusion and chaos of modern life.

Revising to Avoid Ambiguity

DIRECTIONS: *Rewrite each ambiguous sentence to make a statement whose meaning is clear.*

1. T. S. Eliot's poems are hard to read, like a dream.

   _____

   _____

2. Eliot's details match his view of modern life: it's all bad.

   _____

   _____

3. I like Rupert Brooke's "The Soldier" because it's easy and patriotic.

   _____

   _____

4. Anyone can understand Seamus Heaney's theme in "Followers," because it's parents.

   _____

   _____

5. The theme of Dylan Thomas's "Do Not Go Gentle into That Good Night" is easy because it repeats.

   _____

   _____

Writing Workshop—Unit 6
Writing Workshop—Unit 6
Exposition: Multimedia Report

Prewriting: Gathering Details

Use the chart below to help you organize the audiovisual elements you will use in your report.

Report Outline:	Audiovisual Materials:
I. Introduction: _____	_____
II. First point: _____	_____
A. Support: _____	_____
B. Support: _____	_____
III. Second point: _____	_____
A. Support: _____	_____
B. Support: _____	_____
IV. Third Point: _____	_____
A. Support: _____	_____
B. Support: _____	_____
V. Conclusion: _____	_____

Drafting: Shaping Your Report

Use your outline to write the text of your report as dialogue. Then, in the *Audio and Video* column, identify the sounds and the images you will use.

Text	Audio and Video

Name _____ Date _____

Multimedia Report: Integrating Grammar Skills

Revise the draft of your report for clarity and coherence. Pay particular attention to transitions, the words that indicate when you are moving on to a new point and should clarify the relationship between one image and the next.

Vague: A major problem was traffic congestion. Here, the situation improved dramatically.

Clear: A major problem was traffic congestion. *The next photo shows how* the situation improved dramatically *after strict driving restrictions were imposed.*

Add Transitions for Clarity and Coherence

DIRECTIONS: *Add transitions to the following draft to improve the clarity and coherence of the ideas presented.*

The crumbling old playground at Eastside Park was a problem. You can see it here. The equipment was falling apart. Little kids were getting hurt there. Parents stopped taking their kids to the park. Older kids started hanging out there and spraying the slides with graffiti. They left litter everywhere. Even fewer parents brought their kids there.

A neighborhood group decided to clean up the park. Parents volunteered to start bringing their little kids there again and to patrol for vandalism. The park began to improve. You can see some of the early results here.

The group started holding fundraisers at the park. These raised money for new equipment. They showed people that a valuable resource was being lost. This is a photo of the Eastside Park Carnival.

The neighbors used the fundraising money. They bought new swings and slides. Everyone is proud of the new playground. They take good care of it. Here it is.

Spelling—Unit 6
Proofreading Practice

DIRECTIONS: *Proofread the following passage, looking for 27 misspelled words. Cross out each misspelled word, and write it correctly in the space above.*

Today, our memorys are cramed with an unresistible caleidoscope, or collaje, of images from decades of Hollywood movies. It is hard to imagine there was ever a time when movie projecters, videotapes, and DVDs did not exist. The origin of the motion picture is hardly anchent history, but it is traceable back to the 1800s.

Movies, or motion pictures, depend on a contineuous succession of statick images projected at many frames per second. Before the invention of photography, these images were drawings. Once photography was invented, film producers had to learn to photograph a series of live actions spontaneously and simultanously. These images then needed to be projected onto a screen so that the actions were reproduced realisticly. The first motion pictures were actually scientificly arranged as a study in kinesiology, the science of motion.

The beginning of motion pictures as entertainment, featuring acters and storys, can be traced to the American inventer Thomas Edison and to the Lumiére brothers of France. Starting in 1897, manufacturers began selling films and projecting equipment to traveling operaters, who screened the films in locateions such as fairgrounds or circus tents. These exhibitors put together programs of narrateion, sound effects, and music, which accompanyed the silent films.

Soon, there were permanent movie theaters, called nickelodeons, which carryed the first great box-office hit, *The Great Train Robery*, a one-reel-film runing 12 minutes in length. Audiences quickly became disatisfied with short films, and longer movies, commanding higher admission prices, were produced. By the early 1920s, millions of American familys were attending the movies every week. Even then, some people were worryed and sceptical about the impact of movies on society. However, there was no turning back. The movies had become an unreplaceable part of the average person's dreams and fantasys.

Name _____ Date _____

Analyzing Bias in News Media

After choosing a news story, fill out the chart to help you analyze the possible bias of the report.

Subject of news story: _____

What is the main idea of the news story?
What techniques, such as inflammatory images or emotionally charged language, are used that indicate bias?
Identify facts and images that reflect only one point of view.
What important information or important perspective was left out of the newscast?
From the information presented, what is your opinion of this news story?

Suggestions for Further Reading—Unit 6

DIRECTIONS: *Think about the books you have read. Then, on a separate piece of paper, answer the discussion questions and take notes for your literature circle.*

Heart of Darkness and The Secret Sharer by Joseph Conrad

Discussion Discuss the theme of *The Secret Sharer*. Explain what general truth about life Conrad suggests through his tale about a "secret sharer."

Connections—Literature Circle Using examples from *Heart of Darkness*, discuss whether or not Kurtz should be regarded as an admirable individual, based on his accomplishments in the jungle.

Lord Jim by Joseph Conrad

Discussion What word or words would you use to describe the end of the novel? Explain your answer drawing on specific examples or quotations from the text.

Connections—Literature Circle In Jim's time, a career in the English merchant marine was a ticket to an adventurous life filled with exotic settings and people. Discuss what careers today might be the equivalent of Jim's choice of the merchant marine?

Pygmalion/My Fair Lady by George Bernard Shaw

Discussion Does Professor Higgins help or hurt Eliza? Support your response with specifics from the play and the text.

Connections—Literature Circle Would it be positive or negative to be able to "design" a person? Explain your answer using examples from history and your own reasoning.

2001: A Space Odyssey by Arthur C. Clarke

Discussion Discuss the ways in which *2001: A Space Odyssey* explores the possibility of non-human intelligence.

Connections—Literature Circle Do you agree that Hal has the ability to think? If so, do you think he thinks like a human being? Support you responses with details from the book.

Dubliners by James Joyce

Discussion Tell which story in *Dubliners* is your favorite, and explain why. Describe elements of the story's setting, characters, imagery, and theme that appeal to you.

Connections—Literature Circle Based on what happens in "Two Gallants" and "The Boarding House," discuss the general insight Joyce offers about the role of love in relationships between men and women.

Unit 6: A Time of Rapid Change
Benchmark Test 12

MULTIPLE CHOICE

Literary Analysis and Reading Skills *Read "Symphony in Yellow" by Oscar Wilde, below.*
Then, answer the questions that follow.

An omnibus° across the bridge   ° **omnibus** bus
Crawls like a yellow butterfly,
And, here and there, a passer-by
Shows like a little restless midge.°   ° **midge** tiny insect similar to a gnat

5 Big barges full of yellow hay
Are moored against the shadowy wharf,
And, like a yellow silken scarf,
The thick fog hangs along the quay.°   ° **quay** pier

The yellow leaves begin to fade
10 And flutter from the Temple° elms,   ° **Temple** London lawyers' building
And at my feet the pale green Thames°   ° **Thames** (temz) London river near the Temple
Lies like a rod of rippled jade.

1. What form does the poem take?
   A. free verse
   B. ballad stanza
   C. iambic tetrameter
   D. villanelle

2. In reading this poem for understanding, where should you make the first pause?
   A. after line 1
   B. after line 2
   C. in the middle of line 3
   D. after line 4

3. Which choice best describes the poet's voice?
   A. He speaks in confused questions.
   B. He speaks in image-packed musical language.
   C. He speaks in blips and pulses.
   D. He speaks in a tumbling rush of words.

Read this short story. Then, answer the questions that follow.

Father, a man of rigid ways, grew even more rigid after Mother died. He sat brooding over the state of England. A diehard Tory, he believed in neither government assistance programs nor charity. "People should do for themselves," was his motto. "Gives them stamina!" Then the Second World War broke out, and even Father realized that he had to pitch in a little. He agreed to house children being evacuated from London's East End, which the Germans were bombing heavily. "Don't know what I'll do with 'em," Father grumbled. "Two lads coming. Foreigners, no doubt. Likely to stink of cabbage and garlic."

Six months later, when I again had leave, I took the train up and found Father at dinner with young Jacob and Leon Sutton. After introductions were made, I noticed several of the dishes. "Cabbage, Father?" I asked.

"Well, yes, like to make the lads feel at home," Father explained a bit sheepishly. "And it turns out I make a nice little cabbage dish!"

"And do I detect garlic in the meat?" I asked, a twinkle in my eye.

"Eat it, Tom; it's good for you," Father ordered. "Gives you stamina!"

4. What change occurs in the story's most dynamic character or characters?
   A. The father loses his rigid attitudes and becomes more open minded.
   B. The son realizes that his father is not the powerful person he once was.
   C. The Sutton boys escape the dangers of war-torn London.
   D. The Germans attack part of the city of London.

5. How does the first-person narration affect our understanding of the story's characters?
   A. We learn all the details of the father's internal conflict.
   B. We learn all the details of the war and its effects on the Sutton boys.
   C. We do not learn all the details of the father's internal conflict.
   D. We do not learn the son's thoughts and perceptions about his father.

6. How does the central conflict help dramatize or illustrate the theme?
   A. The father's internal struggle with his prejudices reflects the theme of social change.
   B. The Sutton boys' struggle to survive reflects the theme of survival during warfare.
   C. The son's struggle with enemy forces reflects his need to understand his father.
   D. The government's request for help from people reflects the change in the nation.

7. How is the theme enhanced by the historical context of World War II?
   A. The war advances the fields of science and technology.
   B. The war brings people in England together, creating a climate for social change.
   C. The war causes the son to reevaluate his relationship with his father.
   D. The war teaches the characters the survival skills they need.

Read this excerpt from a story. Then, answer the questions that follow.

After years of hard work, Gandar had built up his business as a Delhi chaat wallah, selling India's popular snacks first from a cart and then from a small storefront. Now his friend Manish had invited him to come to America and run one of Manish's restaurants. Gandar's wife Amita was thrilled, but his mother was not. "You will hate it there!" she warned. "You will feel out of place."

"Perhaps. But it's just a five-year agreement. If we do not like life there, we can return after that."

"Five years!" wailed his mother. "Your father is ill now!"

"Don't worry," Amita said, reassuringly. "Of course we will visit you. That is what airplanes are for!"

"You are really going, then?" his mother asked nervously.

"Such a chance comes once in a lifetime. To be able to find decent work outside Delhi, where I have spent my whole life. To see something of the world—it would be cowardly not to," Gandar replied.

8. Which of these is a likely response to the character of Gandar?
   A. Most readers will find him overly ambitious and greedy.
   B. Most readers will find him very selfish for leaving his mother.
   C. Most readers will sympathize with his desire to better himself and see the world.
   D. Most readers will find him foolish for listening at all to his wife and mother.

9. Which detail of background information could most help you understand the selection?
   A. knowing that Indians of the Hindu faith are usually vegetarians
   B. knowing that India is a nation with a large population
   C. knowing that Hindi is one of the main languages of India
   D. knowing that a wallah is a vendor of a certain product

10. How does the story's central conflict relate to its cultural context and theme?
    A. Gandar is torn between two cultures and has to make a decision about them.
    B. Gandar struggles to survive in the poor city of Delhi.
    C. Gandar is torn between love of country and love for his mother.
    D. Gandar's mother and wife are in a struggle to control him.

11. Which of these questions would most help you evaluate Gandar's decision?
    A. What is the climate in the part of America where Gandar and his wife are moving?
    B. At what time of the year will Gandar and his wife be moving?
    C. Will Gandar and his wife have the time and money to visit India as planned?
    D. What is the relationship like between Gandar's mother and his wife?

12. Reading between the lines, why does the mother to refer to her husband's illness?
    A. She hopes that Gandar will cure him.
    B. She is suggesting that Gandar pay his father's medical bills.
    C. She fears that he may die before Gandar returns and that Gandar will never see him again.
    D. She fears that the shock of Gandar's departure will affect his chances of recovery.

Read this brief prophetic essay. Then, answer the questions that follow.

(1) In the not-too-distant future, computer use will become even more widespread than it is today. (2) Tiny computer chips in your clothing will monitor your health and body temperature; computer chips in your wristwatch will allow you to use the Internet. (3) Your refrigerator will tell you when you are low on milk and will even contact the local supermarket computer to place your order.

(4) Yet the Computer Age is not without its drawbacks. (5) Computer usage will limit physical exercise, so that obesity is bound to become even more of a health problem. (6) In addition, the use of computers will mean a loss of millions of jobs. (7) For example, instead of using a travel agent to book a trip, more people will book it directly on the Internet. (8) Computerized robots will come to assist more and more workers. (9) However, jobs requiring judgment and common sense will still be done by human beings.

13. Which statement best summarizes the prediction the writer makes in this essay?
    A. Computers will be used more in the future, bringing both advantages and drawbacks.
    B. In the near future, there will be more computer chips practically everywhere.
    C. The Computer Age is not without its drawbacks.
    D. Computers can never replace human beings in tasks requiring judgment.

14. Which of the following sentences gives the strongest warning about a problem in the future?
    A. sentence 2
    B. sentence 3
    C. sentence 4
    D. sentence 5

15. In judging the writer's message in sentence 5, which of these personal experiences would it be best for the reader to consider?
    A. experiences with high-protein crash diets
    B. experiences with weight problems caused by lack of exercise
    C. experiences with using computers for on-line shopping
    D. experiences learning how to drive

16. In challenging the statement in sentence 6, which phrase should you most question?
    A. In addition
    B. the use of computers
    C. a loss
    D. millions of

Vocabulary

17. Given the meaning of -vol- and the context clues in this sentence, what does *volition* means?

    No persuasion was necessary; she did her homework based on her own *volition*.

    A. self-control
    B. enjoyment
    C. forced behavior
    D. free will

18. Based on your knowledge of Latin roots, why do you think some dogs are named *Fido*?
    A. to emphasize their speed
    B. to emphasize their beauty
    C. to emphasize their loyalty
    D. to emphasize their loud bark

19. Which of the following is a *patronizing* remark?
    A. That's a nice gold chain you're wearing; I didn't realize you could afford one.
    B. I never buy gold chains because I cannot afford them.
    C. I am not sure why people bother wearing gold chains instead of buying more sensible things.
    D. I couldn't afford to buy a gold chain, but I could afford a silver one.

20. From your knowledge of the prefix *a-*, how do you think *atonal* music would sound?
    A. sweet and melodic
    B. harsh and clashing
    C. memorable
    D. catchy but loud

21. From your knowledge of the word parts *-duc-* and *-ible*, what is a *deductible* expense?
    A. one that you can remove from the total
    B. one that you add to the total
    C. one that you would like to avoid
    D. one that you cannot avoid

22. Explain how the meaning of the Latin root *-fil-* is reflected in the word *affiliation*.
    A. An affiliation suggests a close relationship.
    B. An affiliation suggests deep feelings of love.
    C. An affiliation suggests involvement in a charity.
    D. An affiliation suggests deep dislike.

Grammar

23. Which choice below combines these two sentences by using an adverb clause?

    Dylan Thomas left Wales. He settled in London.

    A. Dylan Thomas left Wales and settled in London.
    B. After he left Wales, Dylan Thomas settled in London.
    C. Dylan Thomas left Wales, and he then settled in London.
    D. Dylan Thomas left Wales; he settled in London.

24. Which sentence uses a verb in the present perfect tense?
    A. By the time of his death, Dylan Thomas had visited the United States several times.
    B. Dylan Thomas won fame with his oral readings of his poetry.
    C. Dylan Thomas has become one of the best-known poets of the twentieth century.
    D. Dylan Thomas will be remembered for many years to come.

25. Which sentence uses pronoun cases correctly?
    A. Jane and me like reading poetry.
    B. Many modern British poets are known to Jane and I.
    C. Philip Larkin is one poet that Jane and me really like.
    D. Larkin's poetry confused Jane and me, but now we understand it better.

26. What is the nominative absolute in this sentence?

    The gentleman stood in his garden, his eyes studying me.

    A. The gentleman stood in his garden
    B. stood in his garden
    C. his eyes studying me
    D. studying me

27. Which sentence contains no errors in the use of *affect or effect*?
    A. What affect does a poet's voice have on your enjoyment of poetry?
    B. What is the affect of free verse on your response to the poem?
    C. How does a poem's meter effect or enhance its meaning?
    D. What new readings may effect a change in your appreciation of poetry?

28. How would you change this paragraph to add to sentence variety?

    The couple took a train. They went to Africa. They saw a craftsman. The craftsman sold pottery.

    A. add another short sentence
    B. combine two sentences into one long sentence
    C. remove one of the short sentences
    D. avoid all changes; the sentences are varied as is

29. Which sentence contains a linking verb with a subject complement?
    A. Ted Hughes was married to fellow author Sylvia Plath.
    B. The author of that poem is Stevie Smith.
    C. Dylan Thomas was in America several times.
    D. Stevie Smith and Philip Larkin both died tragically young.

ESSAY

30. Recall an event you witnessed or a scene you observed that, on reflection, has had a deeper meaning for you. It might be something from the world of nature or something involving human interaction. On your paper or a separate sheet, write a short reflective essay about the incident and its deeper meaning.

31. Jot down your ideas for the script of a multimedia presentation that uses visual or audio aids to describe someone whom you consider to be a remarkable person. Describe the media your presentation will include to help capture the qualities or achievements that make the person remarkable.

32. On your paper or a separate sheet, write a proposal for a program that would benefit teenagers in your community. It could be a school program or something run by the local government or another local institution.

ANSWERS

Diagnostic Test 10, p. 2

MULTIPLE CHOICE

1. ANS: D
2. ANS: A
3. ANS: A
4. ANS: C
5. ANS: A
6. ANS: B
7. ANS: C
8. ANS: B
9. ANS: A
10. ANS: B
11. ANS: C
12. ANS: D
13. ANS: C
14. ANS: D
15. ANS: A

Unit 6 Introduction

Names and Terms to Know, p. 5

A. 1. D; 2. G; 3. F; 4. A; 5. C; 6. E; 7. B

B. Sample Answers

1. Trench warfare in World War I included the horrors of poison gas attacks and massive artillery barrages.
2. During World War II, the German invasion of Russia in 1941 killed soldiers and civilians by the millions.
3. Many Modernists used images as symbols, leading to indirect, evocative work.
4. Two of the most effective postmodernist playwrights have been Harold Pinter and Tom Stoppard, both of whom are noted for their experiments with dialogue, sequencing, and the relationships between literature and reality.

Focus Questions, p. 6

Sample Answers

1. The British were expecting an easy victory in World War I, and they were not prepared for the harsh realities of trench warfare, such as poison gas attacks and intense artillery barrages. In World War II, the darkest days for Britain came in 1940, when Britain alone bore the brunt of German air attacks.
2. The Modernists often presented human experience as fragmented, and they used images as symbols. Eliot's *The Waste Land* makes daring use of a collage of "voices" to link the past with the present. The postmodernist playwrights Pinter and Stoppard have experimented with dialogue, sequence, and the relationships of literature to reality.

Poetry of William Butler Yeats

Vocabulary Warm-up Exercises, p. 8

A. 1. twilight
2. glade
3. sensual
4. consume
5. core
6. innocence
7. amid
8. murmur

B. Sample Answers

1. F; *Monuments* are things built in memory of an event or a person.
2. T; Something that is very beautiful might also be described as magnificent, so it might impress you with its *magnificence*.
3. F; A *revelation* is something that is made known, especially something that is surprising.
4. F; Something that *vexed* you would annoy you, not amuse you.
5. F; A person with a fine *intellect* is smart.
6. T; Dogs require a great deal of attention, so if you *neglect* them, they would not like it.
7. F; You would *commend* your friend for some wonderful accomplishment, not for a mistake.
8. T; If something is *mysterious*, then it is difficult to understand or explain.

Reading Warm-up A, p. 9

Sample Answers

1. graceful; lovely; long, bendable necks; *Sensual* means "having to do with the body or the senses."
2. (center); In the *core* of an apple, I would find seeds.
3. the tall trees; The grasshopper was hiding *amid* the tall pieces of grass.
4. (forest); You might see forest animals resting in a *glade*.
5. low sounds; If I were to *murmur* something to my best friend, it might be, "Let's go get a snack."
6. (covered in white feathers); I consider a baby lamb a symbol of *innocence*.
7. sunset; When it is *twilight*, I am usually helping my mom and dad fix dinner.
8. (a diet of aquatic insects and mollusks); I normally *consume* a sandwich, a piece of fruit, and a glass of milk at lunchtime.

Reading Warm-up B, p. 10

Sample Answers

1. Great Pyramid of Khufu in Egypt; Two famous *monuments* that I have visited are the Lincoln Memorial and Mount Rushmore.

2. (for a job well done); I wish someone would *commend* me for learning to play basketball better this year.

3. <u>grandeur</u>; The *magnificence* of the palace took my breath away.

4. (with the head of a human and the body of a lion; *Mysterious* means "difficult to explain or understand."

5. <u>fail to care for</u>; Once I had to *neglect* my dog because I had to study for a test.

6. <u>brainpower</u>; I admire the *intellect* of my Aunt Louise, a woman who is always researching topics in which she is interested.

7. <u>the Sphinx talked to him, saying he was vexed because of the sand that was choking him. He asked Thutmose to clear the sand away, and his reward would be a kingship</u>; The fact that Irma was 54 years old was a *revelation* to me because she looks so much younger.

8. (because of the sand that was choking him); Once I was *vexed* when I couldn't untangle a knot in my shoelaces.

Literary Analysis: Symbolism, p. 11

Sample Responses

1. The fact that Eve is referred to as "a beautiful maid" indicates that the poet is speaking symbolically of all women.

2. Traditionally, women were predestined to become wives, even before they were born. Because their entire lives were devoted to their husbands and families, the poet maintains that they were never actually "born" in the sense of having fully separate identities.

Reading Strategy: Apply Literary Background, p. 12

Possible Responses

1. It's easy to assume this is Yeats's prediction for Gonne; language like "glad grace" and "loved your beauty with love false or true" and "pilgrim soul" fit squarely with Gonne's appearance and career.

2. Yeats's many summers gave him much opportunity to watch, reflect on, and feel the coming autumn at Coole.

3. Lines 3–8, with their reference to things falling apart seem to refer to the fall of the Tsars who had ruled Russia for centuries. Wave after wave of bloodthirsty vengeance by those fighting for control foreshadowed for Yeats an ugly modern world with much violence, a redefined authority, and an absence of belief—exactly the state Russia was becoming.

4. Yeats's dreamy fascination with an ancient city provides him a place of imaginative escape that turns up in his poem as a place safe from physical decay.

Vocabulary Builder, p. 13

A. 1. quest; 2. request

B. 1. C; 2. A; 3. B; 4. D; 5. B; 6. C

Grammar and Style: Noun Clauses, p. 14

A. 1. In "When You Are Old," the speaker expresses an idea of what the thoughts of a woman he once loved might one day be. (object of preposition)

2. Who you are may determine whether you believe "The Lake Isle of Innisfree" refers to a type of place or a kind of work. (subject)

3. Knowledge that the world will go on without you, that stark recognition, glides also across the water in "The Wild Swans at Coole." (appositive)

B. Sample Responses

1. Subject: That Yeats is the best Irish poet of the twentieth century seems beyond question.

2. Complement: The use of graceful, carefully chosen language is how Yeats creates memorable images.

3. Direct object: Some may find what Yeats says about aging cruel, but he was feeling himself aging as he wrote "Sailing to Byzantium."

Enrichment: Philosophy, p. 17

Sample Responses

1. Advantages: Eclecticism can include diverse elements unaccounted for by any individual system of belief. It can reconcile minor doctrinal differences. It allows much variety and leads to tolerance. It includes all human experience and history.

Disadvantages: Eclecticism can be so flexible as to have no actual philosophical center. Sometimes, to combine or reconcile beliefs, an element's central idea is compromised. Inconvenient or inconsistent ideas may be dismissed or ignored.

2. Although spirituality is present in these poems, there is no hint of salvation or hope for an afterlife, central tenets of Christian belief.

3. Yeats explains history as a spiral, derived from the philosophy of Mato and Vico. The Second Coming is Christian terminology, although the poem is not about the Savior predicted by that religion. The Egyptian figure of the Sphinx combines with the story of Bethlehem to tell of a new and brutal world order.

4. Answers include: idea of soul beyond the body, holy city of Byzantium, God's holy fire, pure intellect as entity unto itself, art as immortality.

Selection Test A, p. 18

Critical Reading

1. ANS: A	DIF: Easy	OBJ: Interpretation
2. ANS: B	DIF: Easy	OBJ: Literary Analysis
3. ANS: C	DIF: Easy	OBJ: Comprehension
4. ANS: C	DIF: Easy	OBJ: Comprehension
5. ANS: D	DIF: Easy	OBJ: Interpretation
6. ANS: A	DIF: Easy	OBJ: Literary Analysis

7. ANS: B	DIF: Easy	OBJ: Comprehension
8. ANS: D	DIF: Easy	OBJ: Interpretation
9. ANS: A	DIF: Easy	OBJ: Reading Strategy
10. ANS: D	DIF: Easy	OBJ: Comprehension
11. ANS: B	DIF: Easy	OBJ: Literary Analysis
12. ANS: C	DIF: Easy	OBJ: Comprehension

Vocabulary and Grammar

13. ANS: B	DIF: Easy	OBJ: Vocabulary
14. ANS: D	DIF: Easy	OBJ: Grammar

Essay

15. Students should mention that the speaker addresses a woman whom he has loved. The speaker tells the woman to think how love was lost and how she never saw this man's love among all the others. The speaker is probably Yeats and the woman in the poem is probably Maude Gonne.

Difficulty: *Easy*

Objective: *Essay*

16. Students should note that the speaker has grown older and sadder. The swans, on the other hand, are not tired. Their hearts have not grown cold, according to the speaker.

Difficulty: *Easy*

Objective: *Essay*

Selection Test B, p. 21

Critical Reading

1. ANS: B	DIF: Easy	OBJ: Comprehension
2. ANS: A	DIF: Average	OBJ: Interpretation
3. ANS: A	DIF: Average	OBJ: Interpretation
4. ANS: D	DIF: Average	OBJ: Reading Strategy
5. ANS: B	DIF: Easy	OBJ: Comprehension
6. ANS: C	DIF: Easy	OBJ: Literary Analysis
7. ANS: D	DIF: Average	OBJ: Comprehension
8. ANS: D	DIF: Challenging	OBJ: Comprehension
9. ANS: A	DIF: Easy	OBJ: Reading Strategy
10. ANS: B	DIF: Average	OBJ: Literary Analysis
11. ANS: B	DIF: Average	OBJ: Interpretation
12. ANS: A	DIF: Challenging	OBJ: Literary Analysis
13. ANS: C	DIF: Challenging	OBJ: Reading Strategy

Vocabulary and Grammar

14. ANS: C	DIF: Easy	OBJ: Vocabulary
15. ANS: D	DIF: Average	OBJ: Vocabulary
16. ANS: C	DIF: Average	OBJ: Grammar

Essay

17. Student essays should clearly identify something longed for in each of the three poems and give examples from chosen poems to indicate evidence of that longing. For example, in "When You Are Old," the speaker longs for unrequited love and the missed opportunity it held. In "The Lake Isle of Innisfree," Yeats explicitly longs for peace. In "The Wild Swans at Coole," the speaker longs for a world that does not change, for in the "nineteenth autumn" of his watching, he recalls when he trod "with a lighter tread."

Difficulty: *Easy*

Objective: *Essay*

18. Students should identify symbols in three of the poems in the selection and describe what each represents in the poem and the world beyond it. For example, in "When You Are Old," the fictional old woman symbolizes the future and lost opportunity in love. The "stars" where love has hidden symbolize artistic endeavor. In "The Lake Isle of Innisfree," the isle and everything described on it symbolize a place of peace, either in itself or made from artistic effort. In "The Wild Swans at Coole," the obvious symbols are the swans, who represent unchanging nature, even as they fly away.

Difficulty: *Average*

Objective: *Essay*

"Preludes," "Journey of the Magi," and "The Hollow Men" by T. S. Eliot

Vocabulary Warm-up Exercises, p. 25

A. 1. deliberate
2. consciousness
3. grimy
4. constituted
5. gesture
6. regretted
7. temperate
8. satisfactory

B. **Sample Answers**

1. foolishness; The *folly* of Frank's plan to write his entire research paper the night before it is due is apparent to everyone but Frank.

2. demanding; Gretchen's *insistent* requests for service earned her a reputation as a demanding diner.

3. shameful; Despite her *sordid* past as a counterfeiter, the heroine of the novel I'm reading is really a good person.

4. strength; The *potency* of the salsa was far too much for Zoe.

5. idea; The architect's *conception* of the proposed building was quite impressive.

6. complaining; The two sisters continued *grumbling* about the chores they had to do.

7. basis; The *essence* of Juan's argument was that he was right and Malcolm was wrong.

Reading Warm-up A, p. 26

Sample Answers

1. 1,000 to 1,200 miles and three to twelve months by camel; *Constituted* means "made up of."

2. cold; One city that enjoys *temperate* weather is Los Angeles.

3. (their decision to make the trip); In *Star Wars*, Luke Skywalker later *regretted* confronting Darth Vader too soon.

4. (dirty); If I were *grimy*, the first thing I would do would be to take a bath.

5. to keep going; *Deliberate* means "thought about or intended."

6. awareness; When I come to *consciousness* in the morning, the first thing I think about is getting up in time to get ready for school.

7. (took turns kneeling); A shrug is a *gesture* that can indicate confusion.

8. acceptable; I would receive a passing grade.

Reading Warm-up B, p. 27

Sample Answers

1. to relax the current anti-Catholic laws; A cat might show *hostile* feelings by hissing or arching its back.

2. The new king of England, James I, had promised to relax the anti-Catholic laws, but it now appeared that he would be even more hostile to the Catholics than the former king had been; I was *grumbling* about having to clean up our campsite.

3. (foul); In the comic book I'm reading, a superhero fights against *sordid* criminals.

4. (to begin a revolution that would restore Catholicism as the official religion of England); *Conception* means "the formation of an idea."

5. enough to blow the House of Lords off its foundations; You can increase the *potency* of chili by adding more chili powder or hot sauce.

6. Another word for *folly* is "foolishness"; I have seen people spend all their money on flashy cars and then have nothing left to buy food.

7. the danger; A person should be *insistent* when someone else is in danger or might do something he or she would regret.

8. (a celebration of the uncovering of the plot); *Essence* means "the basic quality" or "that which makes something what it is."

Literary Analysis: Modernism, p. 28

Suggested Responses

1. Students should understand that the clear images, presented without the commentary of the author, are characteristic of Modernism. Students should also understand that the bleak outlook on urban life and the lives of people is a common Modernist theme.

2. The clear images reflect the Modernist style, but unlike the other poems, the people in this work find meaning in their lives. They are guided by a religious belief that helps them through the chaotic world.

3. The world is described as "hollow," "broken," and "lost." People seem unable to communicate or understand themselves and their surroundings. Like "Preludes," the poem uses clear images intended to create emotion in readers and it presents a sad view of modern life.

Reading Strategy: Interpret, p. 29

Suggested Responses

1. Students might list some of the following images: "The grimy scraps of withered leaves about your feet"; "The showers beat on broken blinds and chimney pots"; "Newspapers from vacant lots"; "A lonely cab horse steams and stamps." Students should notice that these images reveal a feeling of quiet, loneliness, and sadness. Eliot seems to be saying that modern, urban life is lonely and depressing.

2. Students might list some of the following images: "With all its muddy feet that press"; "One thinks of all the hands / That are raising dingy shades."; "You curled the papers from your hair, / Or clasped the yellow soles of feet / In the palms of both soiled hands"; "And short, square fingers stuffing pipes." These images show only parts of people, as they focus on simple tasks. The people are fragmented, and words such as "muddy," "dingy," "soiled," and "yellow" give the impression that their lives are tarnished and unhappy.

3. Students might list some of the following details: "The ways deep and the weather sharp"; "the camels galled, sore-footed, and refractory"; ". . . the night-fires going out, and the lack of shelters"; ". . . the cities hostile and the towns unfriendly / And the villages dirty and charging high prices . . ." These images suggest that the journey is difficult, and that the Magi would not endure it if not for an important reason.

4. The Magi are left thinking about birth and death, and they have a sense of unease when they return home to old traditions. The journey changed their lives, and the images imply that the birth they were honoring will have an important effect on the world.

5. The hollow men have a "headpiece filled with straw," "dried voices" that are "quiet and meaningless," and they are "sightless." They are also described as a "paralyzed force, gesture without motion." These images emphasize the misery of the hollow men, who have no self-knowledge and no ability to reach out to find meaning in their lives.

Vocabulary Builder, p. 30

A. 1. fractional; 2. fractious; 3. refract
B. 1. C; 2. A; 3. B; 4. C; 5. C

Grammar and Style: Adjectival Modifiers, p. 31

A. 1. "of withered leaves" modifies *scraps;* prepositional phrase
2. "gathering fuel" modifies *ancient women;* participial phrase
3. "who have crossed" modifies *those;* adjective clause
4. "from vacant lots" modifies *newspapers;* prepositional phrase
5. "that press" modifies *feet;* adjective clause
6. "cursing and grumbling" modifies *men;* participial phrase

B. Sample Response

The poem "Preludes," features a city of despair. The poet writes of showers beating on blinds, a lonely horse stamping and steaming, and the smell of steaks. Morning brings hands that raise dingy shades and the sad masquerades of humans.

Enrichment: Music, p. 34

Suggested Responses

Encourage students to concentrate and use their imaginations as they listen to the classical and modernist pieces. They should record their thoughts on the unique sounds of each piece, the similarities and differences in the musical structures of each time period, and opinions on how the pieces reflect the modernist movement's use of fragments, its exploration of meaninglessness, and its willingness to risk annoying or confusing its audience.

Selection Test A, p. 35

Critical Reading

1. ANS: A	DIF: Easy	OBJ: Comprehension
2. ANS: D	DIF: Easy	OBJ: Interpretation
3. ANS: B	DIF: Easy	OBJ: Literary Analysis
4. ANS: C	DIF: Easy	OBJ: Reading Strategy
5. ANS: B	DIF: Easy	OBJ: Comprehension
6. ANS: D	DIF: Easy	OBJ: Reading Strategy
7. ANS: C	DIF: Easy	OBJ: Interpretation
8. ANS: D	DIF: Easy	OBJ: Literary Analysis
9. ANS: C	DIF: Easy	OBJ: Interpretation
10. ANS: B	DIF: Easy	OBJ: Comprehension
11. ANS: B	DIF: Easy	OBJ: Literary Analysis

Vocabulary and Grammar

12. ANS: D	DIF: Easy	OBJ: Vocabulary
13. ANS: A	DIF: Easy	OBJ: Grammar

Essay

14. Students should recognize that the tone changes in different parts and even in different lines throughout the poem. They might for example, describe the tone in much of "Prelude I" as detached or objective. The tone changes to pity near the end when the speaker mentions the gentle and suffering thing and the old women collecting fuel in vacant lots.
Difficulty: *Easy*
Objective: *Essay*

15. Students should note that the magi were wise men who traveled a great distance to visit the infant Jesus right after he was born. The speaker describes the extreme hardship of the winter journey. Finally, they came to a pleasant valley and located the place they were seeking. The birth brought change to the world, and when they returned to their kingdoms, they were no longer comfortable there.
Difficulty: *Easy*
Objective: *Essay*

Selection Test B, p. 38

Critical Reading

1. ANS: C	DIF: Easy	OBJ: Comprehension
2. ANS: A	DIF: Average	OBJ: Comprehension
3. ANS: C	DIF: Average	OBJ: Literary Analysis
4. ANS: B	DIF: Challenging	OBJ: Interpretation
5. ANS: D	DIF: Easy	OBJ: Interpretation
6. ANS: A	DIF: Easy	OBJ: Reading Strategy
7. ANS: C	DIF: Average	OBJ: Interpretation
8. ANS: B	DIF: Challenging	OBJ: Interpretation
9. ANS: D	DIF: Challenging	OBJ: Literary Analysis
10. ANS: B	DIF: Average	OBJ: Reading Strategy
11. ANS: D	DIF: Average	OBJ: Literary Analysis
12. ANS: B	DIF: Average	OBJ: Comprehension

Vocabulary and Grammar

13. ANS: C	DIF: Easy	OBJ: Vocabulary
14. ANS: A	DIF: Average	OBJ: Vocabulary
15. ANS: D	DIF: Easy	OBJ: Grammar
16. ANS: B	DIF: Average	OBJ: Grammar
17. ANS: D	DIF: Average	OBJ: Grammar

Essay

18. Students should understand that the journey of the Magi is long and difficult. It is important to them because, despite hardships, difficult people, and self-doubt, they press onward. Students should name specific images of the journey's hardships, such as "The ways deep and the weather sharp," the "sore-footed camels," and the "cities hostile and the towns unfriendly." The journey changes their lives in that it affirms their faith and helps them to

anticipate change in the world around them. They are no longer at ease with the "old dispensations," or belief systems, of people.

Difficulty: *Easy*

Objective: *Essay*

19. Both poems represent a break from traditional types of verse in that they convey meaning through simple but meaningful images intended to have a powerful emotional effect. These images reflect the Modernist view of the world in their depiction of chaos, spiritual emptiness, and dirtiness. In "Preludes," the poet describes a rainy, cold city in which people—described as only hands and feet—are fragmented and lost. In daylight, people walk around without direction and in masquerade. At night, they are haunted by a thousand sordid images. At the end of the poem, Eliot expresses the hope that the human spirit can rise above and beyond the sordid circumstances of their lives. In "The Hollow Men," Eliot expresses the meaningless, repetitive behaviors people display in modern life. They are inhibited by corruption, disillusionment, and an inability to connect to their spiritual selves. These themes are emphasized by images of sightlessness, images of a tired, broken, world, and images of people being paralyzed and unable to save themselves.

Difficulty: *Challenging*

Objective: *Essay*

"In Memory of W. B. Yeats" and "Musée des Beaux Arts" by W. H. Auden
"Carrick Revisited" by Louis MacNeice
"Not Palaces" by Stephen Spender

Vocabulary Warm-up Exercises, p. 42

A. 1. intolerant
2. isolation
3. leisurely
4. rapture
5. miraculous
6. emphasis
7. concealment
8. interlude

B. Sample Answers
1. T; The roof, being part of the building, is an *architectural* element.
2. T; A room with an *accumulation* of dust has dust all over everything and has to be dusted.
3. F; An *acquired* talent is something one has to work at to learn.
4. T; If you heard a bear roar, you might feel that you were in danger, which would be a *dreadful* feeling.
5. F; A crowd would probably shout angrily, not *reverently*, to a losing team.

6. F; When you *tamper* with something, you are likely to break it.
7. F; Wealthy and stylish people would be attracted to a *fashionable* place.
8. F; If you refuse to change your mind, you have not *modified* your attitude at all.

Reading Warm-up A, p. 43

Sample Answers
1. (he simply would not allow it); He banished Daedalus and Icarus to the Labyrinth.
2. (being alone all the time); A time I found myself in *isolation* was when I had the measles and had to be kept away from my brother and sister.
3. Labyrinth; If I wanted to be sure of the *concealment* of a small treasure, I would put it in a box under my bed.
4. (stressing); One safety rule that I think deserves great *emphasis* is to always wear a seatbelt in a moving car.
5. (seemingly impossible); In ancient times, a solar eclipse was seen as a *miraculous* event.
6. slowly; One activity that I do *leisurely* is take a bath.
7. delight; After dreaming all his life about skydiving, the *rapture* Jamal felt when he leaped from the plane was unbelievable.
8. (he flew higher and higher); An *interlude* I would enjoy would be a drive out to the beach for a picnic.

Reading Warm-up B, p. 44

Sample Answers
1. building designers; windows or doors in a building
2. (popular); Low-rise jeans are *fashionable*.
3. Because they were not immediately fashionable but became more popular over time; *Acquired* means to gain possession of.
4. (collection); If I had an *accumulation* of old CDs, I would sell them in an online auction.
5. German culture; If I were to *tamper* with a camera, I might break it.
6. ("cosmopolitan rubbish"); I know my favorite old jeans look *dreadful*, but I wear them anyway because they are so comfortable.
7. changed; I would expect to see a different hairstyle than the one she had before.
8. (highly respected)

Literary Analysis: Theme, p. 45

Sample Responses
1. A central idea in the poem is that Yeats's death blurs the line between Yeats himself and his poetry. Auden's word choice implies the theme: "wholly given over to unfamiliar affections" and "words of a dead man / Are modified in the guts of the living."
2. The poem's theme—tragedy matters only to those who are affected by it—is indirectly expressed. Auden's word

choice and tone—"expensive delicate ship" and "sailed calmly on"—imply the theme.

3. These lines express the theme directly. The speaker grapples with his identity, and the lines describe these different identities. The poet's tone, which is both angry and melancholy, implies the theme.

Reading Strategy: Paraphrase, p. 46

A. Possible Responses

1. Nature is indifferent to human suffering.
2. Returning to a place we know mostly from memory limits our perception of the place.
3. Art cannot be kept and collected. It must be created, with energy, if there is any hope that art can change the world.

B. Suggested Responses

1. The phrase "dogs go on with their doggy life" emphasizes nature's indifference to human suffering.
2. The imagery of sea and land underscore the speaker's feelings of ambivalence about the truth of memory.
3. The juxtaposition of "filtered dusts" with "stamping," "emphasis," and "Drink from here energy" sharply contrasts the old and new ideas about art.

Vocabulary Builder, p. 47

A. 1. C; 2. A
B. 1. D; 2. C; 3. B; 4. C; 5. A

Grammar and Style: Parallel Structure, p. 48

A. 1. taught; 2. as; 3. consider; 4. promoting
B. Sample Responses

1. Yeats died on a day that was dark and cold.
2. The "Old Masters" refers to artists from Belgium, Holland, and Italy.
3. Bruegel enjoyed painting scenes of laborers, including harvesters and hunters.
4. The speaker in "Carrick Revisited" admires the landscape and remembers his childhood.

Enrichment: Social Studies, p. 51

Sample Responses

1. At the time, England and Europe were still experiencing the effects of the Great Depression. The "dogs of Europe" might refer to militarists in Germany and Italy, countries that were poised for war.
2. Throughout the 1930s, many people experienced "human unsuccess" as they lost their jobs and means of supporting themselves and their families.

Selection Test A, p. 52

Critical Reading

1. ANS: C	DIF: Easy	OBJ: Comprehension
2. ANS: B	DIF: Easy	OBJ: Reading Strategy

3. ANS: D	DIF: Easy	OBJ: Literary Analysis
4. ANS: C	DIF: Easy	OBJ: Comprehension
5. ANS: A	DIF: Easy	OBJ: Interpretation
6. ANS: B	DIF: Easy	OBJ: Reading Strategy
7. ANS: C	DIF: Easy	OBJ: Literary Analysis
8. ANS: C	DIF: Easy	OBJ: Comprehension
9. ANS: D	DIF: Easy	OBJ: Comprehension
10. ANS: A	DIF: Easy	OBJ: Literary Analysis

Vocabulary and Grammar

11. ANS: B	DIF: Easy	OBJ: Vocabulary
12. ANS: A	DIF: Easy	OBJ: Grammar

Essay

13. Students may note that the theme of "In Memory of W. B. Yeats" is that Yeats is dead, but his poetry inspires readers. The theme of "Musée des Beaux Arts" is that people suffer, but life goes on. The theme of "Carrick Revisited" is the desire people have to know how their past influences their lives. The theme of "Not Palaces" is that in the past, art was for the few; now it should be for all people. Students should cite images, symbols, and other evidence from the poem that supports the theme.
Difficulty: *Easy*
Objective: *Essay*

14. Students should recognize that Auden had great respect and admiration for Yeats. As an example, he creates the image of the cold winter day when Yeats died. He also says that history forgives the failings of people who produce great poetry. Yeats created poetry that did not change the world, but it helped people know themselves and learn to be free.
Difficulty: *Easy*
Objective: *Essay*

Selection Test B, p. 55

Critical Reading

1. ANS: A	DIF: Average	OBJ: Interpretation
2. ANS: A	DIF: Average	OBJ: Comprehension
3. ANS: D	DIF: Challenging	OBJ: Reading Strategy
4. ANS: C	DIF: Average	OBJ: Literary Analysis
5. ANS: B	DIF: Average	OBJ: Interpretation
6. ANS: C	DIF: Average	OBJ: Literary Analysis
7. ANS: B	DIF: Easy	OBJ: Comprehension
8. ANS: C	DIF: Average	OBJ: Reading Strategy
9. ANS: D	DIF: Challenging	OBJ: Literary Analysis
10. ANS: B	DIF: Easy	OBJ: Comprehension
11. ANS: B	DIF: Easy	OBJ: Reading Strategy

Vocabulary and Grammar

12. ANS: B	DIF: Easy	**OBJ**: Vocabulary
13. ANS: D	DIF: Average	**OBJ**: Vocabulary
14. ANS: A	DIF: Easy	**OBJ**: Grammar
15. ANS: C	DIF: Average	**OBJ**: Grammar

Essay

16. Students must focus on two poems. Statements of theme must be supported with relevant lines from the poems. For example, students might note that the theme of "Musée des Beaux Arts" is that tragedy matters only to those who are affected by it. Students should realize that Auden states the theme both directly and indirectly. Lines 1–4, which note that human suffering takes place while ordinary events happen, state this theme directly. Auden's detached tone and word choice—"walking dully along," "innocent," and "lei-surely," for example—convey the theme indirectly.

Difficulty: *Average*

Objective: *Essay*

17. Students must state the views of two poets and compare and contrast them. For example, students might feel an affinity with Auden's view that "poetry makes nothing happen" and contrast it with Spender's fervent belief that poetry can rally people toward a "purpose which the wind engraves."

Difficulty: *Challenging*

Objective: *Essay*

"Shooting an Elephant" by George Orwell

Vocabulary Warm-up Exercises, p. 59

A.
1. miserable
2. intention
3. alternative
4. motives
5. certainty
6. invariably
7. futility
8. committed

B. Sample Answers

1. Two things in nature that are *innumerable* are the stars in the sky and the grains of sand on the beaches.
2. If a group of people were *oppressed*, one of their complaints might be that their freedom of speech had been taken away.
3. The difference between *petty* theft and grand theft is the value of the item or items that were stolen; a petty theft would be the theft of a small amount.
4. If I could have talents *comparable* to those of someone I admire, those talents would be the ability to write well and to speak eloquently in public.

5. The best way to stop the *tyranny* of a bully is to stand up to him or her.
6. One type of food that makes me feel a bit *squeamish* is snails.
7. If a government *inflicted* unfair taxes, the people might elect different representatives.
8. If I met a *Buddhist* priest, I would like to ask him about the basic beliefs of his religion.

Reading Warm-up A, p. 60

Sample Answers

1. Tusks grow throughout the lifetime of the animal; *Invariably* means "without change."
2. to live alone or in small bachelor herds; My *intention* is to complete this project today.
3. (bananas) (sugar); An *alternative* to cereal for breakfast might be eggs.
4. (harvesting their tusks); *Motives* means "reasons or causes that make a person act."
5. ivory is still traded legally in Japan; The *futility* of our efforts to put out the fire soon became clear.
6. (that the sale of ivory helps local and national economies); One thing that I think is a certainty is that I will graduate from high school.
7. starvation and misery; *Wretched* means "completely miserable."
8. (any ivory trade will lead to increased poaching); One goal to which I am *committed* is to learn how to play the piano.

Reading Warm-up B, p. 61

Sample Answers

1. in the logging and tourism industries; Words that mean about the same as *innumerable* are *infinite* or *uncountable*.
2. (in size and strength, the two creatures are not even comparable); A *petty* fault that a friend of mine has is that she is lazy when it comes to keeping her room tidy.
3. the elephant is at least ten times larger; Two items in the classroom that are *comparable* in size and shape are a pen and a pencil.
4. (oppression); *Tyranny* means "absolute power used unfairly."
5. easily shocked; My *squeamish* cousin refuses to eat oysters.
6. by being forced to work; Being given too much homework might make me feel as if I were being *oppressed*.
7. (hardship and danger); *Inflicted* means "gave by striking" or "caused injuries or damage."
8. (holy days); The *Buddhist* temple was the most interesting-looking building in the small town.

Literary Analysis: Irony, p. 62

Sample Responses

1. One would expect a certain respect to be shown toward priests. Orwell believes they are oppressed, but he also thinks of them as "evil spirited" and has fantasies of killing them.
2. The British seem heavily armed—Orwell has several types of rifles—against a population that has no weapons, but the Burmese control the behavior of the British.
3. "Grinning" connotes happiness in a situation that is morbid.
4. The crowd showed little interest in the elephant while it was ravaging the bazaar.
5. Orwell feels compelled to kill the elephant, even though he knows its worth is far greater living than dead.
6. The situation is anything but "perfectly clear." Orwell's original resolve not to kill the animal becomes clouded by many concerns, such as embarrassment and pressure from the crowd.
7. A dangerous weapon, which Orwell uses to perform an unseemly task, contrasts sharply with traditional ideas of beauty.
8. The death of the coolie, who was not valued, gave Orwell an excuse for doing something he did not really want to do—shooting the valuable elephant.

Reading Strategy: Recognize the Writer's Attitudes, p. 63

Sample Responses

1. attitudes toward Burmese: perplexed, upset by hatred; knows they're oppressed; "wretched prisoners"; "rage against the evil-spirited little beasts"; "prostrate peoples"; wants to drive bayonet into Buddhist priest; Conclusion: Orwell believes the Burmese are oppressed by the British and, logically, can understand their hatred. However, part of him wants to react to their hatred with rage and revenge.
2. attitudes toward killing elephant: "vaguely uneasy"; no intention of shooting it; feels pressure of crowd's expectations; "absurd puppet"; wears a mask and is not himself; later rationalizes his action; Conclusion: If the decision were left to him, Orwell would not have shot the elephant. However, he felt pressured by the expectation of the crowd and his own perception of what he should do, as a representative of the ruling group.

Vocabulary Builder, p. 64

A. Sample Response

While serving as a police officer in Burma, Orwell came to despise imperialism. He viewed it as a despotic form of government. He noted the irony in the supposed dominion the colonizers had over the colonized.

B. 1. B; 2. F; 3. E; 4. A; 5. D; 6. C

Grammar and Style: Participial Phrases: Restrictive and Nonrestrictive, p. 65

A. 1. hooted after me when I was at a safe distance; restrictive; insults
2. winding all over a steep hillside; nonrestrictive; labyrinth
3. violently shooing away a crowd of naked children; nonrestrictive; woman
4. sharply twisted to one side; restrictive; head
5. standing in front of the unarmed native crowd; nonrestrictive; I

B. Sample Response

At my first violin recital I was very nervous and uncomfortable. My fingers, drenched in sweat, slipped on my violin strings. I rarely looked up from the pages clipped to my music stand.

Enrichment: Social Studies, p. 68

Possible Responses

1. Instead of being ruled by an outside minority, as under imperialism, the Burmese control their own government under self-rule.
2. Even without imperialism, oppression still exists in the country. The "wretched prisoners huddling in the stinking cages of the lockups" referred to by Orwell could well be today's political prisoners.

Selection Test A, p. 69

Critical Reading

1. ANS: B	DIF: Easy	OBJ: Reading Strategy
2. ANS: C	DIF: Easy	OBJ: Comprehension
3. ANS: A	DIF: Easy	OBJ: Reading Strategy
4. ANS: B	DIF: Easy	OBJ: Reading Strategy
5. ANS: A	DIF: Easy	OBJ: Interpretation
6. ANS: D	DIF: Easy	OBJ: Literary Analysis
7. ANS: A	DIF: Easy	OBJ: Comprehension
8. ANS: D	DIF: Easy	OBJ: Comprehension
9. ANS: C	DIF: Easy	OBJ: Interpretation
10. ANS: C	DIF: Easy	OBJ: Literary Analysis
11. ANS: A	DIF: Easy	OBJ: Comprehension

Vocabulary and Grammar

12. ANS: B	DIF: Easy	OBJ: Vocabulary
13. ANS: A	DIF: Easy	OBJ: Grammar

Essay

14. Students should mention that Orwell is referring to the role that white imperialists are forced into as tyrants. Even a man like Orwell, who does not want to be a sahib or tyrant, is forced to act like one. He looks at the faces of the Burmese and sees that they expect him to shoot

the elephant. Their expectation pushes him into behavior that he knows is wrong and unnecessary.

Difficulty: *Easy*

Objective: *Essay*

15. Students may note that Orwell's attitude carries a strong awareness of the evils of imperialism and how it affects the Burmans and their attitudes toward Europeans. He also shows some pity at the death of the Burman as well as for the suffering of the elephant. In light of this attitude, it is difficult to think that Orwell was truly happy that the Burman had died.

Difficulty: *Easy*

Objective: *Essay*

Selection Test B, p. 72

Critical Reading

1. ANS: B	DIF: Average	OBJ: Reading Strategy
2. ANS: D	DIF: Average	OBJ: Reading Strategy
3. ANS: C	DIF: Average	OBJ: Interpretation
4. ANS: D	DIF: Average	OBJ: Literary Analysis
5. ANS: C	DIF: Easy	OBJ: Comprehension
6. ANS: B	DIF: Average	OBJ: Literary Analysis
7. ANS: C	DIF: Challenging	OBJ: Reading Strategy
8. ANS: B	DIF: Challenging	OBJ: Literary Analysis
9. ANS: B	DIF: Easy	OBJ: Interpretation
10. ANS: A	DIF: Average	OBJ: Interpretation
11. ANS: D	DIF: Average	OBJ: Comprehension

Vocabulary and Grammar

12. ANS: C	DIF: Easy	OBJ: Vocabulary
13. ANS: D	DIF: Average	OBJ: Vocabulary
14. ANS: D	DIF: Average	OBJ: Grammar
15. ANS: A	DIF: Average	OBJ: Grammar

Essay

16. Students should recognize that the real motives Orwell names are the fear of appearing weak or foolish and the desire to impress the subjugated. Students might cite examples such as Orwell's self-consciousness in front of the crowd, his realization that he is an "absurd puppet," his fear of being laughed at, and the contradiction in killing an animal that is no longer a threat.

Difficulty: *Easy*

Objective: *Essay*

17. Students should note that Orwell primarily uses irony of situation in his essay. The inherent assumption behind Orwell's statement is that tyrants destroy the freedom of those they control. The irony, therefore, is that the tyrants destroy their own freedom as well, in an attempt to maintain an appearance of authority, power, and control. Orwell's disillusioning knowledge that he must act as the crowd expects him to act—as a representative

of imperialism—conveys this loss of freedom. As a member of the ruling class, he presumably has freedom of choice. However, from the moment he is called to investigate the problem, he becomes part of a chain of events seemingly beyond his control.

Difficulty: *Challenging*

Objective: *Essay*

"The Demon Lover" by Elizabeth Bowen

Vocabulary Warm-up Exercises, p. 76

A. 1. alight
2. caretaker
3. dependability
4. perplexed
5. knowledgeably
6. apprehension
7. heightening
8. assent

B. Sample Answers

1. On a scale from one to ten, I would rate the *acuteness* of pain from a paper cut as "one," because it does not hurt very much.

2. If a *sinister* man spoke to me, I would feel frightened because he would be giving off an aura of evil and danger.

3. If a storyteller was *resuming* her story after a short break, I would wait because that means she would continue the story.

4. To *console* a friend for losing a game, I might say he played well but just had bad luck.

5. If my friend had *accelerating* spending habits, I would tell her to slow down and not waste her money so foolishly.

6. If the *ventilation* in a room were poor, I would suggest opening the windows to let more air in.

7. If a child hurt her knee, her mother might offer the *consolation* of a hug and some tender words.

8. If two people *resumed* their friendship, they would likely make more phone calls because they would be continuing the relationship.

Reading Warm-up A, p. 77

Sample Answers

1. confused, wondering; I once felt perplexed when I couldn't figure out how to play the violin.

2. (supervises and takes care of property that someone else occupies); Something I would want a caretaker to do at my home would be to clean out the garage.

3. worry; One thing that gives me some apprehension is the thought of sharks in the water when I go surfing.

4. (good answer); Clay's experience with motors enabled him to answer knowledgeably Aaron's question about why the car died.

5. <u>reliability</u>; One aspect of my life in which I demonstrate <u>dependability</u> is keeping up with my homework.

6. (increasing); I usually react to <u>heightening</u> demands on my time and patience by making a list of what I have to do and crossing items off as I do them.

7. (common areas); <u>Alight</u> means "lighted."

8. <u>agreement</u>; I would eagerly give my <u>assent</u> to a job offer as a ballerina.

Reading Warm-up B, p. 78

Sample Answers

1. <u>make him feel better</u>; When I am unhappy, a good hug can <u>console</u> me.

2. (stopped following her only when he saw an officer of the law nearby); <u>Sinister</u> means "threatening."

3. (reminded John about how nervous she had been); I'll be <u>resuming</u> my chores after I eat lunch.

4. <u>comfort</u>; When a friend of mine was feeling unhappy, I offered to treat her to dinner to give her some <u>consolation</u>.

5. (it was probably just a coincidence that the guy stopped when he did); An activity that I once dropped and then <u>resumed</u> was knitting a sweater.

6. <u>pace of life</u>; <u>Accelerating</u> means "increasing in speed."

7. <u>circulation</u>; Two ways to improve the <u>ventilation</u> in a room are to turn on a fan and to open the windows.

8. (sharpness); A feeling that once hit me with great <u>acuteness</u> was the feeling of missing my Aunt Mary after we moved away.

Literary Analysis: The Ghost Story, p. 79

Sample Responses

outside Mrs. Drover's house: *normal:* deserted because of war, autumn so humid and rainy; *unusual:* "unfamiliar queerness" due to street's lack of activity

inside Mrs. Drover's house: *normal:* dark because windows boarded up, usual things are visible (smoke stain, ring on desk, bruise in wallpaper); *unusual:* she is "perplexed," one door is ajar

the letter: *normal:* letters were not uncommon; *unusual:* how it came to be delivered and laid on hall table, vaguely sinister message from former lover who is presumed dead

the farewell, 25 years ago: *normal:* saying good-bye to a soldier would have been a common scene during a war; *unusual:* his face not visible, pressure of buttons on hand, she eager to have the farewell done with, "sinister troth" made

Mrs. Drover's marriage and family: *normal:* courtship, marriage, home, and children, she busy being utterly dependable for her family; *unusual:* [no "unusual" details are given]

catching the taxi: *normal:* the street is busy as usual, the taxi is right where it should be; *unusual:* taxi seems to be waiting for her, starts up without instructions, Mrs. Drover screams when she sees the driver's face, taxi speeds off into the deserted streets

Reading Strategy: Respond, p. 80

Sample Responses

Student reactions to the story will depend on their own life experiences. Be sure that students go beyond their own responses to evaluate whether the author intended that response, and why.

Vocabulary Builder, p. 81

A. 1. locality
2. localism
3. allocation

B. 1. B; 2. E; 3. C; 4. A; 5. D

Grammar and Style: Sentence Beginnings: Participial Phrases, p. 82

A. Sentences 2 and 4, begin with participial phrases.
2. "Proceeding upstairs" modifies *Mrs. Drover.*
4. "Annoyed at the caretaker" modifies *she.*

B. Sample Response

Described as a writer of "finely wrought prose," Elizabeth Bowen is highly praised for her stories. Her characters are mostly from the upper middle class in England and Ireland. Born into that class, Bowen "knew" her characters well. Her novel *The Hotel*, published in 1927, contains a typical Bowen heroine. Trying to cope with a life for which she is not prepared, the girl might remind some of a young Elizabeth Bowen.

Enrichment: Social Studies, p. 85

Suggested Response

Students may choose to research the effect of the Blitz on London architecture. Students should note that the German bombing continued throughout the war but not as aggressively as during the Blitz. When Germany surrendered on May 7, 1945, much of London lay in ruins, and about 30,000 Londoners had been killed. Property losses included the Guildhall, the House of Commons, most of the Inns of Court, many churches, and about eighty percent of London's houses.

Selection Test A, p. 86

Critical Reading

1. ANS: D	DIF: Easy	OBJ: Reading Strategy
2. ANS: B	DIF: Easy	OBJ: Comprehension
3. ANS: D	DIF: Easy	OBJ: Comprehension
4. ANS: C	DIF: Easy	OBJ: Comprehension
5. ANS: B	DIF: Easy	OBJ: Interpretation
6. ANS: A	DIF: Easy	OBJ: Interpretation
7. ANS: A	DIF: Easy	OBJ: Interpretation
8. ANS: C	DIF: Easy	OBJ: Literary Analysis
9. ANS: A	DIF: Easy	OBJ: Reading Strategy
10. ANS: C	DIF: Easy	OBJ: Interpretation

11. ANS: B   DIF: Easy   OBJ: Interpretation

Vocabulary and Grammar

12. ANS: C   DIF: Easy   OBJ: Vocabulary
13. ANS: D   DIF: Easy   OBJ: Grammar

Essay

14. Students who think he is a demon may argue that he was first described as having a "spectral" glimmer in his eye back when he was first introduced. Mrs. Drover's inability to remember what he looks like also suggests that he may have been something other than human. Students who argue that he is a living person may say that a ghost would not have to open a basement window to enter or leave the house. He is also last seen driving a taxi.

Difficulty: *Easy*

Objective: *Essay*

15. Students should mention that the deserted neighborhood and house creates a mood of suspense because Mrs. Drover is all alone. Anything can happen to her, and there is no one to help or even to notice. No one is supposed to be in the house except Mrs. Drover, but she feels a presence. The vacant neighborhood contributes to the mood as well, because she is only able to see one taxi.

Difficulty: *Easy*

Objective: *Essay*

Selection Test B, p. 89

Critical Reading

1. ANS: D   DIF: Easy   OBJ: Comprehension
2. ANS: A   DIF: Average   OBJ: Interpretation
3. ANS: C   DIF: Challenging   OBJ: Literary Analysis
4. ANS: C   DIF: Average   OBJ: Literary Analysis
5. ANS: A   DIF: Average   OBJ: Reading Strategy
6. ANS: B   DIF: Average   OBJ: Literary Analysis
7. ANS: C   DIF: Average   OBJ: Comprehension
8. ANS: B   DIF: Average   OBJ: Interpretation
9. ANS: C   DIF: Easy   OBJ: Reading Strategy
10. ANS: A   DIF: Easy   OBJ: Interpretation
11. ANS: B   DIF: Average   OBJ: Reading Strategy
12. ANS: A   DIF: Easy   OBJ: Interpretation

Vocabulary and Grammar

13. ANS: B   DIF: Easy   OBJ: Vocabulary
14. ANS: B   DIF: Average   OBJ: Grammar

Essay

15. Some students may choose to state that Bowen uses the war to create tension in her stories, to serve as the unhappy background for unhappy people. They may interpret this as opportunism, perhaps therefore acceptance. Or they may say that because Bowen experienced the war herself, its events don't seem noteworthy or interesting to her. Other students may note that all of the strangeness in the story is the result of Mrs. Drover's family being "dislocated' from their normal life by the bombings. The unhappiness and tension that exists in Mrs. Drover are Bowen's way of showing how war breaks people down.

Difficulty: *Easy*

Objective: *Essay*

16. Students should point out the "queerness" of Mrs. Drover's street. Mrs. Drover is "perplexed" by being in her own home. The presence of the letter, as well as its message, is disturbing. The circumstances of her long-ago meeting with her fiancé were a bit odd, as were her years of "dislocation" afterward. She cannot remember his face. She feels a draft of cold air from downstairs. The taxi seems to be waiting for her and starts up without her instructions. All of these "unnatural" elements serve to build suspense so that the reader is expecting catastrophe but still taken by surprise when the taxi speeds off with the screaming Mrs. Drover.

Difficulty: *Average*

Objective: *Essay*

Benchmark Test 10, p. 92

MULTIPLE CHOICE

1. ANS: D
2. ANS: B
3. ANS: B
4. ANS: D
5. ANS: A
6. ANS: D
7. ANS: A
8. ANS: C
9. ANS: D
10. ANS: B
11. ANS: C
12. ANS: A
13. ANS: A
14. ANS: C
15. ANS: B
16. ANS: D
17. ANS: A
18. ANS: D

19. ANS: B
20. ANS: C
21. ANS: C
22. ANS: B
23. ANS: A
24. ANS: D
25. ANS: D
26. ANS: C
27. ANS: C
28. ANS: D
29. ANS: C
30. ANS: B
31. ANS: B
32. ANS: A

ESSAY

33. Students should write a critical sentence concerning a selection in the test. Their responses should be clear and should be followed by two relevant supporting details or examples from the selection.

34. Students' poems should describe some aspect of a water fountain.

35. Students should clearly identify a book, story, or movie. Their overviews should be clear, succinct, and logical.

Diagnostic Test 11, p. 98

MULTIPLE CHOICE

1. ANS: D
2. ANS: B
3. ANS: B
4. ANS: C
5. ANS: D
6. ANS: A
7. ANS: D
8. ANS: C
9. ANS: C
10. ANS: A
11. ANS: D
12. ANS: C
13. ANS: B
14. ANS: D
15. ANS: A

"The Soldier" by Rupert Brooke
"Wirers" by Siegfried Sassoon
"Anthem for Doomed Youth" by Wilfred Owen
"Birds on the Western Front"
by Saki (H. H. Munro)

Vocabulary Warm-up Exercises, p. 102

A. 1. indulge
2. battlefield
3. artillery
4. doubtless or probably
5. clods
6. solitary
7. doubtless or probably
8. wary

B. Sample Answers

1. The *accommodation* offered to the stranger was a guest bedroom with a double bed. This room can *accommodate* two people comfortably.

2. Marcia finds it difficult to *cope* with all the stresses of her job. Tom and Elaine *cope* so well with all their hardships that they are an inspiration to all.

3. The electric fence *deterred* the cows from grazing in the other field. The threat of detention is a *deterrent* to most students who think about breaking the rules.

4. Vanessa lives in the general *locality* of the park. The owner is opening another restaurant at a better *location* next year.

5. The sign told us that admission was *restricted* to members only. Dan's illness *restricted* his activities for a month.

6. Barry is very *sensitive* to loud noises. Terry's *sensitivity* to her sister's needs is clear by the way she helps her.

7. Hector enjoyed his *tranquil* afternoon, fishing at the lake. The *tranquil* moment was interrupted by the sound of a leaf blower.

Reading Warm-up A, p. 103

Sample Answers

1. missing their loved ones and longing for the comforts of home; This weekend I will *doubtless* be doing laundry.

2. (trenches); We visited a Civil War *battlefield* and read the historic plaque there.

3. one; A *solitary* experience I once enjoyed was a bike ride along the river.

4. of shaking hands with men they had been trying to kill just the day before; If a dog were *wary* of me, it might back away with its tail between its legs.

5. (a game of football); I like to *indulge* in a bubble bath whenever I get the chance.

6. (nearly frozen ground); *Clods* are lumps of earth.

7. sound; *Artillery* means "large mounted guns."

8. sound of artillery fire would . . . fill the air once again; One thing I will *probably* do after school today is take a guitar lesson.

Reading Warm-up B, p. 104

Sample Answers

1. they can be found in rainforests, grasslands, wooded areas, and tundras; *Restricted* means "limited or confined."
2. (homes); The *accommodation* my family offers guests who visit our home for a few days is a guest room with a double bed.
3. area; The *locality* of the Johnsons's home is near the beach.
4. *Deterred* means "prevented from doing something."
5. (calm); If I am in a *tranquil* mood, I like to relax in a hammock.
6. deal with; *handle, face, manage*
7. (Owls' wings have downy fringes that muffle the sound as they fly); owls can easily sneak up on their prey; *Consequently* means "as a result."
8. A job that would probably be best for a person with very *sensitive* taste buds would be tasting foods for a company that makes new kinds of snacks.

Literary Analysis: Tone, p. 105

Sample Responses

"Wirers" *Details:* Doomed soldier carried off in great pain; Cost of life to repair barb-wire fence. Impact of image is horror. *Word Choice:* "Moaning" "lurch" are direct and graphic. "No doubt he'll die today" is matter-of-fact. *Voice:* Voice is direct plain speech, a credible soldier, and an understated account of death. Bitter in last line. *Tone:* Overall tone is stark in reporting the casual details of death, turning bitter as the lost life is measured against the minor gain of fence repair

"Birds on the Western Front" *Details:* Narrator falls on nestlings. Two were dead, the others uninjured. Underscores random nature of death in wartime, and the absurdity of war as nature tries to go on. *Word Choice:* "with some abruptness" rather than a terrified dive; "rather a battered condition" means dead; "tranquil and comfortable," even for a bird, seems incredible in the circumstances. *Voice:* Formal diction of an upper class, as if writing a letter back to a local birdwatching club. The voice is gently absurd in these conditions. *Tone:* Overall tone is ironic, focusing closely on birds while in mortal peril.

Reading Strategy: Make Inferences, p. 106

Possible Responses

Setting: War zone; "seems to be very little corresponding disturbance," eyewitness account

Speaker: Observer of some sort, then clearly a soldier; eyewitness observations, then, "I once saw a pair of crows," "throw myself down with abruptness" indicating he is a soldier.

Action/Topic: Bird behavior in wartime; any of various bird behaviors in scarred landscape.

Tone: Ironic and detached; studied language and formal expression, as if in a club or over dinner rather than on a battlefield.

Theme: Absurdity of war, a life and death struggle, as contrasted against bird behavior, also a life and death struggle. Gentle satire of English reserve and mannerisms.

Vocabulary Builder, p. 107

A. 1. laud; 2. laudation; 3. laudatory
B. 1. A; 2. D; 3. B; 4. D; 5. C; 6. C; 7. B

Grammar and Style: Use of *Who* and *Whom* in Adjective Clauses, p. 108

A. 1. who; 2. whom; 3. whom
B. Sample Responses

1. Rupert Brooke was one of many talented writers who died in World War I.
2. Siegfried Sassoon, whom the world first noticed in war, wrote of peace in later life.
3. The families whom the soldiers left behind are on the mind of Wilfred Owen in "Anthem for Doomed Youth."

Enrichment: Social Studies, p. 111

1. The most obvious change is the disappearance of the Austro-Hungarian Empire, which was divided into Austria, Hungary, Czechoslovakia, and Yugoslavia.
2. Part of Germany went to Poland, newly independent from Russia, and the Alsace-Lorraine region went to France.
3. Estonia, Finland, Latvia, Lithuania, and Poland became independent states, and Rumania gained some Ukranian territory.
4. Italy gained some territory in the north from Austria-Hungary.

Selection Test A, p. 112

Critical Reading

1. ANS: B	DIF: Easy	OBJ: Interpretation
2. ANS: C	DIF: Easy	OBJ: Reading Strategy
3. ANS: A	DIF: Easy	OBJ: Literary Analysis
4. ANS: D	DIF: Easy	OBJ: Reading Strategy
5. ANS: B	DIF: Easy	OBJ: Reading Strategy
6. ANS: C	DIF: Easy	OBJ: Literary Analysis
7. ANS: D	DIF: Easy	OBJ: Comprehension
8. ANS: B	DIF: Easy	OBJ: Interpretation
9. ANS: A	DIF: Easy	OBJ: Interpretation
10. ANS: B	DIF: Easy	OBJ: Reading Strategy
11. ANS: D	DIF: Easy	OBJ: Comprehension
12. ANS: A	DIF: Easy	OBJ: Comprehension

Vocabulary and Grammar

13. ANS: B   DIF: Easy   OBJ: Vocabulary
14. ANS: A   DIF: Easy   OBJ: Grammar

Essay

15. Students may note that Brooke expresses a sadness over war, but he still believes in the justification for the war and in the heroism of the English soldiers. In the poems of Sassoon and Owen, students should see their bitterness over the destruction caused by the war. Saki's observations of the birds show the violence of war.

Difficulty: *Easy*

Objective: *Essay*

16. Students may choose "Wirers" or "Anthem for Doomed Youth" as the poem that expresses the modern view of warfare and that most Americans will most nearly agree with. They will argue that war is now seen as destructive and not a glorious adventure. Others may choose Brooke's "The Soldier" for expressing the view that when soldiers die, people regard them as heroes.

Difficulty: *Easy*

Objective: *Essay*

Selection Test B, p. 115

Critical Reading

1. ANS: D   DIF: Average   OBJ: Comprehension
2. ANS: C   DIF: Average   OBJ: Interpretation
3. ANS: B   DIF: Average   OBJ: Reading Strategy
4. ANS: D   DIF: Easy   OBJ: Literary Analysis
5. ANS: A   DIF: Easy   OBJ: Comprehension
6. ANS: A   DIF: Easy   OBJ: Interpretation
7. ANS: D   DIF: Average   OBJ: Interpretation
8. ANS: B   DIF: Challenging   OBJ: Reading Strategy
9. ANS: B   DIF: Average   OBJ: Interpretation
10. ANS: C   DIF: Easy   OBJ: Literary Analysis
11. ANS: D   DIF: Challenging   OBJ: Literary Analysis
12. ANS: A   DIF: Average   OBJ: Reading Strategy

Vocabulary and Grammar

13. ANS: C   DIF: Average   OBJ: Vocabulary
14. ANS: C   DIF: Easy   OBJ: Vocabulary
15. ANS: B   DIF: Average   OBJ: Grammar
16. ANS: D   DIF: Challenging   OBJ: Grammar

Essay

17. The only similarity between "The Soldier" and "Wirers" is that both seem to assume no other fate than death for a soldier. The fundamental difference between the two is in whether the cause is worth the sacrifice: to Brooke it is; to Sassoon it's not. Brooke focuses on the beauty of English life that prepares him for this sacrifice, that the

"pulse in the eternal mind" bear more of an English rhythm. Sassoon's "Wirers", by contrast, sets grim images of exhausted men stumbling in terror beside a matter-of-fact attitude about death. The death of young Hughes gains only a wire "safely mended," which will need to be mended again.

Difficulty: *Average*

Objective: *Essay*

18. Saki's tone comes from two primary factors: a cheerful voice making casual comments and a faintly bizarre topic interspersed with details about the real scenery. Focusing on bird behavior, the narrator still points out "a wealth of ruined buildings" or notes he had "occasion to throw myself abruptly on my face." These off-center descriptions of destruction and danger point to the absurd nature of the topic. The tone of normalcy in the most abnormal of situations implies a contrast between war and normal life. The detailed description of bird behavior in these conditions also implies a contrast between the natural life of the inhabitants and that of the combatants.

Difficulty: *Challenging*

Objective: *Essay*

"Wartime Speech" by Winston Churchill
"Defending Nonviolent Resistance"
by Mohandas K. Gandhi

Vocabulary Warm-up Exercises, p. 119

A.
1. agricultural
2. totality
3. exertions
4. supplement
5. contribution
6. voluntary
7. fulfilled
8. Similarly

B. Sample Answers

1. The speaker seemed determined to stir up agitation. The child was nervous and agitated.
2. Vivian's income is inadequate for her lifestyle. Stan puts in inadequate amounts of time on his homework.
3. Several occurrences the past week have aroused suspicion. After that embarrassing scene occurred, Hazel left town.
4. The city braced itself for the next onslaught of stormy weather. James refused to listen to another onslaught of verbal abuse.
5. The judge sentenced the criminal to ten years—the maximum penalty allowed by law. If you arrive late, the penalty is that you will not be seated until after the first act.

6. Mona was worried that her <u>resources</u> would run out before the project was completed. The millionaire's <u>resources</u> would not be enough to cover his losses.

7. The company has the <u>utmost</u> respect for its founder. Inez gave her <u>utmost</u> efforts to the cause.

Reading Warm-up A, p. 120

Sample Answers

1. his famous <u>"march to the sea"</u>; A *contribution* I recently made to a project was doing some research for a group presentation.

2. (Gandhi had been campaigning quite publicly and vocally for an end to British rule); After two hours of difficult *exertions*, Suzy was tired.

3. <u>rural</u>; *Agricultural* means "relating to the science of farming."

4. (entirely); *part, unit*

5. <u>salt</u>; One *supplement* someone might add to his diet on a daily basis is wheat grass juice.

6. <u>walked with him for 23 days and over 240 miles to the Indian coast</u>; Once I participated in a project, on a *voluntary* basis, to clean up litter on the beach.

7. <u>his promise</u>; *Fulfilled* means "carried out, as a promise or prediction."

8. (began picking up salt everywhere along the coast); Dave has three brothers; *similarly*, Sue has three sisters.

Reading Warm-up B, p. 121

Sample Answers

1. <u>Hitler's armies had already invaded Holland, Belgium, and the northern areas of France</u>; Troublemakers were stirring up *agitation* about conditions in the cafeteria.

2. (it split the British and French forces fighting there); *Onslaught* means "a very violent attack."

3. <u>the German army trapped the British forces at Dunkirk</u>; Two *occurrences* in the past week that I enjoyed were a birthday party for my best friend and a bike ride by the river.

4. One of my goals is to learn to play the piano. The *resources* I need in order to accomplish it are a piano, money for lessons, a good teacher, and time to practice.

5. (completely); *incompletely, partially*

6. <u>were exhausted</u>; The last time I put forth my *utmost* effort was during the playoff game against Jefferson High School.

7. <u>lacking</u>; Frank wants to bake a cake, but he has an *inadequate* amount of sugar for it.

8. (losing their lives); A fair *penalty* for failing to pay a debt in time is extra interest.

Literary Analysis: Speech, p. 122

Possible Responses

1. *Churchill:* ". . . solemn hour for the life of our country, of our Empire, of our Allies, and above all, of the cause of

Freedom. A tremendous battle is raging in France and Flanders."
Gandhi: ". . . I entirely endorse the learned advocate-general's remarks in connection with my humble self. I think he was entirely fair to me . . ."

2. *Churchill:* Status, followed by cause for hope, followed by praise for forces, followed by expectation of battle in Britain, followed by call for commitment, concluded by invocation of history.
Gandhi: Admission of guilt by law; history of his own loyalty, disaffection through chronology of abuse, details, reiteration of guilt by immoral law, appeal to higher morality.

3. *Churchill:* "clawing down three to four to one of our enemies," "foulest and most soul-destroying."
Gandhi: "mad fury of my people," "to invite and cheerfully submit."

4. *Churchill:* Specifics of battles; request for munitions; call for labor.
Gandhi: Any examples from history of Gandhi's service to the Empire.

5. *Churchill:* Roll call of conquered nations; appeal to British history on Trinity Sunday.
Gandhi: Reiteration of guilt; acceptance of penalties; appeal to judge to step down and not participate in injustice.

Reading Strategy: Identify Main Points and Support, p. 123

Sample Responses

Main Idea	We must not be intimidated by these developments.
S1	If they're behind our front, we're behind theirs.
S2	All armies are in danger, so the battle may be even.
S3	French and British armies will be well handled.
S4	The French have a genius for counter-attack.
S5	The British Army has always shown dogged endurance.
S6	The situation could therefore improve suddenly.

Vocabulary Builder, p. 124

A. 1. duration; 2. obdurate; 3. durability

B. 1. invincible; 2. formidable; 3. intimidated; 4. retaliate; 5. diabolical; 6. excrescence; 7. endurance; 8. disaffection; 9. extenuating

Grammar and Style: Parallel Structure, p. 125

A. 1. And if the French Army, and our own Army, are well handled, as I believe they will be; if the French retain that genius for recovery and counter-attack for which they have so long been famous, and if the British Army shows the dogged endurance of which there have been so many examples in the past—then a

sudden transformation might spring into being.
Adverbial clause

2. Only a very small part of that splendid army has yet been heavily engaged; and only a very small part of France has yet been invaded. *Adjective phrase*

3. After this battle in France abates its force, there will come the battle for our island—for all that Britain is, and all that Britain means. *Noun clause*

4. Nonviolence is the first article of my creed. It is also the last article of my faith. *Complement*

5. No sophistry, no jugglery in figures can explain away the evidence that the skeletons in many villages present to the naked eye. *Subject*

B. 1. Churchill wanted to explain the situation, to encourage the Army, to reassure the people, to prepare and to inspire them for the long struggle he foresaw.

2. Gandhi did not dispute the charges against him, but he disputed British right of administration, British application of law, British imposition of justice, and British rule of India.

Enrichment: Community Action, p. 128

Suggested Response

1. Students should select a topic that is appropriate and manageable for the community, the classroom, and a speech. Avoid topics too large, personal, or inflammatory.

2. Students' creativity can show in the introductory "hook" but be sure that the specific topic is also identified.

3. Students should identify a main idea in a manageable form. A specific thesis statement is best.

4. Support features should be distinguishable, relevant, and logical. Avoid hyperbole and the entire range of logical fallacies.

5. Make sure the conclusion follows or summarizes what has gone before in the speech. The conclusion should wrap up the topic as well as call for agreement or action.

Selection Test A, p. 129

Critical Reading

1. ANS: C	DIF: Easy	OBJ: Comprehension
2. ANS: A	DIF: Easy	OBJ: Comprehension
3. ANS: B	DIF: Easy	OBJ: Literary Analysis
4. ANS: D	DIF: Easy	OBJ: Reading Strategy
5. ANS: D	DIF: Easy	OBJ: Literary Analysis
6. ANS: D	DIF: Easy	OBJ: Literary Analysis
7. ANS: C	DIF: Easy	OBJ: Comprehension
8. ANS: D	DIF: Easy	OBJ: Interpretation
9. ANS: B	DIF: Easy	OBJ: Reading Strategy
10. ANS: C	DIF: Easy	OBJ: Comprehension

Vocabulary and Grammar

11. ANS: A	DIF: Easy	OBJ: Vocabulary
12. ANS: C	DIF: Easy	OBJ: Grammar

Essay

13. Students should understand that Churchill thinks the conflict with Germany is a time when freedom is challenged by evil. As a result, it is an opportunity for people to perform heroically in defense of freedom and civilization. Churchill calls Germany a barbaric state and mentions the people of Poland, Denmark, and other nations who will become victims.

Difficulty: *Easy*

Objective: *Essay*

14. Gandhi realized that the government would never change its treatment of Indians. Laws were passed that took away more of the people's freedoms. There were then massacres of Indians and the passage of new laws that humiliated Indians. Finally, he realized that the British administrators did not even know they were acting criminally toward the Indians. As a result of these discoveries, Gandhi decided on his practice of promoting disaffection and nonviolent resistance.

Difficulty: *Easy*

Objective: *Essay*

Selection Test B, p. 132

Critical Reading

1. ANS: A	DIF: Easy	OBJ: Comprehension
2. ANS: C	DIF: Average	OBJ: Interpretation
3. ANS: C	DIF: Average	OBJ: Literary Analysis
4. ANS: B	DIF: Average	OBJ: Reading Strategy
5. ANS: A	DIF: Challenging	OBJ: Literary Analysis
6. ANS: B	DIF: Easy	OBJ: Interpretation
7. ANS: D	DIF: Average	OBJ: Comprehension
8. ANS: A	DIF: Easy	OBJ: Interpretation
9. ANS: B	DIF: Easy	OBJ: Literary Analysis
10. ANS: C	DIF: Easy	OBJ: Reading Strategy
11. ANS: A	DIF: Average	OBJ: Literary Analysis
12. ANS: B	DIF: Average	OBJ: Reading Strategy

Vocabulary and Grammar

13. ANS: D	DIF: Average	OBJ: Grammar
14. ANS: B	DIF: Easy	OBJ: Vocabulary
15. ANS: D	DIF: Average	OBJ: Vocabulary

Essay

16. The purpose of the speech is a clear explanation of the causes and goals of Gandhi's actions against British rule. First, he traces the rise of his disaffection with British rule by citing incidents of racism and repression, although noting service to the Empire. Second, he points to the current condition of the Indian people under British rule, who are powerless, weak, and poor. Third, he states the principle that it is a virtue to oppose a government that has caused the damage he has

already cited, a "sin to have affection" for such a system. The credibility of the first two points makes the logic of the third seem ironclad, and so he considers it a "precious privilege" to oppose such authority. In agreeing to the charges on grounds of morality, he reinforces the notion that the government that makes the laws is immoral.

Difficulty: *Easy*

Objective: *Essay*

17. Churchill's purpose in the speech is to meet the emotional needs of his audience by addressing what the situation is and preparing Britons for what it will be. First, he reports facts, acknowledging what people already know, that France is in trouble, and thus he seems in touch and in control. Second, he further calms a troubled audience by noting the efforts and qualities of the French and British troops. Third, he offers limited hope, suggesting ways things could turn out well and what it might take, although noting it would be "foolish to disguise" what will probably happen. Then he shifts to preparing for war alone and calls on the nation to prepare and produce for the "battle for our island" in the name of "right and freedom." He closes by invoking centuries of British valor and history to emphasize the like nature of this moment.

Difficulty: *Average*

Objective: *Essay*

"Follower" and "Two Lorries" by Seamus Heaney
"Outside History" by Eavan Boland

Vocabulary Warm-up Exercises, p. 136

A. 1. expert
2. conceit
3. reins
4. ordeal
5. pluck
6. strained
7. heft
8. angled

B. Sample Answers

1. Two colors I'd be likely to find in a piece of *sod* are green and brown.
2. If I *stumbled* and fell in front of an audience, I would feel embarrassed.
3. The *myth* about Echo and Narcissus is my favorite.
4. To buy *shafts*, I would go to a horse supply store.
5. If company were coming soon, I might go into a *flurry* of house-cleaning.
6. I might plow a *furrow* to prepare the ground for a vegetable garden.
7. If I were to *tally* the times I brushed my teeth this week, the final number would be fourteen.
8. One great *nuisance* in my life is ironing.

Reading Warm-up A, p. 137

Sample Answers

1. <u>a person who knows</u>; I would like to become an *expert* in the field of sports medicine.
2. (skill); Helen's *conceit* about her beauty is a bit silly.
3. <u>if a horse gets sores</u>; *Ordeal* means "a very difficult or trying experience."
4. (pull them off easily); A rider might give a *pluck* to a horse's reins to have the horse change direction.
5. (slanted); One reason a person might have *angled* a car while driving is to fit into a parking space.
6. <u>to control the horse</u>; If a rider lost the *reins* while riding, the horse might go the wrong way.
7. <u>Lift</u>; It took two cheerleaders to *heft* the third one up into the air.
8. (take too much effort); Once I *strained* myself when carrying a box of books up the stairs.

Reading Warm-up B, p. 138

Sample Answers

1. <u>green earth</u>; The new *sod* that made up the lawn was soaked by the rainstorm.
2. (she planned the trip, packed, got a passport, bought a plane ticket, and was off); *Flurry* means "a sudden commotion of movement."
3. <u>transporting her luggage from one inn to the next</u>; One thing in my life that I consider a *nuisance* is having to make my bed every day.
4. (long and straight); A farmer would plow a *furrow* just before planting a crop.
5. <u>to harness the horse to the plow</u>; Another piece of equipment besides *shafts* that a horse-owner might have to buy is a saddle.
6. (doing so would give a person the gift of eloquence); One god from Greek *myth* is Zeus.
7. <u>tripped</u>; If I *stumbled* while jogging, I might fall and scrape my knees.
8. (add up); If you *tally* the costs, you will find that the meal was not very expensive.

Literary Analysis: Diction and Style, p. 139

Sample Responses

Diction: The contractions lend an informal feeling to this scene-setting, story-telling first stanza. The question in line 5, in which the speaker adopts the coalman's voice, adds to the conversational feeling.

Imagery: Vivid, concrete images of the scene: rain, black coal, warm wet ashes, tire-marks, old lorry, Belfast accent

Rhythm: The stanza does not have rhyme. The rhythm is irregular.

Form: The poem is in six-line stanzas.

Reading Strategy: Summarize, p. 140

Sample Responses

Stanza 1: coalman sweet-talking my mother

Stanza 2: mother "moved" by coalman

Stanza 3: mother goes back to work, cleaning stove

Stanza 4: a lorry blows up a bus station

Stanza 5: I imagine my mother dead after the explosion in Magherafelt

Stanza 6: Which lorry is it?

Stanza 7: the coalman now represents death or violence

Summary: The speaker has two memories or visions of a lorry. In one lorry is a coalman who flirts with his mother. Another lorry at another time blows up a bus station. The speaker imagines his mother dead in the aftermath. The coalman, representing death, returns.

Vocabulary Builder, p. 141

A. 1. B; 2. A; 3. C

B. 1. A; 2. C; 3. A; 4. D; 5. B

Grammar and Style: Concrete and Abstract Nouns, p. 142

A. 1. *expert*—A; *wing*—C; *sod*—C; *headrig*—C; *reins*—C; *team*—C; *land*—C

   2. *films*—C; *conceit*—A; *mother*—C; *business*—A; *ashes*—C; *cheek*—C; *lorry*—C; *Magherafelt*—C

B. Possible Responses

   1. The farmer works with a horse plow and plows a straight furrow.

   2. The boy knows his father is strong and an expert at what he is doing.

   3. The boy stumbles over the furrows and sod, following in his father's wake.

Enrichment: Contemporary Farmer, p. 145

Sample Responses

1. plow, drawn by a team of horses

2. how to take care of his horses, how to plow a straight furrow, when to plant his crops, when to harvest

3. Contemporary farmers need to know about finances (investments, loans, etc.), market conditions, crop, soil, and livestock science, hiring and labor management, and so on.

Selection Test A, p. 146

Critical Reading

1. ANS: A	DIF: Easy	OBJ: Comprehension
2. ANS: C	DIF: Easy	OBJ: Reading Strategy
3. ANS: B	DIF: Easy	OBJ: Comprehension
4. ANS: D	DIF: Easy	OBJ: Interpretation
5. ANS: C	DIF: Easy	OBJ: Reading Strategy

6. ANS: B	DIF: Easy	OBJ: Interpretation
7. ANS: D	DIF: Easy	OBJ: Comprehension
8. ANS: C	DIF: Easy	OBJ: Reading Strategy
9. ANS: A	DIF: Easy	OBJ: Literary Analysis
10. ANS: B	DIF: Easy	OBJ: Interpretation

Vocabulary and Grammar

11. ANS: C	DIF: Easy	OBJ: Vocabulary
12. ANS: A	DIF: Easy	OBJ: Grammar

Essay

13. Students may say that it means that parents grow old and end up depending on their children. In another interpretation, students might say that it is the memory of the father that follows after the speaker. He cannot escape these memories, which follow him always.

   Difficulty: *Easy*

   Objective: *Essay*

14. Students may summarize "Follower" as follows: The speaker's father was an expert in plowing his farm and the speaker followed along, stumbling and falling in the furrows. Now that the speaker is older, it is his father who follows. "Two Lorries" might be summarized in this way: A young coalman asks the speaker's mother, asking her to go to a film in Magherafelt. Many years later, another lorry, this one carrying explosives, blows up the bus station there. The event makes the speaker recall meeting his mother at that station. "Outside History" might be summarized as follows: The speaker notes that there are always outsiders. The stars, for example, have always been outsiders because their light happened thousands of years ago. The speaker decides to become involved and become part of the human ordeal.

   Difficulty: *Easy*

   Objective: *Essay*

Selection Test B, p. 149

Critical Reading

1. ANS: D	DIF: Easy	OBJ: Comprehension
2. ANS: B	DIF: Average	OBJ: Interpretation
3. ANS: D	DIF: Average	OBJ: Interpretation
4. ANS: C	DIF: Challenging	OBJ: Literary Analysis
5. ANS: A	DIF: Average	OBJ: Reading Strategy
6. ANS: A	DIF: Easy	OBJ: Reading Strategy
7. ANS: B	DIF: Average	OBJ: Comprehension
8. ANS: B	DIF: Easy	OBJ: Interpretation
9. ANS: C	DIF: Average	OBJ: Literary Analysis
10. ANS: D	DIF: Average	OBJ: Literary Analysis
11. ANS: C	DIF: Challenging	OBJ: Reading Strategy

Vocabulary and Grammar

12. ANS: A   DIF: Easy   OBJ: Vocabulary
13. ANS: B   DIF: Average   OBJ: Vocabulary
14. ANS: B   DIF: Average   OBJ: Grammar
15. ANS: B   DIF: Average   OBJ: Grammar

Essay

16. Students should be able to relate to the poem's informal, conversational style well enough to recognize it as such. The storytelling quality and the many concrete nouns add to the friendliness of the poem. The imagery, too, is concrete and accessible. Readers can see the horse, the plow, the strong man working, the young boy stumbling, the rough dirt opened up behind the plow, then the old man following the now-grown boy. Students should be able to recall that alternating lines rhyme in each stanza. The form is traditional four-line stanzas.

Difficulty: *Easy*

Objective: *Essay*

17. In "Two Lorries," once the second lorry is introduced, everything in the poem becomes death and ashes. Heaney's image implies that the violence is deceitful—who would expect a lorry to be doing anything but delivering things? He also finds the violence particularly destructive—the only thing that reemerges from the explosion, as it were, is the "driver," who may represent death, violence, or terrorists in general. In "Outside History," Boland refers to "that ordeal" as a darkness that is clogging the roads and rivers with dead bodies. Her feeling that "we are always too late" implies that the violence will go on in spite of efforts to stop it. Students should conclude that Heaney and Boland express similar views on Ireland's troubles.

Difficulty: *Average*

Objective: *Essay*

"No Witchcraft for Sale" by Doris Lessing

Vocabulary Warm-up Exercises, p. 153

A.
1. hundredth
2. chinks
3. vigorously
4. unreasonable
5. exaggerated
6. punctures
7. commotion
8. inevitable

B. Sample Answers
1. The *scorching* ground burned Amy's feet.
2. Danielle was *irritated* by the screeching of the cats.
3. The identical twin brothers shared many *hereditary* traits.

4. The *flustered* speaker nervously delivered his speech.
5. Percy's face, *distorted* by puffiness and pain, was almost unrecognizable.
6. *Discomfort* from the flu made Carla's afternoon very unpleasant.
7. Pat's *distasteful* duty was to fire his friend from a high-paying job.

Reading Warm-up A, p. 154

Sample Answers

1. a snake can be as friendly as a dog or cat; An *exaggerated* claim I have heard about an advertised product is that a certain toothpaste would give me perfectly white teeth.
2. (a dog or cat); If I heard an unusual *commotion* outside my home at night, I would tell my father about it.
3. (energetically); A house-cleaning job that I might do *vigorously* is vacuuming.
4. to expect that anyone interested in having a snake as a pet will take time to research its needs; *Unreasonable* means "not sensible."
5. it cannot be avoided; One thing in life that is *inevitable* is getting older.
6. (holes); I could patch *chinks* in a wall with spackle.
7. injuries; The many *punctures* in the wall showed where the people who lived here before had hung pictures.
8. (ninety-nine); An activity of mine that would not bore me, even after the *hundredth* time I did it, is looking at a sunset.

Reading Warm-up B, p. 155

Sample Answers

1. summer; My favorite activity on a *scorching* day is swimming.
2. (stupidity); *Hereditary* means "passed on from parents to their children."
3. provoked; Something a friend once did that *irritated* me was constantly cracking his knuckles.
4. (panic); Once I got *flustered* when I had to give a speech in front of my class.
5. cutting the skin and trying to suck out the venom; Another word for *distasteful* is "unpleasant."
6. pain; Jane's *discomfort* was apparent by the way she was rubbing her shoulder.
7. pain; *Writhing* means "twisting or distorting the body, as in pain."
8. (agony); In the *Lord of the Rings* movies, the distorted faces of the orcs and goblins were horrifyingly ugly.

Literary Analysis: Cultural Conflict, p. 156

Possible Responses

The Farquars' Attitudes

Others could benefit from this medicine.

It would be nice if something good came about because of them.

There is no reason not to share this "miracle" with others.

The Scientist's Attitudes

Perhaps a handful of these native cures are any good; most of them are pure imagination.

There is money to be made if there is any truth in one of these cures or medicines.

Gideon's Attitudes

Knowledge of the medicine belongs to him and his culture.

The British have their own medicine and don't really believe in the efficacy of African medicines.

1. Their feelings about the medicine and the "miracle" were deep and religious. They were uncomfortable when the scientist talked about money.

2. When they ask a servant a question, they expect a prompt and truthful answer. They don't understand Gideon's resistance, especially after explaining what good the medicine could do. They view Gideon as stubborn and selfish.

3. He is skeptical about the usefulness of any of the native African medicines or cures about which amazing stories were told. He *assumes* that Gideon will not reveal the source of the medicine, which just proves his point about the lack of usefulness of African medicines.

Reading Strategy: Analyze Cultural Differences, p. 157

A. Sample Responses

Farquars: believe white people to be superior to African natives; believe it would be best for Gideon to reveal source of his medicine; are "at home" on their homestead

Farquars and Gideon (in circle intersection): belief in Christian God; devoted to Teddy; shared understanding that the destiny of a white child is different from that of a black child; share some belief in the efficacy of herbal medicines

Gideon: trained by his medicine-man father; conscious of his "place" despite family's affection for him; refuses to reveal source of medicine; is comfortable in bush

B. Possible Response

Without the cultural differences, the story would be about a child's run-in with a poisonous snake. The parents' and the cook's attitudes about the accident and about the cure would be the same. The disagreement over revealing the source of the medicine would not occur. The story could still be engaging, but it would carry much less impact.

Vocabulary Builder, p. 158

A. 1. skeptic; 2. skeptically; 3. skepticism

B. 1. D; 2. B; 3. A; 4. B; 5. C

Grammar and Style: Correct Use of *Like* and *As*, p. 159

A. 1. I; 2. I; 3. C; 4. C; 5. I

B. Possible Responses

1. Like other young children, Teddy was thrilled with the speed of his scooter.

2. Mrs. Farquar was horrified, as most other mothers would be, by Teddy's accident with the snake.

3. Teddy treated Gideon's son disrespectfully, as he had probably seen other colonists do.

4. Gideon, like Mrs. Farquar, reacted strongly to Teddy's injury.

Enrichment: Science, p. 162

Sample Responses

1. Inherent risks involve safety and efficacy. Much of the evidence of benefit is anecdotal, and those substances not proven safe can be dangerous. Some may be harmless but expensive, and some may be outright frauds. Laetrile is an example.

2. Whatever the limitations of western science, the controlled study with large groups measured carefully over long periods of time is indispensable.

3. Students may choose whatever position they wish. Those who support payment for alternative medicine will cite its growing efficacy and economy (relative to hospital costs). Those who oppose such payment will cite difficulty of management and lack of proven worth.

Selection Test A, p. 163

Critical Reading

1. ANS: C	DIF: Easy	OBJ: Comprehension
2. ANS: A	DIF: Easy	OBJ: Interpretation
3. ANS: C	DIF: Easy	OBJ: Literary Analysis
4. ANS: B	DIF: Easy	OBJ: Interpretation
5. ANS: D	DIF: Easy	OBJ: Literary Analysis
6. ANS: A	DIF: Easy	OBJ: Comprehension
7. ANS: C	DIF: Easy	OBJ: Comprehension
8. ANS: D	DIF: Easy	OBJ: Reading Strategy
9. ANS: B	DIF: Easy	OBJ: Interpretation
10. ANS: A	DIF: Easy	OBJ: Reading Strategy
11. ANS: C	DIF: Easy	OBJ: Literary Analysis
12. ANS: D	DIF: Easy	OBJ: Comprehension

Vocabulary and Grammar

13. ANS: D	DIF: Easy	OBJ: Vocabulary
14. ANS: B	DIF: Easy	OBJ: Grammar

Essay

15. Students should note that the title refers to Gideon's refusal to identify the secret plant he used to cure Teddy's eyes. His knowledge is considered witchcraft because it is a native practice closely associated with magic. Gideon probably did not share the secret because he felt he would have been selling out his culture.

    Difficulty: *Easy*

    Objective: *Essay*

16. Students should mention that the scientist was interested in the story because he thought there was a possibility that the native cure might actually work. The scientist doubts that the plant exists but is willing to investigate nonetheless. When Gideon finally hands him a plant, the scientist knows it is not a cure. The episode reinforces his doubt in the usefulness of witchcraft and native cures.

    Difficulty: *Easy*

    Objective: *Essay*

Selection Test B, p. 166

Critical Reading

1. ANS: C	DIF: Easy	OBJ: Comprehension
2. ANS: B	DIF: Average	OBJ: Interpretation
3. ANS: A	DIF: Easy	OBJ: Interpretaion
4. ANS: A	DIF: Average	OBJ: Literary Analysis
5. ANS: B	DIF: Average	OBJ: Reading Strategy
6. ANS: C	DIF: Average	OBJ: Comprehension
7. ANS: D	DIF: Easy	OBJ: Reading Strategy
8. ANS: B	DIF: Easy	OBJ: Interpretation
9. ANS: B	DIF: Average	OBJ: Reading Strategy
10. ANS: C	DIF: Challenging	OBJ: Literary Analysis
11. ANS: A	DIF: Easy	OBJ: Literary Analysis
12. ANS: B	DIF: Challenging	OBJ: Reading Strategy

Vocabulary and Grammar

13. ANS: B	DIF: Easy	OBJ: Vocabulary
14. ANS: D	DIF: Average	OBJ: Vocabulary
15. ANS: C	DIF: Easy	OBJ: Grammar
16. ANS: A	DIF: Challenging	OBJ: Grammar

Essay

17. Student essays should reflect that they understand the conflict of cultures. The Farquars see themselves as masters who run things. Mrs. Farquar rewards Gideon with money, in keeping with his status. Teddy assumes a ruling status after terrorizing a black child. However kind they choose to be, the world is a place they run. Gideon wishes not to run the world but live peacefully in it. His comments on the separate cultures reveal sadness, and he is disappointed but not surprised at Teddy's acts. The fundamental misunderstanding of his

healing art offends him, for the knowledge is not a trick; it is integrally linked to him and his people and he refuses to separate it. Their view is disrespectful to him and they cannot understand.

Difficulty: *Easy*

Objective: *Essay*

18. Gideon cured the child because he cared for him, because it was an emergency, and because he knew he could do so. The motivation was never use of or demonstration of his power. When the Farquars and the scientist ask him how he did it, they are offending him because in so doing they call into question his motivation and his skill. It should be enough that a good thing happened. He has sought no reward. Neither has he anything to prove and is offended to be asked to do so. He is surrounded, he feels, by "yelping dogs," who have little sense of who he is. Under no circumstance will he allow his culture or himself to be invaded and his art taken away.

Difficulty: *Challenging*

Objective: *Essay*

"The Lagoon" by Joseph Conrad
"Araby" by James Joyce

Vocabulary Warm-up Exercises, p. 170

A.
1. fascination
2. discreetly
3. noiselessly
4. offensive
5. somber
6. fringing
7. withstand
8. enchantment

B. Sample Answers

1. If I had two *placid* cats, I do not think they would fight all the time because they would be too peaceful.

2. The senses of smell and sight would be most stimulated by *jasmine*.

3. A *monotonous* song would not be likely to make it to number one because it would be too boring.

4. A *ceaseless* buzzing in my ears would be a good reason to see a doctor because hearing a sound all the time like that might indicate a serious problem.

5. I would not expect people in the middle of *strife* to have dinner together because they would not be friendly.

6. If I swam *energetically*, I would certainly burn a lot of calories.

7. I like to have *periodic* visits with my Aunt Sally every three months or so.

8. A recent *calamity* I heard about in the news was the tsunami in Indonesia.

Reading Warm-up A, p. 171

Sample Answers

1. interest; One thing that holds great *fascination* for me is astronomy.
2. (daze); A story in which *enchantment* plays a part is Cinderella.
3. strung beads
4. (dark); I would wear a *somber* outfit to a funeral.
5. (if Polly dropped it on a hard tile floor); The worst kind of weather my town has had to *withstand* is a hailstorm.
6. that she would tell such an obvious lie to make a sale; They become angry and might speak out against whatever was so *offensive*.
7. silently; It would be important to move *noiselessly* in a library.
8. (tactfully); A time I had to act *discreetly* was when I had to tell my friend she had spinach on her teeth.

Reading Warm-up B, p. 172

Sample Answers

1. calm; This fish was caught in the *placid* waters of Pyramid Lake.
2. (continual); Something that goes on in a *ceaseless* fashion around my home is the chirping of my pet birds.
3. boring; I might pep up an exercise routine that is getting *monotonous* by trying a new activity.
4. (scent), (fragrant), (growing outside the hotel window), (perfume); Hotel owners would want to have jasmine around because it is so pretty and smells so good.
5. (hike); People usually practice sports *energetically* at school.
6. happen with some regularity; Birthdays are a *periodic* event that families often celebrate together.
7. disaster; I can help people who have suffered from a natural *calamity* by donating food or clothing.
8. (conflict); My friends are being very nice to each other today in an effort to avoid *strife*.

Literary Analysis: Plot Devices, p. 173

Sample Responses

1. Quotation marks around Arsat's narrative signal the beginning and the end of the story within the story.
2. Arsat's story is occasionally interrupted by observations from the omniscient narrator. The effect is to remind the reader of the present situation—that the two men sit surrounded by darkness and groping with their own inner darkness as well.
3. Arsat's story told on its own would not have the same effect. It conveys deeper meaning within the context of the outside story in which the white man has a history with Arsat and the reader learns what has become of Arsat since his choice.
4. The boy realizes that his desires will never be satisfied.

5. The boy is standing in the empty hall and looking up into the darkness.

Reading Strategy: Picture Action and Situation, p. 174

Possible Responses

1. The white man contemplates the people in his life he has left behind, losses for which he cannot accept responsibility and for which he has not allowed himself to grieve.
2. When he hears his uncle at the door, the boy instantly feels excited because he can now go to the bazaar. When he hears the signs of his uncle's drunkenness, however, his heart sinks. He knows that he will have to wait longer and negotiate for something his uncle had promised earlier.
3. The boy's small frame looks even smaller in the midst of the hall's immense darkness and barrenness. He is overcome by feelings of uncertainty, disappointment, and sadness.

Vocabulary Builder, p. 175

A. 1. invincibility; 2. convince; 3. evince
B. 1. C; 2. B; 3. C; 4. A; 5. B; 6. C; 7. B; 8. C; 9. A

Grammar and Style: Adverb Clauses, p. 176

A. 1. as he asked, without any words of greeting—"Have you medicine, Tuan?"; composed
2. as if dead; still
3. since the sun of today rose; hears
4. when no friendship is to be despised; had known
5. When we returned to the street; had filled
6. because there would be a retreat that week in her convent; could not go
7. When he was midway through his dinner asked

B. Sample Responses
1. The white man stays with Arsat because he once fought with him in the war.
2. When the others are distracted by the fish hunt, Arsat and his brother kidnap the young woman.
3. The boy feels as if Mangan's sister is a force moving him beyond his control.
4. The boy cannot go to the bazaar until his uncle returns home.

Enrichment: Fine Art, p. 179

Sample Responses

Photographs ("The Lagoon")

1. a river in the jungle; a tropical island
2. the thick jungle foliage; bright beach
3. Jungle is close up, feels like viewer is on the river; the island is distant.
4. Light and shadow sharply contrasted in jungle; the beach is bright in the darker water.

5. Jungle creates a claustrophobic mood, hot atmosphere; the island creates eerily isolated mood.

6. Perspective and the play of light and shadow have the greatest effect on creating either a claustrophobic or isolated mood.

St. Patrick's Close by Walter Osborne ("Araby")

1. a narrow, dingy urban street filled with shabbily-dressed people

2. the church steeple

3. perspective creates illusion for the viewer of walking down street

4. colors are predominantly dark, with only brightness around steeple

5. mood combines the beauty of morning with the grimness of the street

6. subject matter—the tight, dirty street—and palette play strongest role in creating mood

Selection Test A, p. 180

Critical Reading

1. ANS: D	DIF: Easy	OBJ: Interpretation
2. ANS: B	DIF: Easy	OBJ: Reading Strategy
3. ANS: C	DIF: Easy	OBJ: Comprehension
4. ANS: C	DIF: Easy	OBJ: Literary Analysis
5. ANS: B	DIF: Easy	OBJ: Comprehension
6. ANS: A	DIF: Easy	OBJ: Literary Analysis
7. ANS: A	DIF: Easy	OBJ: Interpretation
8. ANS: B	DIF: Easy	OBJ: Comprehension
9. ANS: A	DIF: Easy	OBJ: Comprehension
10. ANS: B	DIF: Easy	OBJ: Reading Strategy
11. ANS: D	DIF: Easy	OBJ: Interpretation
12. ANS: C	DIF: Easy	OBJ: Interpretation

Vocabulary and Grammar

13. ANS: C	DIF: Easy	OBJ: Vocabulary
14. ANS: A	DIF: Easy	OBJ: Grammar

Essay

15. Students should say that the line means that we are really living in a world of illusions. In the story, Arsat knew exactly what he wanted. He wanted to be with Diamelen, and he was sure of that, even when it meant he must sacrifice his brother's life to get her. When she dies, he sees that all he has done and wanted was an illusion.
Difficulty: *Easy*
Objective: *Essay*

16. Students should mention that the narrator is, at first, a joyful young boy who has fun playing with his friends. Then he falls in love, probably for the first time. Events do not work out. He finds nothing to buy Mangan's sis-

ter at Araby. He realizes in the final line how foolish he has been to think his dream of a gift and of pleasing Mangan's sister could be fulfilled.
Difficulty: *Easy*
Objective: *Essay*

Selection Test B, p. 183

Critical Reading

1. ANS: B	DIF: Average	OBJ: Comprehension
2. ANS: C	DIF: Challenging	OBJ: Interpretation
3. ANS: A	DIF: Average	OBJ: Interpretation
4. ANS: B	DIF: Easy	OBJ: Reading Strategy
5. ANS: A	DIF: Average	OBJ: Comprehension
6. ANS: B	DIF: Average	OBJ: Literary Analysis
7. ANS: C	DIF: Easy	OBJ: Comprehension
8. ANS: C	DIF: Average	OBJ: Reading Strategy
9. ANS: A	DIF: Average	OBJ: Interpretation
10. ANS: D	DIF: Challenging	OBJ: Reading Strategy
11. ANS: A	DIF: Challenging	OBJ: Literary Analysis
12. ANS: A	DIF: Average	OBJ: Literary Analysis

Vocabulary and Grammar

13. ANS: A	DIF: Average	OBJ: Vocabulary
14. ANS: C	DIF: Challenging	OBJ: Vocabulary
15. ANS: B	DIF: Average	OBJ: Grammar
16. ANS: B	DIF: Easy	OBJ: Grammar

Essay

17. Students analyzing "The Lagoon" should recognize that the dark and isolated setting of the lagoon provides clues to Arsat's mental state; he has chosen to "live amongst the spirits that haunt the places abandoned by mankind." The dying fire by which Arsat tells his tale symbolizes Arsat's burning passion for Diamelen, a passion that soon fades in the face of Arsat's terrible choice. Students analyzing "Araby" should note that the grim Dublin setting weighs heavily against the boy and his chances to succeed. The boy lives on a "blind," or dead-end street, and by the end of the story he comes to realize that his life is a dead end as well.
Difficulty: *Easy*
Objective: *Essay*

18. Students should note that Conrad uses a story within a story and that Joyce uses an epiphany. In analyzing Conrad's plot device, students might explain that placing Arsat's tale within a larger framework provides a meaningful context and allows the reader to make connections between Arsat's inner struggle, which the character articulates, and the white man's inner struggle, which is left unspoken. Students might point out that Joyce's use of epiphany strikes a stronger emotional chord than merely stating a lesson learned or summa-

rizing a moral. The boy's sudden, painful revelation conveys anger, humiliation, frustration, and resignation all within a single moment.

Difficulty: *Average*

Objective: *Essay*

"The Lady in the Looking Glass: A Reflection"
by Virginia Woolf
"The First Year of My Life" by Muriel Spark

Vocabulary Warm-up Exercises, p. 187

A. 1. intimacy
2. Oriental
3. cleansed
4. rendezvous
5. sayings
6. pitiless
7. barricade
8. bowels

B. Sample Answers
1. unlimited; The number of grains of sand on the beaches is unlimited.
2. genuineness; The genuineness of the signature on the check was verified.
3. slightest; The slightest smile could be detected on Mona's face.
4. bendable; The gymnast's body was extremely bendable.
5. endlessness; Percy hopes his poetry will assure the endlessness of his fame.
6. understanding; Alma's understanding of the passage is murky at best.
7. delicate; The delicate pattern in the lace was difficult to achieve.

Reading Warm-up A, p. 188

Sample Answers
1. children should be seen and not heard; One of my favorite old *sayings* is "All that glitters is not gold."
2. (clean); Sally *cleansed* her palate by sampling the sherbet between courses.
3. let a child cry for any length of time without trying to make the child clean, comfortable, and happy; *Pitiless* means "without pity; cruel; ruthless."
4. (bladder); Doctors recommend a balanced diet for the health of the *bowels*.
5. so the child cannot leave the area; To keep a dog inside a yard, I might use a fence as a *barricade*.
6. (intricate patterns); My favorite type of *Oriental* food is Japanese sushi.
7. meeting; Recently, I had a *rendezvous* with my friend Jake—we met for a movie.
8. (affection); Jane enjoys the *intimacy* of her friendship with Sheila.

Reading Warm-up B, p. 189

Sample Answers
1. busy; After a *hectic* day, I relax by reading a magazine.
2. (gardening schedule); A *flexible* schedule is easier to live with than a rigid schedule because it allows for unusual events that may occur.
3. understanding; One way to study that aids in *comprehension* is to ask yourself questions about the text as you read it.
4. (barely noticeable); This stew has the *subtlest* hint of rosemary as flavoring.
5. so numerous; *Infinite* means "having no limits; endless or boundless."
6. guarantees; If I doubted the *authenticity* of a signature, I might check it against one that I knew was genuine.
7. (extremely beautiful); My mother's ruby ring is *exquisite*.
8. (forever); Shakespeare achieved a kind of *immortality* when he wrote his plays.

Literary Analysis: Point of View—Modern Experiments, p. 190

Sample Responses
1. One stream-of-consciousness passage begins with "One must put oneself in her shoes" and ends with "But one was tired of the things that she talked about at dinner." The narrator begins with a figurative saying, addresses its literal meaning, and from there speculates about Isabella's actions and thoughts.
2. Although the narrator bases her information about Isabella on the items in Isabella's room, her impressions have no real basis in reality. They are all imagination and speculation until Isabella appears before the looking glass.
3. Woolf might have chosen this type of narrator to comment on the unreliability of appearance when searching for meaning.
4. The narrator is super-omniscient, claiming not only to remember everything from the moment of her birth but also to have known everything that was going on in the world, including the thoughts of any given person.
5. The narrator's observations create a brisk, amused tone that contrasts with the grim reality of World War I.
6. This narrator allows Spark to comment on the atrocities of war without sounding didactic. This point of view invites the reader to consider the issue from an ironic perspective.

Reading Strategy: Question, p. 191

Possible Responses
1. Question: Why would these inanimate objects know more about Isabella?; Answer: Because they observe her when she doesn't think she's being observed.
2. Question: Why does Woolf use the word *acid*?; Answer: Because it implies stripping to the bone, or the truth, of a person.

3. Question: Why does the narrator think the song is silly?; Answer: Because on her other "frequencies," she is tuning in to the war's mass destruction.

4. Question: Why is it "essential to know the worst"?; Answer: Because the atrocities on the Western Front have the most impact on the human consciousness to which the narrator is attuned.

Vocabulary Builder, p. 192

A. 1. translucent; 2. transom; 3. transmutation; 4. transatlantic

B. 1. E; 2. A; 3. G; 4. B; 5. C; 6. H; 7. F; 8. D

Grammar and Style: Subject-Verb Agreement in Inverted Sentences, p. 193

A. 1. Here are a letter and an invitation delivered by the postman.
2. There was a suggestion of depth and intelligence in the occupant's room.
3. In the end, there are no interesting thoughts in Isabella's brain.
4. There were many soldiers scarred and killed by poisonous gas during the war.
5. In this anthology are poems by Wilfred Owen and Alan Seegar.
6. Here is an interesting theory on infant development.

B. Sample Response

The first birthday party I recall is my fourth. There were red balloons, red and white streamers, and brightly colored party hats. There was a clown performing magic tricks. In this picture are my mother and father, lighting the four candles on my cake.

Enrichment: Science, p. 196

Sample Responses

1. The reflected image would be of poor quality because the polished metal would not be smooth enough or reflect sufficient light.

2. Improvements such as the use of polished glass and coating with thin metals have increased the quality of reflected images.

3. A reflected image is an illusion in the sense that it presents something as "there" which is actually elsewhere. It does represent reality accurately, however.

4. Literally, the mirror is a decorative and functional object in the woman's room. Figuratively, the mirror reflects what the viewer—in this case, the narrator—wants to see.

5. The mirror is a fitting metaphor because it gives only a perception of reality, not reality itself and Woolf explores the various ways in which the mind constructs its picture of another person.

Selection Test A, p. 197

Critical Reading

1. ANS: D	DIF: Easy	OBJ: Reading Strategy
2. ANS: B	DIF: Easy	OBJ: Literary Analysis
3. ANS: A	DIF: Easy	OBJ: Comprehension
4. ANS: C	DIF: Easy	OBJ: Comprehension
5. ANS: A	DIF: Easy	OBJ: Interpretation
6. ANS: D	DIF: Easy	OBJ: Literary Analysis
7. ANS: C	DIF: Easy	OBJ: Comprehension
8. ANS: D	DIF: Easy	OBJ: Interpretation
9. ANS: B	DIF: Easy	OBJ: Reading Strategy
10. ANS: A	DIF: Easy	OBJ: Interpretation
11. ANS: C	DIF: Easy	OBJ: Interpretation

Vocabulary and Grammar

12. ANS: D	DIF: Easy	OBJ: Vocabulary
13. ANS: B	DIF: Easy	OBJ: Grammar

Essay

14. Students should note that readers can conclude that Isabella is an empty, worn-out, dull, and probably lonely old woman. Throughout, the narrator has been comparing the images she sees in Isabella's room with what she sees in the looking glass, which reveals the truth.
Difficulty: *Easy*
Objective: *Essay*

15. Students should mention that Woolf uses stream-of-consciousness, and the narrative is entirely internal, telling what the narrator thinks from moment to moment. Spark uses an omniscient narrator. The reader learns what the narrator is thinking but is not let in on her moment-to-moment mental processes.
Students should explain why they think either experiment was successful.
Difficulty: *Easy*
Objective: *Essay*

Selection Test B, p. 200

Critical Reading

1. ANS: B	DIF: Average	OBJ: Interpretation
2. ANS: C	DIF: Easy	OBJ: Reading Strategy
3. ANS: A	DIF: Challenging	OBJ: Literary Analysis
4. ANS: A	DIF: Average	OBJ: Comprehension
5. ANS: D	DIF: Easy	OBJ: Literary Analysis
6. ANS: D	DIF: Average	OBJ: Comprehension
7. ANS: C	DIF: Average	OBJ: Literary Analysis

8. ANS: B	DIF: Average	OBJ: Interpretation
9. ANS: B	DIF: Challenging	OBJ: Reading Strategy
10. ANS: A	DIF: Average	OBJ: Reading Strategy
11. ANS: C	DIF: Average	OBJ: Interpretation

Vocabulary and Grammar

12. ANS: A	DIF: Average	OBJ: Vocabulary
13. ANS: D	DIF: Average	OBJ: Vocabulary
14. ANS: A	DIF: Average	OBJ: Grammar
15. ANS: B	DIF: Easy	OBJ: Grammar

Essay

16. Most of Woolf's story is consumed with imagination. The narrator wants to determine Isabella's true character and tries to do so by imagining what her belongings reveal about her. However, when Isabella appears in front of the looking glass, the illusion the narrator has created disappears and the reality of Isabella's emptiness is exposed. Spark bases her story on the imaginative supposition that babies are completely omniscient. With this premise, Spark seems to suggest that only imagination can filter the grim reality of war.

Difficulty: *Easy*
Objective: *Essay*

17. Through stream-of-consciousness narration, Woolf forces the reader to question perceptions of reality. For example, the narrator assumes that the "masklike indifference of [Isabella's] face" reveals greater passion. When Isabella is eventually unmasked, the narrator's judgment is exposed as mere fancy. Spark also wants readers to question reality. Her omniscient narrator reduces human activity to two categories—meaningful or irrelevant. What many assume to be meaningful—the baby's development—is irrelevant in the face of the war's horrors. In the end, the reality behind the narrator's smile is not contentment or amusement but contempt for those who cannot accept reality.

Difficulty: *Average*
Objective: *Essay*

"The Rocking-Horse Winner" by D. H. Lawrence
"A Shocking Accident" by Graham Greene

Vocabulary Warm-up Exercises, p. 204

A.
1. furnishings
2. noiselessly
3. moderately
4. inevitably
5. colleagues
6. distinguished
7. extraordinarily
8. commiseration

B. Sample Answers
1. If someone got credit for something I did, I might make the <u>assertion</u> that I was the one who was responsible for it.
2. In the fall, a maple tree would have brightly colored red and orange leaves; <u>successive</u> seasons would show bare branches, then branches slowly budding with new leaves, and finally branches fully covered with leaves.
3. A dog would react to a <u>shortage</u> of food in its bowl by barking.
4. A <u>potential</u> problem that a family might face at an amusement park would be a lost child.
5. One <u>inspiration</u> I have for an interesting party theme is to come as your favorite fictional character.
6. If I brought a snake into the kitchen, I might hear <u>exclamations</u> of "Cool!" from my little sister and "NOOOOO!" from my mom.
7. A status symbol that led to a <u>frenzy</u> of buying among my friends was a certain video game.
8. If I <u>appeased</u> every demand a child made, the child would get spoiled.

Reading Warm-up A, p. 205
Sample Answers
1. ("big boy" bed) (dresser); *Furnishings* means "furniture or appliances, as for a room."
2. <u>well-groomed</u>; The *distinguished* gentleman gave a rousing speech.
3. (only the best); An animal that jumps *extraordinarily* high is a kangaroo.
4. <u>appeared to be having a meeting in the center of the floor</u>
5. (All) (Every one); One thing that will *inevitably* happen today is that the sun will set.
6. <u>as if an actual horse had been badly recorded</u>; I go to a local department store to buy *moderately* priced clothing.
7. <u>the difficulty of finding a traditional horse</u>; When my great-grandmother died, *commiseration* with a friend comforted me.
8. (snort) (neigh); *Noiselessly*, I tiptoed into my baby brother's room to check on him.

Reading Warm-up B, p. 206
Sample Answers
1. <u>taking a pig for a pet</u>; Once I had a sudden <u>inspiration</u> to go body-surfing in the moonlight.
2. (these animals); *Shortage* means "a lack in the number or amount needed."
3. An idea of mine that could lead to <u>potential</u> profits is offering to walk the dogs of the people in my neighborhood.
4. Four <u>successive</u> generations in my family are represented by people who are still living: my great-grandparents, my grandparents, my parents, and my generation.

5. <u>craze</u>; The sharks seemed to be on a feeding *frenzy*.

6. <u>what wonderful pets they make</u>; If I gave a friend a thoughtful gift, I would expect to hear *exclamations* of gratitude and appreciation.

7. (aggression); If someone pushed in front of me on a line, I would make the *assertion* that he or she should go to the back of the line.

8. (their relentless demands for food); *Appeased* means "satisfied."

Literary Analysis: Theme and Symbol, p. 207

Possible Responses

1. The rocking horse is an expensive toy. Although it looks like a real horse, it cannot go anywhere; it simply rocks back and forth.

2. The rocking horse symbolizes the futility of materialism. The horse may look good, but it is false and it gets the rider nowhere. The faster Paul rocks, the more frenzied he becomes; his actions harm him rather than help him.

3. This symbol underscores the notion that the pursuit of money is useless and self-destructive.

4. The falling pig that kills Jerome's father symbolizes the absurdity of life. Many events in life cannot be predicted or prepared for, and death is one of them.

Reading Strategy: Identify With a Character, p. 208

Sample Responses

1. Paul wants to relieve his mother's anxiety about being lucky and is hurt that she doesn't believe him or appreciate his actions on her behalf. Like Paul, a reader might resolve to prove himself right.

2. Paul's anxiety increases. He had hoped that his earnings would alleviate problems, and now he worries that there will never be enough money. In this situation, a reader might wish to escape the house that is the source of such anxiety.

3. Jerome feels embarrassed and isolated from his classmates. Due to circumstances he could not control, he is now an object of ridicule. In this situation, a reader might resolve not to let his feelings show to others.

4. Jerome feels conflicting emotions: he wants to be closer to Sally yet he fears a negative reaction from her. By delaying the story, he increases his own anxiety. A reader might have similar feelings or perhaps would decide to confront the problem directly.

Vocabulary Builder, p. 209

A. 1. obscures; 2. object; 3. obstacles

B. 1. A; 2. C; 3. B; 4. C; 5. D; 6. C; 7. B; 8. A; 9. D

Grammar and Style: Subjunctive Mood, p. 210

A. 1. were; 2. be; 3. were; 4. were; 5. be; 6. respond

B. Sample Response

In my family, it is important that everyone be focused on a goal. My goal is to become a pilot. If I were older, I could take flying lessons.

Enrichment: Greek Notion of Fate, p. 213

Sample Responses

1. The three goddesses symbolize the idea that people do not actually control what is of most consequence to them—the direction and length of their lives and the moment of their death.

2. Paul's mother shares this deterministic viewpoint. She tells Paul that "it's better to be born lucky than rich" and says she was born unlucky.

3. Paul's fate is to be born to parents who are consumed with money and care little for his well being.

4. Paul attempts to avoid his fate by riding the rocking horse, believing that "the horse could take him where there was luck, if only he forced it."

5. It is Paul's fate to live a life ruled by his mother's unhappiness: riding the horse does not free him from that fate, but ensures that he dies trying to bring in more money for the family.

6. In one sense, Paul's plan defies the Greek notion of fate; he is determined to find his own luck. In another sense, it is his fate to be destroyed by his parents' selfish desires.

Selection Test A, p. 214

Critical Reading

1. ANS: C	DIF: Easy	OBJ: Comprehension
2. ANS: A	DIF: Easy	OBJ: Reading Strategy
3. ANS: B	DIF: Easy	OBJ: Interpretation
4. ANS: D	DIF: Easy	OBJ: Comprehension
5. ANS: B	DIF: Easy	OBJ: Literary Analysis
6. ANS: A	DIF: Easy	OBJ: Literary Analysis
7. ANS: C	DIF: Easy	OBJ: Interpretation
8. ANS: D	DIF: Easy	OBJ: Comprehension
9. ANS: C	DIF: Easy	OBJ: Reading Strategy
10. ANS: A	DIF: Easy	OBJ: Comprehension
11. ANS: D	DIF: Easy	OBJ: Reading Strategy
12. ANS: B	DIF: Easy	OBJ: Literary Analysis

Vocabulary and Grammar

13. ANS: A	DIF: Easy	OBJ: Vocabulary
14. ANS: B	DIF: Easy	OBJ: Grammar

Essay

15. Students should understand that Uncle Oscar means that Paul is not well adjusted to life. In a way, he is better off dead than trying to survive in this world. Stu-

dents may or may not agree with this position. They should give reasons to explain their opinions.

Difficulty: *Easy*

Objective: *Essay*

16. Students should note that the problem is that a pig fell from the balcony of a home, hit Jerome's father in the head, and killed him. His father's death is a problem for Jerome because people cannot help laughing when they hear the story. Most students will say that they would feel embarrassed and uncomfortable if they were Jerome.

Difficulty: *Easy*

Objective: *Essay*

Selection Test B, p. 217

Critical Reading

1. ANS: B	DIF: Average	OBJ: Comprehension
2. ANS: C	DIF: Average	OBJ: Comprehension
3. ANS: D	DIF: Average	OBJ: Literary Analysis
4. ANS: B	DIF: Average	OBJ: Reading Strategy
5. ANS: A	DIF: Average	OBJ: Interpretation
6. ANS: A	DIF: Average	OBJ: Literary Analysis
7. ANS: B	DIF: Easy	OBJ: Comprehension
8. ANS: A	DIF: Easy	OBJ: Interpretation
9. ANS: C	DIF: Average	OBJ: Reading Strategy
10. ANS: C	DIF: Average	OBJ: Literary Analysis
11. ANS: B	DIF: Challenging	OBJ: Reading Strategy
12. ANS: A	DIF: Challenging	OBJ: Interpretation

Vocabulary and Grammar

13. ANS: C	DIF: Average	OBJ: Vocabulary
14. ANS: B	DIF: Average	OBJ: Vocabulary
15. ANS: D	DIF: Average	OBJ: Grammar
16. ANS: C	DIF: Easy	OBJ: Grammar

Essay

17. Paul is deeply affected by his parents' materialism. He senses their anxiety about money and status and assumes the responsibility of resolving it. His anxiety, desire to please, and fierce sense of loyalty make him an easy character to identify with. Jerome, too, is affected by an event beyond his control—the bizarre details of his father's death. The reader seems to feel more sympathy for Jerome because he doesn't view himself as a pitiable person—he thinks the circumstances of his father's death "were still part of the mystery of life." Jerome's main discomfort and unhappiness arise from his inability to view the world as others around him do. The reader hopes that Jerome will find peace or understanding with another person.

Difficulty: *Easy*

Objective: *Essay*

18. Students should identify the rocking horse as the primary symbol in Lawrence's story and realize that it conveys several meanings. For instance, its stationary form symbolizes the futile struggle of materialism; Paul's mother creates a frenzy over money but gets nowhere. Paul's fierce attachment to the rocking horse, even after he outgrows it, echoes his mother's unrealistic attachment to the ideals of wealth and status. Through this symbolism, Lawrence condemns the superficiality of the British elite and highlights the psychological damage wrought by materialism.

Difficulty: *Challenging*

Objective: *Essay*

Benchmark Test 11, p. 220

MULTIPLE CHOICE

1. ANS: B
2. ANS: C
3. ANS: A
4. ANS: D
5. ANS: B
6. ANS: A
7. ANS: D
8. ANS: C
9. ANS: A
10. ANS: C
11. ANS: D
12. ANS: D
13. ANS: A
14. ANS: A
15. ANS: D
16. ANS: B
17. ANS: A
18. ANS: C
19. ANS: D
20. ANS: B
21. ANS: C
22. ANS: A
23. ANS: A
24. ANS: C
25. ANS: D
26. ANS: A
27. ANS: A
28. ANS: C
29. ANS: D

ESSAY

30. Students should clearly identify the problem and give one or more practical suggestions for solving it. They should support their ideas with reasons and examples. To make

Unit 6 Resources: A Time of Rapid Change

their ideas more persuasive, students should take into account the occasion, purpose, and audience, especially if they are producing a speech. They may also use persuasive devices, such as emotional language and parallelism.

31. Students should identify the product and describe it accurately, using vivid sensory language and spatial terms to help readers picture it clearly in their minds. Students should choose appropriate details and diction to convey their feelings about the product. Poems may be free verse or more patterned.

32. Students should clearly state the image, symbol, or theme and cite details from the poem or story to support general statements about it. In the case of a theme, they should logically trace the details that point to the theme and may include their opinions of the theme's validity. In the case of an image or a symbol, they should focus on the effectiveness with which the image or symbol conveys themes, as well as moods or feelings.

Diagnostic Test 12, p. 226
MULTIPLE CHOICE
1. ANS: D
2. ANS: A
3. ANS: C
4. ANS: C
5. ANS: B
6. ANS: A
7. ANS: C
8. ANS: D
9. ANS: B
10. ANS: B
11. ANS: A
12. ANS: D
13. ANS: B
14. ANS: A
15. ANS: B

"Do Not Go Gentle into That Good Night" and "Fern Hill" by Dylan Thomas
"The Horses" and "The Rain Horse" by Ted Hughes

Vocabulary Warm-up Exercises, p. 230
A. 1. unaccustomed
2. rectangular
3. barricade
4. tortuous
5. blundering
6. fierce
7. bombardment
8. sodden

B. Sample Answers
1. T; If you complete a circuit, you get back to where you started because a circuit is a route that turns back to where it began.
2. F; If you are attentive when someone is speaking, you will probably catch most of what the person says.
3. F; The backdrop is the background, not the foreground.
4. F; Medicines that give instantaneous relief would relieve the suffering of patients.
5. F; After a dry, sunny, hot day, the ground would not be awash—on the contrary, it would be dry.
6. T; A sleepwalker seems to be in a trance.
7. F; One way to show boredom is to yawn and act sleepy.
8. F; If you play variations of a song, you change it each time you play it.

Reading Warm-up A, p. 231
Sample Answers
1. unfamiliar; Tracey was unaccustomed to eating in fine restaurants.
2. (winds in and out and up and down); Once I took a ride in a bus on a tortuous road—I thought we would drive off the road and over the cliff.
3. angry; One common occurrence in nature that I would describe as fierce is a hurricane.
4. (heavy raindrops and maybe even hail); Bombardment means "the act of attacking persistently."
5. (terrible error); Once I regretted blundering by assuming that Glenda really liked Richard and acting as if they were already a couple.
6. picnic table; One thing in the classroom that is rectangular is the teacher's desktop.
7. blocking; In a zoo, the bars of the cages usually act as a barricade between people and animals.
8. (rain-soaked); I can prevent getting sodden shoes if I go walking in the rain by wearing rubber boots.

Reading Warm-up B, p. 232
Sample Answers
1. pasture; A backdrop is a background or a setting.
2. (daze); A person in a trance might stare straight ahead without seeing.
3. observant, alert; Roger was attentive to all of Heather's moods.
4. (wooden posts and rails) (plain wire secured to wooden posts); Two variations of tops I might wear with jeans are T-shirts and sweaters.
5. rain or flooding; A wash means "covered or overflowing with water."
6. Once I suffered from boredom when I had to spend three weeks with my cousin Alfred—all he wanted to do was play computer games.

7. *Instantaneous* means "happening in a moment."; There was an *instantaneous* explosion.

8. (track); A *circuit* I can walk to get exercise is a loop around a small lake near my house.

Literary Analysis: Voice, p. 233

Sample Responses

Line: "And honored among wagons . . . / And once below a time . . ."; diction; Thomas "piles" images with lots of *and*'s.

Line: "the spellbound horses walking warm / Out of the whinnying green stable"; word choice / diction; the repeated *w* sounds pull the image together and help create a warm, gentle feeling, suitable for the reflection in the poem.

Line: "My wishes raced through the house-high hay"; diction; the repeated *h*'s give a "stacked-up" feeling, like the hay.

Line: "green and golden" (lines 15 and 44); word choice; both of the colors bring up images of youth, freshness, vitality.

Reading Strategy: Judge the Message, p. 234

Possible Responses

"Do Not Go Gentle into That Good Night"

Message: One should fight against dying rather than accepting its inevitability. Judgment: Students may agree, or they may say that accepting death makes it easier, both for the dying and for the survivors.

"Fern Hill"

Message: Childhood is lovely and brief, and we don't realize it until we are past it. Judgment: Some students may disagree with the poet's very agreeable image of childhood. Students may state that children do sometimes, at least, recognize the loveliness of childhood, if not its brevity.

"The Horses"

Message: The poet expresses appreciation of and gratitude for a vivid memory in the midst of a life that is now less "vivid" or satisfying. Judgment: Students may be able to relate to this message through a vivid memory of their own, from an earlier time in their lives when they were less responsible, less burdened with school or work or concerns about the future.

Vocabulary Builder, p. 235

A. 1. voluntarism; 2. volition; 3. voluntarily

B. 1. C; 2. B; 3. D; 4. A; 5. B

Grammar and Style: Sentence Beginnings: Adverb Clauses, p. 236

A. Sentences 2 and 4 contain adverb clauses.

  2. As he went—modifies *broke*

  4. Whenever it seemed to be drawing off— modifies *listened*

B. Sample Responses

  1. After he reached the top of the hill, he paused.

  2. As if the horse had been waiting, it bore down on him.

Enrichment: Preservation of Wilderness Lands, p. 239

Suggested Response

Students who argue for "using" the land may cite independence from foreign oil and mineral sources as one reason for doing so. Or they may cite support of the growing American population as a reason for logging, pumping, and/or mining. Students who argue for leaving the land untouched may cite wildlife endangerment and extinction statistics, natural beauty, and other ecological reasons. Those who argue for a balance may suggest limited harvest of resources along with preservation of strictly wilderness areas.

Selection Test A, p. 240

Critical Reading

1. ANS: B	DIF: Easy	OBJ: Interpretation
2. ANS: C	DIF: Easy	OBJ: Comprehension
3. ANS: D	DIF: Easy	OBJ: Interpretation
4. ANS: B	DIF: Easy	OBJ: Reading Strategy
5. ANS: C	DIF: Easy	OBJ: Interpretation
6. ANS: A	DIF: Easy	OBJ: Literary Analysis
7. ANS: D	DIF: Easy	OBJ: Literary Analysis
8. ANS: B	DIF: Easy	OBJ: Interpretation
9. ANS: A	DIF: Easy	OBJ: Comprehension
10. ANS: D	DIF: Easy	OBJ: Literary Analysis
11. ANS: A	DIF: Easy	OBJ: Interpretation

Vocabulary and Grammar

12. ANS: C	DIF: Easy	OBJ: Vocabulary
13. ANS: A	DIF: Easy	OBJ: Grammar

Essay

14. Students may or may not agree with the message, but they should give reasons based on their experience and reading that support their judgment.

  Difficulty: *Easy*

  Objective: *Essay*

15. Students should note that both the narrator's choice of inappropriate clothing and the horse's behavior support the theme of the narrator's loss of a connection to his childhood home and to the natural world. He no longer knows how to dress for a walk in the country. In addition, the horse does not fear or respect the narrator.

  Difficulty: *Easy*

  Objective: *Essay*

Selection Test B, p. 243

Critical Reading

1. ANS: C	DIF: Easy	OBJ: Comprehension
2. ANS: D	DIF: Challenging	OBJ: Comprehension
3. ANS: D	DIF: Average	OBJ: Reading Strategy

4. ANS: B	DIF: Average	OBJ: Interpretation
5. ANS: A	DIF: Average	OBJ: Interpretation
6. ANS: D	DIF: Average	OBJ: Interpretation
7. ANS: A	DIF: Challenging	OBJ: Literary Analysis
8. ANS: A	DIF: Easy	OBJ: Comprehension
9. ANS: B	DIF: Average	OBJ: Reading Strategy
10. ANS: A	DIF: Challenging	OBJ: Literary Analysis
11. ANS: D	DIF: Average	OBJ: Comprehension
12. ANS: A	DIF: Average	OBJ: Interpretation

Vocabulary and Grammar

13. ANS: C	DIF: Easy	OBJ: Vocabulary
14. ANS: A	DIF: Average	OBJ: Vocabulary
15. ANS: B	DIF: Easy	OBJ: Grammar

Essay

16. Students should recall that the man's initial response is nothingness, boredom. He had apparently spent time here as a boy hunting rabbits and apparently knew his way around well. As the episode develops with the horse, his anger at the strangeness of the land is transferred to the horse as he tries to outsmart it and get away from it. Students may conclude that the horse *did* appear on this day and serves as a symbol or sign that the man no longer "belongs" there. Other students may argue that the incident with the horse happened twelve years ago and the man simply relives the whole thing, including the final scene in the farmer's shed. Or, perhaps because of his long absence and detachment from the land, the man had *never* met a horse in that field, and he imagined the whole thing, again symbolizing that he no longer belonged.
Difficulty: *Easy*
Objective: *Essay*

17. In "Do Not Go Gentle," Thomas urges resistance to dying. People should not accept death willingly but should fight against it. In "Fern Hill," Thomas expresses a fondness for childhood as a "green and golden" time. He also expresses regret at its passing. Students may or may not accept Thomas's attitudes about the "golden" nature of childhood, citing lack of similar "natural" or pleasurable, free experiences such as Thomas describes. Students may agree or disagree with Thomas's attitudes toward death. Students should focus on the attitude of the *dying* toward death, not of the survivors.
Difficulty: *Average*
Objective: *Essay*

"An Arundel Tomb" and "The Explosion"
by Philip Larkin
"On the Patio" by Peter Redgrove
"Not Waving but Drowning" by Stevie Smith

Vocabulary Warm-up Exercises, p. 247

A.
1. trough
2. moaning
3. comfort
4. blurred
5. vaguely
6. persisted
7. lodged
8. prolong

B. Sample Answers
1. F; If you see someone *dart* out into the street, that person is moving quickly.
2. T; I could make *pellets* out of snow because pellets are small, round balls.
3. T; A *tremor* in the earth signals shaking and is a sign of an earthquake.
4. F; It would not be *absurd* to expect a thank-you note for a gift—it would be reasonable.
5. F; You could not ride down a mountain trail on a *stationary* bike because a stationary bike does not move.
6. F; People who dance *rigidly* are the opposite of graceful and fluid in their movements.
7. T; If you blow up a balloon too much, you are sure to see an *explosion*.
8. F; If you *damage* a painting, it goes down in value.

Reading Warm-up A, p. 248

Sample Answers
1. refusing to give it up; One activity in which I have *persisted* is gymnastics.
2. (the ditch beside the road); A *trough* is a long, narrow depression, such as a ditch or a wheel rut.
3. large farm equipment operating in the fields; *Moaning* is a long, low sound like the one people make when they are in pain or very sad.
4. (pebbles); Marisol lodged a rock under the door to keep it from closing and locking behind her.
5. the passing miles; A word that means about the same as *vaguely* would be *unclearly*.
6. (her ride); People usually want to *prolong* anything that is enjoyable, such as a celebration.

7. age and weather; Jiggling the camera when taking a picture might cause a photograph to be *blurred*.

8. she had a cell phone in her pocket and could call for help if she needed to; A lost person might take *comfort* in having a map or seeing people nearby who might be able to help.

Reading Warm-up B, p. 249

Sample Answers

1. morning exercises; *Stationary* means "unmoving."
2. (in a hurry); Look at the children *dart* from one side of the playground to the other!
3. movement; One thing that might cause you to feel a *tremor* in the ground is an earthquake.
4. (unreasonable); An *absurd* childhood fear is thinking there are monsters under the bed.
5. no explosion of any kind had ever taken place; An *explosion* is a sudden blowing up or bursting of something.
6. harm; One time I accidentally did some *damage* to a camera by leaving it out in the rain.
7. (small, round pebbles); *Pellets* of hail landed on the patio.
8. he never changed his attitude; A word that means the opposite of *rigidly* is *flexibly*.

Literary Analysis: Free Verse and Meter, p. 250

Possible Responses

1. The first line of the poem starts out in trochees instead of iambs, and is half a foot short. The meter of the first phrase emphasizes the words "side by side."
2. Scárfed as ín a héat-haze, dímmed. Line 15 is in trochees, but is half a foot short. It emphasizes the fact that something unnatural has happened; something has thrown things out of kilter, even if just "for a second," as stated in line 14.

Reading Strategy: Read in Sentences, p. 251

A. Stanzas 4–7 of "An Arundel Tomb"

Sentence 1: They would not guess how early in their supine stationary voyage the air would change to soundless damage, turn the old tenantry away; how soon succeeding eyes begin to look, not read.

Sentence 2: Rigidly they persisted, linked, through lengths and breadths of time.

Sentence 3: Snow fell, undated.

Sentence 4: Light each summer thronged the glass.

Sentence 5: A bright litter of birdcalls strewed the same bone-riddled ground.

Sentence 6: And up the paths the endless altered people came, washing at their identity.

Sentence 7: Now, helpless in the hollow of an unarmorial age, a trough of smoke in slow suspended skeins above their scrap of history, only an attitude remains: Time has transfigured them into untruth.

Sentence 8: The stone fidelity they hardly meant has come to be their final blazon, and to prove our almost-instinct almost true: What will survive of us is love.

B. Suggested Responses

With the stanzas written out in narrative form, students may need to be cautioned about reading too quickly. Emphasize the need to find meaning in the lines, not to get to the end of the sentence.

Vocabulary Builder, p. 252

A. 1. A; 2. C; 3. B
B. 1. fidelity; 2. effigy; 3. larking; 4. supine
C. 1. C; 2. D; 3. D; 4. A

Grammar and Style: Sequence of Tenses, p. 253

A. 1. present perfect; 2. present; 3. past
B. Sample Responses

1. I had read the novel before the movie version came out.
2. In the morning I dress before I eat my breakfast.
3. Yesterday, however, I altered my routine and ate breakfast first.

Enrichment: Social Studies, p. 256

Sample Responses

1. The family might feel grateful for decades of steady work and a steady source of income. They might also feel resentful because of the difficulty and danger of the work and the fact that it probably paid relatively little.
2. The technological advances that were being made at the time included some improvements in mining conditions. In addition, the boom probably increased wages somewhat, and the increase in jobs must have been attractive to workers.
3. Most people were utterly dependent on the mines for their livelihoods. They likely had few other skills and no money to move and begin life somewhere else. With the majority of the population affected by the decrease in mining activity, there would have been few community resources to aid those who were left penniless once the mines shut down.

Selection Test A, p. 257

Critical Reading

1. ANS: D	DIF: Easy	OBJ: Comprehension
2. ANS: A	DIF: Easy	OBJ: Reading Strategy
3. ANS: B	DIF: Easy	OBJ: Literary Analysis
4. ANS: C	DIF: Easy	OBJ: Comprehension
5. ANS: D	DIF: Easy	OBJ: Interpretation
6. ANS: C	DIF: Easy	OBJ: Literary Analysis
7. ANS: A	DIF: Easy	OBJ: Interpretation
8. ANS: D	DIF: Easy	OBJ: Reading Strategy
9. ANS: D	DIF: Easy	OBJ: Interpretation

Vocabulary and Grammar

10. ANS: D   DIF: Easy   OBJ: Vocabulary
11. ANS: A   DIF: Easy   OBJ: Grammar

Essay

12. Students should mention that "On the Patio" is about a thunderstorm and a downpour. The speaker watches as the rain pours down, filling a wineglass left on a rusty steel table. The surprise is the speaker's act of darting out onto the patio, drinking the glass empty, and then putting it back, waiting for it fill again.

    Difficulty: *Easy*

    Objective: *Essay*

13. Students should mention that the message of the poem is that the dead man, and possibly most people, found life cold and threatening and always a little too difficult. In saying "I was much too far out all my life / And not waving but drowning," he says he was alone and his actions were the actions of someone desperate.

    Difficulty: *Easy*

    Objective: *Essay*

Selection Test B, p. 260

Critical Reading

1. ANS: D   DIF: Easy   OBJ: Comprehension
2. ANS: D   DIF: Easy   OBJ: Reading Strategy
3. ANS: A   DIF: Challenging   OBJ: Literary Analysis
4. ANS: A   DIF: Average   OBJ: Comprehension
5. ANS: B   DIF: Average   OBJ: Interpretation
6. ANS: C   DIF: Average   OBJ: Literary Analysis
7. ANS: D   DIF: Challenging   OBJ: Literary Analysis
8. ANS: B   DIF: Easy   OBJ: Comprehension
9. ANS: A   DIF: Average   OBJ: Interpretation
10. ANS: C   DIF: Easy   OBJ: Comprehension
11. ANS: D   DIF: Average   OBJ: Interpretation
12. ANS: B   DIF: Easy   OBJ: Interpretation

Vocabulary and Grammar

13. ANS: D   DIF: Easy   OBJ: Vocabulary
14. ANS: B   DIF: Average   OBJ: Vocabulary
15. ANS: C   DIF: Average   OBJ: Grammar
16. ANS: D   DIF: Average   OBJ: Grammar

Essay

17. Students should recognize that the central idea of the poem is that this person has felt like an outsider all his life. He has felt "much too far" outside the company of other people and has been waving to try to get their attention. They didn't notice, just as they didn't notice

him waving when he was out in the water. "They" in the poem talk about the dead man as if he weren't there; they apparently ignored him when he was alive as well. The use of first person for the dead man's thoughts makes readers feel closer to him than to the other persons and makes them sympathize with the dead man.

Difficulty: *Easy*

Objective: *Essay*

18. Students should recognize that the central visual image is the effigy on the tomb of an earl and a countess. Most importantly, the effigy shows the earl fondly holding the countess's hand. The speaker reveals this, at the end of the second stanza, with apparent surprise, as if he is sharing his initial discovery of the fact with readers. The speaker feels that this small detail, created by a sculptor, is the only detail that later generations will notice. He says the gesture, the "fidelity" is an untruth, preserved by the sculptor, but latched onto by viewers as truth because they want to believe that love survives.

Difficulty: *Average*

Objective: *Essay*

"B. Wordsworth" by V. S. Naipaul

Vocabulary Warm-up Exercises, p. 264

A.
1. botanical
2. particularly
3. constellation
4. existed
5. tragedy
6. poet
7. poetry
8. rate

B. Sample Answers

1. F; A visitor would expect to hear *calypso* in the West Indies, not Alaska.
2. F; *Humanity* includes all the human beings, not all the living things.
3. F; A *hospitable* host at a party would make a guest feel very welcome, not uncomfortable.
4. T; If I hoped to get a bargain, I would certainly *negotiate* terms with the seller.
5. T; Parents and grandparents often want to attend the *rite* of graduation because it is an important step in the child's life.
6. T; Because a *mango* is a tropical fruit, it is often used to flavor sherbets.
7. F; You could not put a whole *coconut* on a toothpick because it is much too big for that and its shell is too hard.
8. F; A person who arrives *punctually* at a bus station would not miss the bus because he or she would be on time.

Reading Warm-up A, p. 265

Sample Answers

1. (William Wordsworth); What I like best about Edgar Allan Poe, my favorite *poet,* is his use of rhythm and repetition.
2. simplifying its language and style; One thing I enjoy about *poetry* is its imaginative use of language.
3. ("I Wandered Lonely as a Cloud"); *Particularly* means "especially."
4. stars; One *constellation* is Orion.
5. (flowers); In a local *botanical* garden, I might find bluebonnets, yucca, and orchids.
6. He became an orphan at age thirteen.; It seemed like a *tragedy* when Helen left home, but it turned out for the better.
7. (sat by the fire, occasionally reciting lines from her brother's poetry); An animal that *existed* in the past but is now extinct is the dodo bird.
8. producing 70,000 lines of poetry; At a *rate* of four miles an hour, I could walk eight miles in two hours.

Reading Warm-up B, p. 266

Sample Answers

1. friendly; A *hospitable* gesture that make guests feel comfortable is offering them a seat.
2. (celebration and fun); One *rite* in which high school seniors usually participate is going to the prom.
3. (songs); Les could tell from the style of the music that the song was a *calypso.*
4. people; A *discovery* that benefited all of humanity was penicillin.
5. (bargain); I might *negotiate* prices at a garage sale by offering less than the asking price and then haggling until we reach an agreement.
6. late; To arrive *punctually* at school, I leave home at 7:45 in the morning.
7. tropical fruit; Marla picked a ripe *mango* from the tree in the yard.
8. (palm tree); A food that has *coconut* as an ingredient is macaroons.

Literary Analysis: First-Person Narrator, p. 267

1. yes
2. no; I could tell B. Wordsworth was glad to see me.
3. no; My mother was angry with me for coming home late from school and asked me where I'd been.
4. yes
5. no; B. Wordsworth told me a story about a girl poet and a boy poet.
6. no; B. Wordsworth and I took long walks through the parks and along the waterfront.

Reading Strategy: Respond to Character, p. 268

Possible Responses

For each character—B. Wordsworth and the narrator—students must note three events and each character's behavior, words, and qualities expressed as they experience this event. Students must explain their response to each character/event. For example, students may note B. Wordsworth's request to "watch bees," and note their response to him as an odd, yet interesting character.

Vocabulary Builder, p. 269

A. 1. patroness; 2. patronizing; 3. patronage; 4. patronize
B. 1. C; 2. D; 3. A; 4. B
C. 1. distill; 2. rogue; 3. keenly; 4. patronize

Grammar and Style: Pronoun Case in Compound Construction, p. 270

A. 1. I; 2. he; 3. he
B. 1. Mr. Wordsworth and *he* take long walks together.
   2. *They* live on the same street.
   3. The relationship between the narrator and *her* is not loving.

Enrichment: Astronomer, p. 273

Sample Responses

1. mathematics, science, physics
2. Astronomers now use sophisticated electronic (CCDS) equipment to record their observations rather than relying on optical devices alone.
3. An astronomer needs to interpret and explain his/her observations for other scientists and laypeople.
4. The field of astronomy connects us to the larger universe by attempting to expand our knowledge of it.

Selection Test A, p. 274

Critical Reading

1. ANS: C	DIF: Easy	OBJ: Literary Analysis
2. ANS: A	DIF: Easy	OBJ: Literary Analysis
3. ANS: B	DIF: Easy	OBJ: Comprehension
4. ANS: C	DIF: Easy	OBJ: Comprehension
5. ANS: D	DIF: Easy	OBJ: Interpretation
6. ANS: A	DIF: Easy	OBJ: Interpretation
7. ANS: D	DIF: Easy	OBJ: Interpretation
8. ANS: C	DIF: Easy	OBJ: Reading Strategy
9. ANS: A	DIF: Easy	OBJ: Interpretation
10. ANS: B	DIF: Easy	OBJ: Reading Strategy
11. ANS: D	DIF: Easy	OBJ: Interpretation
12. ANS: C	DIF: Easy	OBJ: Comprehension

Vocabulary and Grammar

13. **ANS:** A   **DIF:** Easy   **OBJ:** Vocabulary
14. **ANS:** A   **DIF:** Easy   **OBJ:** Grammar

Essay

15. Students should realize that the narrator would not use the word *I* or share his or her feelings and thoughts with the reader. Students might say their response to the boy would change because he would no longer be speaking directly to them. Their response to B. Wordsworth would not change because his character is already described in the third person.
   Difficulty: *Easy*
   Objective: *Essay*

16. Students should note that the boy cries because he cares about B. Wordsworth, knows he is dying, and knows also that he will never see B. Wordsworth again. He cries like a poet because he has developed a sensitive nature and sees the tragedy and sadness in life and, in particular, in B. Wordsworth's life. The boy understands or senses this sadness, which is why he cries.
   Difficulty: *Easy*
   Objective: *Essay*

Selection Test B, p. 277

Critical Reading

1. **ANS:** A   **DIF:** Easy   **OBJ:** Comprehension
2. **ANS:** C   **DIF:** Average   **OBJ:** Interpretation
3. **ANS:** D   **DIF:** Easy   **OBJ:** Comprehension
4. **ANS:** C   **DIF:** Easy   **OBJ:** Reading Strategy
5. **ANS:** B   **DIF:** Average   **OBJ:** Interpretation
6. **ANS:** A   **DIF:** Average   **OBJ:** Literary Analysis
7. **ANS:** C   **DIF:** Challenging   **OBJ:** Literary Analysis
8. **ANS:** A   **DIF:** Average   **OBJ:** Interpretation
9. **ANS:** B   **DIF:** Challenging   **OBJ:** Reading Strategy
10. **ANS:** C   **DIF:** Average   **OBJ:** Interpretation
11. **ANS:** D   **DIF:** Average   **OBJ:** Reading Strategy
12. **ANS:** C   **DIF:** Challenging   **OBJ:** Literary Analysis

Vocabulary and Grammar

13. **ANS:** B   **DIF:** Easy   **OBJ:** Vocabulary
14. **ANS:** C   **DIF:** Average   **OBJ:** Vocabulary
15. **ANS:** D   **DIF:** Average   **OBJ:** Grammar
16. **ANS:** A   **DIF:** Challenging   **OBJ:** Grammar

Essay

17. Students may note any number of events or details to show the narrator's response to Wordsworth, including the fact that he is comforted by the poet, his desire to see the poet again, and his sadness as the poet ages. Students should conclude that the narrator is full of

affection for the poet and is quite impressed by his personality and by what he says.
Difficulty: *Easy*
Objective: *Essay*

18. Students should note that if "B. Wordsworth" were written from an omniscient point of view, information about specific characters and events would not be limited. For example, an omniscient narrator would relate what other characters, specifically B. Wordsworth, see, hear, think, imagine, and assume. Students will probably conclude, however, that the story is effective written in first person because, through the wondering and thoughtful mind of the young narrator, the reader empathizes with his experience, from which he grows.
Difficulty: *Average*
Objective: *Essay*

"The Train from Rhodesia" by Nadine Gordimer

Vocabulary Warm-up Exercises, p. 281

A.
1. careered
2. oneself
3. coordinated
4. sinews
5. compartments
6. associated
7. Incredulous
8. bargaining

B. Sample Answers
1. F; An <u>imprint</u> of a hand in wet cement will show when the cement dries.
2. T; <u>Readiness</u> for kindergarten would include not only familiarity with the alphabet, but also knowledge of basic shapes and colors.
3. F; Dreams that <u>recur</u> are dreams that you have over and over again.
4. T; Earthquake <u>preparedness</u> would include having a supply of water and some food.
5. F; <u>Dwindling</u> supplies are supplies that are getting used up.
6. F; A <u>chalet</u> is a Swiss house with wide eaves.
7. T; <u>Interrogating</u> means "asking questions," so the interrogator would be looking for answers.
8. F; <u>Rhythmical</u> music is easy to dance to because of the repeated beat.

Reading Warm-up A, p. 282

Sample Answers
1. <u>one</u>; Belief in *oneself* is necessary for success.
2. <u>may not believe that train travel can be comfortable</u>; *Incredulous* means "feeling or having doubt or disbelief."
3. <u>muscles, bones</u>; Another word for *sinews* is *tendons*.

4. (sleeping); *Compartments* might be useful in a kitchen drawer because they would make it easy to keep different kinds of utensils together.

5. aches and pains; The foods usually *associated* with Thanksgiving are turkey, mashed potatoes, gravy, cranberry sauce, and pumpkin pie.

6. (work together); One game in which *coordinated* effort is necessary in order to win is football.

7. (negotiate); I once used *bargaining* as a tool to get a better price on a skateboard at a flea market.

8. moved at great speed; I once saw a horse that *careered* down a country road, and the rider could barely control him.

Reading Warm-up B, p. 283
Sample Answers

1. wood and a carving tool; *Readiness* for college includes mastery of one's high school courses.

2. (a pattern, graphite paper, and protection for your fingers); Some first-aid *preparedness* that you should bring along on a hike include bandages, sunscreen, and snake-bite medicine.

3. (repeatedly); Two events that *recur* in my daily schedule are lunch at 12:30 and English at 2:00.

4. Swiss . . . decorative details and wide eaves; We stayed in a Swiss *chalet* for two nights.

5. by tracing it on graphite paper; *Imprint* means "a mark made by printing, stamping, or pressing."

6. which way the grain should go; If I were *interrogating* an instructor in an art class, I would ask where I can get quality art supplies.

7. in a repeated pattern; One sport in which I would use *rhythmical* movements is swimming.

8. carve . . . cutting and rubbing it; *decreasing, diminishing*

Literary Analysis: Conflict and Theme, p. 284
Sample Responses

1. The character's inner struggle with reality and unreality, symbolized by her husband and carved animals and baskets, dramatizes the conflict between the realities of two cultures—non-African and African—and how each is out of place when put in the other.

2. The character's dawning awareness of the conflict is dramatized in her "seeing something different" when looking at the lion.

3. The husband's success at buying the lion for a cheap amount and degrading the artist by not taking it decently, dramatizes the colonization of Africa and Africans by exploitive Europeans.

Reading Strategy: Read Between the Lines, p. 285
Suggested Response

For each event students identify in the first column, they must explain the meaning or significance of in the second column. For example, students may record the incident of the lion's mouth "opened in an endless roar too terrible to be heard." By reading between the lines, students may determine that the lion's roar is the cry of native Africans, grieving their loss of independence and dignity.

Vocabulary Builder, p. 286

A. 1. amoral; 2. atonal; 3. atypical
B. 1. C; 2. A; 3. E; 4. B; 5. D
C. Sample Responses

1. Her memories of the incident were impressionistic.

2. After long hours on the train, he felt his muscles begin to atrophy.

3. The suitcase fell, splaying its contents across the corridor.

4. The journey was more restful because it was segmented.

5. Her face sagged, elongated by fatigue.

Grammar and Style: Nominative Absolutes, p. 287

A. 1. the stiff wooden legs sticking up in the air

2. Joints not yet coordinated

3. the wonderful ruff of fur facing her

4. his hands hanging at his sides.

5. her face slumped in her hand

B. Possible Responses

1. The train, a sleek black machine humming with life, pulled into the station.

2. The piccanins and dogs circling her, the young woman stood on the platform.

3. The stationmaster rang the bell, an urgent call heeded by the waiting passengers.

Enrichment: Social Studies, p. 290

1. C; 2. A; 3. C

Selection Test A, p. 291
Critical Reading

1. ANS: A	DIF: Easy	OBJ: Reading Strategy
2. ANS: A	DIF: Easy	OBJ: Comprehension
3. ANS: B	DIF: Easy	OBJ: Reading Strategy
4. ANS: B	DIF: Easy	OBJ: Comprehension
5. ANS: C	DIF: Easy	OBJ: Comprehension
6. ANS: C	DIF: Easy	OBJ: Literary Analysis
7. ANS: D	DIF: Easy	OBJ: Comprehension
8. ANS: B	DIF: Easy	OBJ: Interpretation
9. ANS: D	DIF: Easy	OBJ: Reading Strategy
10. ANS: D	DIF: Easy	OBJ: Literary Analysis
11. ANS: D	DIF: Easy	OBJ: Interpretation

Vocabulary and Grammar

12. ANS: B   DIF: Easy   OBJ: Vocabulary
13. ANS: D   DIF: Easy   OBJ: Grammar

Essay

14. Students should understand that the young wife is angry because she is confused and probably feeling guilty. She sees the poverty of the local people and feels wealthy in comparison. She feels that her husband has taken advantage of the old man.
    Difficulty: *Easy*
    Objective: *Essay*

15. Students may say that the old man was taken advantage of because he is desperate, taking what he could get only as a last resort and knowing his carving was worth more. Other students may point out that he is smiling and that bargaining was part of the marketing culture at the station.
    Difficulty: *Easy*
    Objective: *Essay*

Selection Test B, p. 294

Critical Reading

1. ANS: A   DIF: Average   OBJ: Comprehension
2. ANS: B   DIF: Average   OBJ: Literary Analysis
3. ANS: D   DIF: Easy   OBJ: Comprehension
4. ANS: B   DIF: Average   OBJ: Literary Analysis
5. ANS: C   DIF: Challenging   OBJ: Interpretation
6. ANS: C   DIF: Average   OBJ: Reading Strategy
7. ANS: B   DIF: Challenging   OBJ: Reading Strategy
8. ANS: D   DIF: Challenging   OBJ: Interpretation
9. ANS: B   DIF: Average   OBJ: Comprehension
10. ANS: C   DIF: Challenging   OBJ: Reading Strategy
11. ANS: A   DIF: Average   OBJ: Literary Analysis

Vocabulary and Grammar

12. ANS: B   DIF: Easy   OBJ: Vocabulary
13. ANS: D   DIF: Average   OBJ: Vocabulary
14. ANS: A   DIF: Average   OBJ: Grammar
15. ANS: A   DIF: Challenging   OBJ: Grammar

Essay

16. Students must understand the train's arrival signals the arrival of wealthy white tourists who provide the townspeople with the money they need for economic survival. Therefore, people gather at the station as if expecting a big event. Students may note that it is due to the colonization of Africa that Africans, at the time of this story, are no longer economically independent. By selling their handmade crafts and begging, native South Africans show their desperate dependence upon whites for economic survival.
    Difficulty: *Easy*
    Objective: *Essay*

17. Whichever passage students select, they must explain how it highlights the inner conflict felt by the young woman as well as the larger conflict central to the story. Students will most likely select a passage from the story's ending, where these conflicts are directly experienced by the young woman.
    Difficulty: *Challenging*
    Objective: *Essay*

from *Midsummer, XXIII* and from *Omeros* from *Chapter XXVIII* by Derek Walcott

Vocabulary Warm-up Exercises, p. 298

A.
1. horizon
2. thatched
3. fronds
4. withered
5. triangular
6. scurry
7. quips
8. ashen

B. Sample Answers

1. Inez was drawn to the *splendor* of the epic oil painting. The *splendor* of the feast set before him was astonishing to William.
2. Ravi wants to *perpetuate* the idea that electric cars are the answer to our energy problems. Toni is working on inventing a *perpetual* motion machine.
3. The *reverberation* of the bell could be heard a block away. The sound of the crashing glass *reverberated* throughout the house.
4. The cause of the dinosaurs' *extinction* is a mystery. The dodo is an *extinct* bird.
5. "Beware the ides of March," was a *prophetic* warning given to Julius Caesar. The man claimed to be a *prophet*, but nothing he said ever came true.
6. The children *seethe* with excitement when they go to the amusement park. Stay away from Michael—he's *seething* with anger.
7. The sun *radiated* in all directions, heating the atmosphere of the nearby planets. The bride looked *radiant*, joy beaming from her face.

Reading Warm-up A, p. 299

Sample Answers

1. witty remarks; Betsy could not keep up with all the clever *quips* of the witty guest.
2. (ran); *Scurry* means "the act of running quickly or hastily."
3. dry and lifeless; When a plant has *withered*, you can water it and give it some fertilizer.

4. (fronds of palm trees); You would be unlikely to find a *thatched* hut in a place with little plant life, like a desert or the tundra.

5. (palm trees); The *fronds* waved gently in the breeze.

6. the fin of a shark; A sailboat's sails are *triangular*.

7. (west); The *horizon* is "the line where the earth and the sky seem to meet."

8. pale gray; An experience that might give me an *ashen* face would be a frightening one, like riding a roller coaster.

Reading Warm-up B, p. 300
Sample Answers

1. magnificence; Marybeth was overwhelmed by the *splendor* of the castle.

2. (bubbling over with the excitement); Ted will just *seethe* with anger when he finds out about his car.

3. it came true; A statement someone once said to me that turned out to be *prophetic* was that I would win the swim meet.

4. (joy); Heat *radiated* in all directions from the space heater.

5. echoing; Once I heard a *reverberation* of thunder that lasted for a good fifteen seconds.

6. (the display); *Muttering* is what people are doing when they mumble in a low voice, making it difficult to tell what they are saying.

7. a universal appreciation for her favorite painter; One idea I would like to *perpetuate* is the importance of recycling as much of our trash as possible.

8. (end); *Extinction* means "the condition of no longer existing."

Literary Analysis: Theme and Context, p. 301
Sample Responses

1. *Midsummer:* roar of a Brixton riot tunneled by water hoses; die for the sun; leaf stems tug at their chains . . . nearer to apartheid; "But the blacks can't do Shakespeare"; Their thick skulls bled with rancor . . . the Moor's eclipse; Calibans howled; barred streets burning.

   Omeros: leg irons; chains; ashen ancestors; scorching decks; tubers withered; dried fronds; curved spines; dead palms were heaved overside, the ribbed corpses floated; burnt branches; crooked fingers; waiter; lances; ruin; suntraction; the hold's iron door rolled over their eyes; bolt rammed home its echo; there went Ashanti . . . brother. The context reflects the colonial history of the Caribbean region.

2. In English society, the privileged are unnaturally separated from (yet, perhaps ironically, respected by) working-class people.

Reading Strategy: Apply Background Information, p. 302
Possible Responses

1. Walcott is a playwright as well as a poet, and a person of color who was in England in 1981; The word "color" here likely means racial integration or diversity, as well as character or tone.

2. A *griot* is a West-African shaman; Walcott's heritage as well as his interest in it probably lead him to employ the authentic term for a speaker of this section of the poem.

Vocabulary Builder, p. 303

A. 1. D; 2. E; 3. B; 4. A; 5. C

B. 1. B; 2. C; 3. A; 4. D

Grammar and Style: Commonly Confused Words: *Affect* and *Effect*, p. 304

A. 1. C; 2. I; 3. I; 4. C

B. Possible Responses

1. The effect of *Omeros* is to make the reader feel as if he or she were on a slave ship.

2. Walcott had hoped to effect an increased diversity in Shakespearean theater in England.

Enrichment: Social Studies, p. 307
Possible Responses

1. The world pays attention because the British monarchy is the only monarchy of a great world power. Royalty, like other forms of celebrity, fascinates people because of the profound tension between public expectation and private life.

2. Because its role is ceremonial, some see the monarchy as outdated in a modern world. A queen or king can effect no real change in English life. People are fiercely loyal out of patriotism or respect for tradition.

Selection Test A, p. 308
Critical Reading

1. ANS: A   DIF: Easy   OBJ: Literary Analysis
2. ANS: D   DIF: Easy   OBJ: Reading Strategy
3. ANS: A   DIF: Easy   OBJ: Literary Analysis
4. ANS: A   DIF: Easy   OBJ: Interpretation
5. ANS: C   DIF: Easy   OBJ: Interpretation

6. ANS: D	DIF: Easy	OBJ: Comprehension
7. ANS: A	DIF: Easy	OBJ: Interpretation
8. ANS: D	DIF: Easy	OBJ: Interpretation
9. ANS: C	DIF: Easy	OBJ: Comprehension
10. ANS: B	DIF: Easy	OBJ: Interpretation

Vocabulary and Grammar

11. ANS: B	DIF: Easy	OBJ: Vocabulary
12. ANS: B	DIF: Easy	OBJ: Grammar

Essay

13. Students may conclude that Walcott is deeply involved in West Indians' struggle for equality. They may also observe that he has been fortunate because as an artist, he has not had to face the discrimination that many other West Indians of his ancestry had to face. He also mentions that his white heritage helped him gain access to white friendships. He seems a little uncomfortable with the privileged position he has gained.

Difficulty: *Easy*

Objective: *Essay*

14. Students should note that the griot's story is a prophecy because he takes the role of a captured slave long ago as he tells the story of the enslavement of Africans. Then, he tells of the present when the black waiter brings a bill. This state, he implies, is what has become of those once-free Africans.

Difficulty: *Easy*

Objective: *Essay*

Selection Test B, p. 311

Critical Reading

1. ANS: B	DIF: Average	OBJ: Comprehension
2. ANS: D	DIF: Average	OBJ: Reading Strategy
3. ANS: B	DIF: Challenging	OBJ: Reading Strategy
4. ANS: D	DIF: Average	OBJ: Comprehension
5. ANS: B	DIF: Challenging	OBJ: Reading Strategy
6. ANS: C	DIF: Easy	OBJ: Literary Analysis
7. ANS: C	DIF: Average	OBJ: Literary Analysis
8. ANS: D	DIF: Average	OBJ: Reading Strategy
9. ANS: A	DIF: Average	OBJ: Literary Analysis

Vocabulary and Grammar

10. ANS: C	DIF: Easy	OBJ: Vocabulary
11. ANS: A	DIF: Average	OBJ: Vocabulary
12. ANS: C	DIF: Average	OBJ: Grammar
13. ANS: D	DIF: Average	OBJ: Grammar

Essay

14. Walcott is a person of color raised in West Indian culture, a culture that is defined by economic, historical, and cultural ties to England. This fact may influence his choices of topic and of perspective. Walcott applies the conventions of the epic, passed to him through a British-style education, to West Indian history in Omeros. He gives an outsider's view of English culture in *Midsummer*.

Difficulty: *Easy*

Objective: *Essay*

15. Walcott mixes British and West Indian traditions, and ironically turns to Shakespeare to understand the fate of English blacks (who some whites say cannot "do" Shakespeare). His vision is complicated by the fact that he has a foot in both worlds and a home in neither. Students' examples should point up the areas in these selections in which the viewpoints of the West Indian, of the British-educated person, and of the "outsider" intersect.

Difficulty: *Average*

Objective: *Essay*

From the Author's Desk

Anita Desai Introduces "A Devoted Son", p. 314

1. A short story captures a moment or episode and is complete in itself.

2. Examples include something a person says standing in line for coffee; an object seen in your grandmother's house; or a field or bridge you saw when you passed in a train.

3. Desai scribbles down a few lines on a piece of paper. Then she puts the paper away, along with other scraps in a file. Sometime later, she takes out her notes and finds that one is ready or ripe for development in a story.

4. The seed occurred when she heard an old, white-haired neighbor sing a hymn at a ceremony held for his new-born grandson. The man had embarrassed his family by wandering the streets and accosting people. Desai decided she wanted to capture a duality: the man's moving hymn of praise vs. his unconventional wild language and gestures.

5. Answers will vary. Encourage students to support their evaluations with facts, reasons, and examples.

Anita Desai

Listening and Viewing, p. 315

Sample answers and guidelines for evaluation:

Segment 1: Anita Desai grew up speaking German, Hindi, and English. She writes in clear, "transparent" English so that the tones and rhythms of German and Hindi come through in the characters' voices. Students may answer that characters are more realistic when their voices reflect their native language.

Segment 2: Anita Desai was inspired to write "A Devoted Son" upon hearing an elderly man sing a hymn during a ceremony for his newborn grandson. It tells the story of the old passing on their roles to the young. Students will write about an experience they had that had particular significance for them.

Segment 3: Desai believes that the need for discipline and practice is as important in writing as it is in music. Students may answer that practice is important because it teaches a writer how to focus and how to improve his or her writing.

Segment 4: After moving to the United States, Anita Desai read classic American literature, such as Twain and Faulkner, which gave her a greater understanding of the world around her and helped her adjust to her new life. Students may answer that reading literature can allow them to live in different worlds, understand other cultures, and learn more about their own experiences and those of others.

"A Devoted Son" by Anita Desai

Vocabulary Warm-up Exercises, p. 317

A. 1. humiliating
2. verandah
3. thereafter
4. amongst
5. panicky
6. distraught
7. Miraculously
8. colleagues

B. Sample Answers
1. upset; Jean was <u>distraught</u> when she lost the watch her grandpa had given her.
2. co-workers; Dinesh enjoyed going out with his <u>colleagues</u> after work.
3. amazingly; The team had been behind by fifteen points, but they <u>miraculously</u> still won.
4. from then on; Duke learned to read; <u>thereafter</u>, he read for hours each day.
5. porch; Sasha sat in her rocker on the <u>verandah</u> and visited with her friend Joyce.
6. fearful; Carla felt quite <u>panicky</u> as she crossed the rickety bridge over the churning river.
7. embarrassing; Dean thought it was <u>humiliating</u> to lose the spelling bee so early.

Reading Warm-up A, p. 318

Sample Answers
1. <u>in turmoil</u>, <u>extremely upset</u>; A situation that might make a person feel *distraught* would be a serious illness.
2. <u>her beloved family</u>; A more common word for *amongst* is *among*.
3. (in front of their home); Lizzy always wanted a house with a *verandah*.

4. (failure); *Humiliating* means "extremely embarrassing."
5. (frightened); I might get a *panicky* feeling if I had to do an impromptu performance in front of thousands of people.
6. <u>she had lived up to that promise to herself</u>; After Roger made that mistake once, he never made it again *thereafter*.
7. (she was on her way to college); One thing I wish would *miraculously* happen in my life is that certain family members would learn to get along.
8. (co-workers); In the future, I would like to work with <u>colleagues</u> who are dedicated to the idea of working with disadvantaged children.

Reading Warm-up B, p. 319

Sample Answers
1. <u>because the necessary education is a long and difficult process</u>; Another word for *adamantly* is *stubbornly*.
2. (with no wasted time); One job that I would like to do with great *efficiency* is cleaning my room.
3. <u>a doctor's education can begin as early as high school</u>; With some *exaggeration*, Clara claimed that four boys had asked her to the prom.
4. <u>Graduating with a four-year degree</u>, <u>four years at medical school</u>, <u>a residency program</u>; *Multitude* means "a great number of persons or things."
5. (doctor of medicine degree); A *prestigious* award I would like to win someday is an Oscar for best actor.
6. <u>performing operations</u>; Inflamed or infected tonsils might require the services of a *surgeon*.
7. (none); The hairs on the old man's head were *sparse* but long.
8. (denied); *Deprived* means "kept from getting, having, or enjoying."

Literary Analysis: Static and Dynamic Characters, p. 320

Sample Responses
1. At the beginning of the story Varma is proud, happy and competent. As he ages, retires, loses his wife, and watches his son take over his household, he becomes resentful and irritated. At the end he is angry and bitter and wants to die.
2. Fifth paragraph (begins "To everyone who came to him . . ."): "He came and touched my feet"; Eleventh paragraph (begins "It was a strange fact . . ."): "He developed so many complaints and fell ill so frequently . . ."; The first complete paragraph on the next to last page (begins "'Let me be,' Varma begged, turning his face away from the pills on the outstretched hand."): "Let me die. It would be better, I do not want to live only to eat your medicines."
3. Rakesh is bland, dutiful, and devoted throughout. He is clearly ambitious, though no overt aggressiveness appears, and he is intent only on his success and repeating the patterns that brought it, throughout the story. No other personality traits appear.

4. First paragraph: ". . . and bowed down to touch his feet." Eight h paragraph (begins "For some years Rakesh worked . . ."); ". . . for he became known not only as the best but the richest doctor in town"; Next to last page (begins "At last the sky-blue Ambassador arrived . . ."); "Ever a devoted son, he went first to the corner where the father sat gazing . . ."

Reading Strategy: Evaluate Characters' Decisions, p. 321

Possible Responses

1. Family's desire to see son succeed and Rakesh's ambition; Acclaim from the community, some jealousy; At this point, pride is the dominant emotion.
2. Rakesh seeks unheard of success; Still pride and acclaim, but father's simpleness is hinted; One now begins to wonder at the ultimate effect.
3. Rakesh's surprising decision seems unclear, but family still proud; Varma begins to be eclipsed, and fame dies down; It seems clear there will be an ultimate consequence.
4. Varma's wife has died and his modern son thinks him a fool; Rakesh completely takes over and Varma is treated like a child; Rakesh's observation of duty seems self-centered, for he isn't really helping Varma.
5. Varma has completely lost his identity and any reason to live; Rakesh treats him all the more as senile and childish; All that Varma lived for, including his pride in his devoted son, is gone.

Vocabulary Builder, p. 322

A. 1. C; 2. A; 3. D; 4. B
B. 1. A; 2. D; 3. B; 4. C; 5. B

Grammar and Style: Sentence Variety, p. 323

A. 1. long, complex, declarative
2. long, compound, declarative
3. short, complex, interrogative, fragment (indirect discourse)
4. short, compound, declarative (indirect discourse)
5. long, complex, declarative
6. The paragraph sandwiches two blunt expressions of Varma's shock between long narrative sentences. The first two describe Varma's condition and the realization that shocks him. The final one describes his stunned aftermath and details of his defeat.

B. Sample Response

Varma's mouth worked hard. As if he had a gob of betel in it, though his supply had been cut off years ago, he spat, sharp and bitter as poison, "Keep your tonic—I want none—I won't take any more of your medicines. None. Never." With a wave of his hand, he swept the bottle out of his son's hand. He was suddenly effective. He was grand.

Enrichment: Physical Education, p. 326

Sample Responses

1. Similarities: pitching the ball; hitting the ball with a bat and running to score runs; game divided by innings; outs at the "bases" or by catching the ball; balls struck out of the field of play are automatic scores; fielders distributed around the field.
2. Cricket is a game too complicated to play quickly and easily, and matches may be extremely long, not suited to the American approach to sports.
3. Varma's grandsons playing cricket represents the transition of Rakesh and his family to the upper class, which sometimes adopted British mannerisms and interests, far removed from Varma's world.

Selection Test A, p. 327

Critical Reading

1. ANS: D	DIF: Easy	OBJ: Comprehension
2. ANS: A	DIF: Easy	OBJ: Interpretation
3. ANS: B	DIF: Easy	OBJ: Comprehension
4. ANS: B	DIF: Easy	OBJ: Reading Strategy
5. ANS: D	DIF: Easy	OBJ: Comprehension
6. ANS: C	DIF: Easy	OBJ: Comprehension
7. ANS: C	DIF: Easy	OBJ: Literary Analysis
8. ANS: A	DIF: Easy	OBJ: Interpretation
9. ANS: B	DIF: Easy	OBJ: Literary Analysis
10. ANS: C	DIF: Easy	OBJ: Interpretation
11. ANS: A	DIF: Easy	OBJ: Interpretation

Vocabulary and Grammar

12. ANS: D	DIF: Easy	OBJ: Vocabulary
13. ANS: C	DIF: Easy	OBJ: Vocabulary
14. ANS: C	DIF: Easy	OBJ: Grammar

Essay

15. Students should mention that the medicines and diet restrictions are meant to improve Varma's health and prolong his life. However, Varma wants to eat food he enjoys. Students may decide that while Rakesh's decision is medically wise, he needs to be more flexible and allow his father to take some comfort and enjoyment in the food he eats.

Difficulty: *Easy*
Objective: *Essay*

16. Students should mention that at the beginning of the story, people admire young Rakesh because he is such a successful student. After he leaves the hospital and opens his own clinic, the admiration begins to lessen. He is probably a less important doctor as head of a small clinic than as a board member of a hospital. By the end of the story, he has lost much of the admiration

because it is no longer obvious that he respects his father and gives him the best care.

Difficulty: *Easy*
Objective: *Essay*

Selection Test B, p. 330

Critical Reading

1. ANS: D	DIF: Average	OBJ: Comprehension
2. ANS: C	DIF: Easy	OBJ: Interpretation
3. ANS: A	DIF: Challenging	OBJ: Reading Strategy
4. ANS: A	DIF: Average	OBJ: Literary Analysis
5. ANS: B	DIF: Average	OBJ: Interpretation
6. ANS: D	DIF: Easy	OBJ: Comprehension
7. ANS: B	DIF: Average	OBJ: Literary Analysis
8. ANS: C	DIF: Easy	OBJ: Comprehension
9. ANS: B	DIF: Average	OBJ: Reading Strategy
10. ANS: A	DIF: Easy	OBJ: Literary Analysis
11. ANS: D	DIF: Challenging	OBJ: Reading Strategy
12. ANS: D	DIF: Challenging	OBJ: Comprehension

Vocabulary and Grammar

13. ANS: C	DIF: Average	OBJ: Vocabulary
14. ANS: C	DIF: Average	OBJ: Vocabulary
15. ANS: B	DIF: Easy	OBJ: Grammar
16. ANS: D	DIF: Average	OBJ: Grammar

Essay

17. Students should trace the progression in Varma's life based on changes his ambitions for his son bring about. Although Rakesh shows outward signs of devotion, his modern ways cause his father's unhappiness. Varma moves from pride, through complaining, to defiance, to a kind of realization of what his son is, to a final outburst of protest.

Difficulty: *Easy*
Objective: *Essay*

18. Students may note that Desai shows that Indians are tempted to incorporate Western ideas into a traditional context, but that this blending often causes unhappiness. Students should point out that, in the story, Western medicine appears first as a route to traditional goals—increased prestige and income for the family. It is only when Rakesh begins to apply his medical knowledge to the care he gives his father that the conflict between Western and Indian ways comes to light. Students should provide examples showing how Rakesh's use of Western ideas in an Indian context—his attention to his father's diet, for instance—is both consistent with and destructive of tradition.

Difficulty: *Challenging*
Objective: *Essay*

from *"We'll Never Conquer Space"*
by Arthur C. Clarke

Vocabulary Warm-up Exercises, p. 334

A.
1. virtual
2. vertically
3. ultimate
4. voyaging
5. analogy
6. separation
7. conservative
8. psychological

B. Sample Answers
1. I will turn fifty in the <u>decade</u> of the 2030s.
2. The maximum <u>velocity</u> allowed when driving in a residential area is 30 miles per hour.
3. One <u>profound</u> thought that guides my life is that life is short and should be enjoyed.
4. One school subject that challenges my skills of <u>comprehension</u> is physics.
5. I would entertain an <u>energetic</u> kitten by giving it some toys.
6. One purchase that would require a <u>substantial</u> amount of money is a laptop computer.
7. If I were getting ready to graduate, I would be expecting <u>dispatches</u> from the school concerning graduation requirements.
8. The <u>restraints</u> that might limit the freedom of prisoners include locked doors, shackles, and handcuffs.

Reading Warm-up A, p. 335

Sample Answers
1. <u>space, the last frontier</u>; Time is a thief that robs us of our youth.
2. <u>the wide, wild ocean</u>; The *ultimate* goal of a sporting event is to have fun.
3. (cautious); *Conservative* means "moderate; cautious."
4. (mental); A great *psychological* victory for a typical teenager might be resisting peer pressure.
5. <u>ocean trip</u>; If I had time and money for *voyaging*, I would like to go to Alaska.
6. (up); It is amazing how some professional basketball players can leap so high *vertically* to dunk the ball in the basket.
7. (from home); Another word that is similar to *separation* is *detachment*.
8. <u>that those six months changed the world</u>; A *virtual* certainty in my life is that my mother will bake a cake for my birthday.

Reading Warm-up B, p. 336

Sample Answers

1. <u>the 1950s</u>; The *decade* in which I was born was the 1980s.
2. (Before the launch of Sputnik I . . . advanced player.); Matt has a *profound* fear of spiders.
3. (significant); A hurricane or a tornado might cause *substantial* wind damage.
4. <u>speed</u>; I think a jet might be able to fly at a *velocity* of 500 miles per hour.
5. (radio signals); The kinds of *dispatches* that might make a traveler want to return home quickly might be messages about a family member's health.
6. <u>hold back</u>; Two kinds of *restraints* that keep people safe are seat belts and door locks.
7. <u>new understanding</u>; Luis showed his *comprehension* of the lesson by earning an "A" on the test.
8. (vigorous); Most people put forth an *energetic* effort in sports activities.

Literary Analysis: Prophetic Essay, p. 337

Sample Responses

Thesis: Space travel will never be easy for lumans.

Support 1: The vastness of solar space prohibits human travel.—fact/speculation

Support 2: Even interplanetary communication will be problematic, if not intolerable.— emotional appeal

Support 3: Nothing can ever travel faster than light.—fact/speculation

Support 4: The size of the universe is simply beyond human comprehension, which contributes to the likelihood that humans will not "conquer" space.—emotional appeal

Reading Strategy: Challenge the Text, p. 338

Possible Responses

1. Will video communication become that accessible?
2. *Have* we "abolished space" on Earth? Perhaps abolishing the space between the stars means simply traversing it, not necessarily traversing it quickly.
3. Is technology moving toward using nuclear energy for spaceflight? How "homely" could the solar system be?

Vocabulary Builder, p. 339

A. 1. C; 2. D; 3. B; 4. A
B. 1. D; 2. B; 3. A; 4. B; 5. B; 6. A

Grammar and Style: Linking Verbs and Subject Complements, p. 340

A. 1. are—otherwise; PA
2. was—wide; PA
3. are—face to face; PA
4. is—limit; PN
5. are—wrong; PA

B. Possible Responses

1. Arthur Clarke is a British citizen.
2. Clarke has been a resident of Sri Lanka for forty years.
3. Clarke seems comfortable with his subject matter.

Enrichment: Science, p. 343

Sample Responses

1. If a space voyage occurred at a rate of speed sufficient to cover a vast distance in a reasonable amount of time, time would slow down for the traveler, but not for those at home. Therefore, people would experience time and aging differentially.
2. Clarke suggests that, because of the almost inconceivable distances involved, the communications between space travelers and Earth would take a very long time traveling back and forth. Though this gap in communications would not prevent people from traveling in space, it would eliminate the possibility of their maintaining close family or business relations with people back on Earth.

Selection Test A, p. 344

Critical Reading

1. ANS: B	DIF: Easy	OBJ: Interpretation
2. ANS: C	DIF: Easy	OBJ: Literary Analysis
3. ANS: D	DIF: Easy	OBJ: Reading Strategy
4. ANS: C	DIF: Easy	OBJ: Literary Analysis
5. ANS: D	DIF: Easy	OBJ: Literary Analysis
6. ANS: A	DIF: Easy	OBJ: Comprehension
7. ANS: B	DIF: Easy	OBJ: Interpretation
8. ANS: D	DIF: Easy	OBJ: Interpretation
9. ANS: A	DIF: Easy	OBJ: Reading Strategy
10. ANS: A	DIF: Easy	OBJ: Interpretation

Vocabulary and Grammar

11. ANS: D	DIF: Easy	OBJ: Vocabulary
12. ANS: A	DIF: Easy	OBJ: Grammar

Essay

13. Most students will agree that Clarke has made a convincing argument. They might offer as evidence his statement that nothing can travel faster than the speed of light, which will make even the closest stars very difficult to reach. Students may also draw on their own knowledge to argue in support of or in opposition to Clarke's statements.
    Difficulty: *Easy*
    Objective: *Essay*
14. Students should note that the time barrier is the limit created by the vast size of the universe and the maximum speed at people may ever travel. Even if human

travel could approach the speed of light, space is so huge that getting from star to star would still take a long time. Even if technology reached the point of making this travel possible, the time barrier would still limit any ability to communicate with people on Earth.

Difficulty: *Easy*

Objective: *Essay*

Selection Test B, p. 347

Critical Reading

1. ANS: D   DIF: Easy   OBJ: Literary Analysis
2. ANS: A   DIF: Average   OBJ: Literary Analysis
3. ANS: B   DIF: Challenging   OBJ: Literary Analysis
4. ANS: D   DIF: Average   OBJ: Interpretation
5. ANS: B   DIF: Easy   OBJ: Comprehension
6. ANS: C   DIF: Challenging   OBJ: Literary Analysis
7. ANS: D   DIF: Average   OBJ: Interpretation
8. ANS: A   DIF: Easy   OBJ: Interpretation
9. ANS: D   DIF: Average   OBJ: Comprehension
10. ANS: A   DIF: Challenging   OBJ: Reading Strategy
11. ANS: C   DIF: Easy   OBJ: Reading Strategy
12. ANS: B   DIF: Average   OBJ: Reading Strategy
13. ANS: B   DIF: Average   OBJ: Comprehension

Vocabulary and Grammar

14. ANS: D   DIF: Average   OBJ: Vocabulary
15. ANS: A   DIF: Easy   OBJ: Grammar

Essay

16. Students should recognize that Clarke predicts that solar and stellar space will never be "easily" traversed as are distances—even great distances—on Earth. He argues that the vastness of space prohibits reasonable communication. He assumes that the laws of physics, as we know them, will not change, and that we will never be able to travel faster than the speed of light. This barrier will prevent colonists from sharing a common life or history with those back home.

Difficulty: *Easy*

Objective: *Essay*

17. Students may take the stand that Clarke sells humans short by assuming we won't come up with the technology to bridge interstellar distances. We have done other things that no one ever thought we could do, so why should mastering space travel be any different? Or students may conclude that Clarke's assertions about the vastness of space are valid and convincing. Without changing the laws of physics and the barrier set by the speed of light, mastering interstellar distances seems unlikely.

Difficulty: *Average*

Objective: *Essay*

Writing About Literature—Unit 6

Evaluate Literary Trends: Integrating Grammar Skills, p. 351

Sample Revisions

1. The quick-changing rush of images in T. S. Eliot's poems are dreamlike and difficult to interpret.
2. Eliot uses grim, sordid details of modern life to express his bleak, despairing vision of the world.
3. I like Rupert Brooke's "The Soldier" because it expresses a soldier's love for his country in details that are easy to understand and appreciate.
4. Anyone can understand Seamus Heaney's theme in "The Follower," because the poem uses vivid details to describe the changing relationship between a parent and a child as they both age.
5. The theme of Dylan Thomas's "Do Not Go Gentle into That Good Night" is hard to miss because it is powerfully expressed in the repeated lines "Do not go gentle into that good night" and "Rage, rage against the dying of the light."

Writing Workshop—Unit 6

Multimedia Report: Integrating Grammar Skills, p. 353

Sample Revision

Two years ago, the crumbling old playground at Eastside Park was a problem. This first photo shows how it looked then. Because the equipment was falling apart, little kids were getting hurt there. As a result, parents stopped bringing their kids to the park. Then older kids started hanging out there, spraying the slides with graffiti, and leaving litter everywhere. As conditions grew worse, even fewer parents brought their kids there.

A year ago, a neighborhood group decided to clean up the park. Parents volunteered to start bringing their kids there again and to patrol for vandalism. Soon, as a result of their efforts, the park began to improve, as you can see in the next photo.

Next, the group started holding fundraisers at the park in order to raise money for new equipment and to show people that a valuable resource was being lost. The Eastside Park Carnival, shown in the next photo, raised thousands of dollars for park improvement.

Finally, the neighbors used the fundraising money to buy new swings and slides for the playground. Now, because the playground is such a great place for children, everyone is proud of it and takes good care of it. The last photo shows how much fun the kids of the Eastside neighborhood are having at the playground that they and their parents helped to rebuild.

Spelling—Unit 6

Proofreading Practice, p. 354

1. memories; 2. crammed; 3. irresistible;
4. kaleidoscope; 5. collage; 6. projectors; 7. ancient;
8. continuous; 9. static; 10. simultaneously;
11. realistically; 12. scientifically; 13. actors;
14. stories; 15. operators; 16. locations;
17. narration; 18. accompanied; 19. carried;
20. *Robbery*; 21. running; 22. dissatisfied;
23. families; 24. worried; 25. skeptical;
26. irreplaceable; 27. fantasies

Benchmark Test 12, p. 357

MULTIPLE CHOICE

1. ANS: C
2. ANS: B
3. ANS: B
4. ANS: A
5. ANS: C
6. ANS: A
7. ANS: B
8. ANS: C
9. ANS: D
10. ANS: A
11. ANS: C
12. ANS: C
13. ANS: A
14. ANS: D
15. ANS: B
16. ANS: D
17. ANS: D
18. ANS: C
19. ANS: A
20. ANS: B
21. ANS: A
22. ANS: A
23. ANS: B
24. ANS: C
25. ANS: D
26. ANS: C
27. ANS: D
28. ANS: B
29. ANS: B

ESSAY

30. Students should begin by describing the scene or event and should then explain how the scene or event has a deeper meaning to them. They should use clear transitions to make their descriptions and comparisons clear.

31. Students should identify the person and the qualities or achievements that make him or her remarkable. They should list and briefly describe photographs, artwork, music, video clips, written materials, and/or sound effects they will use in a multimedia presentation that conveys the person's qualities and achievements.

32. Students should clearly describe the program and its goals. They should explain how the program would solve the problems or enhance the experiences of teenagers in the community. They should also include some information on the practicality of the program, such as where it can be conducted, what staff might be needed, how much it might cost, or where the money would come from.